CASENOTE® Legal Briefs®

BUSINESS ORGANIZATIONS

Keyed to Courses Using

Bainbridge's
Business Associations: Cases and Materials on Agency, Partnerships, LLCs, and Corporations
Twelfth Edition

Authored by: Publisher's Editorial Staff

ASPEN PUBLISHING

This publication is designed to provide accurate and authoritative information in regard to the subject matter covered. It is sold with the understanding that the publisher is not engaged in rendering legal, accounting, or other professional services. If legal advice or other expert assistance is required, the services of a competent professional person should be sought.

—From a Declaration of Principles adopted jointly by a Committee of the American Bar Association and a Committee of Publishers and Associates

To contact Customer Service, e-mail customer.service@aspenpublishing.com, call 1-800-950-5259, or mail correspondence to:

Aspen Publishing
Attn: Order Department
1 Wall Street
Burlington, MA 01803

1 2 3 4 5 6 7 8 9 0

ISBN 979-8-8941-0436-2

ABOUT ASPEN PUBLISHING

Aspen Publishing is a leading provider of legal education content and digital learning solutions in the United States and globally. Our innovative products and platforms—designed based on best practices in learning science—engage students and enhance outcomes. From textbooks and audiobooks authored by renowned experts to digital platforms and products like LEAF, Connected eBooks, Connected Quizzing, PracticePerfect, and JD-Next, we empower the next generation of legal professionals with innovative, trusted, and accessible resources.

The Aspen Casebook Series, affectionately known as the "red and black" casebooks among law faculty and students, includes hundreds of highly regarded textbooks across more than 80 disciplines. These range from foundational courses like Torts and Contracts to emerging electives such as Sustainability and the Law of Policing. Our study aids, including the popular *Examples & Explanations* series, help law students master complex topics with clarity and confidence.

Aspen's expertise extends to undergraduate education with our Paralegal, Criminal Justice, and Business Law series, offering the same hallmark quality to a broader audience. JD-Next, our groundbreaking online law school prep course and admissions test, provides a realistic preview of law school, equips students with essential skills for academic success, and evaluates their readiness for legal studies.

Aspen Publishing Is Proud to Be a UWorld Company

Since 2003, UWorld has been a global leader in developing high-quality learning tools for students preparing for high-stakes exams. With a commitment to excellence, UWorld has helped millions of students in undergraduate, graduate, and professional programs in fields such as medicine, nursing, finance, and law achieve their academic and career goals.

Founded by Chandra S. Pemmasani, M.D., during his medical residency, UWorld began focusing on medical education and has since expanded into various academic fields, including law. In 2020, UWorld launched its Legal vertical, starting with its comprehensive Multistate Bar Exam (MBE®) Question Bank, followed by the acquisition of Themis Bar Review, which integrated resources to provide a complete bar exam preparation experience. In 2024, UWorld expanded its offerings by acquiring Aspen Publishing, enhancing its suite of legal education products.

Today, UWorld offers an unparalleled range of study materials that blend active learning methods with expert content, ensuring students and educators can access the most effective resources. From bar preparation to law school success, UWorld is committed to supporting the next generation of legal professionals. Learn more at uworld.com.

Format for the Casenote® Legal Brief

Nature of Case: This section identifies the form of action (e.g., breach of contract, negligence, battery), the type of proceeding (e.g., demurrer, appeal from trial court's jury instructions) or the relief sought (e.g., damages, injunction, criminal sanctions).

Palsgraf v. Long Island R.R. Co.

Injured bystander (P) v. Railroad company (D)

N.Y. Ct. App., 248 N.Y. 339, 162 N.E. 99 (1928).

NATURE OF CASE: Appeal from judgment affirming verdict for plaintiff seeking damages for personal injury.

FACT SUMMARY: Helen Palsgraf (P) was injured on R.R.'s (D) train platform when R.R.'s (D) guard helped a passenger aboard a moving train, causing his package to fall on the tracks. The package contained fireworks which exploded, creating a shock that tipped a scale onto Palsgraf (P).

RULE OF LAW

The risk reasonably to be perceived defines the duty to be obeyed.

FACTS: Helen Palsgraf (P) purchased a ticket to Rockaway Beach from R.R. (D) and was waiting on the train platform. As she waited, two men ran to catch a train that was pulling out from the platform. The first man jumped aboard, but the second man, who appeared as if he might fall, was helped aboard by the guard on the train who had kept the door open so they could jump aboard. A guard on the platform also helped by pushing him onto the train. The man was carrying a package wrapped in newspaper. In the process, the man dropped his package, which fell on the tracks. The package contained fireworks and exploded. The shock of the explosion was apparently of great enough strength to tip over some scales at the other end of the platform, which fell on Palsgraf (P) and injured her. A jury awarded her damages, and R.R. (D) appealed.

ISSUE: Does the risk reasonably to be perceived define the duty to be obeyed?

HOLDING AND DECISION: (Cardozo, C.J.) Yes. The risk reasonably to be perceived defines the duty to be obeyed. If there is no foreseeable hazard to the injured party as the result of a seemingly innocent act, the act does not become a tort because it happened to be a wrong as to another. If the wrong was not willful, the plaintiff must show that the act as to her had such great and apparent possibilities of danger as to entitle her to protection. Negligence in the abstract is not enough upon which to base liability. Negligence is a relative concept, evolving out of the common law doctrine of trespass on the case. To establish liability, the defendant must owe a legal duty of reasonable care to the injured party. A cause of action in tort will lie where harm, though unintended, could have been averted or avoided by observance of such a duty. The scope of the duty is limited by the range of danger that a reasonable person could foresee. In this case, there was nothing to suggest from the appearance of the parcel or otherwise that the parcel contained fireworks. The guard could not reasonably have had any warning of a threat to Palsgraf (P), and R.R. (D) therefore cannot be held liable. Judgment is reversed in favor of R.R. (D).

DISSENT: (Andrews, J.) The concept that there is no negligence unless R.R. (D) owes a legal duty to take care as to Palsgraf (P) herself is too narrow. Everyone owes to the world at large the duty of refraining from those acts that may unreasonably threaten the safety of others. If the guard's action was negligent as to those nearby, it was also negligent as to those outside what might be termed the "danger zone." For Palsgraf (P) to recover, R.R.'s (D) negligence must have been the proximate cause of her injury, a question of fact for the jury.

ANALYSIS

The majority defined the limit of the defendant's liability in terms of the danger that a reasonable person in defendant's situation would have perceived. The dissent argued that the limitation should not be placed on liability, but rather on damages. Judge Andrews suggested that only injuries that would not have happened but for R.R.'s (D) negligence should be compensable. Both the majority and dissent recognized the policy-driven need to limit liability for negligent acts, seeking, in the words of Judge Andrews, to define a framework "that will be practical and in keeping with the general understanding of mankind." The Restatement (Second) of Torts has accepted Judge Cardozo's view.

Quicknotes

FORESEEABILITY A reasonable expectation that change is the probable result of certain acts or omissions.

NEGLIGENCE Conduct falling below the standard of care that a reasonable person would demonstrate under similar conditions.

PROXIMATE CAUSE The natural sequence of events without which an injury would not have been sustained.

Fact Summary: This is included to refresh your memory and can be used as a quick reminder of the facts.

Rule of Law: Summarizes the general principle of law that the case illustrates. It may be used for instant recall of the court's holding and for classroom discussion or home review.

Facts: This section contains all relevant facts of the case, including the contentions of the parties and the lower court holdings. It is written in a logical order to give you a clear understanding of the case. The plaintiff and defendant are identified by their proper names throughout and are always labeled with a (P) or (D).

Issue: The issue is a concise question that brings out the essence of the opinion as it relates to the section of the casebook in which the case appears. Both substantive and procedural issues are included if relevant to the decision.

Party ID: Quick identification of the relationship between the parties.

Concurrence/Dissent: All concurrences and dissents are briefed whenever they are included by the casebook author.

Analysis: This last paragraph gives you a broad understanding of where the case "fits in" with other cases in the section of the book and with the entire course. It is a hornbook-style discussion indicating whether the case is a majority or minority opinion and comparing the principal case with other cases in the casebook. It may also provide analysis from restatements, uniform codes, and law review articles.

Holding and Decision: This section offers a clear and in-depth discussion of the rule of the case and the court's rationale. It is written in easy-to-understand language and answers the issue presented by applying the law to the facts of the case. When relevant, it includes a thorough discussion of the exceptions to the case as listed by the court, any major cites to the other cases on point, and the names of the judges who wrote the decisions.

Quicknotes: Conveniently defines legal terms found in the case.

Note to Students

Aspen Publishing is proud to offer *Casenote® Legal Briefs*—continuing thirty years of publishing America's best-selling legal briefs.

Casenote® Legal Briefs are designed to help you save time when briefing assigned cases. Organized under convenient headings, they show you how to abstract the basic facts and holdings from the text of the actual opinions handed down by the courts. Used as part of a rigorous study regimen, they can help you spend more time analyzing and critiquing points of law than on copying bits and pieces of judicial opinions into your notebook or outline.

Casenote® Legal Briefs should never be used as a substitute for assigned casebook readings. They work best when read as a follow-up to reviewing the underlying opinions themselves. Students who try to avoid reading and digesting the judicial opinions in their casebooks or online sources will end up shortchanging themselves in the long run. The ability to absorb, critique, and restate the dynamic and complex elements of case law decisions is crucial to your success in law school and beyond. It cannot be developed vicariously.

In addition to *Casenote® Legal Briefs*, Aspen Publishing offers the following study aids:

- *Casenote® Legal Briefs*
- *Emanuel Law Outlines®*
- Emanuel® *Law in a Flash Flash Cards*
- Emanuel *CrunchTime® Series*

Each of these series is designed to provide you with easy-to-understand explanations of complex points of law. Each volume offers guidance on the principles of legal analysis and, consulted regularly, will hone your ability to spot relevant issues. We have titles that will help you prepare for class, prepare for your exams, and enhance your general comprehension of the law along the way.

To find out more about our law school tools for success, visit us at *www.AspenPublishing.com* or e-mail us at *customer.service@aspenpublishing.com*. We'll be happy to assist you.

How to Brief a Case

A. Decide on a Format and Stick to It

Structure is essential to a good brief. It enables you to arrange systematically the related parts that are scattered throughout most cases, thus making manageable and understandable what might otherwise seem to be an endless and unfathomable sea of information. There are, of course, an unlimited number of formats that can be utilized. However, it is best to find one that suits your needs and stick to it. Consistency breeds both efficiency and the security that when called upon you will know where to look in your brief for the information you are asked to give.

Any format, as long as it presents the essential elements of a case in an organized fashion, can be used. Experience, however, has led *Casenote® Legal Briefs* to develop and utilize the following format because of its logical flow and universal applicability.

NATURE OF CASE: This is a brief statement of the legal character and procedural status of the case (e.g., "Appeal of a burglary conviction").

There are many different alternatives open to a litigant dissatisfied with a court ruling. The key to determining which one has been used is to discover *who is asking this court for what.*

This first entry in the brief should be kept as *short as possible.* Use the court's terminology if you understand it. But since jurisdictions vary as to the titles of pleadings, the best entry is the one that addresses who wants what in this proceeding, not the one that sounds most like the court's language.

RULE OF LAW: A statement of the general principle of law that the case illustrates (e.g., "An acceptance that varies any term of the offer is considered a rejection and counteroffer").

Determining the rule of law of a case is a procedure similar to determining the issue of the case. Avoid being fooled by red herrings; there may be a few rules of law mentioned in the case excerpt, but usually only one is *the* rule with which the casebook editor is concerned. The techniques used to locate the issue, described below, may also be utilized to find the rule of law. Generally, your best guide is simply the chapter heading. It is a clue to the point the casebook editor seeks to make and should be kept in mind when reading every case in the respective section.

FACTS: A synopsis of only the essential facts of the case, i.e., those bearing upon or leading up to the issue.

The facts entry should be a short statement of the events and transactions that led one party to initiate legal proceedings against another in the first place. While some cases conveniently state the salient facts at the beginning of the decision, in other instances they will have to be culled from hiding places throughout the text, even from concurring and dissenting opinions. Some of the "facts" will often be in dispute and should be so noted. Conflicting evidence may be briefly pointed up. "Hard" facts must be included. Both must be *relevant* in order to be listed in the facts entry. It is impossible to tell what is relevant until the entire case is read, as the ultimate determination of the rights and liabilities of the parties may turn on something buried deep in the opinion.

Generally, the facts entry should not be longer than three to five *short* sentences.

It is often helpful to identify the role played by a party in a given context. For example, in a construction contract case the identification of a party as the "contractor" or "builder" alleviates the need to tell that that party was the one who was supposed to have built the house.

It is always helpful, and a good general practice, to identify the "plaintiff" and the "defendant." This may seem elementary and uncomplicated, but, especially in view of the creative editing practiced by some casebook editors, it is sometimes a difficult or even impossible task. Bear in mind that the *party presently* seeking something from this court may not be the plaintiff, and that sometimes only the cross-claim of a defendant is treated in the excerpt. Confusing or misaligning the parties can ruin your analysis and understanding of the case.

ISSUE: A statement of the general legal question answered by or illustrated in the case. For clarity, the issue is best put in the form of a question capable of a "yes" or "no" answer. In reality, the issue is simply the Rule of Law put in the form of a question (e.g., "May an offer be accepted by performance?").

The major problem presented in discerning what is *the* issue in the case is that an opinion usually purports to raise and answer several questions. However, except for rare cases, only one such question is really the issue in the case. Collateral issues not necessary to the resolution of the matter in controversy are handled by the court by language known as *"obiter dictum"* or merely *"dictum."* While dicta may be included later in the brief, they have no place under the issue heading.

To find the issue, ask *who wants what* and then go on to ask *why did that party succeed or fail in getting it.* Once this is determined, the "why" should be turned into a question.

The complexity of the issues in the cases will vary, but in all cases a single-sentence question should sum up the issue. *In a few cases,* there will be two, or even more rarely, three issues of equal importance to the resolution of the case. Each should be expressed in a single-sentence question.

Since many issues are resolved by a court in coming to a final disposition of a case, the casebook editor will reproduce the portion of the opinion containing the issue or issues most relevant to the area of law under scrutiny. A noted law professor gave this advice: "Close the book; look at the title on the cover." Chances are, if it is Property, you need not concern yourself with whether, for example, the federal government's treatment of the plaintiff's land really raises a federal question sufficient to support jurisdiction on this ground in federal court.

The same rule applies to chapter headings designating sub-areas within the subjects. They tip you off as to what the text is designed to teach. The cases are arranged in a casebook to show a progression or development of the law, so that the preceding cases may also help.

It is also most important to remember to *read the notes and questions* at the end of a case to determine what the editors wanted you to have gleaned from it.

HOLDING AND DECISION: This section should succinctly explain the rationale of the court in arriving at its decision. In capsulizing the "reasoning" of the court, it should always include an application of the general rule or rules of law to the specific facts of the case. Hidden justifications come to light in this entry: the reasons for the state of the law, the public policies, the biases and prejudices, those considerations that influence the justices' thinking and, ultimately, the outcome of the case. At the end, there should be a short indication of the disposition or procedural resolution of the case (e.g., "Decision of the trial court for Mr. Smith (P) reversed").

The foregoing format is designed to help you "digest" the reams of case material with which you will be faced in your law school career. Once mastered by practice, it will place at your fingertips the information the authors of your casebooks have sought to impart to you in case-by-case illustration and analysis.

B. Be as Economical as Possible in Briefing Cases

Once armed with a format that encourages succinctness, it is as important to be economical with regard to the time spent on the actual reading of the case as it is to be economical in the writing of the brief itself. This does not mean "skimming" a case. Rather, it means reading the case with an "eye" trained to recognize into which "section" of your brief a particular passage or line fits and having a system for quickly and precisely marking the case so that the passages fitting any one particular part of the brief can be easily identified and brought together in a concise and accurate manner when the brief is actually written.

It is of no use to simply repeat everything in the opinion of the court; record only enough information to trigger your recollection of what the court said. Nevertheless, an accurate statement of the "law of the case," i.e., the legal principle applied to the facts, is absolutely essential to class preparation and to learning the law under the case method.

To that end, it is important to develop a "shorthand" that you can use to make marginal notations. These notations will tell you at a glance in which section of the brief you will be placing that particular passage or portion of the opinion.

Some students prefer to underline all the salient portions of the opinion (with a pencil or colored underliner marker), making marginal notations as they go along. Others prefer the color-coded method of underlining, utilizing different colors of markers to underline the salient portions of the case, each separate color being used to represent a different section of the brief. For example, blue underlining could be used for passages relating to the rule of law, yellow for those relating to the issue, and green for those relating to the holding and decision, etc. While it has its advocates, the color-coded method can be confusing and time-consuming (all that time spent on changing colored markers). Furthermore, it can interfere with the continuity and concentration many students deem essential to the reading of a case for maximum comprehension. In the end, however, it is a matter of personal preference and style. Just remember, whatever method you use, underlining must be used sparingly or its value is lost.

If you take the marginal notation route, an efficient and easy method is to go along underlining the key portions of the case and placing in the margin alongside them the following "markers" to indicate where a particular passage or line "belongs" in the brief you will write:

N	(NATURE OF CASE)
RL	(RULE OF LAW)
I	(ISSUE)
HL	(HOLDING AND DECISION, relates to the RULE OF LAW behind the decision)
HR	(HOLDING AND DECISION, gives the RATIONALE or reasoning behind the decision)
HA	(HOLDING AND DECISION, applies the general principle(s) of law to the facts of the case to arrive at the decision)

Remember that a particular passage may well contain information necessary to more than one part of your brief, in which case you simply note that in the margin. If you are using the color-coded underlining method instead of marginal notation, simply make asterisks or checks in the margin next to the passage in question in the colors that indicate the additional sections of the brief where it might be utilized.

The economy of utilizing "shorthand" in marking cases for briefing can be maintained in the actual brief writing process itself by utilizing "law student shorthand" within the brief. There are many commonly used words and phrases for which abbreviations can be substituted in your briefs (and in your class notes also). You can develop abbreviations that are personal to you and which will save you a lot of time. A reference list of briefing abbreviations can be found on page x of this book.

C. Use Both the Briefing Process and the Brief as a Learning Tool

Now that you have a format and the tools for briefing cases efficiently, the most important thing is to make the time spent in briefing profitable to you and to make the most advantageous use of the briefs you create. Of course, the briefs are invaluable for classroom reference when you are called upon to explain or analyze a particular case. However, they are also useful in reviewing for exams. A quick glance at the fact summary should bring the case to mind, and a rereading of the rule of law should enable you to go over the underlying legal concept in your mind, how it was applied in that particular case, and how it might apply in other factual settings.

As to the value to be derived from engaging in the briefing process itself, there is an immediate benefit that arises from being forced to sift through the essential facts and reasoning from the court's opinion and to succinctly express them in your own words in your brief. The process ensures that you understand the case and the point that it illustrates, and that means you will be ready to absorb further analysis and information brought forth in class. It also ensures you will have something to say when called upon in class. The briefing process helps develop a mental agility for getting to the *gist* of a case and for identifying, expounding on, and applying the legal concepts and issues found there. The briefing process is the mental process on which you must rely in taking law school examinations; it is also the mental process upon which lawyers rely in serving their clients and in making a living.

Abbreviations for Briefs

acceptance ... acp
affirmed ... aff
answer ... ans
assumption of risk ... a/r
attorney ... atty
beyond a reasonable doubt ... b/r/d
bona fide purchaser ... BFP
breach of contract ... br/k
cause of action ... c/a
common law ... c/l
Constitution ... Con
constitutional ... con
contract ... K
contributory negligence ... c/n
cross ... x
cross-complaint ... x/c
cross-examination ... x/ex
cruel and unusual punishment ... c/u/p
defendant ... D
dismissed ... dis
double jeopardy ... d/j
due process ... d/p
equal protection ... e/p
equity ... eq
evidence ... ev
exclude ... exc
exclusionary rule ... exc/r
felony ... f/n
freedom of speech ... f/s
good faith ... g/f
habeas corpus ... h/c
hearsay ... hr
husband ... H
injunction ... inj
in loco parentis ... ILP
inter vivos ... I/v
joint tenancy ... j/t
judgment ... judgt
jurisdiction ... jur
last clear chance ... LCC
long-arm statute ... LAS
majority view ... maj
meeting of minds ... MOM
minority view ... min
Miranda rule ... Mir/r
Miranda warnings ... Mir/w
negligence ... neg
notice ... ntc
nuisance ... nus
obligation ... ob
obscene ... obs
offer ... O
offeree ... OE
offeror ... OR
ordinance ... ord
pain and suffering ... p/s
parol evidence ... p/e
plaintiff ... P
prima facie ... p/f
probable cause ... p/c
proximate cause ... px/c
real property ... r/p
reasonable doubt ... r/d
reasonable man ... r/m
rebuttable presumption ... rb/p
remanded ... rem
res ipsa loquitur ... RIL
respondeat superior ... r/s
Restatement ... RS
reversed ... rev
Rule Against Perpetuities ... RAP
search and seizure ... s/s
search warrant ... s/w
self-defense ... s/d
specific performance ... s/p
statute ... S
statute of frauds ... S/F
statute of limitations ... S/L
summary judgment ... s/j
tenancy at will ... t/w
tenancy in common ... t/c
tenant ... t
third party ... TP
third party beneficiary ... TPB
transferred intent ... TI
unconscionable ... uncon
unconstitutional ... unconst
undue influence ... u/e
Uniform Commercial Code ... UCC
unilateral ... uni
vendee ... VE
vendor ... VR
versus ... v
void for vagueness ... VFV
weight of authority ... w/a
weight of the evidence ... w/e
wife ... W
with ... w/
within ... w/i
without ... w/o
without prejudice ... w/o/p
wrongful death ... wr/d

Table of Cases

CHAPTER 1

Agency

Quick Reference Rules of Law

PAGE

1. *Gorton v. Doty.* Where one undertakes to transact some business or manage some affair for another by authority and on account of the latter, the relationship of principal and agent arises. 3

2. *A. Gay Jenson Farms Co. v. Cargill, Inc.* A creditor who assumes control of their debtor's business may be held liable as principal for the acts of the debtor in connection with the business. 4

3. *Mill Street Church of Christ v. Hogan.* A person possesses implied authority as an agent to hire another worker where such implied authority is necessary to implement the agent's express authority. 5

4. *Ackerman v. Sobol Family Partnership, LLP.* An attorney whose client is one of several litigants, all of whom are on the same side of litigation, has apparent authority to bind all those litigants to a global settlement agreement where the attorney, although not retained by all the litigants, has represented all the litigants in settlement negotiations for an extended period of time and has indicated to the opponents that the attorney is fully authorized to negotiate settlement terms on behalf of all the litigants; where the litigants have held the attorney out as having authority to negotiate a settlement on their behalf and have knowingly permitted the attorney to act as having such authority; and where the opponents in good faith reasonably believe that the attorney has such authority. 6

5. *Watteau v. Fenwick.* When one holds out another as an agent, that agent can bind the principal on matters normally incident to such agency, even if that agent was not authorized for a particular type of transaction. 10

6. *Botticello v. Stefanovicz.* (1) An agency relationship cannot be established where the fair preponderance of the evidence does not indicate that the purported principal has authorized or agreed to the purported agent acting on their behalf. (2) A person cannot ratify a prior act where the person neither intends to do so nor has full knowledge of all the material circumstances. 11

7. *Hoddeson v. Koos Bros.* To establish apparent agency, the appearance of authority must be shown to have been created by the manifestations of the alleged principal and not solely by the supposed agent. 13

8. *Atlantic Salmon A/S v. Curran.* It is the duty of an agent, in order to avoid personal liability on a contract entered into on behalf of the principal, to disclose not only that the agent is acting in a representative capacity, but also the identity of the principal. 15

9. *Humble Oil & Refining Co. v. Martin.* A party may be liable for a contractor's torts if the party exercises substantial control over the contractor's operations. 16

10. *Hoover v. Sun Oil Company.* A franchisee is considered an independent contractor of the franchisor if the franchisee retains control of inventory and operations. 17

11. *Kerl v. Rasmussen.* A franchisor may be held vicariously liable for the tortious conduct of its franchisee only if the franchisor has control or a right of control over the daily operation of the specific aspect of the franchisee's business that is alleged to have caused the harm for which the franchisor is sought to be held liable. 18

Gorton v. Doty

Father of injured student (P) v. Owner of vehicle (D)

Idaho Sup. Ct., 57 Idaho 792, 69 P.2d 136 (1937)

NATURE OF CASE: Appeal from a judgment in favor of guardian ad litem in a vehicle accident case.

FACT SUMMARY: Doty (D) loaned her car to Russell Garst, a high school football coach, to transport members of the team to a game. When Garst had a traffic accident in which Richard Gorton (P) was injured, Richard's father, as guardian ad litem, sued Doty (D), arguing that Garst was Doty's (D) agent while transporting the team in Doty's (D) car, hence Doty (D), as principal in the agency relationship, was liable for the injuries resulting from the accident.

RULE OF LAW

Where one undertakes to transact some business or manage some affair for another by authority and on account of the latter, the relationship of principal and agent arises.

FACTS: Richard Gorton (P), a minor, was a member of his high school's football team that was scheduled to play a game at another school. Russell Garst was his football coach. Doty (D) knew of the game and volunteered her car for use in transporting team members to and from the game. Doty (D) told Garst that he could use her car if he drove it. She (D) was not promised compensation for the use of her car and did not receive any. The school district paid for the gasoline used, although Doty (D) had "not employed" Garst and had not at any time "directed his work or his services, or what he was doing." On route, Garst was involved in a traffic accident, resulting in injuries to Richard Gorton (P), a passenger. Richard's father, as guardian ad litem, brought suit against Doty (D), arguing that Garst was her agent at the time of the accident and that she was accordingly liable as the principal. Judgment was rendered in favor of Richard Gorton (P), and Doty (D) appealed. The state's highest court granted review.

ISSUE: Where one undertakes to transact some business or manage some affair for another by authority and on account of the latter, does the relationship of principal and agent arise?

HOLDING AND DECISION: [Judge not stated in casebook excerpt.] Yes. Where one undertakes to transact some business or manage some affair for another by authority and on account of the latter, the relationship of principal and agent arises. Here, Doty (D) volunteered the use of her car to Garst, the school football coach, for the purpose of furnishing transportation of the team to and from its game site. She "designated Garst," and, in so doing, made it a condition precedent that the person she designated should drive her car. That she thereby consented that Garst should act for her and in her behalf, in driving her car on that occasion, is clear from her act in volunteering the use of her car upon the express condition that he should drive it, and further, that Garst consented to so act for Doty (D) is equally clear by his act in driving the car. Furthermore, the fact of the car's ownership alone (conceded here), regardless of the presence or absence of the owner in the car at the time of the accident, establishes a prima facie case against the owner for the reason that the presumption arises that the driver is the agent of the owner. Affirmed.

DISSENT: (Budge, J.) Agency means more than mere passive permission. It involves request, instruction, or command. Here, Doty (D) simply loaned her car to Garst to enable him to furnish transportation for the team. It was nothing more nor less than a kindly gesture on her part to be helpful to Garst.

ANALYSIS

In the *Gorton* case, the court noted that it is not essential to the existence of authority that there be a contract between principal and agent or that the agent promise to act as such, nor is it essential to the relationship of principal and agent that they, or either, receive compensation.

Quicknotes

AGENCY A fiduciary relationship whereby authority is granted to an agent to act on behalf of the principal in order to effectuate the principal's objective.

AGENT An individual who has the authority to act on behalf of another.

GUARDIAN AD LITEM Person designated by the court to represent an infant or ward in a particular legal proceeding.

PRINCIPAL A person or entity who authorizes another (the agent) to act on its behalf and subject to its authority to the extent that the principal may be held liable for the actions of the agent.

A. Gay Jenson Farms Co. v. Cargill, Inc.

Farm (P) v. Grain dealer (D)

Minn. Sup. Ct., 309 N.W.2d 285 (1981)

NATURE OF CASE: Appeal from judgment awarding damages for breach of contract.

FACT SUMMARY: Cargill, Inc. (D), in addition to loaning funds to Warren Grain & Seed Co. (Warren) (D), also took control of the day-to-day operations of Warren (D).

RULE OF LAW

A creditor who assumes control of their debtor's business may be held liable as principal for the acts of the debtor in connection with the business.

FACTS: Warren Grain & Seed Co. (Warren) (D) operated a seed elevator and, as a result thereof, purchased grain and seed from local farmers. Cargill, Inc. (D) provided working capital to Warren (D). Warren (D) slowly became less and less sound financially and Cargill (D) became more and more involved in its daily operations. Eventually, Cargill (D) essentially took over the day-to-day operations of Warren (D). Nonetheless, Warren (D) eventually defaulted on two million dollars' worth of purchase contracts it had executed with local farmers (P). Eighty-six individual and corporate farmers (P) sued both Warren (D) and Cargill (D). A jury rendered a verdict against both Warren (D) and Cargill (D). Cargill (D) appealed, contending that it had not been a principal of Warren (D). The state's highest court granted review.

ISSUE: May a creditor who assumes control of their debtor's business become liable as principal for the acts of the debtor in connection with the business?

HOLDING AND DECISION: [Judge not stated in casebook excerpt.] Yes. A creditor who assumes control of their debtor's business may be held liable as principal for the acts of the debtor in connection with the business. Agency is a fiduciary relationship that results from the manifestation of consent by one person to another that the other shall act on their behalf and subject to their control, and consent of the other to so act. In order to create an agency relationship, the principal must consent to the agency, the agent must act on behalf of the principal, and the principal must exercise control of the agent. All three elements were found in the particular circumstances of this case. Warren (D) acted on Cargill's (D) behalf in procuring grain for Cargill (D), and Cargill (D) interfered in Warren's (D) internal affairs. Affirmed.

ANALYSIS

The court, in reaching its decision, noted that Cargill (D) and Warren (D) had a unique relationship that transcended the normal debtor-creditor situation. Cargill (D) financed Warren (D) to establish a source of grain for its business, not to make money as a lender. Cargill (D) was receiving significant amounts of grain and, notwithstanding the risk, the operation was considered profitable.

Quicknotes

AGENT An individual who has the authority to act on behalf of another.

FIDUCIARY RELATIONSHIP Person holding a legal obligation to act for the benefit of another.

PRINCIPAL A person or entity who authorizes another (the agent) to act on its behalf and subject to its authority to the extent that the principal may be held liable for the actions of the agent.

Mill Street Church of Christ v. Hogan

Insured employer (D) v. Injured worker (P)

Ky. Sup. Ct., 785 S.W.2d 263 (1990)

NATURE OF CASE: Petition for review of a workers' compensation board's holding that a worker was a company's employee, and thus entitled to workers' compensation benefits.

FACT SUMMARY: The Mill Street Church of Christ (the Church) (D) hired Bill Hogan to paint its church building. Bill hired his brother, Sam Hogan (P), to help in completing a difficult part of the job. While painting, Sam (P) broke his leg and filed a claim with the workers' compensation board. The board held that Sam (P) was an employee of the Church (D) (hence entitled to workers' compensation benefits) since Bill had the implied authority to hire Sam (P) because such implied authority was necessary to implement Bill's express authority as an agent of the Church (D) to complete the painting job.

RULE OF LAW

A person possesses implied authority as an agent to hire another worker where such implied authority is necessary to implement the agent's express authority.

FACTS: The Mill Street Church of Christ (the Church) (D) hired Bill Hogan to paint its church building. In the past, the Church (D) had allowed Bill to hire his brother, Sam Hogan (P), to assist if any assistance were needed. After Bill had painted most of the church himself, he realized that he needed assistance to paint the baptistry portion of the church, which was very high and difficult to paint. Bill thereupon hired his brother, Sam (P), to help in completing the painting job. The Church (D) supplied the tools, materials, and supplies necessary to complete the project. While painting, a leg of the ladder Sam (P) was using broke, causing Sam (P) to fall and break his left arm. After the accident, Sam (P) filed a claim under the Workers' Compensation Act. The New Workers' Compensation Board, reversing a ruling of the Old Workers' Compensation Board, held that Sam (P), at the time of his injury, was an employee of the Church (D), hence entitled to workers' compensation benefits. The Church (D) petitioned for review.

ISSUE: Does a person possess implied authority as an agent to hire another worker where such implied authority is necessary to implement the agent's express authority?

HOLDING AND DECISION: [Judge not stated in casebook excerpt.] Yes. A person possesses implied authority as an agent to hire another worker where such implied authority is necessary to implement the agent's express authority. Here, Bill Hogan had the implied authority of the Church (D) to hire Sam Hogan (P) as his helper. First, in the past, the Church (D) had allowed Bill Hogan to hire his brother (P) or other persons whenever he needed assistance on a project. Even though the Board of Elders discussed a different arrangement this time, no mention of this discussion was ever made to Bill Hogan or to Sam Hogan (P). Furthermore, Bill Hogan needed to hire an assistant to complete the job for which he had been hired. The interior of the church simply could not be painted by one person. Maintaining a safe and attractive place of worship clearly is part of the church's function, and one for which it would designate an agent to ensure that the building is properly painted and maintained. Finally, here, Sam Hogan (P) believed that Bill Hogan had the authority to hire him as had been the practice in the past. The treasurer of the Church (D) had even paid Bill Hogan for the half hour of work that Sam Hogan (P) had completed prior to the accident. Affirmed.

ANALYSIS

It is important to distinguish implied and apparent authority. Implied authority is actual authority circumstantially proven, which the principal actually intended the agent to possess and includes such powers as are practically necessary to carry out the duties actually designated. Apparent authority, on the other hand, as noted in the *Mill Street Church* case, is not actual authority, but is the authority the agent is held out by the principal as possessing. It is a matter of appearances on which third parties come to rely.

Quicknotes

AGENCY A fiduciary relationship whereby authority is granted to an agent to act on behalf of the principal in order to effectuate the principal's objective.

APPARENT AUTHORITY The authority granted to an agent to act on behalf of the principal in order to effectuate the principal's objective, which may not be expressly granted, but which is inferred from the conduct of the principal and the agent.

EXPRESS AUTHORITY Authority that is delegated pursuant to expressly stated words.

IMPLIED AUTHORITY Inferred power granted, but not expressly given, to an agent to act on behalf of the principal in order to effectuate the principal's objective.

Ackerman v. Sobol Family Partnership, LLP

Attorney's client (P) v. Family partnership (D)

Conn. Sup. Ct., 298 Conn. 495 (2010)

NATURE OF CASE: Appeal from decision enforcing a purported settlement agreement.

FACT SUMMARY: Attorney Glenn Coe (Coe) was retained by some, but not all, of the plaintiffs in litigation regarding a family partnership and family trusts. However, Coe represented all the plaintiffs in mediation and in negotiations to settle the litigation. Coe's clients and the other plaintiffs seemed to authorize such representation and seemed to clothe Coe with authority to negotiate a settlement agreement on their behalf. Coe believed he had such authority, and the defendants in the case also believed he had such authority. Coe eventually made a settlement offer that was accepted by the defendants. However, when it came time to enforce the settlement agreement, the plaintiffs claimed that there was no agreement, and contended that Coe did not have apparent authority to make settlement proposals, engage in settlement discussions, and bind the plaintiffs to a global settlement agreement with the defendants. The defendants countered that there was an agreement, and that Coe did have apparent authority to bind the plaintiffs to that agreement.

RULE OF LAW

An attorney whose client is one of several litigants, all of whom are on the same side of litigation, has apparent authority to bind all those litigants to a global settlement agreement where the attorney, although not retained by all the litigants, has represented all the litigants in settlement negotiations for an extended period of time and has indicated to the opponents that the attorney is fully authorized to negotiate settlement terms on behalf of all the litigants; where the litigants have held the attorney out as having authority to negotiate a settlement on their behalf and have knowingly permitted the attorney to act as having such authority; and where the opponents in good faith reasonably believe that the attorney has such authority.

FACTS: In a series of disputes and actions over a period of years concerning the management and oversight of a family partnership and various family trusts, there were multiple plaintiffs and multiple defendants. The plaintiffs were Rena Sobol Ackerman (Rena), Tamar Ackerman, Sara Ackerman, Jason Ackerman, Tzvi Rakoszynski (Rakoszynski), Mical Sobol Mann (Mann), and Alfred Casella (collectively, "the plaintiffs") (P). The defendants were Ruth Sobol, the Sobol Family Partnership, LLP, Ephraim Sobol and Sobol Property Management, LLC (collectively, "the Sobol defendants") (D); and the Bank of America, N.A. (Bank of America) (D). Glenn Coe (Coe) served as the retained attorney for Rena (P) and the other plaintiffs except for Rakoszynski (P) and Mann (P). On May 29, 2008, Coe, who was a seasoned negotiator, represented all the plaintiffs at a scheduled mediation. At the time the mediation was concluded, a settlement had not been reached. However, negotiations continued, and Coe made a detailed offer of settlement by way of a letter dated June 16, 2008, which was addressed to Attorneys Robert Wyld (Wyld), Dina Fisher (Fisher), and Steven Ecker (Ecker), who represented the Sobol defendants. Wyld responded by rejecting the settlement offer. Negotiations continued, and in a series of conversations that took place on June 26 and June 27, 2008, with Wyld and Attorney David Schneider (Schneider), who represented Bank of America (D), Coe made a different offer to settle the litigation. During that two-day period, Coe expressly assured the defendants' attorneys on separate occasions in response to direct questioning that the settlement offer proposed by him at that time was fully authorized by his clients as well as the other plaintiffs' attorneys, and that if accepted by the defendants, the settlement would resolve the litigation in all respects. Coe had been speaking on behalf of all the plaintiffs regarding settlement with the knowledge and authority of his own clients, as well as the attorneys who represented the other plaintiffs, and that had been the case since the time of the mediation on May 29, 2008. In fact, defense counsel had observed Rena (P) in Coe's presence during the mediation process and knew that Coe was consulting with her concerning negotiations based upon Coe's feedback. Moreover, Rena (P) was very involved in every aspect of the case, including settlement. All the defendants accepted Coe's settlement offer by July 1, 2008. Rena (P), Rakoszynski (P), and Mann (P) were present when Bank of America (D) accepted the offer on July 1. At no time prior to the acceptance of the settlement proposal were the defendants or their attorneys notified that the offer had been withdrawn, unauthorized, or otherwise ineffective. During that same period Rena (P) never manifested to the defendants or their attorneys that Coe's settlement authority was limited or had been terminated. On July 3, 2008, the defendants moved to enforce the settlement agreement. On July 8, the trial court conducted a hearing to determine if the settlement agreement was enforceable. At that hearing, however, the plaintiffs argued that there was no agreement, contending that Coe did not have

Continued on next page.

apparent authority to make settlement proposals, engage in settlement discussions, and bind the plaintiffs to a global settlement agreement with the defendants. The trial court, contrary to the plaintiffs' assertions, determined that Coe did have apparent authority to make and conclude the settlement agreement, and that the defendants' counsel reasonably believed that Coe was, in fact, authorized by the plaintiffs to make the settlement offer at issue. Although Rena (P) testified that Coe had no authority to enter into the settlement, the trial court found her testimony was not credible. Based on its findings and conclusions, the trial court granted the defendants' motions to enforce the settlement agreement. The plaintiffs appealed, and the state's highest court transferred the appeal (consolidated with another appeal) from the state's intermediate appellate court.

ISSUE: Does an attorney whose client is one of several litigants, all of whom are on the same side of litigation, have apparent authority to bind all those litigants to a global settlement agreement where the attorney, although not retained by all the litigants, has represented all the litigants in settlement negotiations for an extended period of time and has indicated to the opponents that the attorney is fully authorized to negotiate settlement terms on behalf of all the litigants; where the litigants have held the attorney out as having authority to negotiate a settlement on their behalf and have knowingly permitted the attorney to act as having such authority; and where the opponents in good faith reasonably believe that the attorney has such authority?

HOLDING AND DECISION: [Judge not stated in casebook excerpt.] Yes. An attorney whose client is one of several litigants, all of whom are on the same side of litigation, has apparent authority to bind all those litigants to a global settlement agreement where the attorney, although not retained by all the litigants, has represented all the litigants in settlement negotiations for an extended period of time and has indicated to the opponents that the attorney is fully authorized to negotiate settlement terms on behalf of all the litigants; where the litigants have held the attorney out as having authority to negotiate a settlement on their behalf and have knowingly permitted the attorney to act as having such authority; and where the opponents in good faith reasonably believe that the attorney has such authority. It is a general rule of agency law that the principal in an agency relationship is bound by, and liable for, the acts in which the agent engages with authority from the principal, and within the scope of the agent's employment. An agent's authority may be actual or apparent. Apparent authority is that semblance of authority that a principal, through the principal's acts or inadvertences, causes or allows third persons to believe the agent possesses. Consequently, apparent authority is to be determined, not by the agent's acts, but by the acts of the agent's principal. In this state, the issue of apparent authority is one of fact to be determined based on two criteria. First, it must appear from the principal's conduct that the principal held the agent out as possessing sufficient authority to embrace the act in question, or knowingly permitted the agent to act as having such authority. Second, the party dealing with the agent must have, acting in good faith, reasonably believed, under all the circumstances, that the agent had the necessary authority to bind the principal to the agent's action. These principles apply to the relationship between attorneys and their clients. Thus, an attorney with apparent authority may enter into a settlement agreement that is binding on the client, although an attorney does not automatically get such apparent authority upon being retained. Instead, manifestations of apparent authority must take the form of conduct by a person, observable by others, that expresses meaning, including silence, which may constitute a manifestation when, "in light of all the circumstances, a reasonable person would express dissent to the inference that other persons will draw from silence." 1 Restatement (Third), Agency, § 1.03 at p. 57. Thus, the failure to express dissent is taken as a manifestation of affirmance. Apparent authority also may be conveyed to third persons from authorized statements of the agent, from documents or other indicia of authority given by the principal to the agent, or from third persons who have heard of the agent's authority through authorized or permitted channels of communication. Likewise, apparent authority can be created by appointing a person to a position that carries with it generally recognized duties to do the things ordinarily entrusted to one occupying such a position.

As to the first criterion for determining apparent authority, a manifestation of a principal's assent or intention does not occur in a vacuum, and the meaning that may reasonably be inferred from it reflects the context in which the manifestation is made. Between particular persons, prior dealings or an ongoing relationship frame the context in which manifestations are made and understood. Here, the trial court's finding that the plaintiffs clothed Coe with apparent authority to settle the litigation is supported by evidence of a course of dealing involving the plaintiffs, the defendants, and the parties' attorneys that was well established before the Sobol defendants (D) and the Bank of America (D) accepted the global settlement offer. It is undisputed that Coe represented all of the plaintiffs at the court-ordered mediation on May 29, 2008, during which settlement terms were discussed and Rena (P) and the other plaintiffs were present. Moreover, it was Coe, acting on behalf of all of the plaintiffs, who subsequently rejected the defendants' written offer. Coe was also the attorney who made a proposed settlement offer in his letter of June 16. It is clear

Continued on next page.

that Coe was authorized to make this offer, which would have settled the entire litigation if accepted, because the letter contained language indicating that it pertained to all of the pending litigation. Additionally, Coe, the other plaintiffs' attorneys, and the defense attorneys all understood that Coe had authority to make the offer, and all the plaintiffs affirmed this understanding. Rena (P), who was very involved in all aspects of the litigation, was present at various hearings, was seen to confer with Coe regarding strategy, and, along with some of the other plaintiffs, was present at Coe's law firm offices when they were waiting for the Bank of America (D) response to the settlement offer. There was no apparent discord or distance in the relationship between Coe and Rena (P). Thus, based on her conduct during the times she was observed with Coe prior to the offer's acceptance, it seems Rena (P) was aware of, and fully supported, the global settlement offer. Additionally, none of the plaintiffs indicated by their conduct prior to the Bank of America's (D) acceptance of the offer that Coe did not have continued authority to settle the litigation, and there was never an express revocation or limitation on Coe's settlement authority. For these reasons, the evidence unequivocally supports the trial court's finding that the plaintiffs held Coe out as possessing the necessary authority to settle the litigation.

As to the second criterion, on the basis of this course of dealing among the parties, the defendants reasonably could have believed that Coe continued to have authority to discuss settlement terms and to make settlement offers during the middle and latter part of June. The defendants queried Coe about his settlement authority on several occasions, on each of which Coe answered their questions plainly and directly and told them at various times throughout the negotiations whether he did or did not have such authority. Coe's conduct was consistent with his representations, as at various times he sought authorization from Rena (P) and the other plaintiffs for settlement terms. Based on their course of conduct with Coe, both Wyld and Schneider testified that they believed Coe had authority to settle the litigation at the end of June, not only because Coe had been acting on behalf of all of the plaintiffs since May 29, but also because Coe had assured Wyld that he had such authority. Wyld and Schneider were further justified in believing that Coe's statements were authorized because attorneys are required to conduct their professional affairs in accordance with rules of professional conduct, so that Wyld and Schneider could reasonably rely on Coe's repeated assurances that he had secured the plaintiffs' consent to the terms of the global settlement offer because an attorney with Coe's abundance of experience and exemplary reputation never would have misrepresented his authority in such a matter in violation of those rules. Coe's assurances were even more authentic in light of his occasional admissions that he did not have authority to agree to certain settlement figures at various times during the final settlement negotiations. Notwithstanding Coe's conceded misunderstanding of the plaintiffs' position, such misunderstanding does not affect the analysis of whether Coe had apparent authority to settle the claim. For these reasons, the evidence was sufficient to support the trial court's conclusion as to Coe's apparent authority under the second prong of the test for apparent authority. Finally, the plaintiffs' argument that because the agreement was not initially in writing, it was not fully authorized, is unavailing; it is well established that an oral settlement agreement that subsequently is to be memorialized in writing is enforceable. Accordingly, Coe had apparent authority to settle the litigation, and the plaintiffs' claim that the settlement agreement is unenforceable has no merit. Affirmed.

ANALYSIS

Under the Restatement approach, apparent authority terminates when a third person has notice that: (1) the agent's authority has terminated; (2) the principal no longer consents to the agent's dealing with the third person; or (3) the agent is acting under a basic error as to the facts. 1 Restatement (Second), Agency § 125, comment (a) (1958). Unless otherwise agreed, there is a notification by the principal to the third person of revocation of an agent's apparent authority or other fact indicating its termination: (a) when the principal states such fact to the third person; or (b) when a reasonable time has elapsed after a writing stating such fact has been delivered by the principal to the other personally. 1 Restatement (Second), § 136(1). In addition, the principal can properly give notification of the termination of the agent's authority by giving publicity by some method reasonably adapted to give the information to such third person. Additionally, if a principal has given an agent general authority to engage in a class of transactions, subject to limits known only to the agent and the principal, third parties may reasonably believe the agent to be authorized to conduct such transactions and need not inquire into the existence of undisclosed limits on the agent's authority. 1 Restatement (Third), Agency, *supra*, at § 3.03, comment (b), pp. 174–75. Based on these factors, the Connecticut Supreme Court concluded that Coe's settlement authority had not been limited or revoked in any way by any of the plaintiffs or their attorneys.

Quicknotes

APPARENT AUTHORITY The authority granted to an agent to act on behalf of the principal in order to effectuate the

Continued on next page.

principal's objective, which may not be expressly granted, but which is inferred from the conduct of the principal and the agent.

GOOD FAITH An honest intention to abstain from taking advantage of another.

MEDIATION A process of alternative dispute resolution engaged in before trial by the parties to a lawsuit either voluntarily or by court order in an attempt to resolve the case.

Watteau v. Fenwick

Supplier (P) v. Pub owner (D)

Q.B., 1 Q.B. 346 (1892)

NATURE OF CASE: Appeal from judgment awarding damages in action for breach of contract.

FACT SUMMARY: Fenwick (D) had authorized Humble as purchasing agent, but only for specific items, an authority Humble then exceeded.

RULE OF LAW

When one holds out another as an agent, that agent can bind the principal on matters normally incident to such agency, even if that agent was not authorized for a particular type of transaction.

FACTS: Fenwick (D) purchased a pub from Humble. Fenwick (D) retained Humble as manager. Part of Humble's duties as manager was purchasing supplies; however, Fenwick (D) authorized Humble to purchase only ale and mineral water. Humble purchased other pub-related items from Watteau (P) over a long period of time, on credit. Watteau (P) later sued to recover the value of the items sold. The trial court granted judgment in favor of Watteau (P). Fenwick (D) appealed, contending that Humble had not been authorized to purchase on his behalf.

ISSUE: When one holds out another as an agent, can that agent bind the principal on matters incident to such agency even if that agent was not authorized for a particular type of transaction?

HOLDING AND DECISION: (Wills, J.) Yes. When one holds out another as an agent, that agent can bind the principal on matters incident to such agency, even if that agent was not authorized for a particular type of transaction. The principal is liable for all the acts of the agent that are within the authority usually confided to an agent of that character, notwithstanding any limitations placed on the agency and not disclosed to third parties. Here, in the context of a public house, one dealing with the manager thereof clearly would expect that such manager would have authority to purchase pub-related items, and therefore Fenwick (D) is liable for the debt incurred by Humble. Appeal dismissed.

ANALYSIS

This case represents an early example of apparent authority. In this context, Humble, having authority to purchase some tavern-related items, had apparent authority to purchase other tavern-related goods, and could bind his principal in doing so. This rule also applies to partnerships; a partner may be held liable for claims made against other partners, even if he does not disclose his identity as a partner and even if the partnership agreement prohibits the transaction underlying the claim.

Quicknotes

AGENT An individual who has the authority to act on behalf of another.

APPARENT AUTHORITY The authority granted to an agent to act on behalf of the principal in order to effectuate the principal's objective, which may not be expressly granted, but which is inferred from the conduct of the principal and the agent.

PRINCIPAL A person or entity who authorizes another (the agent) to act on its behalf and subject to its authority to the extent that the principal may be held liable for the actions of the agent.

Botticello v. Stefanovicz

Purchaser of property (P) v. Sellers of property (D)

Conn. Sup. Ct., 177 Conn. 22, 411 A.2d 16 (1979)

NATURE OF CASE: Appeal by property sellers from an order for specific performance in favor of the property purchaser.

FACT SUMMARY: Mary and Walter Stefanovicz (D) were tenants in common of a farm. Botticello (P) wanted to purchase the farm. Botticello (P) and Walter (D) agreed upon a price of $85,000 for a lease with an option to purchase and signed papers to that effect, but Botticello (P) did not know at the time that Walter (D) did not own the property outright. When Mary (D) and Walter (D) subsequently refused to honor the option agreement, Botticello (P) sued them for specific performance. Mary (D) and Walter (D) contended that Walter (D) was not Mary's (D) agent, so that the agreement was not binding upon her.

RULE OF LAW

(1) An agency relationship cannot be established where the fair preponderance of the evidence does not indicate that the purported principal has authorized or agreed to the purported agent acting on their behalf.

(2) A person cannot ratify a prior act where the person neither intends to do so nor has full knowledge of all the material circumstances.

FACTS: Mary and Walter Stefanovicz (D) were tenants in common of a farm. Botticello (P) visited the farm and offered $75,000 to purchase it. At that time, Mary (D) stated that there was "no way" she could sell it for that amount. Ultimately, Botticello (P) and Walter (D) agreed upon a price of $85,000 for a lease with an option to purchase. The informal agreement was finalized with the assistance of counsel for both Walter (D) and Botticello (P). Neither Botticello (P) nor his attorney, nor Walter's (D) attorney, was then aware of the fact that Walter (D) did not own the property outright. After execution of the lease and option-to-purchase agreement, Botticello (P) took possession of the property and made substantial improvements on it. When Mary and Walter Stefanovicz (D) refused to honor the option agreement, Botticello (P) sued them for specific performance. The trial court ordered specific performance, holding that although Mary (D) was not party to the lease and option-to-purchase agreement, its terms were nonetheless binding on her because Walter (D) had acted as her authorized agent in the negotiations, discussions, and execution of the written agreement. The court also held that even if Walter (D) had not acted as Mary's (D) agent, Mary (D), through her subsequent conduct, ratified the agreement. The state's highest court granted review.

ISSUE:

(1) Can an agency relationship be established where the fair preponderance of the evidence does not indicate that the purported principal has authorized or agreed to the purported agent acting on their behalf?

(2) Can a person ratify a prior act where the person neither intends to do so nor has full knowledge of all the material circumstances?

HOLDING AND DECISION: [Judge not stated in casebook excerpt.]

(1) No. An agency relationship cannot be established where the fair preponderance of the evidence does not indicate that the purported principal has authorized or agreed to the purported agent acting on their behalf. The existence of an agency relationship is a question of fact. The burden of proving agency is on the plaintiff, and it must be proven by a fair preponderance of the evidence. Marital status cannot in and of itself prove an agency relationship, so here, the mere fact that Mary (D) and Walter (D) were married does not prove such a relationship. The fact that one person owns property with another by itself also does not establish agency, so that Mary and Walter's (D) common ownership of the land does not make one the agent for the other. Although Mary (D) remarked that she would not sell the farm for less than $85,000, a statement that one will not sell for less than a certain amount is by no means the equivalent of an agreement to sell for that amount. Moreover, the fact that one spouse tends more to business matters than the other does not, absent other evidence of agreement or authorization, constitute the delegation of power as to an agent. Furthermore, although Mary (D) may have acquiesced in Walter's (D) handling of many business matters, Walter (D) never signed any documents as agent for Mary (D) prior to the time of the alleged farm sale. Mary (D) had consistently signed any deed, mortgage, or mortgage note in connection with their jointly held property. All these facts, taken together, demonstrate the absence of an agency relationship between Walter (D) and Mary (D). Specific performance against Mary (D) is precluded. Reversed as to this issue.

(2) No. A person cannot ratify a prior act where the person neither intends to do so nor has full knowledge of all the material circumstances. Ratification is defined as "the affirmance by a person of a prior act which

Continued on next page.

did not bind them but which was done or professedly done on their account" and it requires acceptance of the results of the act with an intent to ratify, and with full knowledge of all the material circumstances. The facts here do not indicate that Mary (D) intended to ratify the agreement, nor do they establish her knowledge of all the material circumstances surrounding the deal. At most, Mary (D) observed Botticello (P) occupying and improving the land; received rental payments from him from time to time; knew that she had an interest in the property; and knew that the use, occupancy, and rentals were pursuant to a written agreement she had not signed. None of these facts is sufficient to support the conclusion that Mary (D) ratified the agreement and thus bound herself to its terms—especially since Walter (D) had the right to lease his undivided one-half interest in the property. Moreover, since Walter (D) never purported to be acting on Mary's (D) behalf, she cannot be deemed to have ratified the agreement by merely accepting its benefits and by failing to repudiate it. That is because if the original transaction was not purported to have been done on account of the principal, the fact that the principal receives its proceeds does not make him a party to it. Specific performance reversed as to Mary (D). Vacated and remanded for a new trial.

ANALYSIS

Agency may be either actual or apparent. Apparent authority is that semblance of authority that a principal, through his own acts or inadvertences, causes or allows third persons to believe his agent possesses. Apparent authority thus must be determined by the acts of the principal rather than by the acts of the agent. Since in this case Botticello (P) admitted that he did not know of Mary's (D) interest in the land at the time the agreement was signed, her actions could not form the basis for a finding of apparent authority, which is likely why Botticello (P) did not pursue that theory of agency.

Quicknotes

SPECIFIC PERFORMANCE An equitable remedy whereby the court requires the parties to perform their obligations pursuant to a contract.

TENANCY IN COMMON An interest in property held by two or more people, each with equal right to its use and possession; interests may be partitioned, sold, conveyed, or devised.

Hoddeson v. Koos Bros.

Customer (P) v. Furniture store (D)

N.J. Super. Ct. App. Div., 47 N.J. Super. 224, 135 A.2d 702 (1957)

NATURE OF CASE: Appeal from a judgment for plaintiff in an action based on an alleged agency. [The complete procedural posture of the case is not indicated in the casebook extract.]

FACT SUMMARY: When Mrs. Hoddeson (P), intending to purchase furniture, gave cash to a man on the sales floor of Koos Brothers furniture store (D) who held himself out to be a salesperson, but later discovered he was not employed by the store but was a con artist who kept the money, she brought suit against the store, on the basis of an agency relationship. [The complete procedural posture of the case is not indicated in the casebook extract.]

RULE OF LAW

To establish apparent agency, the appearance of authority must be shown to have been created by the manifestations of the alleged principal and not solely by the supposed agent.

FACTS: Mrs. Hoddeson (P) and her relatives went to Koos Brothers furniture store (D) and purchased furniture from a man on the sales floor who she assumed was a salesperson of the store. He guided Hoddeson (P) and her family to the furniture she desired to purchase, withdrew from his pocket a pad on which he presumably recorded her order and calculated the total purchase price to be $168.50. Hoddeson (P) handed to him the $168.50 in cash. He told her the articles would be delivered but gave her no receipt. Subsequently when the articles were not delivered, Hoddeson (P) contacted the store and discovered there was never any such sale. Neither she nor her relatives were later able to recognize the salesman among any of the store's regularly employed sales force. Hoddeson (P) brought suit against Koos Brothers (D), based on a theory of agency. Koos Brothers (D) defended by contending that the purported salesman was in fact a con artist, arguing that, therefore, there could not have been an agency relationship. The trial court found in favor of Hoddeson (P). Koos Brothers (D) appealed, and the state's intermediate appellate court granted review. [The complete procedural posture of the case is not indicated in the casebook extract.]

ISSUE: To establish apparent agency, must the appearance of authority be shown to have been created by the manifestations of the alleged principal and not solely by the supposed agent?

HOLDING AND DECISION: [Judge not stated in casebook excerpt.] Yes. To establish apparent agency, the appearance of authority must be shown to have been created by the manifestations of the alleged principal and not solely by the supposed agent. Where a party seeks to impose liability upon an alleged principal on a contract made by an alleged agent, as here, the party must assume the obligation of proving the agency relationship. It is not the burden of the alleged principal to disprove it. Here, Hoddeson's (P) evidence did not substantiate the existence of any basic express authority or project any question implicating implied authority. The law cannot permit apparent authority to be established by the mere proof that a dishonest person in fact exercised it. Accordingly, the judgment must be reversed. Nevertheless, the rule that those who bargain without inquiry with an apparent agent do so at the risk and peril of an absence of the agent's authority has a patently impracticable application to the customers who patronize modern department stores. The duty of a store proprietor encompasses the exercise of reasonable care and diligence to protect a customer from loss occasioned by the deceptions of an apparent salesman. Therefore, Hoddeson (P) should be permitted, in a new trial, to prove that Koos Brothers (D) should be estopped from denying apparent agency. In doing so, the following rule of estoppel should apply: Where a proprietor of a place of business by their dereliction of duty enables one who is not their agent conspicuously to act as such and ostensibly to transact the proprietor's business with a patron in the establishment, the appearances being of such a character as to lead a person of ordinary prudence and circumspection to believe that the impostor was in truth the proprietor's agent, in such circumstances the law will not permit the proprietor defensively to avail themself of the impostor's lack of authority and thus escape liability for the consequential loss thereby sustained by the customer. Reversed and new trial allowed.

ANALYSIS

In *Hoddeson*, the action was one in assumpsit, where Hoddeson (P) sought to establish privity of contract through an agency relationship. The lower court granted judgment on a jury finding that the person who sold the furniture to Hoddeson (P) was in fact an employee of Koos Brothers (D), but, as the holding in this decision shows, the appellate court found the evidence legally insufficient for such a finding. Thus, the court held that apparent agency had not been established

Continued on next page.

by the plaintiff, who bears the burden of proving that matter. Nonetheless, the court, finding that a "proprietor's duty of care and precaution for the safety and security of the customer encompasses more than the diligent observance and removal of banana peels from the aisles," and additionally encompasses the exercise of reasonable care and diligence to protect a customer from loss occasioned by the deceptions of an apparent salesman, set forth the standard for agency by estoppel by which Hoddeson (P) could prevail on her claim if she were able to prove the elements of agency by estoppel in a new trial. To do so, she would have to prove that Koos Brothers (D) had been derelict in its duty to identify and prevent the supposed imposter from acting as a salesperson on its premises, perhaps by adducing evidence that Koos Brothers (D) did not regularly monitor its sales force or did not have a policy of doing so. On the other hand, Koos Brothers (D) could defend such a claim by showing that it did regularly monitor its sales operations to a reasonable degree necessary to prevent imposters from acting as salespeople. In any event, the court in this decision did not entertain those questions but left them to a new trial—assuming Hoddeson (P) wanted to pursue one.

Quicknotes

ASSUMPSIT An oral or written promise by one party to perform or pay another.

ESTOPPEL An equitable doctrine precluding a party from asserting a right to the detriment of another who justifiably relied on the conduct.

EXPRESS AUTHORITY Authority that is delegated pursuant to expressly stated words.

IMPLIED AUTHORITY Inferred power granted, but not expressly given, to an agent to act on behalf of the principal in order to effectuate the principal's objective.

Atlantic Salmon A/S v. Curran

Wholesale sellers of salmon (P) v. Agent of partially disclosed principal (D)

Mass. App. Ct., 32 Mass. App. Ct. 488, 591 N.E.2d 206 (1992)

NATURE OF CASE: Appeal of a judgment in favor of the agent of a salmon purchaser in a suit by the salmon wholesaler for recovery of contractual costs.

FACT SUMMARY: Atlantic Salmon A/S (Atlantic) (P) and Salmonor A/S (Salmonor) (P) sued Curran (D) for $153,788.50 and $101,759.65, respectively, owing on a contract that Curran (D) had purportedly made as the agent of Boston International Seafood Exchange, but which in fact Curran (D) had made with another company (Marketing Designs, Inc.) as a partially disclosed principal.

RULE OF LAW

It is the duty of an agent, in order to avoid personal liability on a contract entered into on behalf of the principal, to disclose not only that the agent is acting in a representative capacity, but also the identity of the principal.

FACTS: Atlantic Salmon A/S (Atlantic) (P) and Salmonor A/S (Salmonor) (P), salmon wholesalers, had for several years dealt with a salmon exporter known as "Boston International Seafood Exchange, Inc." or "Boston Seafood Exchange, Inc." Payment checks to the plaintiffs were imprinted with the name "Boston International Seafood Exchange, Inc." and signed by Curran (D), using the designation "Treas.," intending thereby to convey the impression that he was treasurer. Wire transfers and payments were also made in the same manner. Curran (D) also gave the plaintiffs business cards that listed him as "marketing director" of "Boston International Seafood Exchange, Inc." Subsequently, a new corporation named "Marketing Designs, Inc.," was organized, and then dissolved. Atlantic (P) was owed $153,788.50 and Salmonor (P) owed $101,759.65 for salmon sold to a business known as "Boston International Seafood Exchange" during the period that such company was actually owned by "Marketing Designs, Inc." Curran (D) had made checks imprinted with the name "Boston International Seafood Exchange, Inc." to plaintiffs as payment for the salmon. Curran never informed the plaintiffs of the existence of "Marketing Designs, Inc.," and the plaintiffs did not know of it until after the commencement of the present litigation. Atlantic (P) and Salmonor (P) sued Curran (D) for the amount owing on the Boston International Seafood Exchange contract. The trial court awarded judgment for Curran (D). Atlantic (P) and Salmonor (P) appealed. The state's intermediate appellate court granted review.

ISSUE: Is it the duty of an agent, in order to avoid personal liability on a contract entered into on behalf of the principal, to disclose not only that the agent is acting in a representative capacity, but also the identity of the principal?

HOLDING AND DECISION: [Judge not stated in casebook excerpt.] Yes. It is the duty of an agent, in order to avoid personal liability on a contract entered into on behalf of the principal, to disclose not only that the agent is acting in a representative capacity, but also the identity of the principal. Here, it is not sufficient that the plaintiffs may have had the means, through a search of the records of the Boston city clerk, to determine the identity of Curran's (D) principal. Actual knowledge is the test. It is not enough that the other party has the means of determining such information. The agent must either bring forward actual knowledge or, what is the same thing—that which to a reasonable person is equivalent to knowledge—or the agent will be bound. There is no hardship to the agent in this rule since the agent always has the power to relieve itself from personal liability by fully disclosing the principal and contracting only in the latter's name. Here, the agent, Curran (D), did not bring forth such information, but in fact had contracted with Atlantic (P) and Salmonor (P) at prior times directly. Reversed.

ANALYSIS

In *Atlantic Salmon*, the court noted that if the other party to a transaction has notice that the agent is or may be acting for a principal, but has no notice of the principal's identity, the principal for whom the agent is acting is a partially disclosed principal. In the instant case, although Atlantic (P) and Salmonor (P) had notice that Curran (D) was purporting to act for a corporate principal, Atlantic (P) and Salmonor (P) had no notice of the identity of the principal. Hence, since the corporate principal was only a partially disclosed principal, Curran (D) was a party to the contract.

Quicknotes

AGENT An individual who has the authority to act on behalf of another.

PRINCIPAL A person or entity that authorizes another (the agent) to act on its behalf and subject to its authority to the extent that the principal may be held liable for the actions of the agent.

Humble Oil & Refining Co. v. Martin

Filling station owner (D) v. Injured bystander (P)

Tex. Sup. Ct., 148 Tex. 175, 222 S.W.2d 995 (1949)

NATURE OF CASE: Appeal from judgment awarding damages for personal injury.

FACT SUMMARY: Martin (P), injured when a car rolled out of a service station owned by Humble Oil and Refining Co. (Humble) (D), sought to hold Humble (D) liable for the station operator's negligence.

RULE OF LAW

A party may be liable for a contractor's torts if the party exercises substantial control over the contractor's operations.

FACTS: Martin (P) and his two children (P) were injured when they were struck by a vehicle that rolled out of a service station owned by Humble Oil and Refining Co. (Humble) (D) and operated by Schneider. Martin (P) sued both Love (D), the owner of the vehicle that struck him, and Humble (D). The evidence showed that Humble (D) exercised substantial control over the details of the station's operation. The trial court rendered judgment against both Love (D) and Humble (D), and the state's intermediate appellate court affirmed. Humble (D) appealed, contending that it was not responsible for the torts of its independent contractors.

ISSUE: May a party be liable for a contractor's torts if the party exercises substantial control over the contractor's operations?

HOLDING AND DECISION: [Judge not stated in casebook excerpt.] Yes. A party may be liable for a contractor's torts if the party exercises substantial control over the contractor's operations. A party is not normally liable for the torts of their contractors. However, when that party so substantially controls the manner of the contractor's operations, the contractor relationship breaks down and a master-servant relationship is formed. Here, Schneider was obligated to perform any duty Humble (D) might impose on him. Humble (D) paid some of Schneider's operating expenses and controlled the station's hours. The evidence showed that Humble (D) mandated much of the day-to-day operations of the station, certainly enough to justify the trial court's finding of a master-servant relationship rather than a contractor relationship. Affirmed.

ANALYSIS

According to the Restatement (Second) of Agency, a master-servant relationship is one in which the servant has agreed to work and be subject to the master's control. An independent contractor, on the other hand, agrees to work, but is not under the principal's control insofar as the manner in which the job is accomplished. In general, liability will not be imputed to the principal for the tortious conduct of an independent contractor. Under the theory of "apparent agency," the mere appearance a master-servant-type relationship may subject the principal to liability.

Quicknotes

INDEPENDENT CONTRACTOR A party undertaking a particular assignment for another who retains control over the manner in which it is executed.

MASTER-SERVANT RELATIONSHIP Relationship where a particular individual agrees to render personal services to another for valuable consideration.

NEGLIGENCE Conduct falling below the standard of care that a reasonable person would demonstrate under similar conditions.

Hoover v. Sun Oil Company

Injured motorist (P) v. Filling station owner (D)

Del. Super. Ct., 58 Del. 553, 212 A.2d 214 (1965)

NATURE OF CASE: Summary judgment motion by defendant in action seeking damages for personal injury.

FACT SUMMARY: Hoover (P) sought to hold franchisor Sun Oil Co. (D) responsible after he was injured in a fire at a service station franchise operated by Barone (D).

RULE OF LAW

A franchisee is considered an independent contractor of the franchisor if the franchisee retains control of inventory and operations.

FACTS: Barone (D) operated as a franchisee of Sun Oil Co. (Sun) (D). The agreement called for a certain level of compliance by Barone (D) with Sun (D) standards, but Barone (D) was left in control of day-to-day operations of the service station and made all inventory decisions. Barone (D) carried primarily Sun (D) products but was allowed to carry products by other companies as well. Hoover (P) suffered burns when a fire started while his vehicle was being filled by an employee at the station. Hoover (P) sued Sun (D) and Barone (D). Sun (D) moved for summary judgment, contending that Barone (D) was an independent contractor, so that Sun (D) could not be liable under any form of vicarious liability.

ISSUE: Is a franchisee considered an independent contractor of the franchisor if the franchisee retains control of inventory and operations?

HOLDING AND DECISION: [Judge not stated in casebook excerpt.] Yes. A franchisee is considered an independent contractor of the franchisor if the franchisee retains control of inventory and operations. The test in such a situation is whether the franchisor retains the right to control the details of the day-to-day operations of the franchisee. A franchisor's control or influence over the results alone, are insufficient to establish a principal-agent relationship. Here, while Sun (D) obviously had some control over the operation of Barone's (D) business, Barone (D) retained full control over his operations, including what inventory to stock. This clearly falls on the contractor side of the issue. Motion granted.

ANALYSIS

It is difficult in cases dealing with the issue here to find one single determinant of whether one will be considered an agent or an independent contractor. Different courts focus on different factors. A franchise agreement that would lead to a result of no vicarious liability in one jurisdiction could well lead to the opposite conclusion in another jurisdiction.

Quicknotes

AGENT An individual who has the authority to act on behalf of another.

FRANCHISEE A party whom a supplier of goods or services agrees to permit to sell the good or service or to otherwise conduct business on behalf of the franchise.

FRANCHISOR A supplier of goods or services who agrees to permit a re-seller to sell the good or service or to otherwise conduct business on behalf of the franchise.

INDEPENDENT CONTRACTOR A party undertaking a particular assignment for another who retains control over the manner in which it is executed.

PRINCIPAL A person or entity who authorizes another (the agent) to act on its behalf and subject to its authority to the extent that the principal may be held liable for the actions of the agent.

SUMMARY JUDGMENT Judgment rendered by a court in response to a motion made by one of the parties, claiming that the lack of a question of material fact in respect to an issue warrants disposition of the issue without consideration by the jury.

VICARIOUS LIABILITY The imputed liability of one party for the unlawful acts of another.

Kerl v. Rasmussen

Shooting victim (P) v. Franchise operator (D)

Wis. Sup. Ct., 682 N.W.2d 328 (2004)

NATURE OF CASE: Appeal in action for vicarious liability of franchisor for franchisee's alleged negligent hiring. [The procedural posture of the case is not presented in the casebook extract.]

FACT SUMMARY: After Harvey Pierce, a work-release inmate who had been hired by DRI (D), a franchisee operator of an Arby's (D) fast-food restaurant, shot and injured Robin Kerl (P), Pierce's former girlfriend, and shot and killed her fiancé, David Jones, Kerl (P) and Jones' estate (P) brought suit, contending, inter alia, that Arby's (D) was vicariously liable for DRI's (D) negligent hiring of Pierce. Arby's (D) countered that it could not be vicariously liable for Pierce's actions where it did not have the right to actively control the hiring and supervision of DRI's (D) employees.

RULE OF LAW

A franchisor may be held vicariously liable for the tortious conduct of its franchisee only if the franchisor has control or a right of control over the daily operation of the specific aspect of the franchisee's business that is alleged to have caused the harm for which the franchisor is sought to be held liable.

FACTS: In 1985, DRI (D) entered into a franchise license agreement with Arby's (D), a national franchisor of fast-food restaurants. Although the agreement contained a plethora of general quality and operational standards and controls on the operation of DRI's (D) restaurant, required DRI (D) to hire, train, maintain, and properly supervise sufficient qualified and courteous personnel for the efficient operation of the restaurant, and required that someone in charge at the restaurant complete a management training seminar conducted by Arby's (D), the agreement gave DRI (D) sole control over the hiring and supervision of its employees. In early 1999, DRI (D) hired Harvey Pierce, a work-release inmate. Several months later, Pierce walked off the job without permission, walked over to a nearby Wal-Mart, and ambushed his former girlfriend, Robin Kerl (P), and her fiancé, David Jones, injuring Kerl (P) and killing Jones. Pierce shot and killed himself. Kerl (P) and Jones' estate (P) brought suit, alleging, inter alia, that Arby's (D) was vicariously liable, as DRI's (D) franchisor, for DRI's (D) negligent supervision of Pierce, under theories of actual or constructive agency and respondeat superior. The state's highest court heard an appeal in the case. [The procedural posture of the case is not presented in the casebook extract.]

ISSUE: May a franchisor be held vicariously liable for the tortious conduct of its franchisee only if the franchisor has control or a right of control over the daily operation of the specific aspect of the franchisee's business that is alleged to have caused the harm for which the franchisor is sought to be held liable?

HOLDING AND DECISION: [Judge not stated in casebook excerpt.] Yes. A franchisor may be held vicariously liable for the tortious conduct of its franchisee only if the franchisor has control or a right of control over the daily operation of the specific aspect of the franchisee's business that is alleged to have caused the harm for which the franchisor is sought to be held liable. Although a person is generally only liable for their own torts, the law will impose vicarious liability on a person or entity who did not commit the tortious conduct but nevertheless is deemed responsible by virtue of the close relationship between that person and the tortfeasor. The doctrine of *respondeat superior* ("let the master answer"), holds a supervisory party liable for the actionable conduct of a subordinate or associate because of a master-servant agency relationship between the two parties. Vicarious liability is a form of strict liability without fault. Under *respondeat superior*, a master may be held vicariously liable for a servant's torts regardless of whether the master's own conduct is tortious. Thus, vicarious liability is imputed liability that is imposed upon an innocent party for the torts of another because the nature of the agency relationship—specifically the element of control or right of control—justifies it. A modern justification for imposing vicarious liability is to spread risk and encourage safety and the exercise of due care by employees/servants by incentivizing masters who control or have the right to control the conduct of their servants to take steps to ensure that their servants exercise due care in carrying out the master's business. However, where the requisite degree of control by a master/principal is lacking, applying vicarious liability cannot be justified, because if a principal does not control or have the right to control the day-to-day physical conduct of the agent, then the opportunity and incentive to promote safety and the exercise of due care are not present, and imposing liability without fault would not be fair. Although *respondeat superior* is applied primarily in the employment context, it has also been applied in the franchising context, but much more sparingly, because it is much more difficult

Continued on next page.

to establish the requisite degree of control of a franchisee by a franchisor than of an employee by an employer. Although franchise agreements typically impose detailed requirements on the franchisee's operations, the existence of these contractual requirements does not mean that franchisors have a role in managing the day-to-day operations of their franchisees. To the contrary, the imposition of quality and operational requirements by contract suggests that the franchisor does not intervene in the daily operation and management of the independent business of the franchisee. Also, because many franchise relationships include a license to use the franchisor's trade or service mark, the detailed quality and operational standards and inspection rights specified in the franchise agreement are integral to the protection of the franchisor's trade or service mark under the federal Lanham Act, the purpose of which, however, is to ensure the integrity of registered trademarks, not to create a federal law of agency. Accordingly, courts that have considered the issue of a franchisor's vicarious liability for a franchisee's negligence have held that the quality and operational standards and inspection rights contained in a franchise agreement do not establish a franchisor's control or right of control over the franchisee sufficient to ground a claim for vicarious liability as a general matter or for all purposes. Vicarious liability in such cases will be imposed only where the franchisor has control or has the right to control the daily conduct or operation of the particular "instrumentality" or aspect of the franchisee's business that is alleged to have caused the harm. Applying these principles here, Arby's (D) did not exercise the degree of control over DRI (D) necessary for the imposition of vicarious liability because Arby's (D) did not have control over the day-to-day supervision of DRI's (D) employees. Although the agreement contained a plethora of general quality and operational standards and controls on the operation of DRI's (D) restaurant, required DRI (D) to hire, train, maintain, and properly supervise sufficient qualified and courteous personnel for the efficient operation of the restaurant, and required that someone in charge at the restaurant complete a management training seminar conducted by Arby's (D), the agreement gave DRI (D) sole control over the hiring and supervision of its employees. Not only did Arby's (D) and DRI (D) stipulate in the license agreement that they did not have an agency relationship, the agreement's provisions regarding the specific issue of personnel were broad and general, so that Arby's (D) could not step in and take over the management of DRI's (D) employees; in other words, there was no "master/servant" relationship. Moreover, Arby's (D) right to terminate the relationship because of an uncured violation of the agreement is not the equivalent of a right to control the daily operation of the restaurant or actively manage DRI's (D) work force. For these reasons, Arby's (D) cannot be held vicariously liable for DRI's (D) negligent supervision of Pierce.

ANALYSIS

Vicarious liability under respondeat superior typically arises in employer/employee relationships but is not confined to this type of agency. A servant need not be under formal contract to perform work for a master, nor is it necessary for a person to be paid to occupy the position of servant. Although a servant need not be paid to expose the master to liability for the servant's torts, it is well-settled that except under certain limited circumstances, a master will only be liable for torts of the servant committed within the scope of the servant's employment. A deviation or stepping away from the master's business—a "frolic and detour" in the language of the early common law—may preclude vicarious liability. The question whether a tortfeasor was acting within the scope of employment at the time the injury was inflicted is normally for the jury to determine. This "scope of employment" question is often the main point of contention in a suit for damages predicated on a theory of vicarious liability. Here, these fact issues are not reached because the court decides there is no master-servant/employer-employee relationship in the first instance, which is also why the court affirms the lower courts' finding that there was no genuine issue of material fact as to whether DRI (D) was Arby's (D) servant when it came to the day-to-day control of DRI's (D) employees.

Quicknotes

AGENCY A fiduciary relationship whereby authority is granted to an agent to act on behalf of the principal in order to effectuate the principal's objective.

AGENT An individual who has the authority to act on behalf of another.

FRANCHISE An agreement whereby one party (the franchisor) grants another (the franchisee) the right to market its product or service.

FRANCHISE AGREEMENT A contract pursuant to which a supplier of goods or services agrees to permit a re-seller to sell the good or service or to otherwise conduct business on behalf of the franchise.

FRANCHISEE A party who a supplier of goods or services agrees to permit to sell the good or service or to otherwise conduct business on behalf of the franchise.

FRANCHISOR A supplier of goods or services who agrees to permit a re-seller to sell the good or service or to otherwise conduct business on behalf of the franchise.

Continued on next page.

PRINCIPAL A person or entity that authorizes another (the agent) to act on its behalf and subject to its authority to the extent that the principal may be held liable for the actions of the agent.

RESPONDEAT SUPERIOR Rule that the principal is responsible for tortious acts committed by its agents in the scope of their agency or authority.

VICARIOUS LIABILITY The imputed liability of one party for the unlawful acts of another.

Miller v. McDonald's Corp.

Restaurant patron (P) v. Franchisor (D)

Or. Ct. App., 150 Or. App. 274, 945 P.2d 1107 (1997)

NATURE OF CASE: Appeal from summary judgment for defendant in tort action.

FACT SUMMARY: Miller (P) argued that McDonald's Corp. (D) was liable for injuries she sustained while eating at a McDonald's franchise owned by 3K Restaurants.

RULE OF LAW

For purposes of determining tort liability, a jury may find that an agency relationship exists between a franchisor and a franchisee where the franchisor retains significant control over the daily operations of the franchisee's business and insists on uniformity of appearance and standards designed to cause the public to think that the franchise is part of the franchisor's business.

FACTS: Miller (P) suffered injuries when she bit into a heart-shaped sapphire stone while eating a Big Mac sandwich purchased at a McDonald's Corp. (McDonald's) (D) restaurant, which in fact was owned by 3K Restaurants (3K), a McDonald's franchisee. Miller (P) brought suit against McDonald's (D). The license agreement under which 3K operated its restaurant required it to operate in a manner consistent with the "McDonald's System." The agreement described the way in which 3K was to operate the restaurant in considerable detail. It expressly required 3K to operate in compliance with McDonald's (D) prescribed standards, policies, practices, and procedures, and 3K had to follow McDonald's (D) specifications and blueprints for the equipment and layout of the restaurant. In short, through its agreement, McDonald's (D) sought to ensure uniformity of appearance, food, service, and standards in all McDonald's (D) restaurants, whether franchised or not. In addition, to ensure compliance with the agreement, McDonald's (D) periodically sent field consultants to the restaurant to inspect its operations. Notwithstanding these efforts, the agreement provided that 3K was not an agent of McDonald's (D) for any purpose, but rather was an independent contractor. Miller (P) claimed that she went to the restaurant, believing that McDonald's (D) owned, controlled, and managed it. As far as she could tell, the restaurant's appearance was similar to that of other McDonald's (D) restaurants that she had patronized, and nothing disclosed to her that any entity other than McDonald's (D) was involved in its operation. The trial court granted summary judgment to McDonald's (D) on the ground it did not own or operate the restaurant. The appellate court granted review.

ISSUE: For purposes of determining tort liability, may a jury find that an agency relationship exists between a franchisor and a franchisee where the franchisor retains significant control over the daily operations of the franchisee's business and insists on uniformity of appearance and standards designed to cause the public to think that the franchise is part of the franchisor's business?

HOLDING AND DECISION: [Judge not stated in casebook excerpt.] Yes. For purposes of determining tort liability, a jury may find that an agency relationship exists between a franchisor and a franchisee where the franchisor retains significant control over the daily operations of the franchisee's business and insists on uniformity of appearance and standards designed to cause the public to think that the franchise is part of the franchisor's business. The kind of actual agency relationship that would make McDonald's (D) vicariously liable for 3K's negligence requires that McDonald's (D) had the right to control the method by which 3K performed its obligations under the agreement. Here, a jury could find that McDonald's (D) retained sufficient control over 3K's daily operations, that an actual agency relationship existed, and that McDonald's (D) had the right to control 3K in the precise part of its business that allegedly resulted in Miller's (P) injuries. That is sufficient to raise an issue of actual agency. Here, too, there is an issue of apparent agency. The crucial issue in that regard is whether the putative principal (McDonald's (D)) holds the third party (3K) out as an agent and whether the plaintiff (Miller (P)) relies on that holding out. In cases from other jurisdictions, the centrally imposed uniformity is the fundamental basis for the courts' conclusion that there was an issue of fact whether the franchisors held the franchisees out as the franchisors' agents. Likewise, here, there is an issue of fact about whether McDonald's (D) held 3K out as its agent. Because there are numerous factors indicating centrally imposed uniformity, McDonald's (D) does not seriously dispute that a jury could find that it held 3K out as its agent. Rather, it argues that there is insufficient evidence that Miller (P) justifiably relied on that holding out, and argues that Miller (P) would have to prove that she went to the restaurant because she believed that McDonald's (D) operated both it and the other McDonald's restaurants that she had previously patronized. McDonald's (D) argument both demands a

Continued on next page.

higher level of sophistication about the nature of franchising than the general public can be expected to have and ignores the effect of its own efforts to lead the public to believe that McDonald's (D) restaurants are part of a uniform national system of restaurants with common products and common standards of quality. A jury could find from Miller's (P) affidavit that she believed that all McDonald's (D) restaurants were the same because she believed that one entity owned and operated all of them or, at the least, exercised sufficient control that the standards that she experienced at one would be the same as she experienced at others. A jury could find that it was McDonald's (D) very insistence on uniformity of appearance and standards, designed to cause the public to think of every McDonald's (D), franchised or unfranchised, as part of the same system, that makes it difficult or impossible for Miller (P) to tell whether her previous experiences were at restaurants that McDonald's (D) owned or franchised. Reversed.

ANALYSIS

In determining whether McDonald's (D) was vicariously liable for 3K's alleged negligence because 3K was McDonald's (D) apparent agent, the court relied on Restatement (Second) of Agency, §267. That section indicates that: "One who represents that another is his servant or other agent and thereby causes a third person justifiably to rely upon the care or skill of such apparent agent is subject to liability to the third person for harm caused by the lack of care or skill of the one appearing to be a servant or other agent as if he were such."

Quicknotes

AGENCY A fiduciary relationship whereby authority is granted to an agent to act on behalf of the principal in order to effectuate the principal's objective.

FRANCHISEE A party whom a supplier of goods or services agrees to permit to sell the good or service or to otherwise conduct business on behalf of the franchise.

FRANCHISOR A supplier of goods or services who agrees to permit a re-seller to sell the good or service or to otherwise conduct business on behalf of the franchise.

SUMMARY JUDGMENT Judgment rendered by a court in response to a motion made by one of the parties, claiming that the lack of a question of material fact in respect to an issue warrants disposition of the issue without consideration by the jury.

TORT A legal wrong resulting in a breach of duty by the wrongdoer, causing damages as a result of the breach.

VICARIOUS The imputed liability of one party for the unlawful acts of another.

Ira S. Bushey & Sons, Inc. v. United States

Drydock owner (P) v. Federal government (D)

398 F.2d 167 (2d Cir. 1968)

NATURE OF CASE: Appeal of a judgment in favor of a drydock owner in its damages suit against the Government for injury to the drydock by a government employee.

FACT SUMMARY: When a drunken Coast Guard seaman turned wheels on a drydock wall, damaging a drydock owned by Ira S. Bushey & Sons (P), the latter sued the Government (D) for compensation.

RULE OF LAW

Conduct of an employee may be within the scope of employment even if the specific act does not serve the employer's interests.

FACTS: While the U.S. Coast Guard vessel *Tamaroa* was being overhauled in a floating drydock, Lane, a Coast Guard seaman returning drunk from shore leave late at night, turned some wheels on the drydock wall, thus flooding the lock, partially sinking the *Tamaroa*, and damaging the drydock owned by Ira S. Bushey & Sons (Bushey) (P). Access from the shore to the ship was provided by a route that went past the security guard at the gate, through the yard, up a ladder to the top of one drydock wall, and along the wall to a gangway leading to the fantail deck, where men returning from leave reported at a quartermaster's shack. Bushey (P) sued the Government (D) and was granted compensation by the federal district court. The Government (D) appealed, arguing that Seaman Lane's conduct was not within the scope of his employment. The court of appeals granted review.

ISSUE: May conduct of an employee be within the scope of employment even if the specific act does not serve the employer's interests?

HOLDING AND DECISION: (Friendly, J.) Yes. Conduct of an employee may be within the scope of employment even if the specific act does not serve the employer's interests. Lane's conduct was not so "unforeseeable" as to make it unfair to charge the Government (D) with responsibility. What is reasonably foreseeable in the context of respondeat superior is quite a different thing from the foreseeable unreasonable risk of harm that spells negligence. The foresight that should impel the prudent person to take precautions is not the same measure as that by which he should perceive the harm likely to flow from his long-run activity in spite of all reasonable precautions on his own part. The proper test here bears far more resemblance to that which limits liability for workers' compensation than to the test for negligence. The employer should be held to expect risks, to the public also, which arise out of, and in the course of, his employment of labor. Here, it was foreseeable that crew members crossing the drydock might do damage, negligently or even intentionally, such as pushing a Bushey (P) employee or kicking property into the water. Moreover, the proclivity of seamen to find solace for solitude by copious resort to the bottle while ashore has been noted in opinions too numerous to warrant citation. Once all this is granted, "it is immaterial that Lane's precise action was not to be foreseen." The risk that seamen going and coming from the *Tamaroa* might cause damage to the drydock is enough to make it fair that the enterprise bear the loss. Affirmed.

ANALYSIS

In the *Bushey* case, the court notes that people do not disregard their personal qualities when they go to work. Into the job they carry their intelligence, skill, habits of care, and rectitude. Just as inevitably, they take along their tendencies to carelessness and camaraderie, as well as emotional make-up. All these expressions of human nature are incidents inseparable from working together. "They involve risks of injury and these risks are inherent in the working environment." The court, in part, based on this observation of human conduct its determination that Lane's conduct was not so "unforeseeable."

Quicknotes

RESPONDEAT SUPERIOR Rule that the principal is responsible for tortious acts committed by its agents in the scope of their agency or authority.

SCOPE OF EMPLOYMENT Those duties performed pursuant to a person's occupation or employment.

Majestic Realty Associates, Inc. v. Toti Contracting Co.

Owner of damaged property (P) v. Demolition company and municipality (D)

N.J. Sup. Ct., 30 N.J. 425, 153 A.2d 321 (1959)

NATURE OF CASE: Appeal from a defense judgment in a property damage suit by a building owner against the employer of an independent contractor.

FACT SUMMARY: When a building owned by Majestic Realty Associates, Inc. (Majestic) (P) and occupied by its tenant, Bohen's Inc. (P) was extensively damaged by demolition work on adjoining buildings performed by Toti Contracting Co. (Toti) (D), Majestic (P) and Bohen's Inc. (P) sued Toti (D) and the Parking Authority of the City of Paterson, New Jersey (D), which had hired Toti (D) to perform the demolition.

RULE OF LAW

Although a person who engages a contractor, who conducts an independent business using its own employees, is not ordinarily liable for negligence of the contractor in the performance of the contract, such person is liable when the contractor performs inherently dangerous work.

FACTS: The Parking Authority of the City of Paterson, New Jersey (Parking Authority) (D), contracted with Toti Contracting Co. (Toti) (D) to demolish several buildings, including one that adjoined a building owned by Majestic Realty Associates, Inc. (Majestic) (P) and occupied by its tenant, Bohen's Inc. (P). In the process of leveling the adjacent buildings, Toti (D) first removed the roofs, then the front and south sidewalls and all the interior partitions and floors. To accomplish the demolition, Toti (D) used a 3500-pound metal ball, suspended from a street crane. During the demolition, Toti (D) caused extensive damage to the building owned by Majestic (P) and occupied by Bohen's Inc. (P). Toti's (D) president said at the time, "I goofed." Both Majestic (P) and Bohen's Inc. (P) sued Toti (D) and the Parking Authority (D). The trial court entered judgment for Toti (D) and the Parking Authority (D). Majestic (P) and Bohen's Inc. (P) appealed, and the Appellate Division reversed. The state's highest court granted review.

ISSUE: Although a person who engages a contractor, who conducts an independent business using its own employees, is not ordinarily liable for negligence of the contractor in the performance of the contract, is such person liable when the contractor performs inherently dangerous work?

HOLDING AND DECISION: [Judge not stated in casebook excerpt.] Yes. Although a person who engages a contractor, who conducts an independent business using its own employees, is not ordinarily liable for negligence of the contractor in the performance of the contract, such person is liable when the contractor performs inherently dangerous work. Inherently dangerous work, which in New York may also be equated with nuisance, is an activity which can be carried on safely only by the exercise of special skill and care, and which involves grave risk of danger to persons or property if negligently done. The New York rule is sound and is hereby adopted. There is no doubt that the line between work that is ordinary, usual, and commonplace, and that which is inherently dangerous because its very nature involves a peculiar and high risk of harm to members of the public or adjoining proprietors of land unless special precautions are taken, "is somewhat shadowy." In demolishing the walls of the building in question, Toti (D) used a large metal ball, weighing 3500 pounds, suspended from a crane that was stationed in the street. Every time the ball would strike a wall, debris and dirt would fly and the Majestic (P) building "rocked." The razing of buildings by demolition is an activity that necessarily involves a peculiar risk of harm, and the razing of buildings in a busy, built-up section of a city is inherently dangerous. Affirmed.

ANALYSIS

The *Majestic* court noted that it is important to distinguish an operation that may be classified as inherently dangerous from one that is ultra-hazardous. The latter is described by the Restatement or Torts § 520 as one that (a) necessarily involves a serious risk of harm to the person, land, or chattels of others that cannot be eliminated by the exercise of the utmost care, and (b) is not a matter of common usage. The distinction is important because liability is absolute where the work is ultra-hazardous.

Quicknotes

INHERENTLY DANGEROUS ACTIVITY An activity that is dangerous at all times so that precautions must be taken to avoid injury.

VICARIOUS LIABILITY The imputed liability of one party for the unlawful acts of another.

Arguello v. Conoco, Inc.

Racial minority consumers (P) v. Gasoline distributor (D)

207 F.3d 803 (5th Cir.), *cert. denied*, 531 U.S. 874 (2000)

NATURE OF CASE: Appeal by civil rights claimants from a summary judgment in favor of an oil company.

FACT SUMMARY: When several Conoco, Inc. (D) stores subjected racial minority consumers, including Arguello (P), to various forms of racial discrimination, the latter brought suit against Conoco (D), alleging racial discrimination in violation of federal legislation while patronizing the Conoco (D) facilities.

RULE OF LAW

To impose liability under civil rights legislation for the discriminatory actions of a third party, the plaintiff must demonstrate an agency relationship between the defendant and the third party.

FACTS: Several racial minority consumers, including Arguello (P), were subjected to various forms of racial discrimination while purchasing gasoline and other services from Conoco, Inc. (D) outlets. The discrimination took the form of refusal of service, racial epithets, and extremely rude treatment by the store clerks clearly based on the race of the consumers who had come to utilize the facilities. The incidents took place at two types of facilities: (1) Conoco-branded stores that were independently owned, and (2) Conoco-owned stores whose clerks were Conoco (D) employees. Arguello (P) and the other racial minority consumers filed suit against Conoco (D), alleging that they were subjected to racial discrimination in violation of federal legislation while patronizing the Conoco (D) facilities. The federal district court granted summary judgment in favor of Conoco (D) on all the claims. Arguello (P) and the other consumers appealed. The court of appeals granted review.

ISSUE: To impose liability under civil rights legislation for the discriminatory actions of a third party, must the plaintiff demonstrate an agency relationship between the defendant and the third party?

HOLDING AND DECISION: [Judge not stated in casebook excerpt.] Yes. To impose liability under civil rights legislation for the discriminatory actions of a third party, the plaintiff must demonstrate an agency relationship between the defendant and the third party. To establish an agency relationship between Conoco (D) and the branded stores, Arguello (P) must show that Conoco (D) had given consent for the branded stores to act on its behalf and that the branded stores were subject to the control of Conoco (D). The Conoco-branded stores were independently owned but entered into Petroleum Marketing Agreements (PMAs), which allowed them to market and sell Conoco brand gasoline and supplies in their stores, although Conoco (D) did not control the daily operations of these stores, including personnel decisions. Here, the PMAs expressly stated that each branded store was an independent business and that its clerks were not employees of Conoco (D). The PMAs further stated that Conoco (D) and the marketer were "completely separate entities" and not partners, general partners, "nor agents of each other in any sense whatsoever and neither has the power to obligate or bind the other." Thus, there was no agency. As to the Conoco-owned stores, however, the employees of these stores were acting within the scope of their employment for Conoco (D) when they engaged in the statutorily discriminatory practices because these clerks were performing authorized duties for Conoco (D) such as conducting sales. These clerks also used their authority to conduct credit card transactions and use the gas station intercom to commit the discriminatory acts in question. Summary judgment is affirmed as to liability of Conoco (D) for the actions of its branded stores because of lack of an agency relationship. On the other hand, Conoco's (D) summary judgment is reversed as to liability for the actions of the employee clerks of the Conoco-owned stores on the basis of an agency relationship. Hence, affirmed in part and reversed in part.

ANALYSIS

In the *Arguello* case, the court noted that, as to the discriminatory actions of the clerks in the branded stores, Conoco (D) could not be held to have ratified their actions by not suspending or firing them since an employer must be aware of an agent's actions before it can ratify such actions.

Quicknotes

AGENCY A fiduciary relationship whereby authority is granted to an agent to act on behalf of the principal in order to effectuate the principal's objective.

DISCRIMINATION Unequal treatment of a class of persons.

SUMMARY JUDGMENT Judgment rendered by a court in response to a motion made by one of the parties, claiming that the lack of a question of material fact in respect to an issue warrants disposition of the issue without consideration by the jury.

Reading v. Regem

British soldier (P) v. British government (D)

K.B., 2 K.B. 268, 2 All E.R. 27 (1948)

NATURE OF CASE: Petition for the return of money.

FACT SUMMARY: When military authorities took possession of bribe money obtained by Reading (P) while an army sergeant, Reading (P) filed a petition for its return.

RULE OF LAW

An agent who takes advantage of the agency to make a profit dishonestly is accountable to the principal for the wrongfully obtained proceeds.

FACTS: During the period that Reading (P) was a sergeant in the Royal Army Medical Corps, he was found to have accepted bribes. Military authorities took possession of the bribe money. Reading (P) brought suit against the Crown (D), arguing that these moneys were his and should be returned to him. The Crown (D) responded that the bribes were received by Reading (P) by reason of his military employment; hence, the money should be retained by the Crown (D).

ISSUE: Is an agent who takes advantage of the agency to make a profit dishonestly, accountable to the principal for the wrongfully obtained proceeds?

HOLDING AND DECISION: [Judge not stated in casebook excerpt.] Yes. An agent, who takes advantage of the agency to make a profit dishonestly, is accountable to the principal for the wrongfully obtained proceeds. It matters not that the master has not lost any profit nor suffered any damage, nor does it matter that the master could not have done the act itself. If the servant has unjustly enriched himself by virtue of his service without the master's sanction, such servant should not be allowed to keep the money. It should belong to the master because the servant obtained it solely by reason of the position the servant occupied as a servant of the master. Here, although there was not a fiduciary relationship because Reading (D) was not acting in the course of his employment when he accepted the bribes, agency is not an essential ingredient of the instant cause of action. The uniform of the Crown (D) and the position of Reading (D) as a servant of the Crown (D) were the only reasons why he was able to get the money; that is sufficient to make him liable to hand it over to the Crown (D). Petition dismissed with costs.

ANALYSIS

The *Reading* court noted that it was unnecessary in this case to draw a distinction between law and equity since here the real cause of action was a claim for the restitution of moneys which, in justice, ought to be paid over.

Quicknotes

AGENCY A fiduciary relationship whereby authority is granted to an agent to act on behalf of the principal in order to effectuate the principal's objective.

BRIBERY The offering, giving, receiving, or soliciting of something of value for the purpose of influencing the action of an official in the discharge of the official's public or legal duties.

Rash v. J.V. Intermediate, Ltd.

Former employee (D) v. Former employer (P)

498 F.3d 1201 (10th Cir. 2007)

NATURE OF CASE: Appeal in action for breach of fiduciary duties. [The complete procedural posture is not presented in the casebook extract.]

FACT SUMMARY: J.V. Intermediate, Ltd. and J.V. Industrial Companies, Ltd. (collectively, JVIC) (P) contended that its former employee, Rash (D), by owning a company that competed and contracted with JVIC (P) without JVIC's (P) knowledge, breached his fiduciary duties to JVIC (P).

RULE OF LAW

An employee has a fiduciary duty, as the employer's agent, to disclose to the employer what the employer, as principal, has a right to know.

FACTS: J.V. Intermediate, Ltd. and J.V. Industrial Companies, Ltd. (collectively, JVIC) (P) in 1999 hired Rash (D) to start and manage a Tulsa, Oklahoma, branch of JVIC's (P) business. For the first two years of the employment relationship, Rash (D) had an employment contract that provided he would "devote [his] full work time and efforts" to JVIC (P). Starting in 2001, Rash (D), without telling JVIC (P) or its president, Vardell, became the owner of several businesses, including Total Industrial Plant Services, Inc. (TIPS), a scaffolding business. At that time, JVIC (P) was not in the scaffolding line of business. Between 2001 and 2004, TIPS bid on projects for JVIC-Tulsa, which often was awarded the business, and during this time period, JVIC (P) paid TIPS over $1 million. At some point during Rash's (D) tenure, JVIC (P) started a scaffolding business, but JVIC-Tulsa never used that business. JVIC (P) sued Rash (D) for breach of fiduciary duties, claiming Rash (D) had a duty to disclose to JVIC (P) his interest in TIPS. The federal district court, interpreting state law, rendered an opinion, and the court of appeals granted review. [The complete procedural posture is not presented in the casebook extract.]

ISSUE: Does an employee have a fiduciary duty, as the employer's agent, to disclose to the employer what the employer, as principal, has a right to know?

HOLDING AND DECISION: [Judge not stated in casebook excerpt.] Yes. An employee has a fiduciary duty, as the employer's agent, to disclose to the employer what the employer, as principal, has a right to know. First, Rash (D) was JVIC's (P) agent, as he was the principal operator and manager of the Tulsa division, and he had contractually agreed to perform the duties of an agent, having agreed to devote his full work time and efforts to JVIC's (P) business. Further, Rash (D) does not deny he was JVIC's (P) agent, but instead argues that the scope of his agency did not include scaffolding-related ventures. Under state law, which has adopted the Restatement (Second) of Agency, an agent is subject to a duty to his principal to act solely for the benefit of the principal in all matters connected with his agency, unless the parties otherwise agree. Accordingly, Rash (D) owed a fiduciary duty to JVIC (P), and the issue becomes what was the scope of that duty. Under state law, the inquiry is whether a fiduciary duty exists with respect to a particular occurrence or transaction. Here, under the particular circumstances of the case, Rash (D) violated his fiduciary duty by failing to disclose his interest in TIPS to JVIC (P). This conclusion flows from the duty an employee has to deal openly with the employer and to fully disclose to the employer information about matters affecting the company's business. Although an employee does not have an absolute duty of loyalty and may prepare to start a competing business while still employed, at the very least, an employee's independent enterprise cannot compete or contract with the employer without the employer's full knowledge. Even if, as Rash (D) contends, Vardell told him he had no problem with Rash (D) forming a business that might contract with JVIC (P), and even if Rash (D) owed no specific duty to JVIC (P) regarding its scaffolding business, Rash (D) nonetheless had a general duty of full disclosure respecting matters affecting JVIC's (P) business. Thus, by failing to inform JVIC (P) of TIPS, Rash (D) breached that general fiduciary duty as a matter of law. The plaintiff is entitled to judgment as a matter of law.

ANALYSIS

As this case illustrates, whether an agency relationship is created in the employment context depends on the particular facts of the case. Here, the court found it significant that Rash (D) was hired to build the Tulsa division of JVIC (P) from scratch and had sole management responsibilities for operations at the branch; that he was charged with finding facilities to operate the business, hiring and training employees, gathering tools and equipment for the branch, and promoting the new venture; that he solicited and received bids for subcontracts and directly received the invoices for those bids; that he set the rates charged to JVIC's (P) customers for work performed by the Tulsa division and kept track of all the costs of the division; and that, in general, he "ran the shop" and was "responsible for generating business

Continued on next page.

for the Tulsa upstart." The key for the court seems to be that the arrangement between Rash (D) and JVIC (P) was not merely an arm's length business arrangement between the two parties entered for their mutual benefit, but instead was a formal employer/employee relationship. It seems that in the court's view, the formality of the relationship created a relationship of special trust between the parties, which in turn supported fiduciary duties being owed by Rash (D) to JVIC (P).

Quicknotes

AGENT An individual who has the authority to act on behalf of another.

BREACH OF FIDUCIARY DUTY The failure of a fiduciary to observe the standard of care exercised by professionals of similar education and experience.

FIDUCIARY DUTY A legal obligation to act for the benefit of another, including subordinating one's personal interests to that of the other person.

RESTATEMENT (SECOND) OF AGENCY, § 1 Agency is a fiduciary relation resulting from consent of one person to have another act on their behalf.

Town & Country House & Home Service, Inc. v. Newbery

Cleaning service company (P) v. Former employee (D)

N.Y. Ct. App., 3 N.Y.2d 554, 147 N.E.2d 724 (1958)

NATURE OF CASE: Appeal from reversal of dismissal of action for unfair competition and from order holding former employees liable for unfair competition against their former employer.

FACT SUMMARY: Certain employees (D) of Town & Country House & Home Service, Inc. (P) left, formed a competing company, and utilized customer lists they had obtained from their former employer to solicit business for their new enterprise.

RULE OF LAW

Former employees may not use confidential customer lists belonging to their former employer to solicit new customers.

FACTS: Town & Country House & Home Service, Inc. (Town & Country) (P) operated a home cleaning service catering to affluent households, who were not readily ascertainable. Newbery (D) and several other employees (D) resigned and formed a competing company. Using customer lists they had obtained while in Town & Country's (P) employ, they began soliciting Town & Country customers for accounts of their own. Town & Country (P) sued for unfair competition. The trial court dismissed on grounds that the former employees were not bound contractually by any negative covenant to not use the customer lists, and that the techniques and methods used by Town & Country (P) were not trade secrets. The state's intermediate appellate court reversed, holding that the employees (D) had conspired to engage in unfair competition and breach of fiduciary duties. The state's highest court granted review.

ISSUE: May former employees use confidential customer lists belonging to their former employer to solicit new customers of their own?

HOLDING AND DECISION: [Judge not stated in casebook excerpt.] No. Former employees may not use confidential customer lists belonging to their former employer to solicit new customers. A customer list is, insofar as it contains information not readily available to the general public, a trade secret. Here, the availability of Town & Country's (P) customers could not be readily ascertainable, and Town & Country (P) had invested many years of business effort and advertising to obtain its customers. Therefore, Town & Country's (P) customer lists were trade secrets. The law does not permit another to use a trade secret that they obtained through employment with the one possessing the secret. Therefore, while there was nothing illegitimate about the employees (D) forming their own competing company, they crossed the line when they used Town & Country's (P) confidential customer list in soliciting business. Town & Country (P) is entitled to an injunction prohibiting further solicitation, and recoupment of profits obtained from use of the list. Affirmed in part, reversed in part.

ANALYSIS

When an employee leaves a company to form a competitor, the customers of the former employer are a natural place to start looking for accounts. Needless to say, the former employer will not take kindly to this. Most states have some sort of prohibition against this type of activity, although total prohibition is not always the case.

Quicknotes

FIDUCIARY DUTY A legal obligation to act for the benefit of another, including subordinating one's personal interests to that of the other person.

TRADE SECRET Consists of any formula, pattern, plan, process, or device known only to its owner and business, which gives an advantage over competitors; a secret formula used in the manufacture of a particular product that is not known to the general public.

UNFAIR COMPETITION Any dishonest or fraudulent rivalry in trade and commerce, particularly imitation and counterfeiting.

CHAPTER 2

Partnerships

Quick Reference Rules of Law

13. *Giles v. Giles Land Company.* (1) In a family partnership, a partner may be dissociated from the partnership where the partner has threatened the other partners; the family relationship between the partner and other partners is broken; and there is only distrust between the partner and other partners. (2) In a family partnership, a partner may be dissociated from the partnership where the partner's conduct toward the other partners has led to a standstill so that the partnership can no longer carry on its business to the mutual advantage of the other partners. *50*

14. *Kovacik v. Reed.* In a joint venture in which one party contributes funds and the other labor, neither party is liable to the other for contribution for any loss sustained. *52*

15. *G & S Investments v. Belman.* (1) The mere filing of a complaint seeking dissolution of a partnership does not require liquidation of the partnership assets and distribution of the net proceeds. (2) A partnership buyout agreement is valid and binding even if the purchase price is less than the value of the partner interest, since partners may agree among themselves by contract as to their rights and liabilities. *53*

16. *In re El Paso Pipeline Partners, L.P. Derivative Litigation.* (1) Where a limited partnership agreement eliminates directors' common-law fiduciary duties and replaces them with contractual obligations, those express obligations are not breached where directors have acted in accord with the contractual obligations. (2) Where a limited partnership agreement does not expressly eliminate the obligation of the general partner to act in good faith, the general partner does not breach the implied covenant of good faith and fair dealing where the agreement suggests that if the parties had addressed the issue, no obligation to act in good faith would have been imposed. *55*

Fenwick v. Unemployment Compensation Commission

Beauty salon manager (P) v. State unemployment agency (D)

N.J. Ct. Err. & App., 133 N.J.L. 295, 44 A.2d 172 (1945)

NATURE OF CASE: Appeal from judgment characterizing business relationship as a partnership.

FACT SUMMARY: The Unemployment Compensation Commission (D) determined that a written agreement fixing compensation between Chesire and her employer, Fenwick (P), owner of the United Beauty Shoppe, did not make her a partner in the shop.

RULE OF LAW

A partnership is an association of two or more persons to carry on as co-owners of a business for profit.

FACTS: Fenwick (P) hired Chesire as a cashier and receptionist for his beauty salon. Cheshire was employed at a salary of $15.00 per week until December 1938, when she requested a raise. Fenwick (P) agreed to pay her a higher wage if the income from the shop warranted it. To that end, an agreement was drawn up by a local attorney. The agreement stated that Chesire and Fenwick (P) associated themselves as a "partnership" for the operation of the shop; however, Chesire would make no capital investment, would have no control over the management of the shop, and would not be liable for any losses of the business. The agreement further provided that her salary would remain the same, but she would receive a year-end bonus of 20 percent of the net profits of the shop, if the business warranted it, and that the partnership could be terminated by either party upon ten days' notice. The relationship was terminated on January 1, 1942. The Unemployment Compensation Commission (UCC) (D) sought to determine whether Chesire was an employee or partner for the year of 1939 for the purpose of assessing Fenwick's (P) liability under an unemployment compensation statute. The UCC (D) held that the agreement was nothing more than an agreement to fix compensation. The trial court, however, found that the parties were partners. The UCC (D) appealed, and the state's highest court granted review.

ISSUE: Is a partnership an association of two or more persons to carry on as co-owners of a business for profit?

HOLDING AND DECISION: [Judge not stated in casebook excerpt.] Yes. A partnership is an association of two or more persons to carry on as co-owners of a business for profit. Although the agreement between Fenwick (P) and Chesire was termed a "partnership" agreement, the essential element of co-ownership was lacking. The agreement was merely one in which Fenwick (P) agreed to share the profits from a business he owned with Chesire. In determining whether a partnership exists, factors to be considered include: the intentions of the parties as evidenced through the language of any written agreements, the right to share in profits, the obligation to share in losses, the ownership and control of the partnership property, control over management of the business, and the rights of the parties on dissolution. Fenwick (P) contributed all the capital, managed the business, and took over all assets on dissolution. Chesire got nothing from the agreement other than a new wage scale and risked nothing from it. Ownership was conclusively with Fenwick (P). Reversed.

ANALYSIS

This case demonstrates that courts will look beyond the mere language of an agreement to determine the true nature of a business association. Similarly, the absence of a written agreement will not preclude a finding that a partnership did exist. Although profit sharing is often strong evidence that a partnership was intended, it is never conclusive.

Quicknotes

PARTNERSHIP A voluntary agreement entered into by two or more parties to engage in business and to share any attendant profits and losses.

Martin v. Peyton

Creditor (P) v. Alleged partner (D)

N.Y. Ct. App., 246 N.Y. 213, 158 N.E. 77 (1927)

NATURE OF CASE: Appeal from judgment holding a business relationship was not a partnership.

FACT SUMMARY: Martin (P), a creditor of the brokerage firm Knauth, Nachod, & Kuhne (KN&K), claimed that investments made by Peyton (D) and his associates (D) in KN&K made them partners in the firm.

RULE OF LAW

Although the absence of an explicit partnership agreement does not itself preclude the creation of a partnership, it must be proven that investors in an enterprise have an intention to carry on as co-owners of the enterprise a business for profit before they can be considered partners of the enterprise.

FACTS: In the spring of 1921, Knauth, Nachod, & Kuhne (KN&K) was having financial difficulties and obtained a loan from Peyton (D) for $500,000 to use as collateral to secure bank advances. When this money was insufficient to cure KN&K's financial woes, it was suggested that Peyton (D) and his associates, Perkins (D) and Freeman (D), become partners to assist KN&K in its recovery. They refused the suggestion. Instead, they drew up an agreement whereby Peyton (D), Perkins (D), and Freeman (D) would loan KN&K $2,500,000 worth of securities and, to insure the lenders against loss, would be given KN&K's more speculative securities, 40 percent of KN&K's profits until the loan was repaid, and an option to join KN&K if they desired. The agreement further provided that Peyton (D), Perkins (D), and Freeman (D) were to be designated as "trustees" and kept advised and consulted on important KN&K matters; that each member of KN&K would have to assign his interest in the firm to the trustees; and that no loans to firm members or distributions of profits were to be made. Martin (P), a creditor of KN&K, filed suit against Peyton (D), Perkins (D), and Freeman (D), claiming that their investments in KN&K made them partners in the firm, which made them liable for KN&K's debts. The trial court found that Peyton (D), Perkins (D) and Freeman (D) were creditors, not partners, and Martin (P) appealed. The state's highest court granted review.

ISSUE: Although the absence of an explicit partnership agreement does not itself preclude the creation of a partnership, must it be proven that investors in an enterprise have an intention to carry on as co-owners of the enterprise a business for profit before they can be considered partners of the enterprise?

HOLDING AND DECISION: [Judge not stated in casebook excerpt.] Yes. Although the absence of an explicit partnership agreement does not itself preclude the creation of a partnership, it must be proven that investors in an enterprise have an intention to carry on as co-owners of the enterprise a business for profit before they can be considered partners of the enterprise. Despite the assertions of the lenders in the documents that they did not intend to become partners, the question still remained whether in fact they agreed to so associate themselves with KN&K as to "carry on as co-owners a business for profit." Here, the facts do not demonstrate such an intention, and the agreements between Peyton (D), Perkins (D), and Freeman (D) and KN&K do not prove that this was their intent. The documents were merely a loan of securities with provisions to insure their collateral. Given the financial troubles KN&K was suffering, it is entirely understandable that the agreement would contain provisions allowing Peyton (D), Perkins (D), and Freeman (D) to closely monitor their investment. Although the option provision of the agreement was somewhat unusual, it alone is not enough to prove that a present partnership was created. The issue is one of degree, and, here, the point where the lenders would have become partners has not been reached. Affirmed.

ANALYSIS

Two types of business associations available in most states today but not available in the 1920s would likely have been attractive options for KN&K: the limited liability company (LLC) and the limited liability partnership (LLP). Like a corporation, an LLC provides liability protection for its members while still allowing for hands-on management. The rules governing LLPs vary by state but generally provide limited liability for debts of the partnership due to negligence but not for contractual obligations.

Quicknotes

COLLATERAL Property that secures the payment of a debt.

CORPORATION A distinct legal entity characterized by continuous existence; free alienability of interests held

Continued on next page.

therein; centralized management; and limited liability on the part of the shareholders of the corporation.

CREDITOR A person or party to whom a debt or obligation is owed.

LIABILITY Any obligation or responsibility.

LIMITED LIABILITY COMPANY (LLC) A business entity combining the features of both a corporation and a general partnership; the LLC provides its shareholders and officers with limited liability, but it is treated as a partnership for taxation purposes.

LIMITED LIABILITY PARTNERSHIP (LLP) A partnership combining characteristics of corporations and partnerships where the partners have limited liability, usually for the negligence, errors, omissions, misconduct, or malpractice of other partners, and usually share equally in the company's management. In some states, LLPs can be formed only for certain professional endeavors, such as accounting or the practice of law.

PARTNERSHIP A voluntary agreement entered into by two or more parties to engage in business and to share any attendant profits and losses.

Southex Exhibitions, Inc. v. Rhode Island Builders Association, Inc.

Business (P) v. Purported business partner (D)

279 F.3d 94 (1st Cir. 2002)

NATURE OF CASE: Appeal from a judgment holding that no partnership existed.

FACT SUMMARY: Southex Exhibitions, Inc. (Southex) (P), as the successor-in-interest of Sherman Exposition Management, Inc. (SEM), sought damages from Rhode Island Builders Association, Inc. (D) for breach of an agreement that Southex (P) contended was a partnership agreement since the agreement used the word "partners."

RULE OF LAW

The existence of a partnership normally must be determined under a totality-of-the-circumstances test.

FACTS: In 1974, the Rhode Island Builders Association, Inc. (RIBA) (D) entered into an agreement with Sherman Exposition Management, Inc. (SEM), a professional show owner and producer, for productions of RIBA (D) home shows. The preamble to the agreement stated that both entities would participate in the shows as "sponsors and partners." The term of the agreement was fixed at five years, renewable by mutual agreement. In contemporaneous conversations relating to the meaning of the term "partners," SEM's president informed RIBA's (D) representative that he "wanted no ownership of the show" and described SEM simply as the "producer" of the RIBA (D) shows. Subsequently, Southex Exhibitions, Inc. (Southex) (P) acquired SEM's interest under the agreement. RIBA (D) later expressed dissatisfaction with Southex's (P) performance and refused to renew the agreement. Southex (P) brought suit against RIBA (D), alleging that the 1974 agreement established a partnership between RIBA (D) and Southex's (P) predecessor-in-interest (i.e., SEM) and that RIBA (D) had breached its fiduciary duties to its co-partner, Southex (P), by its wrongful dissolution of their partnership and its subsequent appointment of another producer. The trial court rendered judgment for RIBA (D). Southex (P) appealed, and the court of appeals granted review.

ISSUE: Must the existence of a partnership normally be determined under a totality-of-the-circumstances test?

HOLDING AND DECISION: [Judge not stated in casebook excerpt.] Yes. The existence of a partnership normally must be determined under a totality-of-the-circumstances test. Here, the original 1974 agreement was simply entitled "Agreement," rather than "Partnership Agreement." Second, rather than an agreement for an identifiable duration, it prescribed a fixed, albeit renewable, term. Third, rather than undertake to share operating costs with RIBA (D), SEM not only agreed to advance all monies required to produce the shows, but to indemnify RIBA (D) for all show-related losses as well. State law normally presumes that partners share equally, or at least proportionately, in partnership losses. Similarly, although RIBA (D) involved itself in some management decisions, SEM was responsible for the lion's share. Further, Southex (P) not only entered into contracts, but conducted business with third parties. As a matter of fact, their mutual association was never given a name. It is also noteworthy that Southex (P) never filed either a federal or state partnership tax return. Similarly, the evidence as to whether either SEM or RIBA (D) contributed any corporate property was highly speculative, particularly since their mutual endeavor simply involved a periodic event, namely, an annual home show, with neither generated, nor necessitated, ownership interests in significant tangible properties, aside from cash receipts. Affirmed.

ANALYSIS

In *Southex*, the court noted that even though the Uniform Partnership Act explicitly identifies profit sharing as particularly probative indicia of partnership formation, and that some courts have even held that the absence of profit sharing compels a finding that no partnership existed, it does not necessarily follow that evidence of profit sharing compels a finding of partnership formation.

Quicknotes

TOTALITY-OF-THE-CIRCUMSTANCES TEST Standard that focuses on all the circumstances of a particular case, instead of individual factors.

Young v. Jones

Investor (P) v. Bank (D)

816 F. Supp. 1070 (D.S.C. 1992), *aff'd sub nom.* Young v. Federal Deposit Insurance Corporation, 103 F.3d 1180 (4th Cir.), *cert. denied*, 522 U.S. 928 (1997)

NATURE OF CASE: Action for damages alleging partnership by estoppel.

FACT SUMMARY: Young (P), a Texas investor who lost $550,000 after relying on a falsified financial audit statement attached to an audit letter by Price Waterhouse–Bahamas (PW-Bahamas) (D), sought to recover damages from Price Waterhouse–U.S. (PW-U.S.) (D), on the grounds there was a partnership by estoppel between PW-Bahamas (D) and PW-U.S. (D).

RULE OF LAW

A person who represents themself, or permits another to represent them, to anyone as a partner in an existing partnership or with others not actual partners, is liable to persons to whom such a representation is made who has given credit to the actual or apparent partnership.

FACTS: Young (P), an investor from Texas, deposited $550,000 in a South Carolina bank on the basis of an unqualified audit letter issued by Price Waterhouse–Bahamas (PW-Bahamas) (D) regarding the financial statement of Swiss American Fidelity and Insurance Guaranty (SAFIG). The letterhead used for the SAFIG audit identified the Bahamian accounting firm only as "Price Waterhouse," and the audit letter also bore a Price Waterhouse trademark and signature. The financial statement turned out to have been falsified, and Young (P) lost the deposited money. Young (P) filed suit to recover the lost funds and investment potential alleging that PW-Bahamas (D) knew that the letter would induce third parties to rely to their detriment on the financial statement. Young (P) asserted that PW-Bahamas (D) and PW-U.S. (D) operated as a partnership, or in the alternative, operated as partners by estoppel, and therefore PW-U.S. (D) should be held liable for the negligent acts of PW-Bahamas (D). PW-Bahamas (D) and PW-U.S. (D) denied that a partnership existed between the two and submitted documents establishing that the two were separately organized.

ISSUE: Is a person who represents themself, or permits another to represent them, to anyone as a partner in an existing partnership or with others not actual partners, liable to persons to whom such a representation is made who has given credit to the actual or apparent partnership?

HOLDING AND DECISION: [Judge not stated in casebook excerpt.] Yes. A person who represents themself, or permits another to represent them, to anyone as a partner in an existing partnership or with others not actual partners, is liable to any such person to whom such a representation is made who has, on the faith of the representation, given credit to the actual or apparent partnership. There is no evidence that the two entities are partners in fact. Therefore, if they are partners at all, they are partners by estoppel. Although Young (P) alleges that Price Waterhouse holds itself out as an international accounting firm, he can point to nothing concrete that should hold the various affiliated entities liable for the acts of others. There is no evidence that Young (P) relied on any act or statement by any PW-U.S. (D) partner indicating the existence of a partnership with PW-Bahamas (D). Even if there were, there has been no evidence presented that any member of PW-U.S. (D) had anything to do with SAFIG's falsified financial statement or any other act related to the lost investment. The allegations of negligence against PW-Bahamas (D) cannot serve to hold members of PW-U.S. (D) liable as partners by estoppel.

ANALYSIS

Perhaps Young (P) would have been more successful had he argued for liability on an agency theory. Provisions of the Uniform Partnership Act (U.P.A.) state that every partner is an agent of the partnership and potentially liable for the unauthorized torts and contracts of a partner. Although PW-U.S. (D) would still have argued that the Bahamian group was a separate entity, the U.P.A. sections on acts involving third parties are extremely favorable to such third parties when they have been injured.

Quicknotes

EQUITABLE ESTOPPEL An equitable doctrine that precludes a person from asserting a right to which the person was entitled, resulting from their action, conduct, or failure to act, that caused another party to justifiably rely on such action, conduct, or failure to act to their detriment.

PARTNERSHIP A voluntary agreement entered into by two or more parties to engage in business and to share any attendant profits and losses.

Meinhard v. Salmon

Partner (P) v. Partner (D)

N.Y. Ct. App., 249 N.Y. 458, 164 N.E. 545 (1928)

NATURE OF CASE: Appeal from judgment enforcing fiduciary rights arising from a joint venture.

FACT SUMMARY: Meinhard (P) filed suit for breach of fiduciary duties against Salmon (D), his coadventurer in a joint venture, after Salmon (D) usurped an opportunity that should have been offered to the venture.

RULE OF LAW

Joint adventurers owe one another the highest fiduciary duty of loyalty while the enterprise is ongoing.

FACTS: In April 1902, Salmon (D) entered into a joint venture with Meinhard (P) to lease a hotel in New York City from Louisa Gerry for a term of 20 years. Under the terms of the agreement, Meinhard (P) provided the majority of the funding for the lease, while Salmon (D) managed and operated the property, although both partners were responsible for any losses. In January 1922, as the old lease was near its end, Elbridge Gerry, who had become owner of the property, approached Salmon (D) with an offer for a new lease. The new lease covered a larger tract of property for a period of 20 years but contained covenants for renewal potentially expanding the deal to a maximum of 80 years. The new lease was signed between Gerry and the Midpoint Realty Company, which was owned and controlled exclusively by Salmon (D). Salmon (D) did not tell Meinhard (P) of the new lease until the deal had already been completed. Meinhard (P) then demanded that the lease be held in trust as an asset of the venture to be shared, but Salmon (D) refused. Meinhard (P) subsequently filed suit to enforce his share, and the trial judge ruled that he was entitled to 25 percent. Following cross-appeals, the state's intermediate appellate court enlarged Meinhard's (P) equitable interest to 50 percent of the whole lease. Salmon (D) appealed, and the state's highest court granted review.

ISSUE: Do joint adventurers owe to one another the highest fiduciary duty of loyalty while the enterprise is ongoing?

HOLDING AND DECISION: (Cardozo, C.J.) Yes. Joint adventurers owe to one another the highest fiduciary duty of loyalty while the enterprise is ongoing. Salmon (D) appropriated to himself, in secrecy and silence, an opportunity that should have belonged to the joint venture. The subject matter of the new lease was an extension and enlargement on the old one. Salmon's (D) conduct excluded his coadventurer Meinhard (P) from any chance to compete or enjoy the opportunity that had come to him alone by virtue of their venture. Salmon (D) need only have advised Meinhard (P) of the opportunity when it arose and then either of them would have been free to compete for the project. The judgment of the appellate court should be generally affirmed but modified to provide for a trust attaching to shares of stock on the lease, with Salmon (D) receiving one share more than Meinhard (P) so that he may retain management control over the new lease. Affirmed, as modified.

DISSENT: (Andrews, J.) The joint venture entered into by Salmon (D) and Meinhard (P) was for a limited scope, object, and duration of time. It was designed to exploit a particular lease and contained no mention of the venture continuing beyond the date of its termination. Had this been a general partnership between the two, the majority's result would have been correct. However, given the limited nature of the venture, Salmon (D) did not act unfairly.

ANALYSIS

Judge Cardozo, in his majority opinion, indicated that the fiduciary duty owed to co-venturers is equal to that owed a partner. The dissent, on the other hand, drew a distinction between the fiduciary duties required by the two. The Uniform Partnership Act and Revised Uniform Partnership Act have roughly incorporated Cardozo's approach.

Quicknotes

COVENANT A written promise to do, or to refrain from doing, a particular activity.

FIDUCIARY DUTY A legal obligation to act for the benefit of another.

JOINT VENTURE Venture undertaken based on an express or implied agreement between the members, common purpose and interest, and an equal power of control.

Sandvick v. LaCrosse

Oil and gas lease co-owner (P) v. Oil and gas lease co-owner (D)

N.D. Sup. Ct., 747 N.W.2d 519 (2008)

NATURE OF CASE: Appeal from judgment that no partnership or joint venture existed between co-owners of oil and gas leases.

FACT SUMMARY: Sandvick (P) and Bragg (P), who had owned with LaCrosse (D) and Haughton (D) oil and gas leases, known as the Horn leases, claimed that LaCrosse (D) and Haughton (D) had breached fiduciary duties to Sandvick (P) and Bragg (P) by purchasing top leases that covered the same acreage as the Horn leases and became effective at the expiration of the Horn leases and by not offering Sandvick (P) and Bragg (P) the opportunity to purchase the top leases with them.

RULE OF LAW

(1) A partnership does not exist where a business undertaking is more limited than a series of acts directed to an end.

(2) A joint venture exists between parties who purchase assets from their credits in a single checking account in equal shares, where the assets are titled in a single entity's name, and where profits, if any, are to be shared.

(3) Joint venturers breach their fiduciary duty of loyalty to co-joint venturers where they take for themselves an opportunity that belongs to the joint venture without giving their co-joint venturers the chance to participate in that opportunity.

FACTS: Sandvick (P), Bragg (P), LaCrosse (D), and Haughton (D) together, in equal shares, purchased oil and gas leases, known as the Horn leases, that had a five-year term. Empire Oil Company, owned by LaCrosse (D), held record title to the leases. The leases were purchased from the parties' credits in the Empire Oil Company JV checking account. Their intent was to sell the leases before the end of the five-year term. Before the Horn leases were set to expire, LaCrosse (D) and Haughton (D), without informing Sandvick (P) and Bragg (P), purchased "top" leases on the Horn property that were set to begin at the expiration of the initial Horn leases. The top leases covered the same acreage as the initial Horn leases and were also for a term of five years. Sandvick (P) and Bragg (P) sued LaCrosse (D) and Haughton (D), contending that LaCrosse (D) and Haughton (D) had breached fiduciary duties to Sandvick (P) and Bragg (P) by not offering Sandvick (P) and Bragg (P) the opportunity to purchase the top leases with them. The trial court held that no partnership or joint venture existed. The trial court found that the parties' undertaking was very limited and did not coincide with the definition of a business. The trial court also found that under the circumstances, the parties had no expectations that the other parties would refrain from investing in the area without offering to the other parties the opportunity to join the investment. The state's highest court granted review.

ISSUE:

(1) Does a partnership exist where a business undertaking is more limited than a series of acts directed to an end?

(2) Does a joint venture exist between parties who purchase assets from their credits in a single checking account in equal shares, where the assets are titled in a single entity's name, and where profits, if any, are to be shared?

(3) Do joint venturers breach their fiduciary duty of loyalty to co-joint venturers where they take for themselves an opportunity that belongs to the joint venture without giving their co-joint venturers the chance to participate in that opportunity?

HOLDING AND DECISION: [Judge not stated in casebook excerpt.]

(1) No. A partnership does not exist where a business undertaking is more limited than a series of acts directed to an end. Under the Revised Uniform Partnership Act, a "business" is defined as a series of acts directed toward an end, and includes every trade, profession, and occupation. Here, the trial court determined that the parties' undertaking was very limited and did not coincide with this definition. The trial court did not err in this conclusion, since, here, the parties entered into the Horn leases for a specific period and the purchase of those leases was a separate act, not a series of acts. Affirmed as to this issue.

(2) Yes. A joint venture exists between parties who purchase assets from their credits in a single checking account in equal shares, where the assets are titled in a single entity's name, and where profits, if any, are to be shared. For a business enterprise to constitute a joint venture, the following four elements must be present: (1) contribution by the parties of money, property, time, or skill in some common undertaking, but the contributions need not be equal or of the same nature; (2) a proprietary interest and right of mutual control over the engaged property; (3) an express or implied agreement for the sharing

Continued on next page.

of profits, and usually, but not necessarily, of losses; and (4) an express or implied contract showing a joint venture was formed. Notwithstanding that the trial court found that no agreement was entered into, express or implied, limiting the parties' abilities to continue activity that did not include the other parties, and that under the circumstances the parties had no expectations that the other parties would refrain from investing in the area without offering to the other parties the opportunity to join the investment, the trial court found several findings that reflected a joint venture. These were that (1) LaCrosse opened a checking account under the name Empire Oil JV Account; (2) the leases were purchased from the parties' credits in the Empire Oil Company JV account in equal shares; (3) title to the leases was held in Empire Oil Company's name; and (4) the parties' intent in acquiring the leases was to sell them. There was also evidence that any profits would have been shared had the Horn leases been sold. Based on these factors, the parties had a joint venture. Reversed as to this issue.

(3) Yes. Joint venturers breach their fiduciary duty of loyalty to co-joint venturers where they take for themselves an opportunity that belongs to the joint venture without giving their co-joint venturers the chance to participate in that opportunity. The fiduciary duties owed in the joint venture flow from the scope of the venture, applying principles of partnership law. Joint venturers, like partners, owe each other the duty of loyalty while the joint venture is ongoing, including the duty to account to the joint venture for opportunities belonging to the joint venture, and to refrain from acting adversely to the venture's interests and from competing with the venture. Here, LaCrosse (D) and Haughton (D) created a conflict of interest by purchasing the top leases prior to the expiration of the original leases without notifying Sandvick (P) and Bragg (P), since it was in LaCrosse's (D) and Haughton's (D) best interest not to sell the original leases during the remaining six months of the original term. Having excluded Sandvick (P) and Bragg (P), LaCrosse (D) and Haughton (D) potentially stood to benefit more by waiting to sell the leases after the original term expired. Accordingly, LaCrosse (D) and Haughton (D), in the exercise of their fiduciary duty of loyalty, should have not purchased the top leases without informing Bragg (P) and Sandvick (P), who should have had an opportunity to purchase the top leases with LaCrosse (D) and Haughton (D).

CONCURRENCE AND DISSENT: (Crothers, J.) The majority is correct in ruling that no partnership was formed. The majority errs, however, in concluding that LaCrosse (D) and Haughton (D) breached their duty of loyalty, even assuming, arguendo, that a joint venture had been formed. The majority fails to honor the trial court's findings and ignores state law that permits partners (and therefore joint venturers) to limit the scope of their duty of loyalty to the remaining partners—and the fact that the parties could have limited this duty—without further inquiry. There was no written contract between the parties, and the parameters of the transaction were unclear. The trial court found that the parties were involved in other oil and gas leases with other third parties, separate and apart from the Horn leases, and that the parties knew Haughton (D) had various leasehold and mineral interests in the area and had reason to believe that he would continue to invest in the area. Therefore, the majority erred in ignoring the trial court's findings of facts and in usurping the fact-finding role.

ANALYSIS

The hallmark of a joint venture is that parties pool financial resources and share control to accomplish a for-profit, limited-time event. There is, however, no definite formula for identifying the joint venture relationship in all cases, and, as this case clearly illustrates, each case will depend upon its own unique facts. Here, the dissent takes the majority to task for casting aside as apparently less persuasive the trial court's findings, which the majority agreed supported the trial court's conclusion that no joint venture existed, in favor of the facts that the majority found more persuasive. Given that the outcome of the case so heavily depends on the unique facts, it is arguable that the majority in this case has ignored the "clearly erroneous" standard of review and has indeed usurped the trial court's fact-finding role.

Quicknotes

BREACH OF FIDUCIARY DUTY The failure of a fiduciary to observe the standard of care exercised by professionals of similar education and experience.

FIDUCIARY Person holding a legal obligation to act for the benefit of another.

FIDUCIARY DUTY A legal obligation to act for the benefit of another, including subordinating one's personal interests to that of the other person.

JOINT VENTURE Venture undertaken based on an express or implied agreement among the members, with a common purpose and interest, and an equal power of control.

Meehan v. Shaughnessy

Attorney (P) v. Former law firm (D)

Mass. Sup. Jud. Ct., 404 Mass. 419, 535 N.E.2d 1255 (1989)

NATURE OF CASE: Appeal from judgment ordering recovery of fees and rejecting breach-of-duty counterclaim.

FACT SUMMARY: Meehan (P) and Boyle (P) commenced an action to determine their rights and liabilities after terminating their relationship with Parker, Coulter, Daley & White (Parker Coulter) (D), their former law firm, to start a firm of their own. Parker & Coulter (D) counterclaimed for breach of fiduciary duty and other claims.

RULE OF LAW

A partner breaches their fiduciary duty to the partnership by using their position of trust and confidence to the disadvantage of the partnership.

FACTS: Meehan (P) and Boyle (P), partners of the law firm Parker, Coulter, Daley & White (Parker Coulter) (D), decided in June 1984 to terminate their relationship with Parker Coulter (D) and start their own firm beginning in January 1985. In preparing to establish their new firm, they decided on who from Parker Coulter (D) they wanted to invite to join them and which clients they would seek to remove to their new firm. Although they originally planned to give notice to Parker Coulter (D) on December 1, 1984, rumors of their departure began to circulate as early as July, and Meehan (P) was approached on several occasions by different partners regarding the rumors. On each occasion Meehan (P) denied that he was leaving, but after being approached by partner Shaughnessy (D) on November 30, Meehan (P) and Boyle (P) decided to distribute their notice that afternoon. The partners of Parker Coulter (D) subsequently asked Boyle (P) to identify the cases he intended to take with him. Boyle (P) did not return the list until two weeks later, by which time he had obtained authorizations from the majority of clients whose cases he planned to take with him, unbeknownst to Parker Coulter (D). Shortly after leaving Parker Coulter (D), Boyle (P) and Meehan (P) commenced an action against Parker Coulter (D) to recover amounts they claimed were owed to them under the firm's partnership agreement. Parker Coulter (D) counterclaimed that Meehan (P) and Boyle (P) had violated their fiduciary duties, breached the partnership agreement, and tortiously interfered with their advantageous business and contractual relationships by engaging in improper conduct in withdrawing cases and clients from Parker Coulter (D) and inducing Parker Coulter (D) employees to join the new firm. The trial court judge rejected all of Parker Coulter's (D) claims and found that Meehan (P) and Boyle (P) were entitled to recover amounts owed to them under the partnership agreement. Parker Coulter (D) appealed. The state's highest court granted review.

ISSUE: Does a partner breach their fiduciary duty to the partnership by using their position of trust and confidence to the disadvantage of the partnership?

HOLDING AND DECISION: [Judge not stated in casebook excerpt.] Yes. A partner breaches their fiduciary duty to the partnership by using their position of trust and confidence to the disadvantage of the partnership. Although fiduciaries may plan to compete with the entity to which they owe allegiance, in the course of such arrangements they must not otherwise violate their fiduciary duties. Meehan (P) and Boyle (P) were entitled to make logistical arrangements such as signing a lease, obtaining financing, and drawing up lists of clients in preparing to establish their new firm. Meehan (P) and Boyle (P) committed no breach of their duties to Parker Coulter (D) during their last several months with the firm with regard to their handling of cases or changes in workload. However, they did breach their fiduciary duties by unfairly acquiring consent from clients to remove cases from Parker Coulter (D). Through their preparation for obtaining clients' consent, their secrecy concerning which clients they intended to take, and the substance and method of their communications with clients, Meehan (P) and Boyle (P) used their position of trust and confidence to obtain an unfair advantage over their former partners in breach of their fiduciary duties. Reversed and remanded.

ANALYSIS

Many partnership agreements contain provisions that expressly prescribe procedures to be followed when a partner leaves to start a new firm or transfers to another firm. Such clauses are becoming increasingly common as attorneys move more and more frequently among firms. Even where such provisions do exist, such changes are inevitably uncomfortable, and some periods of secrecy are unavoidable. This case is one example of where the line is between acceptable secrecy and unacceptable secrecy in cases of partnership disassociation.

Continued on next page.

Quicknotes

COUNTERCLAIM An independent cause of action brought by a defendant to a lawsuit in order to oppose or deduct from the plaintiff's claim.

FIDUCIARY DUTY A legal obligation to act for the benefit of another, including subordinating one's personal interests to that of the other person.

UNIFORM PARTNERSHIP ACT § 20 Partners have an obligation to provide true and full information of all things affecting the partnership to any partner.

Lawlis v. Kightlinger & Gray

Former partner (P) v. Law firm (D)

Ind. Ct. App., 562 N.E.2d 435 (1990)

NATURE OF CASE: Appeal from summary judgment for defendant in a suit for damages for breach of contract.

FACT SUMMARY: Although Lawlis (P) successfully battled his problem with alcohol abuse, the law firm of Kightlinger & Gray (D) voted to expel him from his senior partnership position.

RULE OF LAW

When a partner is involuntarily expelled from a business, the partner's expulsion must have been in good faith for dissolution to occur without violating the partnership agreement.

FACTS: Lawlis (P) was a partner in the law firm of Kightlinger & Gray (the Firm) (D) for ten years, until 1982. In that year, he became an alcohol abuser. The Firm (D) agreed to allow Lawlis (P) to continue as a partner while he sought treatment, stipulating that there was to be no second chance. Lawlis (P) was, however, given a second chance when later resumed the consumption of alcohol. Although remaining a partner of the Firm (D), Lawlis's (P) workload was greatly reduced. Because he had not consumed alcohol since his second trip to the clinic, Lawlis (P) believed his previous status should be restored. The Firm (D), however, voted to sever his relationship with the Firm (D), allowing him a weekly draw and retaining his status as a senior partner to facilitate his transition to other employment. When Lawlis (P) refused to agree to this arrangement, the Firm (D) voted to expel him. Lawlis (P) filed suit for damages for breach of contract. Summary judgment was for the Firm (D). Lawlis (P) appealed, and the state's intermediate appellate court granted review.

ISSUE: When a partner is involuntarily expelled from a business, must the partner's expulsion have been in good faith for dissolution to occur without violating the partnership agreement?

HOLDING AND DECISION: [Judge not stated in casebook excerpt.] Yes. When a partner is involuntarily expelled from a business, the partner's expulsion must have been in good faith for dissolution to occur without violating the partnership agreement. Where the remaining partners in a firm deem it necessary to expel a partner under a no-cause expulsion clause in a partnership agreement, the expelling partners are deemed to have acted in good faith if their conduct does not cause a wrongful withholding of money or property legally due the expelled partner. That the Firm (D) in this case recommended a step-down severance over six months rather than immediate severance, as permitted under the partnership agreement, demonstrates a compassionate, not greedy, purpose. Contrary to Lawlis's (P) argument, his expulsion did not contravene the partnership agreement's duty of good faith and fair dealing, as it is clear he was not expelled for the predatory purpose of increasing the Firm's (D) lawyer to partner ratio. Affirmed.

ANALYSIS

Potential damage to partnership business may be a consideration where no-cause expulsion of a partner from a law firm takes place. Under the partnership agreement in existence in the instant case, a two-thirds majority of the senior partners could, at any time, expel any partner from the partnership. Lawlis (P) was the only partner who voted against his own expulsion.

Quicknotes

DISSOLUTION Annulment or termination of a formal or legal bond, tie, or contract.

FIDUCIARY RELATIONSHIP Person holding a legal obligation to act for the benefit of another.

In re Fulton

[Parties not identified.]

43 B.R. 273 (Bankr. M.D. Tenn. 1984)

NATURE OF CASE: Proceeding in bankruptcy to determine ownership and distribution of property.

FACT SUMMARY: Carroll (P) claimed that his former partner, Fulton (D), a debtor in bankruptcy, wrongfully characterized as Fulton's (D) personal asset a trailer that had belonged to the partnership.

RULE OF LAW

(1) The intent of partners at the time property is acquired controls whether the property is partnership property or separate property.

(2) When a partnership is dissolved, its property must be used to pay its liabilities in the priority established by partnership law.

FACTS: Carroll (P) and Fulton (D) established a trucking company, C&F Trucking, as a partnership, with Carroll (P) providing the capital and a semi-truck, and Fulton (D) driving the truck. The partners were to split any profits. In July 1982, Carroll's (P) grandmother, Holcomb (P), wired to him $9,000, of which he used $4,600 to purchase a trailer for the partnership. The invoice listed C&F Trucking as the purchaser, and the certificate of title, signed by Fulton (D), listed the partnership as the owner. Fulton (D) used the trailer in furtherance of the business. About five months later, Fulton (D) filed for personal bankruptcy under Chapter 7. He scheduled the trailer as an asset of the bankruptcy estate. Carroll (P) and Holcomb (P) contested, asserting that the trailer did not belong to Fulton (D). The bankruptcy court held a hearing to decide to whom the trailer belonged, and the extent, if any, to which the bankruptcy estate had an interest therein.

ISSUE:

(1) Does the intent of partners at the time property is acquired control whether the property is partnership property or separate property?

(2) When a partnership is dissolved, must its property be used to pay its liabilities in the priority established by partnership law?

HOLDING AND DECISION: [Judge not stated in casebook excerpt.]

(1) Yes. The intent of partners at the time property is acquired controls whether the property is partnership property or separate property. Such intention must be shown by the facts and circumstances surrounding the transaction of purchase, along with the parties' conduct toward the property after the purchase. Here, the evidence established that Carroll (P) and Fulton (D) conducted their business as a partnership. The evidence also established that the trailer was purchased for the partnership and used in furtherance of partnership business. Thus, the trailer did not belong exclusively to Fulton (D).

(2) Yes. When a partnership is dissolved, its property must be used to pay its liabilities in the priority established by partnership law. Since a partnership is a legal entity separate from its partners, a partner cannot claim title in partnership property. The partner may claim only the rights in specific partnership property as bestowed upon the partner under partnership law. Under partnership law, when a partnership is dissolved, debts to creditors other than partners are paid first, debts to partners for contributions other than for capital and profits are paid second, debts owing to partners in respect of capital contributions are paid third, and, finally, debts owing to partners in respect of profits are paid last. When a partner files for bankruptcy, the partner's estate obtains whatever partnership interest was held by the filing partner. Here, Fulton's (D) bankruptcy had the effect of dissolving the partnership as a matter of law. Because Holcomb (P) loaned the money used to purchase the trailer to Carroll (P), and not the partnership, Carroll's (P) purchase of the trailer and contribution thereof to the partnership constituted a capital contribution. The equity in the trailer, therefore, must be distributed in the order provided for in the partnership law.

ANALYSIS

To effect the court's ruling, the parties would have to provide an accounting of the trailer's equity that described its distribution in accordance with partnership law, giving priority to debts to creditors other than partners; then debts to partners for contributions other than for capital and profits; then debts owing to partners in respect of capital contributions (thus Carroll (P), who the court held had contributed the trailer as a capital contribution, would receive any amounts left over from the payment of the first two types of debt); and then, finally, debts owing to partners in respect of profits (here, Fulton (D) would be entitled to any amount left over from the payment of the first three types of debt if he were owed anything on account of profits).

Continued on next page.

Quicknotes

BANKRUPTCY A legal proceeding whereby a debtor, who is unable to pay their debts as they become due, is relieved of their obligation to pay their creditors, either by liquidation and distribution of their remaining assets or through reorganization and payment from future income.

CAPITAL In tax, often used synonymously with basis; in accounting, an account that represents the equity (ownership) interests of the owners, i.e., the amounts they would obtain if the business were liquidated.

PARTNERSHIP A voluntary agreement entered into by two or more parties to engage in business and to share any attendant profits and losses.

PROFIT An amount gained above those monies or value paid in the form of costs.

National Biscuit Company v. Stroud

Food distributor (P) v. Grocery partner (D)

N.C. Sup. Ct., 249 N.C. 467, 106 S.E.2d 692 (1959)

NATURE OF CASE: Appeal from judgment for plaintiff in suit to recover for goods sold.

FACT SUMMARY: Stroud (D) advised National Biscuit Company (National) (P) that he (D) would not be responsible for any bread National (P) sold to his partner. Nevertheless, National (P) continued to make deliveries ordered by Freeman, Stroud's (D) partner.

RULE OF LAW

A partner may not escape liability for debts incurred by a co-partner merely by advising the creditor, in advance, that the partner will not be responsible for those debts.

FACTS: Stroud (D) and Freeman entered into a general partnership to sell groceries under the name of Stroud's Food Center. Both partners apparently had an equal right to manage the business. The partnership periodically ordered bread from National Biscuit Company (National) (P). Eventually, however, Stroud (D) notified National (P) that he (D) would not be responsible for any additional bread National (P) sold to Stroud's Food Center. Nevertheless, National (P) sent, at Freeman's request, additional bread of a total value of $171.04. On the day of the last delivery, Stroud (D) and Freeman dissolved their partnership. Most of the firm's assets were assigned to Stroud (D), who agreed to liquidate the assets of the partnership and to discharge its liabilities. National (P) eventually sued Stroud (D) to recover the value of the bread that had been delivered but never paid for. Stroud (D) denied liability for the price of the bread, contending that his notice to National (P) that he (D) would not be responsible for further deliveries had relieved him of any obligation to pay for the bread. The trial court rendered judgment in favor of National (P), and Stroud (D) appealed. The state's highest court granted review.

ISSUE: May a partner escape liability for debts incurred by a co-partner merely by advising the creditor, in advance, that the partner will not be responsible for those debts?

HOLDING AND DECISION: [Judge not stated in casebook excerpt.] No. A partner may not escape liability for debts incurred by a co-partner merely by advising the creditor, in advance, that the partner will not be responsible for those debts. The acts of a partner, if performed on behalf of the partnership and within the scope of its business, are binding upon all co-partners. According to the appropriate provisions of the Uniform Partnership Act, all partners are jointly and severally liable for all obligations incurred on behalf of the partnership. If a majority of the partners disapprove of a transaction before it is entered into, then they may escape liability for whatever obligations that transaction ultimately incurs. But Freeman and Stroud (D) were equal partners, with neither possessing the power to exercise a majority veto over the acts of the other. Freeman's acts were entered into on behalf of the partnership, were within the scope of its ordinary business, and probably conferred a benefit upon both Freeman and Stroud (D) as partners. Under these circumstances, it is proper to hold Stroud (D) liable for the price of the bread delivered by National (P) even after Stroud's (D) notice that he (D) would not be held responsible for additional shipments. Affirmed.

ANALYSIS

The rule adopted by the Uniform Partnership Act is consistent with traditional principles of agency law. In the absence of a contrary provision in the parties' partnership agreement, each partner acts as the agent of the partnership and of each other partner. Of course, only acts performed on behalf of the partnership and consistent with the partnership's purposes are binding on other partners. However, even an act that is outside the scope of a partner's duties may bind the partner's co-partners if they ratify it.

Quicknotes

AGENT An individual who has the authority to act on behalf of another.

NORTH CAROLINA UNIFORM PARTNERSHIP ACT All partners are jointly and severally liable for the acts and obligations of the partnership.

PRINCIPAL A person or entity who authorizes another (the agent) to act on its behalf and subject to its authority to the extent that the principal may be held liable for the actions of the agent.

Summers v. Dooley

Partner (P) v. Partner (D)

Idaho Sup. Ct., 94 Idaho 87, 481 P.2d 318 (1971)

NATURE OF CASE: Appeal from judgment granting partial relief to plaintiff in action for reimbursement of partnership funds.

FACT SUMMARY: In Summers's (P) suit against his partner Dooley (D) for reimbursement of his expenditure of $11,000 for the purpose of hiring an employee, Dooley (D) contended that because he did not approve of hiring the additional employee, the majority of partners did not consent to his hiring, and that Summers (P) should not be reimbursed for his unilateral hiring decision.

RULE OF LAW

Business differences in a partnership must be decided by a majority of the partners provided no other agreement between the partners speaks to the issues.

FACTS: Summers (P) and Dooley (D) entered into a partnership for the purpose of operating a trash collection business. The two men operated the business. When either of them was unable to work, the non-working partner provided a replacement at his own expense. Dooley (D) became unable to work, and Summers (P), at his own expense, hired an employee to take Dooley's (D) place. Four years later, Summers (P) approached Dooley (D) regarding the hiring of an additional employee, but Dooley (D) refused. Summers (P), on his own, then hired another person and paid him out of his own pocket. Dooley (D) objected and refused to pay for the new person out of partnership funds. Summers (P) kept the man employed but filed an action against Dooley (D) for reimbursement of Summers's (P) expenditures of $11,000 in hiring the extra employee. Dooley (D) argued that the majority of partners had not approved of the hiring, and that Summers (P) should not be reimbursed for his unilateral hiring decision. The trial court denied Summers (P) all the relief he requested, granting him only partial relief, and he appealed. The state's highest court granted review.

ISSUE: Must business differences in a partnership be decided by a majority of the partners provided no other agreement between the partners speaks to the issues?

HOLDING AND DECISION: [Judge not stated in casebook excerpt.] Yes. Business differences in a partnership must be decided by a majority of the partners provided no other agreement between the partners speaks to the issues. Here, the record shows that although Summers (P) requested Dooley's (D) acquiescence in the hiring of the extra employee, such requests were not honored. In fact, Dooley (D) made it clear that he was "voting no" with regard to the hiring of an additional employee. An application of Idaho law to the factual situation presented here indicates that the trial court was correct in its disposal of the issue since a majority of the partners did not consent to the hiring of the extra man. Dooley (D) continually voiced objection to the hiring. He did not sit idly by and acquiesce to Summers's (P) actions. Thus, it would be unfair to permit Summers (P) to recover for an expense that was incurred individually, not for the benefit of the partnership, but rather for the benefit of one partner. Affirmed.

ANALYSIS

The rule that any difference arising as to ordinary matters connected with the partnership business may be decided by a majority of the partners is subject to any agreement between them. Partnership agreements often contain provisions vesting management in a managing partner or management committee. The same result, however, may be reached without explicit agreement on the basis of course of conduct.

Day v. Sidley & Austin

Former partner (P) v. Law firm (D)

394 F. Supp. 986 (D.D.C. 1975), *aff'd sub nom.* Day v. Avery, 548 F.2d 1018 (D.C. Cir. 1976), *cert. denied*, 431 U.S. 908 (1977)

NATURE OF CASE: Motion for summary judgment in action for damages.

FACT SUMMARY: Day (P), a former partner in the law firm of Sidley & Austin (S & A) (D), filed suit following approval of S & A's (D) merger with another firm and the changes that resulted from the merger.

RULE OF LAW

Partners have a fiduciary duty to make a full and fair disclosure to other partners of all information that may be of value to the partnership.

FACTS: Day (P) was a senior partner at the Washington office of the law firm Sidley & Austin (S & A) (D) from 1963 to 1972. Day (P) was a senior underwriting partner entitled to a certain percentage of the firm's profits and was privileged to vote on certain matters as specified in the partnership agreement. Day (P) was not a member of S & A's (D) executive committee, which managed day-to-day business. A 1970 partnership agreement vested management in the executive committee, and that agreement made no special provisions for Day (P), whereas it did for some of the other partners. In early 1972, the executive committee began exploring the idea of a merger with another firm. Each partner, including Day (P), voiced approval of the merger idea. Several other meetings of the underwriting partners were held before the final agreement was drawn up, but Day (P) chose not to attend any of them. The final amended Partnership Agreement, dated October 16, 1972, was executed by all S & A (D) partners, including Day (P). Day (P) resigned from the firm effective December 31, 1972, claiming that the changes that occurred after the merger in the Washington office made continued service with S & A (D) intolerable. Day (P) contended that the firm had made several active misrepresentations about the merger proposal, which amounted to fraud and breach of fiduciary duty owed to him as a partner. In particular, he claimed S & A (D) asserted that no partner would be worse off in any way as a result of the merger, including positions on committees. S & A (D) filed a motion for summary judgment asserting that Day's (P) factual allegations failed to support a cause of action.

ISSUE: Do partners have a fiduciary duty to make a full and fair disclosure to other partners of all information that may be of value to the partnership?

HOLDING AND DECISION: [Judge not stated in casebook excerpt.] Yes. Partners have a fiduciary duty to make a full and fair disclosure to other partners of all information that may be of value to the partnership. First, as to Day's (P) fraud claim, the alleged misrepresentation he asserts cannot support a fraud cause of action because he was not deprived of any legal right as the result of his reliance on the statement, since the 1970 partnership agreement set forth in detail the relationships among the partners and the structure of the firm, but it made no special provision for Day (P) to continue as the Washington office's chairman. Moreover, Day (P) could not have reasonably believed that no changes would be made in the office since the S & A (D) agreement gave complete authority to the executive committee to decide questions of firm policy. Also, S & A (D) did not breach any fiduciary duty owed to Day (P). No court has recognized a fiduciary duty to disclose the type of information handled by the executive committee involving the merger, the concealment of which does not produce any profit for the offending partners nor any financial loss for the partnership as a whole. Day's (P) breach of contract claims also fail to support a cause of action for which a legal remedy is available. Day (P) had no reasonable expectation that no changes would be made in the office since the firm's partnership agreement gave complete authority to the executive committee to decide questions of firm policy. As an able and experienced attorney, it should have been clear to Day (P) that the differences and misunderstandings that developed with his former partners were the type of business risks that, although not uncommon, are not resolvable by judicial proceedings. S & A's (D) alleged activities did not amount to illegality, and any personal humiliation was a risk he assumed when he joined the partnership. S & A's (D) motion for summary judgment is granted.

ANALYSIS

Courts are extremely reluctant to become involved in claims such as this one where a partnership agreement clearly defines the parties' rights as relating to one another. As the court pointed out, the primary and perhaps only injury Day (P) suffered was a bruised ego. A court is more likely to intervene when a third party is involved who was not privy to the standard operating

Continued on next page.

procedures of the partnership, or a less savvy plaintiff than a seasoned attorney, like Day (P).

Quicknotes

FIDUCIARY DUTY A legal obligation to act for the benefit of another.

FRAUD A false representation of facts with the intent that another will rely on the misrepresentation to their detriment.

MISREPRESENTATION A statement or conduct by one party to another that constitutes a false representation of fact.

PARTNERSHIP A voluntary agreement entered into by two or more parties to engage in business and to share any attendant profits and losses.

Giles v. Giles Land Company

General partner (P) v. Partnership (D)

Kan. Ct. App., 47 Kan. App. 2d 744, 279 P.3d 139 (2012)

NATURE OF CASE: In a books and records action brought by a general partner, appeal from judgment granting a counterclaim to dissociate the general partner from the partnership.

FACT SUMMARY: Kelly Giles (Kelly) (P), a general partner in Giles Land Co. (D), a family farming partnership, contended that he should not have been dissociated from the partnership because he neither engaged in wrongful conduct that adversely and materially affected the partnership, nor engaged in conduct relating to the partnership that made it not reasonably practicable to carry on the business in partnership with him.

RULE OF LAW

(1) In a family partnership, a partner may be dissociated from the partnership where the partner has threatened the other partners; the family relationship between the partner and other partners is broken; and there is only distrust between the partner and other partners.

(2) In a family partnership, a partner may be dissociated from the partnership where the partner's conduct toward the other partners has led to a standstill so that the partnership can no longer carry on its business to the mutual advantage of the other partners.

FACTS: The Giles Land Co. (the partnership) (D) was a family farming partnership whose partners, both general and limited, were members of the Giles family. Norman and Dolores, the parents, along with their seven children, were partners. One of the children, Kelly Giles (Kelly) (P), was continually at odds with the other family members. At some point, the other members wanted to convert the partnership to a limited liability company (LLC). Kelly (P), unable to attend the conversion meeting, sought production of all partnership books and records. Unsatisfied with the records provided to him, Kelly (P) filed suit seeking court-ordered production of all records he was seeking. As part of that suit, the other partners (i.e., his parents and siblings), counterclaimed to dissociate Kelly (P) from the partnership (D). They presented evidence that Kelly (P) had threatened them by turning to each of the general partners and saying that they would each die, in turn, and that he would be the last man standing and that he would then get to control the partnership (D). Kelly (P) also had said that "paybacks are hell" and that he intended to get even with his partners. There was also evidence that none of the partners could communicate with Kelly (P) regarding partnership business. From this, the trial court concluded that the familial relationship between Kelly (P) and other partners was broken, and that there was no trust between the partners and Kelly (P), and that, therefore, it was not practicable to carry on the business so long as Kelly (P) was a partner. The trial court was also presented with evidence that Kelly (P) berated, belittled, and yelled and cursed at his father, Norman, which led Norman to conclude that Kelly's (P) involvement in the partnership (D) had led to a standstill and was no longer tenable. There was also evidence that Kelly (P) had frustrated the partnership's (D) opportunities to purchase more land. From this, the trial court concluded that Kelly (P) had engaged in wrongful conduct that adversely and materially affected the partnership's (D) business. For these reasons, the trial court granted the counterclaim to dissociate Kelly (P) from the partnership (D). The trial court also ruled that the partnership (D) had provided Kelly (P) with sufficient books and records. Kelly (P) appealed the ruling on dissociation, and the state's intermediate appellate court granted review.

ISSUE:

(1) In a family partnership, may a partner be dissociated from the partnership where the partner has threatened the other partners; the family relationship between the partner and other partners is broken; and there is only distrust between the partner and other partners?

(2) In a family partnership, may a partner be dissociated from the partnership where the partner's conduct toward the other partners has led to a standstill so that the partnership can no longer carry on its business to the mutual advantage of the other partners?

HOLDING AND DECISION: [Judge not stated in casebook excerpt.]

(1) Yes. In a family partnership, a partner may be dissociated from the partnership where the partner has threatened the other partners; the family relationship between the partner and other partners is broken; and there is only distrust between the partner and other partners. One of the statutory standards permitting dissociation of a partner states that a partner may be dissociated where: "the partner engaged in conduct relating to the partnership business which makes it not reasonably practicable to carry on the business in partnership with the partner." Kelly (P) contends that his threats and broken ties with his family did

Continued on next page.

not constitute "conduct related to the partnership business." Because the partnership at issue is a family partnership, it is relevant that personal family issues were affecting the business. Given the mutual animosity and distrust harbored by Kelly (P) and the partners, it is clear the parties could no longer do business with each other. The partnership had reached an impasse regarding important business because of a lack of communication between Kelly (P) and his partners. Moreover, Kelly's (P) statement predicting the deaths of his general partners, his statement that "paybacks are hell," and his statement that he would "get even" showed a naked ambition on his part to control the partnership (D), contrary to the interests of the other partners. Accordingly, under this statutory standard, the trial court did not err in ordering Kelly (P) dissociated from the partnership (D). Affirmed as to this issue.

(2) Yes. In a family partnership, a partner may be dissociated from the partnership where the partner's conduct toward the other partners has led to a standstill so that the partnership can no longer carry on its business to the mutual advantage of the other partners. Another statutory standard permitting dissociation of a partner states that a partner may be dissociated where: "the partner engaged in wrongful conduct that adversely and materially affects the partnership business." Kelly (P) argues that his conduct was not wrongful, and that even if it was wrongful, it did not adversely and materially affect the business. In the context of a family partnership, Kelly's (P) making threats or trying to intimidate and abuse his father into giving him what he wanted, constitutes wrongful conduct. Such conduct also led to a standstill in partnership business, as the partners could no longer communicate with Kelly (P) about partnership business, and he frustrated business opportunities because he could not agree with the other partners as to the partnership's (D) direction. Accordingly, Kelly's (P) conduct satisfied this statutory standard, and the trial court did not err in in ordering Kelly (P) dissociated from the partnership (D) based on this standard. Affirmed as to this issue.

ANALYSIS

Under the Uniform Partnership Act (UPA), under which this case was decided, the effect of a partner's dissociation is generally that the partner's right to participate in the management and conduct of the partnership business terminates, as does the partner's duty of loyalty, which continues only with regard to matters arising and events occurring before the partner's dissociation, unless the partner participates in winding up the partnership's business. Thus, after dissociation, a partner is free to appropriate to his own benefit any new business opportunity thereafter coming to his attention, even if the partnership continues.

Quicknotes

PARTNERSHIP A voluntary agreement entered into by two or more parties to engage in business and to share any attendant profits and losses.

Kovacik v. Reed

Investor (P) v. Superintendent (D)

Cal. Sup. Ct., 49 Cal. 2d 166, 315 P.2d 314 (1957)

NATURE OF CASE: Suit for an accounting and to recover one-half the losses sustained by the parties' joint venture.

FACT SUMMARY: Kovacik (P) asked Reed (D) to be his superintendent on several remodeling jobs; when the jobs were unprofitable, Kovacik (P) asked Reed (D) to share equally in the losses and Reed (D) refused.

RULE OF LAW

In a joint venture in which one party contributes funds and the other labor, neither party is liable to the other for contribution for any loss sustained.

FACTS: Kovacik (P) asked Reed (D) to be his superintendent on several remodeling jobs. Kovacik (P) told Reed (D) that he had approximately $10,000 to invest and that if Reed (D) would superintend and estimate the jobs, he would share the profits with him on a 50-50 basis. They did not discuss the apportionment in the event of any losses. Reed (D) accepted the proposal and began working. Several months later Kovacik (P) informed Reed (D) that the venture lost money and demanded Reed (D) contribute to the losses. Reed (D) refused and Kovacik (P) filed suit for an accounting and to recover from Reed (D) one-half the losses. The trial court concluded the parties were to "share equally all their joint venture profits and losses" and, following an accounting, awarded plaintiff $4,340, representing one-half the losses found to have been incurred by Kovacik (P). Reed (D) appealed, and the state's highest court granted review.

ISSUE: In a joint venture, in which one party contributes funds and the other labor, is either party liable to the other for contribution for any loss sustained?

HOLDING AND DECISION: [Judge not stated in casebook excerpt.] No. In a joint venture, in which one party contributes funds and the other labor, neither party is liable to the other for contribution for any loss sustained. The general rule is that in the absence of an agreement to the contrary, the law presumes partners and joint venturers intended to participate equally in profits and losses of the common enterprise, irrespective of the amounts contributed, each sharing in the loss in the same proportion as they would in the profits. However, that presumption applies only in cases in which each party had contributed capital or was to receive compensation to be paid to them before computation of the losses or profits. This was not such a case. Reversed.

ANALYSIS

The court also stated that the party who contributed money or other capital to the venture was not entitled to recovery from the party who contributed his labor. The rationale for the rule is that in the event of a loss, each party would lose his investment—one, money, and the other, labor. Another basis for the rule is that the parties have valued their contributions equally and thus have sustained equivalent losses.

Quicknotes

CONTRIBUTION The right of a person or party who has compensated a victim for their injury to seek reimbursement from others who are equally responsible for the injury in proportional amounts.

JOINT VENTURE Venture undertaken based on an express or implied agreement between the members, common purpose and interest, and an equal power of control.

G & S Investments v. Belman

General partner (P) v. Executor of partner's estate (D)

Ariz. Ct. App., 145 Ariz. 258, 700 P.2d 1358 (1984)

NATURE OF CASE: Appeal from judgment for plaintiffs initially seeking to dissolve a partnership and subsequently invoking right to continue partnership upon partner's death.

FACT SUMMARY: G & S Investments (G & S) (P), a general partner in a limited partnership with Nordale, wanted to dissolve the partnership pursuant to the buy-out provision in their agreement due to Nordale's wrongful conduct, but then continued the partnership after Nordale died.

RULE OF LAW

(1) The mere filing of a complaint seeking dissolution of a partnership does not require liquidation of the partnership assets and distribution of the net proceeds.

(2) A partnership buyout agreement is valid and binding even if the purchase price is less than the value of the partner interest, since partners may agree among themselves by contract as to their rights and liabilities.

FACTS: G & S Investments (G & S) (P) sought a judicial dissolution of their limited partnership with Nordale after he began using cocaine and started making irrational and bad business decisions. Nordale died after the filing of the complaint, and G & S (P) filed a supplemental complaint invoking their right to continue the partnership and acquire Nordale's interest. The trial court entered judgment in favor of G & S (P), finding that it had the right to continue the partnership and that the estate was owed $4,867 pursuant to a formula contained in the partnership agreement. Belman (D), as executor of Nordale's estate, claimed that the mere filing of the original complaint acted as a dissolution of the partnership, requiring the liquidation of the assets and distribution of the net proceeds to the partners, and appealed. Belman (D) also claimed that the term "capital account" in the partnership agreement was ambiguous because it was not clear whether the cost basis or the fair market value of the partnership's assets should be used in determining the capital account. The state's intermediate appellate court granted review.

ISSUE:

(1) Does the mere filing of a complaint seeking dissolution of a partnership require liquidation of the partnership assets and distribution of the net proceeds?

(2) Is a partnership buyout agreement valid and binding even if the purchase price is less than the value of the partner interest, since partners may agree among themselves by contract as to their rights and liabilities?

HOLDING AND DECISION: [Judge not stated in casebook excerpt.]

(1) No. The mere filing of a complaint seeking dissolution of a partnership does not require liquidation of the partnership assets and distribution of the net proceeds. Nordale's conduct was in contravention of the partnership agreement. His conduct affected the carrying on of the business and made it impracticable to continue in partnership with him. It was his conduct, not G & S's (P) filing of the original complaint, which gave the court the power to dissolve the partnership and allow G & S (P) to carry on the business on its own.

(2) Yes. A partnership buyout agreement is valid and binding even if the purchase price is less than the value of the partner interest, since partners may agree among themselves by contract as to their rights and liabilities. The Articles of Partnership provided that upon the death, retirement, insanity, or resignation of one of the general partners the surviving or remaining partners were permitted to continue the partnership business, and that they had to purchase the interest of the departed partner. Such buyout agreements are valid and binding. Modern business practices allow parties to be bound by a contract they enter willingly, absent fraud or duress. The term "capital account" is not ambiguous and clearly means the partner's capital account as it appears on the books of the partnership, and not the fair market value of the interest. Affirmed.

ANALYSIS

The court in this case relied on a decision in an earlier case. In the case of *Cooper v. Isaacs,* 448 F.2d 1202 (D.C. Cir. 1971), the court had rejected the contention that the mere filing of a complaint acted as a dissolution of a partnership. Dissolution was found to occur only when decreed by the court or when brought about by other acts.

Continued on next page.

Quicknotes

ARTICLES OF PARTNERSHIP A written agreement, specifying the terms of a partnership.

CAPITAL In tax, is often used synonymously with basis; in accounting, refers to an account that represents the equity (ownership) interests of the owners, i.e., the amounts they would obtain if the business were liquidated.

COST BASIS The value paid for an asset.

DISSOLUTION Annulment or termination of a formal or legal bond, tie, or contract.

DURESS Unlawful threats or other coercive behavior by one person or party that causes another to commit acts that they would not otherwise do.

FAIR MARKET VALUE The price of particular property or goods that a buyer would offer and a seller accept in the open market, following full disclosure.

FRAUD A false representation of facts with the intent that another will rely on the misrepresentation to their detriment.

PARTNERSHIP A voluntary agreement entered into by two or more parties to engage in business and to share any attendant profits and losses.

In re El Paso Pipeline Partners, L.P. Derivative Litigation

[Parties not identified.]

Del. Ct. Ch., 2014 WL 2768782 (2014)

NATURE OF CASE: Cross-motions for summary judgment in action for breach of express contractual obligations and the implied covenant of good faith and fair dealing in a limited partnership agreement.

FACT SUMMARY: Limited partnership investors claimed that a "drop-down" transaction, whereby El Paso Corporation (El Paso Parent) sold assets to El Paso MLP, which was controlled by El Paso Pipeline GP Company, L.L.C., the general partner of El Paso MLP (the General Partner), which in turn was 100 percent owned by El Paso Parent, breached express contractual obligations as well as the implied covenant of good faith and fair dealing in El Paso MLP's limited partnership agreement.

RULE OF LAW

(1) Where a limited partnership agreement eliminates directors' common-law fiduciary duties and replaces them with contractual obligations, those express obligations are not breached where directors have acted in accord with the contractual obligations.

(2) Where a limited partnership agreement does not expressly eliminate the obligation of the general partner to act in good faith, the general partner does not breach the implied covenant of good faith and fair dealing where the agreement suggests if the parties had addressed the issue, no obligation to act in good faith would have been imposed.

FACTS: El Paso MLP was a publicly owned master limited partnership (MLP) that owned interests in companies that operated natural gas pipelines, liquid natural gas (LNG) terminals, and storage facilities throughout the United States. El Paso Corporation (El Paso Parent) was El Paso MLP's sponsor. A sponsor initially contributes a block of assets to the MLP and, over time, sells additional assets to the MLP. Because the assets move from the sponsor level down to the MLP level, the sales are referred to colloquially as "drop-downs." El Paso Parent controlled El Paso Pipeline GP Company, L.L.C. (the General Partner), the sole general partner of El Paso MLP. Thus, El Paso Parent also controlled El Paso MLP. Because of the resulting potential for conflict-of-interest transactions for the General Partner, El Paso MLP's limited partnership agreement (LPA) provided that El Paso MLP could proceed with a transaction that presented a conflict of interest for the General Partner if a conflict-of-interest transaction received "Special Approval." The LPA defined this form of approval as "approval by a majority of the members of the Conflicts Committee acting in good faith." The Conflicts Committee was defined as a committee of the General Partner's board, and its members had to meet the independence standards required of directors who serve on an audit committee of a publicly traded company. At El Paso MLP, the Conflicts Committee was not a standing committee of the General Partner Board, but rather a committee constituted on an ad hoc basis to consider specific conflict-of-interest transactions. In early 2010, El Paso Parent offered to sell El Paso MLP interests in two LNG companies, Southern LNG and Elba Express, for total value of $1.053 billion (the "Drop-Down" transaction). The revenue of these two companies came primarily from long-term agreements (Service Agreements) with subsidiaries of Shell and British Gas. Despite the contracts, Shell and British Gas had the practical option of walking away from the Service Agreements if they became unprofitable, as the subsidiaries that were parties to the Service Agreements were judgment-proof shell companies with no assets. At the time of the proposed Drop-Down, the market for LNG had faltered, and El Paso Parent faced a significant risk that Shell and British Gas would choose to breach the Service Agreements. Because the proposed Drop-Down created a conflict of interest for the General Partner, a Conflicts Committee comprised of three outside directors was formed. The committee hired a legal advisor and a financial advisor. The Conflicts Committee met five times to review El Paso Parent's proposal, and, along with its financial advisor, reviewed the proposed transaction and Southern LNG's and Elba Express's assets, including a summary of the Service Agreements. The Committee was able to obtain some concessions from El Paso Parent, and, after the financial advisor opined that the transaction was fair from a financial point of view to the El Paso MLP's limited partners, the Conflicts Committee unanimously recommended that El Paso MLP enter into the Drop-Down at a value that represented an Earnings Before Interest Taxes Depreciation and Amortization (EBITDA) multiple of around 12.2x. Unbeknownst to the Conflicts Committee, at the same time that El Paso Parent was proposing to sell LNG assets to El Paso MLP and touting their value, El Paso Parent was turning down an opportunity to buy LNG assets (Gulf LNG) for itself at an EBITDA multiple of 9.1x. After the Drop-Down was consummated, limited partners brought suit claiming that the Conflicts Committee had acted in bad faith, and, therefore, had breached the LPA's express obligations, as

Continued on next page.

well as the implied covenant of good faith and fair dealing. The LPA expressly abrogated all common-law duties that the General Partner and its board members might otherwise owe to El Paso MLP and its limited partners, including fiduciary duties, and it replaced those duties with contractual commitments. The LPA also provided that any conflict-of-interest transaction would be deemed approved by all partners and would not constitute a breach of the LPA or any duty stated or implied by law or equity as long as the action was approved by Special Approval. The plaintiffs contended that El Paso Parent's decision not to acquire an LNG asset at a lower implied EBITDA multiple while at the same time selling its own LNG assets to El Paso MLP for a higher implied EBITDA multiple was highly material information that should have been provided to the Conflicts Committee. The plaintiffs contended that the deal that El Paso Parent rejected illustrated arm's-length pricing for a comparable LNG asset, such that the Conflicts Committee's decision to buy a similar LNG asset at a significantly higher implied EBITDA multiple gave rise to an inference of bad faith. The plaintiffs further contended that the members of the Conflicts Committee failed to appreciate how easy it would be for Shell and British Gas to walk away from the Service Agreements, that Shell and British Gas would have a significant economic incentive to do so given the weakness in the domestic gas market, and that the value of the projected revenue under the Service Agreements had to be discounted significantly in light of that risk. The parties cross-moved for summary judgment. The Chancery Court reviewed the motions.

ISSUE:

(1) Where a limited partnership agreement eliminates directors' common-law fiduciary duties and replaces them with contractual obligations, are those express obligations breached where directors have acted in accord with the contractual obligations?

(2) Where a limited partnership agreement does not expressly eliminate the obligation of the general partner to act in good faith, does the general partner breach the implied covenant of good faith and fair dealing where the agreement suggests if the parties had addressed the issue, no obligation to act in good faith would have been imposed?

HOLDING AND DECISION: [Judge not stated in casebook excerpt.]

(1) No. Where a limited partnership agreement eliminates directors' common-law fiduciary duties and replaces them with contractual obligations, those express obligations are not breached where directors have acted in accord with the contractual obligations. Under Delaware law, the standard for good faith that applies to the Conflicts Committee requires a subjective belief that the determination or other action is in the best interests of El Paso MLP. Contrary to plaintiff's claims, the Conflicts Committee acted in good faith because it understood the state of the natural gas industry and did not consciously disregard the risk that Shell and British Gas might breach their service agreements. The Conflicts Committee considered the revenue risk and believed that the guarantees were meaningful and that even if the guarantees covered only a portion of the Service Agreements' revenue, neither Shell nor British Gas would default. While reasonable minds could disagree about the judgment made by the Conflicts Committee in this regard, the Conflicts Committee's judgment was not so extreme that it could support a potential finding of bad faith, nor was the committee's process sufficiently egregious to support such an inference. Moreover, that El Paso Parent did not inform the Conflicts Committee of its decision to forgo purchasing a stake in another LNG terminal for a substantially lower price had no bearing on the Conflicts Committee's subjective good faith. Although a price differential could imply bad faith in some circumstances, the Conflicts Committee members would have had to have known about such pricing issues in order for a factual dispute regarding good faith to be raised—and here, the plaintiffs conceded that the members did not know about the pricing differential. For these reasons, the Drop-Down did not violate the express requirements of the LPA. Summary judgment for defendants.

(2) No. Where a limited partnership agreement does not expressly eliminate the obligation of the general partner to act in good faith, the general partner does not breach the implied covenant of good faith and fair dealing where the agreement suggests if the parties had addressed the issue, no obligation to act in good faith would have been imposed. Here, the LPA did not expressly eliminate the obligation of the General Partner or El Paso Parent to act in good faith. Thus, the court must fill the gap and determine what the parties would have agreed to had they addressed the issue. Looking at the LPA's express provisions and its structure, it is likely no such obligation would have been imposed. Therefore, the LPA has not been breached. Summary judgment for defendants.

ANALYSIS

Even if the Conflicts Committee or its advisors knew about El Paso Parent's rejection of the Gulf LNG deal and the data point it represented when they were determining whether to endorse the Drop-Down, knowledge of the pricing disparity between the Gulf LNG deal and the Drop-Down might have been sufficient to support

Continued on next page.

an inference of subjective bad faith. Nevertheless, such a ruling by the court would not mean that the defendants necessarily would lose and be held liable, only that a trial would be necessary to resolve a disputed question of fact as to their intent. This is because the ultimate inquiry must focus on the subjective belief of the specific directors accused of wrongful conduct. The directors' personal knowledge and experience will be relevant to a subjective good faith determination, which must focus on measuring the directors' approval of a transaction against their knowledge of the facts and circumstances surrounding the transaction.

Quicknotes

IMPLIED COVENANT OF GOOD FAITH AND FAIR DEALING An implied warranty that the parties will deal honestly in the satisfaction of their obligations and without an intent to defraud.

LIMITED PARTNERSHIP A voluntary agreement entered into by two or more parties whereby one or more general partners are responsible for the enterprise's liabilities and management and the other partners are liable only to the extent of their investment.

CHAPTER 3

The Nature of the Corporation

Quick Reference Rules of Law

Boilermakers Local 154 Retirement Fund v. Chevron Corporation

Shareholder (P) v. Corporation (D)

Del. Ct. Ch., 73 A.3d 934 (2013)

NATURE OF CASE: Consolidated actions challenging the adoption of forum selection bylaws by a corporation's board as statutorily and contractually invalid.

FACT SUMMARY: The boards of the corporations Chevron (D) and FedEx (D), independently of each other, adopted bylaws that provided litigation relating to the internal affairs of the companies should be conducted in Delaware, the state where each company was incorporated. Stockholders (P) of each company brought separate suits challenging the bylaws, contending that the adoptions were statutorily invalid because they were beyond the boards' statutory authority, and were contractually invalid because the boards unilaterally adopted the bylaws. The actions were consolidated.

RULE OF LAW

(1) Where a corporation's certificate of incorporation empowers its board to adopt, amend, or repeal bylaws, a bylaw adopted by the board that requires litigation relating to the corporation's internal affairs to be brought in the corporation's state of incorporation is not statutorily invalid.

(2) Where a corporation's certificate of incorporation empowers its board to adopt, amend, or repeal bylaws, a bylaw unilaterally adopted by the board that requires litigation relating to the corporation's internal affairs to be brought in the corporation's state of incorporation is not contractually invalid.

FACTS: The boards of the corporations Chevron (D) and FedEx (D), independently of each other, unilaterally adopted "forum selection" bylaws that provided litigation relating to the internal affairs of the companies should be conducted in Delaware, the state where each company was incorporated. Delaware's law governs the internal affairs of each company because the companies are incorporated there. The forum selection bylaws applied to breach of fiduciary suits, derivative actions, actions arising under the Delaware General Corporation Law (DGCL), or any action asserting a claim governed by the internal affairs doctrine. Under the DGCL, 8 Del. C. § 109(a), the power to adopt, amend, or repeal bylaws resides in the stockholders, but a corporation's certificate of incorporation may confer that power on the directors. However, such a provision in the certificate of incorporation does not divest the shareholders of their bylaw powers. The DGCL, 8 Del. C. § 109(b), also provides that bylaws may contain any provision not inconsistent with law or with the certificate of incorporation, relating to the business of the corporation, the conduct of its affairs, and its rights or powers or the rights or powers of its stockholders, directors, officers, or employees. Both Chevron's (D) and FedEx's (D) certificates of incorporation conferred on the boards the power to adopt bylaws. In adopting the bylaws, the boards asserted that they were responding to corporations being subject to litigation over a single transaction or a board decision in more than one forum simultaneously, so-called "multi-forum litigation," and that the bylaws would significantly reduce needless duplicative litigation costs. Stockholders (P) of each company brought separate suits challenging the bylaws, contending that the adoptions were statutorily invalid because they were beyond the boards' statutory authority, and were contractually invalid because the boards unilaterally adopted the bylaws. The Court of Chancery consolidated the actions to determine whether the forum selection bylaws were facially invalid, either statutorily or contractually.

ISSUE:

(1) Where a corporation's certificate of incorporation empowers its board to adopt, amend, or repeal bylaws, is a bylaw adopted by the board that requires litigation relating to the corporation's internal affairs to be brought in the corporation's state of incorporation, statutorily invalid?

(2) Where a corporation's certificate of incorporation empowers its board to adopt, amend, or repeal bylaws, is a bylaw unilaterally adopted by the board that requires litigation relating to the corporation's internal affairs to be brought in the corporation's state of incorporation, contractually invalid?

HOLDING AND DECISION: [Judge not stated in casebook extract.]

(1) No. Where a corporation's certificate of incorporation empowers its board to adopt, amend, or repeal bylaws, a bylaw adopted by the board that requires litigation relating to the corporation's internal affairs to be brought in the corporation's state of incorporation is not statutorily invalid. As a matter of plain language, the forum selection bylaws address the rights of stockholders, because they regulate where stockholders can exercise their right to bring certain internal affairs claims against the corporation and its directors and officers. They also plainly relate to

Continued on next page.

the conduct of the corporation by channeling internal affairs cases into the courts of the state of incorporation. The argument that the bylaws regulate an "external" matter must be rejected. 8 Del. C. § 109(b) has long been understood to allow the corporation to set self-imposed rules and regulations that the board deems are necessary for the corporation's functioning, and the forum selection bylaws here fit this description. They are process-oriented, because they regulate where stockholders may file suit, not whether the stockholder may file suit or the kind of remedy that the stockholder may obtain. The bylaws also pertain to cases that relate to the business of the corporation, the conduct of its affairs, and the rights or powers of stockholders, directors, officers, or employees. The potential claims covered are the kind of claims most central to the relationship between those who manage the corporation and the corporation's stockholders. Additionally, other types of bylaws regulate how stockholders may exercise their rights as stockholders, e.g., an advance notice bylaw that requires stockholders to give notice of their intent to present proposals or nominations. Thus, even if the bylaws at issue are a novel use of statutory authority, such use is not prohibited merely because it is novel, since merely because the DGCL does not address a specific matter does not mean that it is necessarily prohibited. Judgment is granted to defendants, and the claim is dismissed with prejudice.

(2) No. Where a corporation's certificate of incorporation empowers its board to adopt, amend, or repeal bylaws, a bylaw unilaterally adopted by the board that requires litigation relating to the corporation's internal affairs to be brought in the corporation's state of incorporation is not contractually invalid. The stockholder plaintiffs (P) argue that, although contractual forum selection clauses are prima facie valid, the forum selection bylaws are contractually invalid because they were adopted by a board, rather than by Chevron's (D) and FedEx's (D) dispersed stockholders. The plaintiffs (P) argue that this method of adopting a forum selection clause is invalid as a matter of contract law, because it does not require the assent of the stockholders who will be affected by it. According to this view, there are two types of bylaws: (i) contractually binding bylaws that are adopted by stockholders; (ii) non-contractually binding bylaws that are adopted by boards using their statutory authority conferred by the certificate of incorporation. This view, however, misapprehends fundamental principles of corporate law, which clearly provides that bylaws constitute a binding part of the contract between a corporation and its stockholders. The stockholders of Chevron (D) and FedEx (D) were on notice that the boards of those corporations could unilaterally act to adopt bylaws regulating matters as authorized by the DGCL. Thus, such bylaws are not extra-contractual simply because the board acts unilaterally. Instead, the bylaws are part of the overarching statutory and contractual regime the stockholders have assented to. The contractual framework established by the DGCL and the certificates of incorporation explicitly recognizes that stockholders will be bound by bylaws adopted unilaterally by their boards. Under that clear contractual framework, the stockholders assent to not having to assent to board-adopted bylaws. It should be remembered, however, that under this framework, the stockholders may join to repeal any bylaw adopted by the board, as they retain their bylaw powers, notwithstanding a board's authority to act unilaterally as to bylaws. In other words, stockholders have powerful rights they can use to protect themselves if they do not want board-adopted forum selection bylaws to be part of the contract between themselves and the corporation. Judgment is granted to defendants, and the claim is dismissed with prejudice.

ANALYSIS

The court in this case resolved only the question of whether the forum selection bylaws were, either statutorily or contractually, facially invalid. If in the future, stockholders believe that these bylaws operate inequitably in a particular scenario, the stockholders facing such a concrete situation will have to challenge the case-specific application of the bylaw. Such an approach regarding bylaws is consistent with the established principle that courts should endeavor to enforce them to the extent that it is possible to do so without violating anyone's legal or equitable rights. This is also consistent with the doctrine laid down by the United States Supreme Court decision in *The Bremen v. Zapata Off-Shore Co.*, 407 U.S. 1 (1972) and its progeny, which requires courts to give as much effect as is possible to forum selection clauses and only deny enforcement of them to the limited extent necessary to avoid some fundamentally inequitable result or a result contrary to positive law.

Quicknotes

BYLAWS Rules promulgated by a corporation regulating its governance.

FORUM SELECTION CLAUSE Provision contained in a contract setting forth the particular forum in which the parties would resolve a matter if a dispute were to arise.

VantagePoint Venture Partners 1996 v. Examen, Inc.

Preferred shareholder (D) v. Corporation (P)

Del. Sup. Ct., 871 A.2d 1108 (2005)

NATURE OF CASE: Appeal from judgment for plaintiff in declaratory judgment action to determine the rights of preferred shareholders voting on a merger.

FACT SUMMARY: VantagePoint Venture Partners 1996 (VantagePoint) (D), a preferred shareholder of Examen, Inc. (P), a Delaware corporation, contended that California had the constitutional right to regulate a shareholder vote on Examen's (P) merger, whereas Examen (P) contended that Delaware law and the company's Certificate of Designations controlled. If Delaware law controlled, VantagePoint (D) would not be entitled to a class vote of its preferred stock, and would not be able to block the merger, whereas if California law controlled, it could.

RULE OF LAW

The internal affairs doctrine requires that a merger vote be governed by the law of the corporation's state of incorporation.

FACTS: Examen, Inc. (P), a Delaware corporation, wanted to merge with another corporation. VantagePoint Venture Partners 1996 (VantagePoint) (D) held 83.4 percent of Examen's (P) preferred stock. Examen (P) brought a declaratory judgment action in Delaware Court of Chancery seeking the court's determination that pursuant to Delaware law and under the company's Certificate of Designations of Series A Preferred Stock ("Certificate of Designations"), VantagePoint (D) was not entitled to a class vote of the Series A Preferred Stock on the proposed merger. A few days later, VantagePoint (D) filed suit in California seeking a declaration that Examen (P) was subject to California law, which would permit VantagePoint (D) to vote its shares in a separate class in connection with the proposed merger. The California court stayed the action pending the Court of Chancery's decision. The Court of Chancery ruled that the case was governed by the internal affairs doctrine, so that the law of the state of incorporation, i.e., Delaware, governed the vote required to approve the merger. The Delaware Supreme Court granted review, and also denied VantagePoint's (D) request to enjoin the merger, which was promptly consummated.

ISSUE: Does the internal affairs doctrine require that a merger vote be governed by the law of the corporation's state of incorporation?

HOLDING AND DECISION: [Judge not stated in casebook excerpt.] Yes. The internal affairs doctrine requires that a merger vote be governed by the law of the corporation's state of incorporation. The internal affairs doctrine is not merely a conflicts-of-law principle. It also has a constitutional dimension, since under the Fourteenth Amendment Due Process Clause corporate directors and officers have a significant right to know what law will be applied to their actions, and shareholders have a right to know by what standards of accountability they may hold those managing the corporation's business and affairs. The United State Supreme Court has similarly indicated that states may regulate the internal affairs of the corporations they create. Here, Examen (D) is a Delaware corporation, and the legal issue, relating to shareholder voting on a merger, clearly involves the relationship among the corporation and its shareholders. Vantage Point's (D) argument, that California's law in this area (Cal. Corp. Code § 2115) is a narrow exception to the internal affairs doctrine, must be rejected. That statute requires that many aspects of a corporation's internal affairs be governed by California law to the exclusion of the law of the state of incorporation. If California law were permitted to control, such a result would be apt to produce inequalities, intolerable confusion, and uncertainty, and intrude into the domain of other states that have a superior claim to regulate the same subject matter. Moreover, it would contravene the United States Supreme Court's mandate that the internal affairs of a corporation must be regulated by one uniform system of regulation. Therefore, Delaware's law must apply here and, under the Commerce Clause, California may not constitutionally regulate Examen's (D) internal affairs since the internal affairs of a corporation may be subject to only one uniform system of regulation—here, Delaware's. Affirmed.

ANALYSIS

California and New York have chosen to exercise their power over corporations that have been called "pseudo-foreign" because they are incorporated in another state but conduct most of their activities and business, and have most of their shareholders, in-state (see *Wilson v. Louisiana-Pacific Resources, Inc.*, 138 Cal. App. 3d 216, 187 Cal. Rptr. 852 (Cal. Ct. App. 1982)). The Delaware Supreme Court's ruling in *VantagePoint*, while not surprising given Delaware's status as the incorporation capital of the country, nonetheless weakens the ability of California and New York to have their regulation of

Continued on next page.

"pseudo-foreign" corporations enforced in other states. If this case had been brought in California, presumably the result would have been different.

Quicknotes

COMMERCE CLAUSE Article 1, Section 8, clause 3 of the United States Constitution, granting Congress the power to regulate commerce with foreign countries and among the states.

DUE PROCESS The constitutional mandate requiring the courts to protect and enforce individuals' rights and liberties consistent with prevailing principles of fairness and justice and prohibiting the federal and state governments from such activities that deprive its citizens of life, liberty, or property interest.

INTERNAL AFFAIRS DOCTRINE A doctrine of law providing that in respect to corporations, the law of the state having the most substantial relationship to the event giving rise to the cause of action and the parties involved governs.

MERGER The acquisition of one company by another, after which the acquired company ceases to exist as an independent entity.

Walkovszky v. Carlton

Injured pedestrian (P) v. Cab company owner (D)

N.Y. Ct. App., 18 N.Y.2d 414, 223 N.E.2d 6 (1966)

NATURE OF CASE: Appeal from reversal of dismissal of action to recover damages for personal injury.

FACT SUMMARY: Walkovszky (P), run down by a taxicab owned by Seon Cab Corporation (Seon) (D), sued Carlton (D), a stockholder of ten corporations, including Seon (D), each of which had only two cabs registered in its name.

RULE OF LAW

Whenever anyone uses control of the corporation to further their own rather than the corporation's business, they will be liable for the corporation's acts, but where a corporation is a fragment of a larger corporate combine that actually conducts the business, a court will not "pierce the corporate veil" to hold individual shareholders liable.

FACTS: Walkovszky (P) was run down by a taxicab owned by Seon Cab Corporation (Seon) (D). In his complaint, Walkovszky (P) alleged that Seon (D) was one of ten cab companies of which Carlton (D) was a shareholder and that each corporation had but two cabs registered in its name. The complaint, by this, implied that each cab corporation carried only the minimum automobile liability insurance required by law ($10,000). It was further alleged that these corporations were operated as a single entity with regard to financing, supplies, repairs, employees, and garaging. Each corporation and its shareholders were named as defendants because the multiple corporate structures, Walkovszky (P) claimed, constituted an unlawful attempt to "defraud members of the general public," and that none of the corporations had a separate existence of their own. Carlton (D) moved to dismiss the action on the grounds that as to him it did not state a cause of action. The trial court granted the motion, but the state's intermediate appellate court reversed. The state's highest court granted review.

ISSUE: Whenever anyone uses control of the corporation to further their own rather than the corporation's business, they will be liable for the corporation's acts, but where a corporation is a fragment of a larger corporate combine that actually conducts the business, will a court "pierce the corporate veil" to hold individual shareholders liable?

HOLDING AND DECISION: (Fuld, J.) No. Whenever anyone uses control of the corporation to further their own rather than the corporation's business, they will be liable for the corporation's acts, but where a corporation is a fragment of a larger corporate combine that actually conducts the business, a court will not "pierce the corporate veil" to hold individual shareholders liable. While the law permits the incorporation of a business for the purpose of minimizing personal liability, this privilege can be abused. Courts will disregard the corporate form ("pierce the corporate veil") to prevent fraud or to achieve equity. General rules of agency—respondeat superior—will apply to hold an individual liable for a corporation's negligent acts. The court here had earlier invoked the doctrine in a case where the owner of several cab companies (and whose name was prominently displayed on the cabs) actually serviced, inspected, repaired, and dispatched them. However, in such instances, it must be shown that the stockholder was conducting the business in his individual capacity. In this respect, Walkovszky's (P) complaint is deficient. The corporate form may not be disregarded simply because the assets of the corporation, together with liability insurance, are insufficient to assure recovery. If the insurance coverage is inadequate, the remedy lies with the legislature and not the courts. It is not fraudulent for the owner of a single cab corporation to take out no more than minimum insurance. Fraud goes to whether Carlton (D) and his associates (D) were shuttling their funds in and out of the corporations without regard to formality and to suit their own convenience. Here, the plaintiff did not adequately state a cause of action against the defendant in his individual capacity. Reversed.

DISSENT: (Keating, J.) The corporations formed by Carlton (D) were intentionally undercapitalized for the purpose of avoiding responsibility for acts that were bound to arise as a result of the operation of a large taxi fleet. During the course of the corporations' existence, all income was continually drained out of the corporations for the same purpose. Given these circumstances, the shareholders (D) should all be held individually liable to Walkovszky (P) for the injuries he suffered. Carlton (D) was incorrect in claiming that, because the minimum amount of insurance required by the statute was obtained, the corporate veil could not and should not be pierced despite the fact that the assets of the corporation that owned the cab were trifling compared with the business to be done and the risks of loss, which were certain to be encountered. In requiring the minimum liability insurance of $10,000, the legislature did not intend to shield those individuals who organized corporations with the specific intent of avoiding responsibility to the

Continued on next page.

public, where the operation of the corporate enterprise yielded profits sufficient to purchase additional insurance. Moreover, it is reasonable to assume that the legislature believed that those individuals and corporations having substantial assets would take out insurance far in excess of the minimum in order to protect those assets from depletion. In addition, it cannot be lightly inferred from the legislature's failure to increase the minimum insurance requirements that the legislature acquiesced in the shareholders' (D) scheme to avoid liability and responsibility to the public. Thus, the court should hold that a participating shareholder of a corporation vested with a public interest, organized with capital insufficient to meet liabilities, which are certain to arise in the ordinary course of the corporation's business, may be held personally responsible for such liabilities. Under such a holding, the only types of corporate enterprises that will be discouraged as a result of a decision allowing the individual shareholder to be sued will be those such as the one in question, designed solely to abuse the corporate privilege at the expense of the public interest.

ANALYSIS

Courts, in justifying disregard of the corporate entity so as to pierce the corporate veil, advance an estoppel argument. If the entity is not respected by the shareholders, they cannot complain if the court, likewise, disregards the corporate arrangement—this is to prevent abuse of the form. Since the corporate veil may be pierced even in instances where there has been no reliance on a company's seeming healthiness, as in tort claims, whether or not creditors have been misled is not of primary importance. Rather, a court will look at the degree to which the corporate shell has been perfected and the corporation's use as a mere business conduit of its shareholders.

Quicknotes

CORPORATE VEIL Refers to the shielding from personal liability of a corporation's officers, directors, or shareholders for unlawful conduct engaged in by the corporation.

EQUITABLE ESTOPPEL An equitable doctrine that precludes a person from asserting a right to which the person was entitled, resulting from their action, conduct, or failure to act, that caused another party to justifiably rely on such action, conduct, or failure to act to their detriment.

NEGLIGENCE Conduct falling below the standard of care that a reasonable person would demonstrate under similar conditions.

RESPONDEAT SUPERIOR Rule that the principal is responsible for tortious acts committed by its agents in the scope of their agency or authority.

Sea-Land Services, Inc. v. Pepper Source

Carrier (P) v. Dissolved corporation (D)

941 F.2d 519 (7th Cir. 1991)

NATURE OF CASE: Appeal from a grant of summary judgment for the plaintiff in an action for money owed.

FACT SUMMARY: When Sea-Land Services, Inc. (Sea-Land) (P) could not collect a shipping bill because Pepper Source (PS) (D) had been dissolved, Sea-Land (P) sought to pierce the corporate veil to hold PS's (D) sole shareholder personally liable.

RULE OF LAW

The corporate veil will be pierced where there is a unity of interest and ownership between the corporation and an individual and where adherence to the fiction of a separate corporate existence would sanction a fraud or promote injustice.

FACTS: After Sea-Land Services, Inc. (Sea-Land) (P), an ocean carrier, shipped peppers for Pepper Source (PS) (D) it could not collect on the substantial freight bill because PS (D) had been dissolved. Moreover, PS (D) apparently had no assets. Unable to recover on a default judgment against PS (D), Sea-Land (P) filed another lawsuit, seeking to pierce the corporate veil and hold Marchese (D), sole shareholder of PS (D) and other corporations, personally liable. PS (D) then took the necessary steps to be reinstated as a corporation in Illinois. Sea-Land (P) moved for summary judgment, which the district court granted. Marchese (D) and Pepper Source (D) appealed. The court of appeals granted review.

ISSUE: Will the corporate veil be pierced where there is a unity of interest and ownership between a corporation and an individual and where adherence to the fiction of a separate corporate existence would sanction a fraud or promote injustice?

HOLDING AND DECISION: (Bauer, C.J.) Yes. The corporate veil will be pierced where there is a unity of interest and ownership between a corporation and an individual and where adherence to the fiction of a separate corporate existence would sanction a fraud or promote injustice. There can be no doubt that the unity of interest and ownership part of the test is met here. Corporate records and formalities have not been maintained, funds and assets have been commingled with abandon, PS (D) was undercapitalized, and corporate assets have been moved and tapped and borrowed without regard to their source. The second part of the test is more problematic, however. An unsatisfied judgment, by itself, is not enough to show that injustice would be promoted. On remand, Sea-Land (P) is required to show the kind of injustice necessary to evoke the court's power to prevent injustice. Reversed and remanded.

ANALYSIS

On remand, judgment for Sea-Land (P) required Marchese (D) to pay the shipping debt plus post-judgment interest. On appeal, the judgment was affirmed, *Sea-Land Services, Inc. v. Pepper Source*, 993 F.2d 1309 (7th Cir. 1993). The court in that case observed that Marchese (D) had received countless benefits at the expense of Sea-Land (P) and others, including loans and salaries paid in such a way as to insure his corporations had insufficient funds with which to pay their debts.

Quicknotes

COMMINGLED ASSETS The combining of money or property into a joint account or asset.

CORPORATE VEIL Refers to the shielding from personal liability of a corporation's officers, directors, or shareholders for unlawful conduct engaged in by the corporation.

Frigidaire Sales Corporation v. Union Properties, Inc.

Manufacturer (P) v. Limited partners (D)

Wash. Sup. Ct., 88 Wash. 2d 400, 562 P.2d 244 (1977)

NATURE OF CASE: Appeal of affirmance of judgment for defendants in action to attach liability to limited partners.

FACT SUMMARY: Frigidaire Sales Corporation (Frigidaire) (P) attempted to hold the limited partners of Commercial Investors (Commercial) generally liable after Commercial breached its contract with Frigidaire (P).

RULE OF LAW

Limited partners do not incur general liability for the limited partnership's obligations simply because they are officers, directors, or shareholders of the corporate general partner.

FACTS: Frigidaire Sales Corporation (Frigidaire) (P) entered into a contract with Commercial Investors (Commercial), a limited partnership. Mannon (D) and Baxter (D) were limited partners of Commercial and also officers, directors, and shareholders of Union Properties (Union) (D), the only general partner of Commercial. Mannon (D) and Baxter (D) controlled Commercial by exercising day-to-day control and management of Union (D). Commercial breached the contract and Frigidaire (P) filed suit against Union (D), Mannon (D), and Baxter (D), asserting that they should incur general liability for the limited partnership's obligations because they exercised day-to-day control and management of Commercial. Mannon (D) and Baxter (D) argued that Commercial was controlled by Union (D), a separate legal entity, and not by them in their individual capacities. The trial court declined to hold Mannon (D) and Baxter (D) generally liable, the state's intermediate appellate court affirmed, and Frigidaire (P) appealed. The state's highest court granted review.

ISSUE: Do limited partners incur general liability for the limited partnership's obligations simply because they are officers, directors, or shareholders of the corporate general partner?

HOLDING AND DECISION: [Judge not stated in casebook excerpt.] No. Limited partners do not incur general liability for the limited partnership's obligations simply because they are officers, directors, or shareholders of the corporate general partner. In Washington, parties may form a limited partnership with a corporation as the sole general partner. To hold that Mannon (D) and Baxter (D) incurred general liability for the limited partnership's obligations would require the court to totally ignore the corporate entity of Union (D), when Frigidaire (P) knew it was dealing with that corporate entity. Although Mannon (D) and Baxter (D) controlled Commercial through their control of Union (D), they scrupulously separated their actions on behalf of Commercial from their personal actions and the corporations were clearly separate entities. Frigidaire (P) knew that Union (D) was the sole general partner of Commercial and that Mannon (D) and Baxter (D) were only limited partners. If Frigidaire (P) had not wished to rely on the solvency of Union (D) as the only general partner, it could have insisted that Mannon (D) and Baxter (D) personally guarantee contractual performance. When the shareholders of a corporation, who are also the corporation's officers and directors, conscientiously keep the affairs of the corporation separate from their personal affairs, and no fraud or manifest injustice is perpetrated upon third persons who deal with the corporation, the corporation's separate entity should be respected. Affirmed.

ANALYSIS

The court's opinion does not preclude a finding of general liability of limited partners where there is a showing of fraud or deception. Other courts have been less lenient in protecting limited partners and have held them generally liable if their actions constituted control of the corporation. In some states, on the other hand, a corporate entity is not permitted to be a general partner because such arrangements are viewed as shams.

Quicknotes

GENERAL PARTNERSHIP A voluntary agreement entered by two or more parties to engage in business whereby each of the parties is to share in any profits and losses therefrom equally and each is to participate equally in the management of the enterprise.

LIMITED PARTNERSHIP A voluntary agreement entered by two or more parties whereby one or more general partners are responsible for the enterprise's liabilities and management and the other partners are only liable to the extent of their investment.

A.P. Smith Mfg. Co. v. Barlow

Corporation (P) v. Shareholder (D)

N.J. Sup. Ct., 13 N.J. 145, 98 A.2d 581, *appeal dismissed*, 346 U.S. 861 (1953)

NATURE OF CASE: Appeal from declaratory judgment affirming corporate authority.

FACT SUMMARY: Barlow (D) and other shareholders of A.P. Smith Mfg. Co. (P) challenged its authority to make a donation to Princeton University, claiming such a contribution was ultra vires and that the state's statutes that expressly authorized the contribution could not constitutionally be applied to the corporation, given that it had been created long before their enactment.

RULE OF LAW

State legislation adopted in the public interest can be constitutionally applied to preexisting corporations under the reserved power.

FACTS: A.P. Smith Mfg. Co. (P) was a New Jersey corporation incorporated in 1896. Over the years it regularly made donations to various community organizations and public universities. In 1951, the board of directors adopted a resolution stating that it was in A.P. Smith Mfg.'s (P) best interest to donate $1,500 to Princeton University's annual fund. Shareholders (D) of A.P. Smith Mfg. (P) questioned the corporation's authority to make the contribution on two grounds: (1) its certificate of incorporation did not expressly authorize the donation and A.P. Smith (P) possessed no implied power to make it; and (2) the New Jersey statutes that would have expressly authorized the contribution did not constitutionally apply to A.P. Smith (P) because it was created long before their enactment. A.P. Smith Mfg. (P) sought a declaratory judgment following the shareholder's challenges. The trial court held that the donation was intra vires, and the shareholders (D) appealed. The state's highest court granted review.

ISSUE: Can state legislation adopted in the public interest be constitutionally applied to preexisting corporations under the reserved power?

HOLDING AND DECISION: [Judge not stated in casebook excerpt.] Yes. State legislation adopted in the public interest can be constitutionally applied to preexisting corporations under the reserved power. Fifty years before the incorporation of A.P. Smith Mfg. (P), the New Jersey legislature provided that every corporate charter thereafter granted would be subject to alteration and modification at the discretion of the legislature. A similar reserved power was incorporated into the state constitution. New Jersey courts have repeatedly recognized where justified by the advancement of the public interest, the reserved power may be invoked to sustain later charter alterations even though they affect contractual rights between the corporation and its stockholders. Therefore, a statute enacted in 1930 encouraging and expressly authorizing reasonable charitable contributions is applicable to A.P. Smith Mfg. (P) and must be upheld as a lawful exercise of A.P. Smith Mfg.'s (P) implied and incidental powers under common-law principles. Affirmed.

ANALYSIS

The court was clearly swayed as much by philanthropic concerns and social policy as by statutory law. It dedicated a large portion of its opinion to discussing the economic and social importance of corporate contributions, particularly those made to universities. The opinion was quite prophetic, as such donations have grown even more significantly in the decades since the opinion was written.

Quicknotes

DECLARATORY JUDGMENT An adjudication by the courts that grants not relief but is binding over the legal status of the parties involved in the dispute.

INTRA VIRES "Within the power" refers to powers that are within the scope of authority of an individual or corporation.

Dodge v. Ford Motor Co.

Shareholder (P) v. Corporation (D)

Mich. Sup. Ct., 204 Mich. 459, 170 N.W. 668 (1919)

NATURE OF CASE: Appeal from order compelling a dividend.

FACT SUMMARY: Shareholders Horace and John Dodge (P) filed suit against Ford Motor Co. (D) after Henry Ford (D), the controlling shareholder, decided not to pay any more special dividends and to instead reinvest the money in the business.

RULE OF LAW

A corporation's primary purpose is to provide profits for its stockholders.

FACTS: Ford Motor Co. (D) was incorporated in 1903 with Henry Ford (D) as the majority shareholder and the Dodge brothers (P) owning 10 percent of the common shares. Ford Motor Co. (D) grew rapidly, profits soared, and from 1911 to 1915 large regular and special dividends were paid to the shareholders. In 1915, the Dodges' (P) share of the regular dividend was $120,000 and their share of the special dividend was $1,000,000, with the prospect of even more increases in the future. In 1913, the Dodges (P) formed a separate auto company, which competed with Ford (D). In 1916, despite having profits of almost $174,000,000 and more than $50,000,000 cash on hand, Henry Ford (D) announced that in the future no special dividends would be paid, profits would be reinvested into the business, and the price of the company's cars would be reduced. After the announcement of the new dividend policy, John Dodge (P) met with Ford (D) to complain about the new policy and offered to sell his and his brother's shares to Ford (D) for $35,000,000. After Ford (D) rejected the buyout offer, the Dodges (P) filed suit, attacking both the dividend policy and Ford's (D) plans to expand manufacturing facilities. The trial court ruled in favor of the Dodges (P), ordering payment of the dividend and enjoining the building of a smelting plant, and Ford (D) appealed. The state's highest court granted review.

ISSUE: Is a corporation's primary purpose to provide profits for its stockholders?

HOLDING AND DECISION: [Judge not stated in casebook excerpt.] Yes. A corporation's primary purpose is to provide profits for its stockholders. The powers of a corporation's directors are to be employed to that end and their discretion is to be exercised in the choice of means to attain that end. However, this discretion does not extend to a change in the end itself, to the reduction of profits, or to the nondistribution of profits among stockholders in order to devote them to other purposes. Given the Ford Motor Co.'s (D) clearly prosperous economic outlook, Ford (D) was not entitled to arbitrarily refuse to pay a dividend that had been established over several years. Although the courts should not interfere with the proposed expansion of Ford Motor Co. (D), the evidence shows that there was a large and consistent daily, weekly, and monthly receipt of cash as well as a large balance on hand. Furthermore, the contemplated expenditures were not to be immediately made, but to be paid over a considerable period of time. The trial court was correct in ruling that a large sum of money should have been distributed to the shareholders. Affirmed as to the dividend policy; reversed as to the company's expansion plans.

ANALYSIS

The court realized that Ford (D) was motivated by more than a desire to expand his company's manufacturing capabilities. Ford (D) clearly wanted to avoid funding his competition's new venture. Perhaps that is why he also refused the Dodge brothers' (P) buyout offer.

Quicknotes

COMMON STOCK A class of stock representing the corporation's ownership, the holders of which are entitled to dividends only after the holders of preferred stock are paid.

DIVIDEND The payment of earnings to a corporation's shareholders in proportion to the amount of shares held.

FIDUCIARY DUTY A legal obligation to act for the benefit of another, including subordinating one's personal interests to that of the other person.

SHAREHOLDER An individual who owns shares of stock in a corporation.

Shlensky v. Wrigley

Minority shareholder (P) v. Majority shareholder (D)

Ill. App. Ct., 95 Ill. App. 2d 173, 237 N.E.2d 776 (1968)

NATURE OF CASE: Appeal from dismissal of a shareholder's purported derivative action.

FACT SUMMARY: Wrigley (D), the majority shareholder in the Chicago Cubs, refused to install lights at Wrigley Field in order to hold night games, and Shlensky (P), a minority shareholder, filed a derivative suit to compel the installation.

RULE OF LAW

A shareholder's derivative suit can only be based on conduct by the directors that borders on fraud, illegality, or conflict of interest.

FACTS: Wrigley (D) was the majority shareholder and a director of the Chicago Cubs baseball team. Shlensky (P), a minority shareholder, sought to bring a shareholders' derivative action to compel the directors to equip Wrigley Field (the Cub's home field) with lights so that night games could be played, and revenues could be increased. The trial court sustained Wrigley's (D) motion to dismiss over Shlensky's (P) contention that the refusal to install lights was a personal decision of Wrigley's (D) and not in the best interest of the shareholders. The state's intermediate appellate court granted review.

ISSUE: Can a shareholders' derivative suit be based on conduct by the directors that does not border on fraud, illegality, or conflict of interest?

HOLDING AND DECISION: [Judge not stated in casebook excerpt.] No. A shareholder's derivative suit can only be based on conduct by the directors that borders on fraud, illegality, or conflict of interest. Shlensky (P) is attempting to use the derivative suit to force a business judgment on the board of directors of the Chicago Cubs, but there is no showing of fraud, illegality, or conflict of interest. There are valid reasons for refusal to install lights in the stadium. Though Shlensky (P) alleges that night games haven't been considered due to Wrigley's (D) personal feelings about the sport, Wrigley (D) has suggested that night games in the Wrigley Field area would have a detrimental effect on the neighborhood. Additionally, there is no showing that night games would significantly increase revenues, or even that additional expenses wouldn't be required. Affirmed.

ANALYSIS

Though the "business judgment rule" is typically stated as relating to the functions of directors, the rule is equally applicable to officers of the corporation while acting in their official capacities; and it may apply to controlling shareholders as well if these persons assert their more extraordinary management functions, e.g., mergers or sale of their complete interest.

Quicknotes

BUSINESS JUDGMENT RULE Doctrine relieving corporate directors and/or officers from liability for decisions honestly and rationally made in the corporation's best interests.

CONFLICT OF INTEREST Refers to ethical problems that arise, or may be anticipated to arise, between an attorney and their client if the interests of the attorney, another client, or a third-party conflict with those of the present client.

FRAUD A false representation of facts with the intent that another will rely on the misrepresentation to their detriment.

SHAREHOLDER'S DERIVATIVE ACTION Action asserted by a shareholder in order to enforce a cause of action on behalf of the corporation.

McRitchie v. Zuckerberg

Diversified shareholder investor (P) v. Director and controlling shareholder (D)

Del. Ch. Ct., 315 A.3d 518 (2024)

NATURE OF CASE: Motion to dismiss for failure to state a claim in action for breach of fiduciary duty against corporate directors, officers, and controlling shareholder on the grounds that the defendants managed the corporation under a firm-specific model rather than a diversified-investor model.

FACT SUMMARY: McRitchie (P), a diversified shareholder of Meta Platforms, Inc. ("Meta" or the "Company"), the world's largest social media network, brought suit contending that Meta's directors (D), officers (D), and controlling shareholder (D) breached their fiduciary duties to shareholders by managing Meta under a firm-specific model rather than a diversified-investor model. The directors (D), officers (D), and controller (D) asserted that they did not have a duty to manage Meta under a diversified-investor model and moved to dismiss McRitchie's (P) suit for failure to state a claim.

RULE OF LAW

Directors, officers, and controlling stockholders of a Delaware corporation do not have a fiduciary duty to seek to maximize value for stockholders who are diversified investors, rather than managing the corporation pursuant to a single-firm model in which the directors, officers, and controllers owe duties to the stockholders as investors in that corporation.

FACTS: McRitchie (P), a diversified shareholder of Meta Platforms, Inc. ("Meta" or the "Company"), a Delaware corporation and the world's largest social media network, brought suit in Delaware Court of Chancery contending that Meta's nine directors (D), its officers (D), and its controlling shareholder and director, Zuckerberg (D), breached their fiduciary duties to shareholders by managing Meta under a firm-specific model rather than a diversified-investor model. Meta has four major social media platforms: Facebook, Instagram, Messenger, and WhatsApp, and it has two classes of stock. Class A shares trade publicly and carry one vote per share, whereas Class B shares are only held by insiders and carry ten votes per share. Meta's public stockholders are broadly diversified institutional investors, most of which are legally required to diversify. Diversification comports with Modern Portfolio Theory. Its proponents have demonstrated through mathematical models that investors can increase returns at lower risk by owning a diversified portfolio of securities. For diversified investors, returns primarily track overall market performance, not the performance of individual companies. Over time, market performance should rise and fall with the performance of the economy as a whole. Assuming gross domestic product (GDP) is a representative measure of the performance of the economy as a whole, a diversified portfolio should rise and fall over time with GDP. Based on the Modern Portfolio Theory, McRitchie (P) argued that because stockholders are investors and because under Modern Portfolio Theory prudent investors diversify, the law must operate on the assumption that a corporation's stockholders are diversified, so that owing fiduciary duties to the corporation and its stockholders must mean owing duties that run to the corporation and its stockholders as diversified equity investors. Furthermore, because the returns that accrue to diversified equity investors should generally track the economy as a whole, complying with fiduciary duties oriented to diversified equity investors must mean managing the corporation based on what would be best for the economy as a whole. Thus, McRitchie (P) concluded that Delaware law currently follows a diversified-investor model, and, if not, the law should change. McRitchie (P) also contended that Zuckerberg and the other Meta directors (D) were concentrated investors, meaning that they benefitted when Meta outperformed the market, but that Meta's other stockholders were diversified investors who benefitted when the market as a whole did well. The interests of concentrated investors and diversified investors can diverge when a company's business generates negative externalities. An externality is an effect or consequence of an activity that is not reflected in the cost of the activity. The existence of externalities means that the person engaging in the activity does not fully internalize all of its effects or consequences. A negative externality harms third parties, and because a business that generates negative externalities does not internalize their cost, the owners of that business benefit from continuing to create them. McRitchie (P) contends that Meta's business generates negative externalities and that Meta consciously and openly prioritizes company-specific value over harm to the economy and society, at the expense of the portfolios of its diversified investors. McRitchie (P) also contends that Meta awards to executives large grants of equity, which incentivize executives to pursue initiatives that promote Meta's value at the expense of the economy, society, and the portfolios of diversified stockholders. Accordingly, McRitchie (P) claims that the defendants breached their fiduciary duties by managing Meta in a manner that ignored the interests of Meta's diversified stockholders and caused harm to them while increasing

Continued on next page.

Meta's share price and bottom line while also failing to consider how Meta's activities and policies effect society and the economy at large and thus the portfolios of its diversified stockholders. The directors (D), officers (D), and Zuckerberg (D) asserted that they did not have a duty to manage Meta under a diversified-investor model and moved to dismiss McRitchie's (P) suit for failure to state a claim.

ISSUE: Do directors, officers, and controlling stockholders of a Delaware corporation have a fiduciary duty to seek to maximize value for stockholders who are diversified investors, rather than managing the corporation pursuant to a single-firm model in which these parties owe duties to the stockholders as investors in that corporation?

HOLDING AND DECISION: [Judge not stated in casebook extract.] No. Directors, officers, and controlling stockholders of a Delaware corporation do not have a fiduciary duty to seek to maximize value for stockholders who are diversified investors, rather than managing the corporation pursuant to a single-firm model in which the directors, officers, and controllers owe duties to the stockholders as investors in that corporation. Under Delaware's board-centric model of governance, directors' fiduciary duties run to the corporation and the stockholders of that corporation—a single-firm model. Although the Delaware Supreme Court's decisions do not expressly address the single-firm model versus the diversified-investor model, a range of the Court's decisions, by necessary implication, establish that fiduciary duties run to firm-specific stockholders in their capacities as firm-specific stockholders and not in any other capacities they may have. First, in cases about stockholders versus stakeholders (e.g., creditors), such as *Unocal Corporation v. Mesa Petroleum Co.*, 493 A.2d 946 (Del. 1985), and *Revlon, Inc. v. MacAndrews & Forbes Holdings, Inc.*, 506 A.2d 173 (Del.1985), the Supreme Court of Delaware, emphasizing that directors have a fiduciary duty to act in the best interests of the corporation's stockholders, neither mentioned stakeholders, nor referred to stockholders in other capacities, such as their capacities as diversified investors. Also, the Court gave no indication that the directors should consider the interests of stockholders as diversified investors whose interests were aligned with the economy as a whole, and looked only to stockholders' economic interests as investors in the corporation that was the subject of the action. In *Revlon*, the Court expressly held that the directors of Revlon could not properly consider the interests of the noteholders, even though only weeks earlier all of the noteholders had been stockholders, and even though it was highly likely that at least some of the noteholders remained stockholders. In *Revlon*, the Court did not contemplate that the directors could consider the interests of the stockholders as investors who also held notes, nor did the Court imply that the directors could consider the interests of stockholders in other capacities, whether as diversified investors, as Revlon employees, or as potential users of Revlon beauty products. Second, the Court has consistently rejected claims brought by stockholder plaintiffs who have asserted claims for breach of fiduciary duty against directors who took action that harmed the plaintiffs in a non-stockholder capacity. Third, the historical development of corporate fiduciary duties throughout the U.S., not just in Delaware, confirms that those duties are firm-specific. Early cases focused on directors' potential breaches of trust involving the misuse or misapplication of the firm-specific capital that the stockholders had contributed or the firm-specific profits the firm had generated. Notably, directors were not held to be fiduciaries for the stockholders as individuals, but, instead, were fiduciaries for the corporation's shares, where each share initially represented a proportionate claim on the aggregate value of the contributed capital and the directors had the duty to grow that value by promoting the value of the firm. Over time, each share represented a proportionate claim on the resulting value of the firm. Stockholders entered the mix only because shares have owners, and the owners of shares benefit when the value of the firm increases because that value accrues proportionately to the shares. Thus, the directors' obligation was an economic one: care for the capital entrusted to the firm, protect and grow the value of the firm, and thereby increase the value of the shares. Fiduciary duties thus properly run to the corporation for the benefit of the shares, making the resulting fiduciary obligation inherently financial and firm-specific. This understanding of directors' fiduciary duties as firm-specific has not changed with time.

Because the weight of the Delaware Supreme Court's precedents indicates that it does not currently follow a diversified-investor model, McRitchie (P) advocates for changing the law so it does. However, McRitchie (P) starts by caricaturing what the single-firm focus requires by positing that a single-firm orientation means that fiduciaries have no duty (or ability) to consider the costs of their decisions on the typical stockholders' portfolios, even if those costs far outweigh any benefit received as holders of company shares. That, however, is not true. Directors must seek to maximize the value of the firm for the ultimate benefit of its stockholders, so that directors may—or even must—consider a broad spectrum of issues, including how a decision affects stakeholders, the economy, and society. Directors who cause their corporation to become a pariah because its actions consistently or profoundly harm the broader economy will not be able to create durable long-term value for firm-specific stockholders. Therefore, directors can and should

Continued on next page.

consider those issues when making decisions about what will promote the value of the firm over the long-term. McRitchie's (P) strongest argument in favor of the diversified-investor model is that the single-firm model is more likely to generate negative externalities. Writing extra-judicially, former Chief Justice Strine called for society to recognize that for-profit corporations will seek profit for their stockholders using all legal means available, so that one way to address negative externalities is by the enactment of strong statutes and regulations to address externality risk and fundamental concerns about appropriate protection of workers and the environment. He also emphasized that within the limits of their discretion, directors must make stockholder welfare their sole end, and that other interests may be taken into consideration only as a means of promoting stockholder welfare. The ability of corporations to pursue profit thus being subjected to the requirement that Delaware corporations only pursue lawful business by lawful acts, gives positive laws and regulations power to constrain negative externalities, with corporate law as a supportive adjunct. Moreover, there is no need to change current law, because Delaware law already permits corporations to opt into a diversified-investor model through private ordering if they so desire. One way this can be achieved is through the use of a limited purpose clause under § 102(a)(3) of the DGCL. Pursuant to a narrow purpose clause, directors could be constrained to operate in a manner that would not harm diversified investors. For example, the corporation's purpose could be stated as pursuing only businesses that benefit diversified equity investors and do not create externalities that benefit the corporation at the expense of the economy as a whole. Under § 102(b)(1), a second method of fiduciary tailoring involves a charter provision that defines, limits, or regulates the powers of the corporation, directors, and stockholders, and allows a corporate charter to contain virtually any provision that is related to the corporation's governance, subject only to the requirement that it not be contrary to Delaware law. Lastly, a third approach to fiduciary tailoring involves explicitly reorienting the duties of directors under § 141(a) of the DGCL, which contains a Board Power Exception, which authorizes a board to depart from Delaware's typical board-centric regime. Thus, using the Board Power Exception, a charter could re-orient the powers and duties of the board of directors toward diversified investors by stating, for example, that "any duties conferred or imposed upon the board of directors of the corporation shall be owed to the corporation for the ultimate benefit of its stockholders as diversified investors." For all the foregoing reasons, McRitchie (P) has failed to state a claim on which relief can be granted, and, accordingly, the case is dismissed with prejudice.

ANALYSIS

As this case shows, in Delaware, the ability of corporations to pursue profit is subject to the requirement that Delaware corporations only pursue lawful business by lawful acts. By imposing this statutory floor, Delaware law squarely rejects the Chicago School concept of "law as price." That concept posits that a firm may find it advantageous to violate a law deliberately and pay the penalty, presumably because it is more advantageous for the corporation to do so. Thus, where the Chicago School's concept prevails, managers have no general obligation to avoid violating regulatory laws and might even have a duty to violate the law if, by doing so, they can maximize profits for stockholders. Delaware law, however, applies a concept that is the opposite of the law-as-price concept by providing that a fiduciary of a Delaware corporation cannot be loyal to a Delaware corporation by knowingly causing it to seek profit by violating the law. Delaware law thus mandates that its entities and the fiduciaries who manage them comply with positive law. That legal requirement promotes legal compliance in its own right, while also providing a mechanism for holding fiduciaries accountable when they knowingly cause an entity to violate positive law.

Quicknotes

BREACH OF FIDUCIARY DUTY The failure of a fiduciary to observe the standard of care exercised by professionals of similar education and experience.

COMMON STOCK A class of stock representing the corporation's ownership, the holders of which are entitled to dividends only after the holders of preferred stock are paid.

DIVERSIFIED INVESTOR An investor who spreads their investments across various asset classes, such as stocks, bonds, and real estate, to reduce risk and enhance potential returns.

FIDUCIARY Person holding a legal obligation to act for the benefit of another.

FIDUCIARY DUTY A legal obligation to act for the benefit of another, including subordinating one's personal interests to that of the other person.

NOTEHOLDER Holder of a note that has the right to receive payment according to the terms of the note.

SHAREHOLDER An individual who owns shares of stock in a corporation.

CHAPTER 4

The Duties of Officers, Directors, and Other Insiders

Quick Reference Rules of Law

CHAPTER 4

Kamin v. American Express Company

Shareholder (P) v. Corporation (D)

N.Y. Sup. Ct., 86 Misc. 2d 809, 383 N.Y.S.2d 807, *aff'd*, N.Y. App. Div., 54 A.D.2d 654, 387 N.Y.S.2d 993 (1976)

NATURE OF CASE: Derivative action for damages for waste of corporate assets.

FACT SUMMARY: Kamin (P) brought a shareholders' derivative suit claiming American Express Company (D) had engaged in waste of corporate assets by declaring a certain dividend in kind.

RULE OF LAW

The decision to declare a dividend or make a distribution is exclusively a matter of business judgment for the board of directors, so that the courts will not interfere with the board's decision as long as it is made in good faith.

FACTS: American Express Company (D) had acquired for investment almost two million shares of common stock in Donaldson, Lufken and Jenrette (DLJ) at a cost of $29.9 million. Kamin (P), a minority stockholder in American Express (D), charged that the subsequent decision to declare a special dividend to all stockholders resulting in a distribution of the shares of DLJ in kind was a negligent violation of the directors' fiduciary duty. He argued that the market value of the DLJ shares was only $4 million and that American Express (D) should have sold the DLJ shares on the market so as to be able to offset the $25 million capital loss against taxable capital gains on other investments and thus obtain an $8 million tax saving that would be otherwise unavailable. In a shareholders' derivative action, Kamin (P) sought a declaration that the dividend in kind constituted a waste of corporate assets and sought damages therefor. American Express (D) moved to dismiss the complaint.

ISSUE: Is the decision to declare a dividend or make a distribution exclusively a matter of business judgment for the board of directors, so that the courts will not interfere with the board's decision as long as it is made in good faith?

HOLDING AND DECISION: [Judge not stated in casebook excerpt.] Yes. The decision to declare a dividend or make a distribution is exclusively a matter of business judgment for the board of directors, so that the courts will not interfere with the board's decision as long as it is made in good faith. It is not enough to charge, as Kamin (P) has in this case, that the directors made an imprudent decision or that some other course of action would have been more advantageous. Such a charge cannot give rise to a cause of action. Thus, the motion for summary judgment and dismissal of the complaint is granted.

ANALYSIS

The "business judgment rule" illustrated in this case expresses the traditional and still valid view of a director's duty of care. This common-law standard is designed to allow the directors a wide berth in conducting the affairs of the corporation so that they can act effectively and efficiently in pursuing the corporation's best interests rather than being constantly influenced by the need to practice "defensive management" to prevent being held liable in this type of action.

Quicknotes

BUSINESS CORPORATION LAW, § 720 Permits an action against directors for failure to perform duties in managing corporate assets.

BUSINESS JUDGMENT RULE Standard of review that presumes that in making a business decision, the directors of a corporation acted on an informed basis, in good faith, and in the honest belief that the action taken was in the best interests of the company.

COMMON STOCK A class of stock representing the corporation's ownership, the holders of which are entitled to dividends only after the holders of preferred stock are paid.

DUTY OF CARE Duty that an officer or director owes to the corporation, by virtue of their fiduciary relationship, to act for the benefit of the corporation.

FIDUCIARY DUTY A legal obligation to act for the benefit of another, including subordinating one's personal interests to that of the other person.

SHAREHOLDER'S DERIVATIVE ACTION Action asserted by a shareholder in order to enforce a cause of action on behalf of the corporation.

Smith v. Van Gorkom

Shareholder (P) v. Chief executive officer (D)

Del. Sup. Ct., 488 A.2d 858 (1985)

NATURE OF CASE: Appeal from defense verdict in a class action suit brought by a corporation's shareholders against its board of directors.

FACT SUMMARY: The board of directors (D) of Trans Union Corporation (D) voted to approve a merger agreement based solely on the representations of Van Gorkom (D), one of its directors.

RULE OF LAW

The business judgment rule shields directors or officers of a corporation from liability only if, in reaching a business decision, the directors or officers acted on an informed basis, availing themselves of all material information reasonably available.

FACTS: Van Gorkom (D), chief executive officer (CEO) and director of Trans Union Corporation (D), approached Pritzker, a corporate takeover specialist, to stage a leveraged buy-out at a proposed per share price of \$55. Van Gorkom (D) consulted no other board members except Petersen, the company's controller, for help in calculating the feasibility of such a takeover. On September 18, 1980, Van Gorkom (D) met with Pritzker, who demanded that Trans Union (D) respond to his offer within three days. Van Gorkom (D) called a special meeting of the company's senior management and of the board (D) for the next day. Despite senior management's adverse reaction to the proposed merger, the board of directors (D) approved the agreement based on Van Gorkom's (D) 20-minute oral presentation. The board (D) did not have sufficient time to study the merger documents, nor did Van Gorkom (D) substantiate the \$55 per share price. Without reviewing its contents, Van Gorkom (D) executed the merger agreement on September 22. Smith (P) and other stockholders (P) subsequently filed a class action suit against Trans Union (D) and the board of directors (D). On February 10, 1981, however, the shareholders voted to approve the merger. The Court of Chancery found the board's (D) actions shielded by the business judgment rule. The state's highest court granted review.

ISSUE: Does the business judgment rule shield directors or officers of a corporation from liability only if, in reaching a business decision, the directors or officers acted on an informed basis, availing themselves of all material information reasonably available?

HOLDING AND DECISION: (Horsey, J.) Yes. The business judgment rule shields directors or officers of a corporation from liability only if, in reaching a business decision, the directors or officers acted on an informed basis, availing themselves of all material information reasonably available. The director has a duty to the corporation's shareholders to make an informed business decision regarding a proposed merger before it is subjected to shareholder approval. Subsequent shareholder ratification does not relieve the director from this duty, unless their approval is also based on an informed decision. In this case, the directors (D) breached their duty of care by failing to conduct further investigation as to the proposed merger, and by submitting the proposal for shareholder approval without providing them with the relevant facts necessary to make an educated decision. Reversed and remanded.

DISSENT: (McNeilly, J.) The board of directors (D) was capable of making prompt, informed business decisions regarding the corporation. The proxy materials provided to the shareholders contained sufficient information from which to ascertain that the value of their stock may be greater than its market value reflected.

ANALYSIS

A director or officer may not passively rely on information provided by other directors or officers, outside advisers, or authorized committees. The director may rely only on credible information provided by competent individuals, after taking reasonable measures to substantiate it. There was widespread reaction to this decision, with many states adopting legislation that permits a corporation to include in its certificate of incorporation a provision that eliminates or limits the personal liability of a director other than for breaches of the duty of loyalty or for acts or omissions not undertaken in good faith or that involve intentional misconduct or a knowing violation of law. Numerous corporations have taken advantage of such provisions.

Quicknotes

BUSINESS JUDGMENT RULE Standard of review that presumes that in making a business decision, the directors of a corporation acted on an informed basis, in good faith,

Continued on next page.

and in the honest belief that the action taken was in the best interests of the company.

CLASS ACTION A suit commenced by a representative on behalf of an ascertainable group that is too large to appear in court, shares a commonality of interests, and will benefit from a successful result.

DUTY OF CARE Duty that an officer or director owes to the corporation, by virtue of their fiduciary relationship, to act for the benefit of the corporation.

Bayer v. Beran

[Parties not identified.]

N.Y. Sup. Ct., 49 N.Y.S.2d 2 (1944)

NATURE OF CASE: Motion to dismiss a complaint alleging breach of fiduciary duty.

FACT SUMMARY: Directors of the Celanese Corporation of America (D) were charged with negligence and self-interest in commencing a radio advertising program.

RULE OF LAW

Policies of business management are left solely to the discretion of the board of directors and may not be questioned absent a showing of fraud, improper motive, or self-interest, even though the decision may later be judged unwise or unprofitable.

FACTS: Prior to 1942, the Celanese Corporation of America (Celanese) (D) engaged in an advertising campaign aimed at developing brand awareness. Following a Federal Trade Commission ruling it must label its products "rayon," Celanese (D) commenced a radio advertising program costing one million dollars per year. This decision was made following studies conducted by Celanese's (D) advertising department, and the employment of both a radio consultant and an advertising agency. Mrs. Dreyfus, wife of Celanese's (D) president, was selected to perform in the radio program. The board (D) was charged with commencing an illegal radio advertising program, negligence in its selection of the program and their decision to renew its contract, and self-interest, by promoting the career of Mrs. Dreyfus, in initiating the program and spending large sums of money in connection with it.

ISSUE: Are policies of business management left solely to the discretion of the board of directors and may not be questioned absent a showing of fraud, improper motive, or self-interest, even though the decision may later be judged unwise or unprofitable?

HOLDING AND DECISION: [Judge not stated in casebook excerpt.] Yes. Policies of business management are left solely to the discretion of the board of directors and may not be questioned absent a showing of fraud, improper motive, or self-interest, even though the decision may later be judged unwise or unprofitable. However, the business judgment rule only protects directors from personal liability for their negligence if they have not violated their duty of loyalty to the corporation. In cases where directors enter into personal transactions with their companies, such transactions are rigorously scrutinized and, upon the showing of any unfair advantage, will be voided. The burden then shifts to the interested director to demonstrate the transaction's good faith and inherent fairness to the corporation. In this case, there is no evidence that the advertising program was inefficient, disproportionate in price, or conducted for the personal gain of Mrs. Dreyfus. Notwithstanding that the radio advertising program was not taken up at any formal meeting of the board, and no resolution approving it was adopted, such informality is not fatal, and does not render the expenditures for the program illegal. The evidence shows that the directors acted in the free exercise of their honest business judgment and that their conduct in approving the radio program did not constitute negligence, waste, or improvidence. Dismissed.

ANALYSIS

When the court invokes the business judgment rule, the directors of the corporation are almost always shielded from liability. However, the court will only invoke the rule following a preliminary determination that the duties of care and loyalty have not been violated. The violation is not limited to direct action taken by the director. Where a relative of a director of a corporation is closely associated with the company's course of action, the motives supporting the transaction will be scrutinized.

Quicknotes

BUSINESS JUDGMENT RULE Standard of review that presumes that in making a business decision, the directors of a corporation acted on an informed basis, in good faith, and in the honest belief that the action taken was in the best interests of the company.

FIDUCIARY DUTY A legal obligation to act for the benefit of another, including subordinating one's personal interests to that of the other person.

Benihana of Tokyo, Inc. v. Benihana, Inc.

Parent corporation (P) v. Subsidiary (D)

Del. Sup. Ct., 906 A.2d 114 (2006)

NATURE OF CASE: Appeal from judgment for defendants in breach of fiduciary action.

FACT SUMMARY: Benihana of Tokyo (P) contended that the directors of its subsidiary, Benihana, Inc. (D), breached their fiduciary duties by authorizing the issuance of convertible preferred stock as part of a transaction to raise capital where one of the board members, Abdo (D), negotiated the deal on behalf of the buyer without the board's knowledge.

RULE OF LAW

(1) A statutory safe harbor for transactions involving interested directors is satisfied where the disinterested directors do not know that the interested director negotiated a financing transaction on behalf of a potential buyer, but know that the interested director is a principal of the buyer and approached the company on behalf of the buyer about entering into the transaction.

(2) An interested director does not breach their fiduciary duty of loyalty where the director neither sets the terms of a transaction nor deceives, nor controls or dominates the disinterested directors' approval of the transaction.

(3) A board validly exercises business judgment where it subjectively believes a transaction it is approving is in the company's best interests and for a proper corporate purpose.

FACTS: Benihana, Inc. (Benihana) (D), a subsidiary of Benihana of Tokyo (BOT) (P), which was owned by a family trust, had two classes of common stock. Benihana (D) needed to raise capital to renovate and upgrade its properties and retained Morgan Joseph as its financial advisor. One of several financing options that Morgan Joseph initially discussed with some executives and Abdo (D), a member of the board and executive committee, was the issuance of convertible preferred stock. The full Benihana (D) board met with Morgan Joseph's representative, who recommended using such financing. At the meeting, the board was given a book that detailed a possible transaction involving such financing. Not even a month later, the board met again to review the terms of the transaction and to clarify their preferences and negotiation strategy. Shortly after that meeting, Abdo (D) contacted Morgan Joseph and indicated that his firm, BFC Financial Corp. (BFC) was interested in purchasing the convertible stock. Abdo (D) negotiated with Morgan Joseph for several weeks and came to agreement on the terms of a transaction. Afterwards, at its next meeting, the board was informed that BFC was the potential buyer. Although the board knew that Abdo (D) was a principal of BFC, it did not know that he had negotiated the deal on BFC's behalf. At the meeting, Abdo (D) made a presentation on BFC's behalf, and then left the meeting. A book distributed to the board by Morgan Joseph indicated that Abdo (D) had approached Morgan Joseph on behalf of BFC. After due deliberation, the board approved the transaction, subject to receipt of a favorable fairness opinion. After Morgan Joseph provided such an opinion, the stock issuance was publicly announced. The family trust (owning BOT) questioned the transaction and urged the board to consider other financing routes. The board considered this request at its next meeting, but general counsel advised that the trust's concerns had merit. Also, Morgan Joseph opined that the transaction was economically fair. The board then approved the transaction. During the next two weeks, the company received three alternative financing proposals, all of which were considered by a committee of outside directors and rejected as inferior. After that, the Stock Purchase Agreement was executed and the stock issuance was authorized. BOT (P) brought suit alleging all Benihana (D) directors (with the exception of one) had breached various fiduciary duties by approving the transaction and stock issuance. The Court of Chancery ruled that the board was authorized to issue the preferred stock, and that the board's approval of the transaction was a valid exercise of its business judgment. The state's highest court granted review.

ISSUE:

(1) Is a statutory safe harbor for transactions involving interested directors satisfied where the disinterested directors do not know that the interested director negotiated a financing transaction on behalf of a potential buyer, but know that the interested director is a principal of the buyer and approached the company on behalf of the buyer about entering into the transaction?

(2) Does an interested director breach their fiduciary duty of loyalty where the director neither sets the terms of a transaction nor deceives, nor controls or dominates the disinterested directors' approval of the transaction?

(3) Does a board validly exercise business judgment where it subjectively believes a transaction it is approving is in the company's best interests and for a proper corporate purpose?

Continued on next page.

HOLDING AND DECISION: [Judge not stated in casebook excerpt.]

(1) Yes. A statutory safe harbor for transactions involving interested directors is satisfied where the disinterested directors do not know that the interested director negotiated a financing transaction on behalf of a potential buyer, but know that the interested director is a principal of the buyer and approached the company on behalf of the buyer about entering into the transaction. Here, a state statute (DGCL § 144(a)(1)) provides a safe harbor for interested transactions if "[t]he material facts as to the director's . . . relationship or interest and as to the contract or transaction are disclosed or are known to the board of directors . . . and the board . . . in good faith authorizes the contract or transaction by the affirmative votes of a majority of the disinterested directors. . . . " After approval by the disinterested directors, the interested transaction is reviewed under the business judgment rule. Here, the board should have been informed about Abdo's (D) involvement so it could make an informed decision, but the evidence shows that it had material information indicating such involvement when it approved the transaction. The board knew BFC was the potential buyer, and the board knew Abdo (D) was BFC's principal. Thus, the directors understood that he was BFC's representative in the transaction, and that the transaction could not proceed without his approval. Accordingly, the disinterested directors possessed all the material information about Abdo's (D) interest in the transaction, and their approval of it satisfied the safe harbor provision. Affirmed, as to this issue.

(2) No. An interested director does not breach their fiduciary duty of loyalty where the director neither sets the terms of a transaction nor deceives, nor controls or dominates the disinterested directors' approval of the transaction. Here, contrary to BOT's (P) assertions, Abdo (D) did not use any confidential company information to negotiate on behalf of BFC. The record shows that Abdo (D) knew the terms a buyer could expect in a transaction such as the one under negotiation. Moreover, the negotiations involved give and take and Benihana (D) prevailed on most of the key terms. Abdo (D) did not set the terms of the deal; he did not deceive the board; and he did not dominate or control the other directors' approval of the transaction. Therefore, Abdo did not breach his duty of loyalty. Affirmed, as to this issue.

(3) Yes. A board validly exercises business judgment where it subjectively believes a transaction it is approving is in the company's best interests and for a proper corporate purpose. The record here supports the Chancery Court's conclusion that the board's approval of the transaction was a valid exercise of its business judgment since the record shows that the primary purpose of the transaction was to provide the company with what the directors believed to be the best financing vehicle available for securing capital for renovating its properties. Conversely, the record does not support BOT's (P) assertion that the primary purpose was to dilute BOT's (P) voting control. Affirmed, as to this issue.

ANALYSIS

The court here rejected an entire fairness standard of review because it found that there had been no breach of the duty of loyalty. However, when a parent engages in a cash-out merger with a partially owned subsidiary, the entire fairness standard will be applied. Under the entire fairness standard – which is stricter than the business judgment standard – the corporation must show that the transaction satisfied both "fair dealing" and "fair price" to the cashed-out minority shareholders.

Quicknotes

BREACH OF FIDUCIARY DUTY The failure of a fiduciary to observe the standard of care exercised by professionals of similar education and experience.

BUSINESS JUDGMENT RULE Standard of review that presumes that in making a business decision, the directors of a corporation acted on an informed basis, in good faith, and in the honest belief that the action taken was in the best interests of the company.

CONVERTIBLE STOCK Stock that may be converted into common stock or some other type of security pursuant to its terms.

ENTIRE FAIRNESS A defense to a claim that a director engaged in an interested director transaction by showing the transaction's fairness to the corporation.

INTERESTED DIRECTOR A director of a corporation who has a personal interest in the subject matter of a transaction between the corporation and another party.

PREFERRED STOCK Shares of stock that are entitled to payment of dividends and other distributions before the holders of common stock.

SAFE HARBOR A tax code provision safeguarding the taxpayer from liability in respect to the payment of taxes, so long as the taxpayer has made an effort to comply with the provisions of the code.

Broz v. Cellular Information Systems, Inc.

Corporate officer (D) v. Corporation (P)

Del. Sup. Ct., 673 A.2d 148 (1996)

NATURE OF CASE: Appeal from a judgment for Cellular Information Systems, Inc. (P) in an action alleging Broz (D) usurped a corporate opportunity.

FACT SUMMARY: Broz (D) utilized a business opportunity for his wholly owned corporation instead of Cellular Information Systems, Inc. (P) for which he served as a member of the board of directors.

RULE OF LAW

The corporate opportunity doctrine is implicated only in cases where the fiduciary's seizure of an opportunity results in a conflict between the fiduciary's duties to the corporation and the self-interest of the director as actualized by the exploitation of the opportunity.

FACTS: Broz (D) owned RFB Cellular, Inc. (RFBC), and he also served on the board of directors of Cellular Information Systems, Inc. (CIS) (P), which was a competitor of RFBC. RFBC owned and operated an FCC license area, known as Michigan-4, wherein RFBC provided cellular telephone service to a geographically defined area. Mackinac Cellular Corp. (Mackinac) owned Michigan-2, which was adjacent to Michigan-4. In an effort to divest itself of Michigan-2, Mackinac contacted Broz (D) in his personal capacity to see if RFBC would be interested in purchasing it. CIS (P), which had divested itself of numerous cellular licenses and which had emerged from bankruptcy, was not offered the opportunity to purchase Michigan-2. In addition, Broz (D) informed CIS's (P) CEO and two of its directors of RFBC's interest in purchasing Michigan-2, and none of them objected. In fact, they all indicated to Broz (D) that CIS (P) was not interested in Michigan-2. In the meantime, another corporation, PriCellular, was attempting to acquire CIS (P). While Broz (D) was submitting written offers to Mackinac, PriCellular began negotiations with Mackinac to arrange for an option to purchase Michigan-2. The option gave PriCellular the right to purchase at a certain price unless another potential buyer offered at least $500,000 more than that exercise price. CIS's (P) CEO was aware of PriCellular's interest in Michigan-2, but nonetheless maintained that CIS (P) was not interested in it. Broz (D) satisfied the option terms (by paying the additional amount) and purchased Michigan-2. Nine days later, PriCellular acquired CIS (P). Afterward, CIS (P) brought suit claiming that Broz (D) had breached his fiduciary duties by usurping for himself (through RFBC) a corporate opportunity that belonged to CIS (P) and that Broz (D) should have formally submitted to the CIS (P) board. The trial court agreed with CIS (P), and the state's highest court granted review.

ISSUE: Is the corporate opportunity doctrine implicated only in cases where the fiduciary's seizure of an opportunity results in a conflict between the fiduciary's duties to the corporation and the self-interest of the director as actualized by the exploitation of the opportunity?

HOLDING AND DECISION: [Judge not stated in casebook excerpt.] Yes. The corporate opportunity doctrine is implicated only in cases where the fiduciary's seizure of an opportunity results in a conflict between the fiduciary's duties to the corporation and the self-interest of the director as actualized by the exploitation of the opportunity. Here, the totality of the circumstances indicates that Broz (D) did not usurp an opportunity that properly belonged to CIS (P). Broz (D) was entitled to utilize a corporate opportunity for the benefit of RFBC, his wholly owned corporation, instead of for CIS (P), for which he served as an outside director because: (1) the opportunity became known to him in his individual and not corporate capacity; (2) the opportunity was related more closely to the business conducted by RFBC than to that engaged in by CIS (P); (3) CIS (P) did not have the financial capacity to exploit the opportunity; and (4) CIS (P) was aware of Broz's (D) potentially conflicting duties toward RFBC and did not object to his actions on RFBC's behalf. Although the Michigan-2 opportunity was within CIS's (P) line of business, CIS (P) did not have a cognizable interest or expectancy in the license. Moreover, contrary to the Chancery Court's determination, Broz (D) was not required to formally reveal the opportunity to CIS (P). Reversed.

ANALYSIS

In Klein and Ramseyer's hornbook on Business Associations, the authors note that a common argument made by executives accused of usurping corporate opportunities is that the corporation lacked the financial capacity to effectively exploit it. However, courts generally reject this defense unless the defendant has explicitly disclosed the corporate opportunity and the corporation rejects it. This case, however, represents the Delaware view that, if a corporation does not have the financial ability to utilize the opportunity, its financial incapacity will weigh against a court finding

Continued on next page.

that the director was required to offer the opportunity to the corporation.

Quicknotes

CORPORATE OPPORTUNITY An opportunity that a fiduciary to a corporation has to take advantage of information acquired by virtue of their position for the individual's benefit.

FEDERAL COMMUNICATIONS COMMISSION (FCC) Created in 1934 to regulate interstate and foreign communications. Its regulatory powers include radio, television, telephone, cable, and satellite communications.

FIDUCIARY DUTY A legal obligation to act for the benefit of another, including subordinating one's personal interests to that of the other person.

TOTALITY OF THE CIRCUMSTANCES TEST Standard that focuses on all the circumstances of a particular case, instead of individual factors.

In re eBay, Inc. Shareholders Litigation

[Parties not identified.]

Del. Ct. Ch., 2004 WL 253521 (2004)

NATURE OF CASE: Motion to dismiss claim of breach of fiduciary duty.

FACT SUMMARY: Shareholders (P) of eBay, Inc. (eBay) brought derivative actions against certain eBay officers and directors (D) for usurping corporate opportunities by accepting from eBay's investment banker, Goldman Sachs Group (D), thousands of initial public offering shares (IPOs) at the initial offering price.

RULE OF LAW

Where a corporation regularly and consistently invests in marketable securities, a claim for usurpation of corporate opportunity is stated where it is alleged that the corporation's officers and directors accepted initial public offering (IPO) share allocations at the initial offering price instead of having those allocations offered to the corporation.

FACTS: eBay retained Goldman Sachs Group (Goldman Sachs) (D) as its underwriting investment banker during a series of IPOs. eBay paid Goldman Sachs (D) millions of dollars for its underwriting services. During this time period, Goldman Sachs (D) "rewarded" individual eBay officers and directors (D) by allocating to them thousands of IPO shares, managed by Goldman Sachs (D), at the initial offering price. Because the IPO market during this particular period of time was extremely active, prices of initial stock offerings often doubled or tripled in a single day. Investors, who were well connected, either to Goldman Sachs (D) or to similarly situated investment banks serving as IPO underwriters, were able to flip these investments into instant profit by selling the equities in a few days or even in a few hours after they were initially purchased. Shareholders (P) of eBay filed derivative actions against those eBay directors and officers (D) who had accepted the IPO shares from Goldman Sachs (D) on the grounds such conduct usurped a corporate opportunity that rightfully belonged to eBay, which regularly invested in marketable securities, and constituted a breach of fiduciary duty of loyalty. The accused officers and directors (D) moved to dismiss for failure to state a claim.

ISSUE: Where a corporation regularly and consistently invests in marketable securities, is a claim for usurpation of corporate opportunity stated where it is alleged that the corporation's officers and directors accepted IPO share allocations at the initial offering price instead of having those allocations offered to the corporation?

HOLDING AND DECISION: (Memorandum Opinion) Yes. Where a corporation regularly and consistently invests in marketable securities, a claim for usurpation of corporate opportunity is stated where it is alleged that the corporation's officers and directors accepted IPO share allocations at the initial offering price instead of having those allocations offered to the corporation. First, eBay financially was able to exploit the opportunities in question. Second, eBay was in the business of investing in securities, as it had hundreds of millions of dollars invested in such investments. Third, eBay was never given an opportunity to turn down the IPO allocations as too risky or to accept them. It is, therefore, unavailing to argue the allocations were collateral investment opportunities that arose by virtue of the inside directors'/officers' (D) status as wealthy individuals. Here, the facts implied that the allocations were offered by Goldman Sachs (D) as financial inducements to maintain and secure corporate business. Because this case involved below-market-price investment opportunities, this was not an instance where a broker offered advice to a director about an investment in a marketable security. Instead, it would seem the highly lucrative IPO allocations were made both to reward the insiders (D) for past business and to induce them to direct future business to Goldman Sachs (D). In addition, this conduct placed the insiders (D) in a position of conflict with their duties to the corporation. Because the allocations can be viewed as a form of commercial discount or rebate for past or future investment banking services, steering such commercial rebates to certain insiders (D) placed those insiders (D) in an obvious conflict between their self-interest and the corporation's interest. Finally, even if one assumes that IPO allocations like those in question here do not constitute a corporate opportunity, a cognizable claim is nevertheless stated on the common-law ground that an agent is under a duty to account for profits obtained personally in connection with transactions related to their company. In other words, the complaint gives rise to a reasonable inference that the insiders (D) accepted a commission or gratuity that rightfully belonged to eBay but that was improperly diverted to them. Thus, even if the complained-of conduct does not run afoul of the corporate opportunity doctrine, it may still constitute a breach of the fiduciary duty of loyalty. Motions to dismiss denied.

Continued on next page.

ANALYSIS

The conduct engaged in by Goldman Sachs (D) in this case is commonly known as "spinning." Such conduct, under circumstances such as those alleged in this case, is widely regarded as unethical. Where there is a quid pro quo between the investment bank and the recipient of the share allocation, whereby the recipient directs business to the bank in return for the allocation, the transaction may be an illegal bribe. In fact, the court in this case noted that Goldman Sachs (D) should have been aware of earlier SEC interpretations that prohibited steering "hot issue" securities to persons in a position to direct future business to the broker-dealer. The court also held that the plaintiffs had made out a case of aiding and abetting a breach of fiduciary duty against Goldman Sachs (D), finding that Goldman Sachs (D) had provided underwriting and investment advisory services to eBay for years, and knew, therefore, that each of the individual insiders (D) owed a fiduciary duty to eBay not to profit personally at eBay's expense and to devote their undivided loyalty to the interests of eBay. Goldman Sachs (D) also knew or should have known that eBay invested its excess cash in marketable securities and debt. Taken together, the court concluded that these allegations alleged a claim for aiding and abetting sufficient to withstand a motion to dismiss.

Quicknotes

AIDING AND ABETTING Assistance given in order to facilitate the commission of a criminal act.

CORPORATE OPPORTUNITY DOCTRINE Prohibits fiduciaries from usurping business opportunities that rightly belong to the corporation.

DUTY OF LOYALTY A director's duty to refrain from self-dealing or to take a position that is adverse to the corporation's best interests.

FIDUCIARY DUTY A legal obligation to act for the benefit of another, including subordinating one's personal interests to that of the other person.

INSIDER Any person within a corporation who has access to information not available to the public.

QUID PRO QUO What for what; in the contract context used synonymously with consideration to refer to the mutual promises between two parties rendering a contract enforceable.

SHAREHOLDERS DERIVATIVE ACTION Action asserted by a shareholder in order to enforce a cause of action on behalf of the corporation.

Fliegler v. Lawrence

Shareholders (P) v. Officers and directors (D)

Del. Sup. Ct., 361 A.2d 218 (1976)

NATURE OF CASE: Appeal in shareholder derivative suit asserting wrongful usurpation of corporate opportunity. [The procedural posture of the case is not presented in the casebook extract.]

FACT SUMMARY: Shareholders (P) of Agau Mines, Inc. (Agau) brought suit against its officers and directors (D) claiming the officers and directors (D) wrongfully usurped a corporate opportunity belonging to Agau and profited thereby.

RULE OF LAW

Ratification of an "interested transaction" by a majority of independent, fully informed shareholders shifts the burden of proof to the objecting shareholder to demonstrate that the terms of the transaction are so unequal as to amount to a gift or a waste of corporate assets.

FACTS: Lawrence (D), president of Agau Mines, Inc. (Agau), acquired certain properties in his individual capacity under a lease option for $60,000. Lawrence (D) agreed to transfer the properties to Agau but, after consulting with Agau's board of directors, agreed that the corporation's legal and financial positions would not allow acquisition and development of the properties at that time. The directors (D) decided to transfer the properties to United States Antimony Corporation (USAC), a closely held corporation formed for this purpose and a majority of whose stock was owned by Agau's directors, so that capital could be raised through the sale of stock, without risk to Agau. Agau was also granted a long-term option to acquire USAC if the properties later became commercially valuable. In 1970, Agau and USAC executed the option. Upon approval by the shareholders and the exercise of the option, Agau was to deliver 800,000 shares of its restricted investment stock for all authorized and issued shares of USAC. The board voted to exercise the option and a majority of the shareholders approved. Shareholders (P) brought a derivative suit on behalf of Agau to recover the 800,000 shares and for an accounting, claiming the officers and directors (D) wrongfully usurped a corporate opportunity and profited thereby. The Court of Chancery held for the defendants, and the state's highest court granted review.

ISSUE: Does ratification of an "interested transaction" by a majority of independent, fully informed shareholders shift the burden of proof to the objecting shareholder to demonstrate that the terms of the transaction are so unequal as to amount to a gift or a waste of corporate assets?

HOLDING AND DECISION: [Judge not stated in casebook excerpt.] Yes. Ratification of an "interested transaction" by a majority of independent, fully informed shareholders shifts the burden of proof to the objecting shareholder to demonstrate that the terms of the transaction are so unequal as to amount to a gift or a waste of corporate assets. The general rule in shareholder derivative suits involving interested director or officer transactions is that the burden of proof is on the defendant director/officer to prove the transaction was intrinsically fair. This court in *Gottlieb v. Hayden Chemical Corp.*, 91 A.2d 57 (1952), noted that when approval is granted by a majority of independent, fully informed shareholders the "entire atmosphere is freshened and a new set of rules invoked." Here that is not the case and the objective fairness test applies. On this basis, the directors (D) have proved the intrinsic fairness of the transaction. Agau received properties of substantial value, a potentially self-financing and profit-generating enterprise, and the interest given to the USAC shareholders was a fair price to pay. Affirmed.

ANALYSIS

The court also rejected the directors' (D) contention that § 144 of the Delaware Code demonstrated the legislature's intent to eliminate the requirement that the ratifying shareholders be disinterested or independent. That section provides, in pertinent part, that a transaction between a corporation and one or more of its directors and officers is not void or voidable solely because of the officer or director's participation, if certain requirements are met. The court interpreted this section as a safeguard against the invalidation of transactions merely because an officer or director of the corporation is involved.

Quicknotes

CORPORATE OPPORTUNITY An opportunity that a fiduciary to a corporation has to take advantage of information acquired by virtue of their position for the individual's benefit.

Continued on next page.

INTRINSIC FAIRNESS TEST A defense to a claim that a director engaged in an interested director transaction by showing the transaction's fairness to the corporation.

SHAREHOLDER'S DERIVATIVE ACTION Action asserted by a shareholder in order to enforce a cause of action on behalf of the corporation.

In re Investors Bancorp, Inc. Stockholder Litigation

Stockholders (P) v. Directors (D)

Del. Sup. Ct., 177 A.3d 1208 (2017)

NATURE OF CASE: Appeal from grant of motion to dismiss.

FACT SUMMARY: The Investors Bancorp Inc. (Investors) equity incentive plan created a pool of equity awards that the directors (D) could later award themselves. This plan was approved by a majority of the stockholders. Some stockholders (P) challenged the equity incentive plan awards to Investors' directors (D) as unfair and excessive.

RULE OF LAW

The stockholder ratification defense is unavailable to boards for discretionary awards to nonemployee directors under stockholder approved equity incentive plans that provide only general parameters restricting the board's discretion.

FACTS: Investors Bancorp Inc. sets director compensation based on the recommendations of the Compensation and Benefits Committee (Committee). The board (D) proposed an equity incentive plan (EIP) with the stated goals of promoting Investors' growth and performance and to entice and retain highly qualified officers, employees, and directors. The EIP provided that the maximum number of all shares that could be awarded to nonemployee directors was 30 percent of all restricted stock available under the EIP. The specifics of any awards under the EIP would not be determined until after stockholder approval. The stockholders duly approved the EIP at Investors' annual meeting. Following stockholder approval, the Committee held a series of meetings approving 7.8 million in restricted shares to the board (D) valued at roughly $51.7 million or $2.16 million per director. In comparison, the prior year the average compensation per director was $133,340. The awards were significantly higher than the awards made to directors at peer companies. The setting of board compensation is self-interested because the board is deciding how much they should pay themselves for their service. Stockholders (P) alleged that directors (D) breached their fiduciary duties by awarding themselves excessive compensation. The board (D) moved for dismissal, arguing that the stockholder approval provided for the more deferential business judgment rule analysis of the compensation awards. The trial court granted the motion and Stockholders (P) appealed.

ISSUE: Is the stockholder ratification defense available to boards for discretionary awards to nonemployee directors under stockholder approved equity incentive plans that provide only general parameters restricting the board's discretion?

HOLDING AND DECISION: [Judge not stated in casebook excerpt.] No. The stockholder ratification defense is unavailable to boards for discretionary awards to nonemployee directors under stockholder approved equity incentive plans that provide only general parameters restricting the board's discretion. Instead, courts will review the awards for fairness to the corporation. An unqualified grant of sole discretion presents the potential for abuse by self-dealing. In this case, the stockholders (P) properly alleged a breach of fiduciary duty in the board's (D) exercise of discretion following stockholder approval of the general parameters of the EIP. The grant of restricted stock to the board (D) is subject to the entire fairness standard. Reversed and remanded.

ANALYSIS

Stockholder ratification is an affirmative defense for specific director awards and when a plan is self-executing and does not allow for discretion. However, when directors retain discretion and make awards only under stockholder approved general parameters the affirmative defense is unavailable. The Delaware Supreme Court rejected the Court of Chancery's allowance of the ratification defense so long as the plan places "meaningful limits" on director discretion. The decision attempts to balance the utility of a ratification defense with the need for judicial review of self-interested discretionary acts. The doctrine of ratification under Delaware law is not of unlimited breadth.

Quicknotes

AFFIRMATIVE DEFENSE A manner of defending oneself against a claim not by denying the truth of the charge, but by introducing some evidence challenging the plaintiff's right to bring the claim; affirmative defenses shift the burden of proof to the defendant to establish all the elements of the defense.

Continued on next page.

BREACH OF FIDUCIARY DUTY The failure of a fiduciary to observe the standard of care exercised by professionals of similar education and experience.

BUSINESS JUDGMENT RULE Standard of review that presumes that in making a business decision, the directors of a corporation acted on an informed basis, in good faith, and in the honest belief that the action taken was in the best interests of the company.

In re The Walt Disney Co. Derivative Litigation

[Parties not identified.]

Del. Sup. Ct., 906 A.2d 27 (2006)

NATURE OF CASE: Appeal from judgment for defendants in derivative action for breaches of fiduciary duties and contract, and for waste.

FACT SUMMARY: Shareholders (P) of The Walt Disney Company (Disney) contended that a $130 million severance package received by Ovitz (D) under his employment agreement (OEA) when he was terminated as Disney's president was the product of breaches of fiduciary duty and contract by Ovitz (D) and Disney's directors (D) and constituted a waste of assets.

RULE OF LAW

(1) An individual cannot be deemed to be a de facto corporate officer where that individual has not assumed or purported to assume the duties of a corporate office.

(2) Due care and bad faith may be treated as separate grounds for denying business judgment rule review.

(3) An entire board of directors does not have to consider and approve an officer's employment agreement.

(4) Members of a compensation committee do not breach their duty of due care where, although they do not follow best practices, they are sufficiently informed about all material facts regarding a decision they make.

(5) Directors do not breach their duty of care in electing an officer where they are informed of all material information reasonably available regarding their decision.

(6) "Intentional dereliction of duty, a conscious disregard for one's responsibilities" is an appropriate legal definition of bad faith.

(7) Where a corporation's governing instruments vest authority in the chief executive officer (CEO)/chairman as well as in the entire board of directors to terminate an officer, the entire board of directors does not breach the fiduciary duties of due care and good faith by failing to terminate an officer and by permitting the CEO/chairman to do so.

(8) A chief executive officer (CEO)/chairman does not breach the duty of care or the duty to act in good faith by making a decision that is based in fact and that is made within their business judgment.

(9) Where directors rely on advice that is accurate, and their reliance is made in good faith, they do not breach any fiduciary duties.

(10) Where payment provisions of a corporate contract have a rational business purpose, directors do not commit waste of corporate assets by making payment under the contract.

FACTS: The Walt Disney Company (Disney) needed a president. Disney's chairman and chief executive officer (CEO), Eisner (D), knew Ovitz (D), who was a founder of, and partner in, Creative Artists Agency (CAA), a very successful Hollywood talent agency. Eisner (D) and Ovitz (D), who knew each other for more than 25 years, had previously discussed the possibility of working together, and Eisner (D) and Russell (D), who was a director and chairman of Disney's compensation committee, approached Ovitz (D) about joining Disney. Ovitz (D) was interested in joining as a co-CEO, and negotiations over Ovitz's employment agreement (OEA) began. Ovitz (D) annually earned between $20 and $25 million from CAA and insisted on downside protections to ensure similar income. The parties worked out a draft OEA that provided Ovitz (D) with a five-year contract and two tranches of options. The first tranche consisted of 3 million options vesting in equal parts in the third, fourth, and fifth years, and if the value of those options at the end of the five years had not appreciated to $50 million, Disney would make up the difference. The second tranche consisted of two million options that would vest immediately if Disney and Ovitz (D) opted to renew the contract. The draft OEA sought to protect both parties in the event Ovitz's (D) employment ended prematurely, and provided that absent defined causes, neither party could terminate the agreement without penalty. If Ovitz (D) left Disney for any reason other than those permitted under the OEA, he would forfeit any benefits remaining under the OEA and could be enjoined from working for a competitor. Likewise, if Disney fired Ovitz (D) for any reason other than gross negligence or malfeasance, he would be entitled to a non-fault payment (NFT), which consisted of his remaining salary, $7.5 million a year for unaccrued bonuses, the immediate vesting of his first tranche of options, and $10 million cash-out payment for the second tranche of options. Ovitz's (D) compensation was designed to induce him to work for Disney by compensating him for remuneration he would be forfeiting by leaving CAA. The parties understood that Ovitz's

Continued on next page.

(D) salary would be at the top level for any corporate officer and significantly above that of even Eisner, the Disney CEO, and that the stock options granted under the OEA would exceed the standards applied within Disney and corporate America and would "raise very strong criticism." The financial terms of the draft OEA were reviewed by an executive compensation consultant and Watson (D), another member of Disney's compensation committee; it was determined that the OEA would approximate Ovitz's (D) annual compensation at CAA—around $24.1 million per year. Also, under the OEA, Ovitz (D) would be president, and not a co-CEO. Ovitz (D) agreed to the draft OEA terms, and these terms were memorialized in a letter agreement (OLA), which expressly provided that a formal contract was subject to approval by the Disney board (D) and compensation committee. Once the OLA was signed, a formal contract was drafted, and then reviewed for an hour by the Disney compensation committee. The committee unanimously recommended the employment agreement. Immediately after the compensation committee meeting, the Disney board (D) met in executive session. After being informed about Ovitz (D) and his proposed compensation package, the board (D) unanimously elected Ovitz (D) as president. Ovitz (D) remained with Disney for about 14 months. It became increasingly clear that he was not a good fit with his fellow executives, and the board (D) was informed of various problems with Ovitz (D). Eisner (D) eventually discussed these problems with Ovitz (D), making it clear that Ovitz (D) was no longer welcome at Disney. Eisner (D) also inquired of counsel, including Litvack (D), a board member, whether Ovitz (D) could be terminated for cause under the OEA, in which case Disney could avoid making the non-fault termination (NFT) payment, but counsel consistently informed Eisner that there was no cause for terminating Ovitz (D). Ovitz (D) was then terminated. His severance package under the OEA amounted to around $130 million. Disney shareholders (P) brought a derivative action, claiming that the severance payout was the product of fiduciary duty and contractual breaches by Ovitz (D), and breaches of fiduciary duty by the Disney directors (D) at the time of the events, and a waste of assets. The Court of Chancery rejected these claims, and the state's highest court granted review.

ISSUE:

(1) Can an individual be deemed to be a de facto corporate officer where that individual has not assumed or purported to assume the duties of a corporate office?
(2) May due care and bad faith be treated as separate grounds for denying business judgment rule review?
(3) Does an entire board of directors have to consider and approve an officer's employment agreement?
(4) Do members of a compensation committee breach their duty of due care where, although they do not follow best practices, they are sufficiently informed about all material facts regarding a decision they make?
(5) Do directors breach their duty of care in electing an officer where they are informed of all material information reasonably available regarding their decision?
(6) Is "intentional dereliction of duty, a conscious disregard for one's responsibilities" an appropriate legal definition of bad faith?
(7) Where a corporation's governing instruments vest authority in the chief executive officer (CEO)/chairman as well as in the entire board of directors to terminate an officer, does the entire board of directors breach the fiduciary duties of due care and good faith by failing to terminate an officer and by permitting the CEO/chairman to do so?
(8) Does a chief executive officer (CEO)/chairman breach the duty of care or the duty to act in good faith by making a decision that is based in fact and that is made within their business judgment?
(9) Where directors rely on advice that is accurate, and their reliance is made in good faith, do they breach any fiduciary duties?
(10) Where payment provisions of a corporate contract have a rational business purpose, do directors commit waste of corporate assets by making payment under the contract?

HOLDING AND DECISION: [Judge not stated in casebook excerpt.]

(1) No. An individual cannot be deemed to be a de facto corporate officer where that individual has not assumed or purported to assume the duties of a corporate office. The shareholders (P) claim that it was an error for the Chancery Court to summarily dismiss their claim that Ovitz (D) breached his fiduciary duties to Disney by negotiating and entering into the OEA. The Chancery Court found that Ovitz (D) was not an officer during this time, so that as a matter of law he could not have had any fiduciary duties to Disney. The shareholders (P) argue that Ovitz (D) was a de facto officer at that time by virtue of his contacts, receipt of confidential information, and request for reimbursement of certain expenses, which vested him with apparent authority. The shareholders' (D) argument lacks merit because a de facto officer is one who has assumed possession of an office under the claim and color of an election or appointment and who is actually discharging the duties of that office. Here, Ovitz's (D) conduct does not meet this definition, either factually or legally, because he did not assume, or purport to assume, the

Continued on next page.

duties of Disney's President until after he signed the OEA. Therefore, the Chancery Court did not err as to this issue. Affirmed, as to this issue.

(2) Yes. Due care and bad faith may be treated as separate grounds for denying business judgment rule review. The shareholders (P) claim that the Chancery Court erred in treating as distinct questions whether they established by a preponderance of the evidence either gross negligence or a lack of good faith. Under the business judgment rule, director action is presumed to have been made on an informed basis, in good faith, and in the honest belief that the action taken is in the corporation's best interest. Those presumptions can be rebutted if the plaintiff shows that the directors breached their fiduciary duty of care or of loyalty or acted in bad faith. If that is shown, the burden then shifts to the director defendants to demonstrate that the challenged act or transaction was entirely fair to the corporation and its shareholders. Here, however, there was no claim of the breach of the duty of loyalty. Therefore, the only way to rebut the business judgment rule presumption is to show that the directors (D) breached their duty of care or had not acted in good faith. The Chancery Court did not err in treating these grounds separately. Affirmed, as to this issue.

(3) No. An entire board of directors does not have to consider and approve an officer's employment agreement. The shareholders (P) argue that the Chancery Court erred in ruling that the entire Disney board (D) was not required to consider and approve the OEA. Where, as here, a corporation's governing instruments allocate that decision to a compensation committee, the entire board does not have to consider and approve that decision. There is nothing in the state's statutes that requires that an entire board of directors make decisions concerning executive compensation. Therefore, the Chancery Court did not err in ruling that only the compensation committee could consider and approve the OEA. Affirmed, as to this issue.

(4) No. Members of a compensation committee do not breach their duty of due care where, although they do not follow best practices, they are sufficiently informed about all material facts regarding a decision they make. The Chancery Court acknowledged that the compensation committee's decision-making process fell far short of corporate governance best practices, but nevertheless ruled that they were adequately informed about the OEA before approving it, so that they did not breach their duty of care. The shareholders (P) claim that the Chancery Court's decision was erroneous because the evidence showed that the compensation committee members did not properly inform themselves of the material facts, so that they were grossly negligent in approving the NFT provisions of the OEA. Under a best practices scenario, the committee members would have considered a matrix of alternative scenarios under the OEA. Instead, they considered a term sheet that summarized the material terms of the OEA. The term sheet disclosed what would happen in case of a non-fault termination. Thus, the compensation committee knew that in the event of an NFT, Ovitz's (D) severance payment alone could be in the range of $40 million cash, plus the value of the accelerated options. The question is whether they were informed that those options could reach a value of more than $90 million; the record shows they were. Although this knowledge was not imparted in one tidy source, such as a spreadsheet—which would have been desirable under a best practices scenario—the information was made available to the compensation committee in various spreadsheets that had been prepared for the committee's meetings. The compensation committee members derived their information about the potential magnitude of an NFT payout from two sources. The first was the value of the "benchmark" options previously granted to other officers, along with their valuations, and the second was the amount of downside protection Ovitz (D) was demanding. The committee members knew that by leaving CAA and coming to Disney, Ovitz (D) would be sacrificing "booked" CAA commissions of $150 to $200 million—an amount that Ovitz (D) demanded as protection against the risk that his employment relationship with Disney might not work out. Ovitz (D) wanted at least $50 million of that compensation to take the form of an "up-front" signing bonus. Because it was decided to not grant such a bonus, the committee members knew that the value of the options had to be greater. They also knew that under the NFT, the earlier in the contract that Ovitz (D) was terminated without cause, the greater the severance payment would be. For these reasons, the Chancery Court did not err in concluding that there was sufficient evidence that the compensation committee members were adequately (if, albeit, not ideally) informed about the potential magnitude of an early NFT severance payout. Affirmed, as to this issue.

(5) No. Directors do not breach their duty of care in electing an officer where they are informed of all material information reasonably available regarding their decision. The shareholders (P) contend that the directors (D) breached their duty of care in electing Ovitz (D) because they were not informed about

Continued on next page.

their decision, and that the Chancery Court erred in ruling to the contrary. The record, however, does not support the shareholders' (P) stance. The directors (D) were well aware about the need for a new president. They knew from Eisner (D) about Ovitz (D) and his qualifications, and that Eisner (D) believed he would work well with Ovitz (D). They also knew that to accept a position at Disney, Ovitz (D) would have to leave CAA, an extremely successful and lucrative business. The directors (D) also knew that the public supported Ovitz's (D) hiring, as did Eisner (D) and other senior officers. The board (D) was also informed of the key terms of the OEA and knew that the compensation committee approved and recommended the OEA. Based on these facts, the Chancery Court did not err in concluding that directors (D) were fully informed of all material facts, and, therefore, did not breach their duty of care. Affirmed, as to this issue.

(6) Yes. "Intentional dereliction of duty, a conscious disregard for one's responsibilities" is an appropriate legal definition of bad faith. This is the definition the Chancery Court used in assessing whether the directors (D) and compensation committee had not acted in good faith, and in holding that they had not acted in bad faith. The Chancery Court noted that this standard of bad faith is not the only one that can be used but is an appropriate definition. The shareholders (P) argue that this is not an appropriate standard. The Chancery Court did not err in using this definition, because there are at least three different categories of fiduciary conduct that can give rise to a bad-faith claim. The first is "subjective bad faith," which is fiduciary conduct motivated by an actual intent to do harm. Such conduct is not claimed to have occurred here. The second category involves lack of due care, which does not involve malevolent intent, but sounds in gross negligence (here, the Chancery Court did not find gross negligence). In any event, gross negligence by itself cannot constitute bad faith, as these are clearly distinguished in common law and by statute. The third category falls between the first two, and this is the category intended to be captured by the Chancery Court's definition. The question is whether such misconduct is properly treated as a non-exculpable, non-indemnifiable violation of the fiduciary duty to act in good faith; the answer is "yes." That is because fiduciary misconduct is not limited to self-interested disloyalty or to gross negligence but may lie somewhere in between these extremes. For example, the fiduciary may intentionally act with a purpose other than that of advancing the best interests of the corporation, may act with the intent to violate applicable positive law, or may intentionally fail to act in the face of a known duty to act, demonstrating a conscious disregard for his duties. Such an intermediate category of bad faith is also recognized statutorily. The Chancery Court's definition of bad faith encompasses this intermediate bad-faith category, and, therefore, is appropriate. Affirmed, as to this issue.

(7) No. Where a corporation's governing instruments vest authority in the chief executive officer (CEO)/chairman as well as in the entire board of directors to terminate an officer, the entire board of directors does not breach the fiduciary duties of due care and good faith by failing to terminate an officer and by permitting the CEO/chairman to do so. The shareholders (P) assert that only the full board (D), but not Eisner (D) alone, could have terminated Ovitz (D). Although the board (D) had the authority to terminate Ovitz (D), it did not have the duty to do so, since Disney's governing instruments could be read to permit Eisner (D) to terminate Ovitz (D) and the board (D) understood this to be the case. Without a duty to act, the board (D) could not have breached any fiduciary duties. Because Eisner (D) had concurrent power with the board (D) to terminate lesser officers, such as Ovitz (D), board (D) approval was not necessary for Eisner (D) to terminate Ovitz (D). Affirmed, as to this issue.

(8) No. A chief executive officer (CEO)/chairman does not breach the duty of care or the duty to act in good faith by making a decision that is based in fact and that is made within their business judgment. The shareholders (P) claim that Ovitz (D) could have been terminated for cause, and therefore Eisner (D), as well as Litvack (D), acted without due care and in bad faith in reaching the contrary conclusion. The factual record does not support the shareholders' (P) assertions that Ovitz (D) intentionally failed to follow Eisner's (D) directives and was insubordinate, that Ovitz (D) was a habitual liar, and that Ovitz (D) violated policies relating to expenses and to reporting gifts he gave while at Disney. Therefore, Eisner (D) correctly concluded that Ovitz (D) could not be terminated for cause. Moreover, Eisner (D) also acted within his business judgment in pursuing termination of Ovitz (D) and triggering the NFT, since the other options were to keep Ovitz (D) as president or to offer him another position at Disney, which would have also triggered the NFT and a possible lawsuit, which would have potentially been very costly. Eisner (D) acted within his business judgment in choosing the course of action he did. Affirmed, as to this issue.

Continued on next page.

(9) No. Where directors rely on advice that is accurate, and their reliance is made in good faith, they do not breach any fiduciary duties. The shareholders (P) argue that the business judgment rule presumptions did not protect the Disney board's acquiescence in the NFT payout, because the board was not entitled to rely upon Eisner's (D) and Litvack's (D) advice that Ovitz (D) could not be terminated for cause. However, the advice given by Eisner (D) and Litvack (D) was accurate, and the directors (D) relied on this advice in good faith. For these reasons, the directors (D) did not breach any fiduciary duties, and their actions were protected by the business judgment rule. Affirmed, as to this issue.

(10) No. Where payment provisions of a corporate contract have a rational business purpose, directors do not commit waste of corporate assets by making payment under the contract. The shareholders (P) argue that the severance payment to Ovitz (D) constituted a waste of corporate assets. This claim is rooted in the doctrine that a plaintiff who fails to rebut the business judgment rule presumptions is not entitled to any remedy unless the transaction constitutes waste. To recover on a claim of corporate waste, a plaintiff must prove that the exchange was "so one-sided that no business person of ordinary, sound judgment could conclude that the corporation has received adequate consideration." This very high standard for waste is a corollary of the proposition that where business judgment presumptions are applicable, the board's decision will be upheld unless it cannot be "attributed to any rational business purpose." The claim that the payment of the NFT amount to Ovitz (D) constituted waste is meritless on its face, because at the time the NFT amounts were paid, Disney was contractually obligated to pay them. Thus, the question becomes whether the OEA NFT severance provisions were wasteful to begin with. Although the shareholders (P) argue that those provisions gave Ovitz (D) every incentive to leave Disney as soon as possible, they ignore that those provisions had a rational business purpose—to induce Ovitz (D) to leave CAA, at what would have been considerable cost to him. Because the provisions had a rational business purpose, the shareholders (P) cannot meet their burden of proving waste. Affirmed, as to this issue.

ANALYSIS

This case demonstrates, among other things, how the duty of directors to act in good faith is an independent duty that is on the same footing as the duties of care and of loyalty, and how that duty interacts with the other independent duties. Although the duty to act in good faith has always been part of corporate governance jurisprudence, it has been only relatively recently that the duty has been viewed as an independent duty, rather than as a duty subsumed within the other fiduciary duties.

Quicknotes

BUSINESS JUDGMENT RULE Standard of review that presumes that in making a business decision, the directors of a corporation acted on an informed basis, in good faith, and in the honest belief that the action taken was in the best interests of the company.

DUTY OF CARE Duty that an officer or director owes to the corporation, by virtue of their fiduciary relationship, to act for the benefit of the corporation.

DUTY OF LOYALTY A director's duty to refrain from self-dealing or to take a position that is adverse to the corporation's best interests.

FIDUCIARY DUTY A legal obligation to act for the benefit of another, including subordinating one's personal interests to that of the other person.

GOOD FAITH COMPLIANCE A sincere or unequivocal intention to fulfill an obligation or to comply with specifically requested conduct.

Francis v. United Jersey Bank

Bankruptcy trustee (P) v. Executor of director's estate (D)

N.J. Sup. Ct., 87 N.J. 15, 432 A.2d 814 (1981)

NATURE OF CASE: Review of Appellate Division decision holding director of corporation liable for clients' losses.

FACT SUMMARY: Lillian Pritchard (D) ignored her duties as a director, allowing her sons to withdraw over $12 million from client trust accounts.

RULE OF LAW

Liability of a corporation's directors to its clients requires a demonstration that: (1) a duty existed; (2) the directors breached that duty; and (3) the breach was a proximate cause of the client's losses.

FACTS: Lillian Pritchard (D) inherited a 48 percent interest in Pritchard & Baird, a reinsurance broker, from her husband. She and her two sons, Charles, Jr. and William, served as directors of the corporation. Her sons withdrew over $12 million in the form of loans from client trust accounts. Mrs. Pritchard (D) was completely ignorant as to the fundamentals of the reinsurance business and paid no attention to the affairs of the corporation. After the misappropriation of client funds by her sons was discovered, and the company became insolvent, Mrs. Pritchard (D) died. A bankruptcy trustee (P), on behalf of Pritchard & Baird's creditors, sued her estate to recover the misappropriated amounts. The trial court held her liable for the clients' losses, finding that although she was competent to act, she had made no effort to exercise her duties as a director. The state's intermediate appellate court affirmed, and the state's highest court granted review.

ISSUE: Does liability of a corporation's directors to its clients require a demonstration that: (1) a duty existed; (2) the directors breached that duty; and (3) the breach was a proximate cause of the client's losses?

HOLDING AND DECISION: [Judge not stated in casebook excerpt.] Yes. Individual liability of a corporation's directors to its clients requires a demonstration that: (1) a duty existed; (2) the directors breached that duty; and (3) the breach was a proximate cause of the client's losses. This is a departure from the general rule that a director is immune from liability and is not an insurer of the corporation's success. The director of a corporation stands in a fiduciary relationship to both the corporation and its stockholders. Inherent in this role is a duty to acquire a basic understanding of the corporation's business and a continuing duty to keep informed of its activities. This entails an overall monitoring of the corporation's affairs, and a regular review of its financial statements. Such a review may present a duty of further inquiry. Here, Mrs. Pritchard (D) failed to exercise supervision over the corporation, including the examination of its financial statements, which would have revealed the misappropriation of funds by her sons. Any duty she has to the company's clients arises from the nature of the company's business and the company's solvency. Here, the company was a reinsurance broker. The hallmark of the reinsurance industry is the unqualified trust and confidence reposed by ceding companies and reinsurers in reinsurance brokers. Thus, it could have rightfully been assumed by the company's clients that Mrs. Pritchard (D), as the company's director, would not sanction the commingling and the conversion of client funds for the personal use of her sons. In effect, therefore, Mrs. Pritchard (D) had a relationship to the company's clientele akin to that of a director of a bank to its depositors—a fiduciary relationship with fiduciary duties. The cumulative effect of her negligence and breach of her fiduciary duties was a substantial factor contributing to, and was a proximate cause of, the clients' losses. Affirmed.

ANALYSIS

Directors do not ordinarily owe a duty of care to third parties unless the corporation is insolvent. However, as this case demonstrates, as a consequence of the nature of certain types of enterprises, the director stands in a fiduciary capacity to third parties. Thus, the question is one of fact and circumstances. Because the reinsurance business relies on the entrustment of capital within the company, and on the transmission of funds to the appropriate parties, Mrs. Pritchard (D) owed a duty of care to third-party clients of Pritchard and Baird.

Quicknotes

FIDUCIARY DUTY A legal obligation to act for the benefit of another, including subordinating one's personal interests to that of the other person.

NEW JERSEY BUSINESS CORPORATION ACT § 14A Directors are obligated to discharge their duties in good faith and with skill of ordinary prudent person in similar position.

PROXIMATE CAUSE The natural sequence of events without which an injury would not have been sustained.

Stone v. Ritter

Shareholder (P) v. Corporate directors (D)

Del. Sup. Ct., 911 A.2d 362 (2006)

NATURE OF CASE: Appeal from judgment dismissing derivative action.

FACT SUMMARY: Shareholders (P) bringing a derivative action against AmSouth Bancorporation directors (D) contended that demand was excused because the directors (D) breached their oversight duty and utterly failed to act in good faith regarding compliance with various banking regulations, thus facing a likelihood of personal liability that would render them incapable of exercising independent and disinterested judgment in response to a demand request.

RULE OF LAW

A derivative action will be dismissed for failure to make demand where alleged particularized facts do not create a reasonable doubt that the corporation's directors acted in good faith in exercising their oversight responsibilities.

FACTS: AmSouth Bancorporation (AmSouth) was a holding company whose wholly owned subsidiary, AmSouth Bank, operated hundreds of banking branches. In 2004, AmSouth and AmSouth Bank paid $40 million in fines and $10 million in civil penalties to resolve government and regulatory investigations pertaining principally to the failure by bank employees to file "Suspicious Activity Reports" (SARs), as required by the federal Bank Secrecy Act (BSA) and various federal anti-money-laundering (AML) regulations. These violations were discovered after a "Ponzi" scheme, which was unwittingly aided by AmSouth branch employees, was uncovered. Although the corporation had in place an extensive information and reporting system, in its investigation, the government concluded that "AmSouth's compliance program lacked adequate board and management oversight." AmSouth shareholders (P) brought a derivative action against the corporation's present and former directors (D) based on these events, without first making demand on the board. AmSouth's Certificate of Incorporation contained a provision that would exculpate its directors for breaches of their duty of care, provided they acted in good faith. The directors (D) moved to dismiss for lack of demand, and the Court of Chancery held that the shareholders (P) had failed to adequately plead that such a demand would have been futile, finding that the directors (D) had not been alerted by any "red flags" that violations of law were occurring. The state's highest court granted review.

ISSUE: Will a derivative action be dismissed for failure to make demand where alleged particularized facts do not create a reasonable doubt that the corporation's directors acted in good faith in exercising their oversight responsibilities?

HOLDING AND DECISION: [Judge not stated in casebook excerpt.] Yes. A derivative action will be dismissed for failure to make demand where alleged particularized facts do not create a reasonable doubt that the corporation's directors acted in good faith in exercising their oversight responsibilities. The allegations made by the shareholders (P) are a classic "*Caremark*" claim—named after *In re Caremark Intl. Deriv. Litig.*, 698 A.2d 959 (Del. Ch. 1996). Such a claim of directorial liability is premised on the directors' ignorance of liability-creating activities (such as criminal conduct or failure to follow regulations) within the corporation. In *Caremark*, the court ruled that directors will face personal liability only where there has been a sustained or systematic failure of the board to exercise oversight, as where there is an utter failure to even attempt to implement or monitor a reasonable information and reporting system. Here, the shareholders (P) assert that because it was likely the directors would face such personal liability, they could not be reasonably expected to exercise independent and disinterested judgment when faced with a pre-suit demand. However, AmSouth's Certificate of Incorporation's exculpatory provision will shield the directors (D) from liability as long as they acted in good faith—so if they acted in good faith, demand would not be excused. Thus, it must be determined whether the directors (D) acted in good faith. The standard for this determination has evolved. The standard in cases such as this is that the board must assure itself that information and reporting systems exist in the corporation that are reasonably designed to provide to senior management and to the board itself timely, accurate information to permit the board, as well as management, to reach informed decisions about the corporation's compliance with law and its business performance. As the *Caremark* court observed, "the duty to act in good faith cannot be thought to require directors to possess detailed information about all aspects of the operation of the enterprise." Thus, only where there is a sustained or systematic failure to ensure an adequate information and reporting system is in place, or, if such a system is in place, where the board consciously fails to monitor it or oversee its operations, will there be a showing of lack of good faith. Additionally, there must be a showing that the directors knew they were not discharging their

Continued on next page.

fiduciary duties. In fact, recent decisions show that this formulation is consistent with examples of bad faith. The Chancery Court applied this standard and was, therefore, correct in doing so. When this standard is applied to the facts pleaded by the shareholders (P), it becomes clear that the directors did not fail to act in good faith. The facts showed that the directors (D) had established a reasonable information and reporting system and had set up numerous departments and committees to oversee AmSouth's compliance with federal banking regulations. This system also permitted the board to periodically monitor such compliance. Here, while it is clear with hindsight that the organization's internal controls were inadequate, there were also no "red flags" to put the board on notice of any wrongdoing. The directors (D) took the steps they needed to ensure a reasonable information and reporting system existed. Therefore, although there ultimately may have been failures by employees to report deficiencies to the board, there is no basis for an oversight claim seeking to hold the directors personally liable for such failures by the employees; a bad (and very costly) outcome does not per se equate to bad faith. Affirmed.

ANALYSIS

The court in this case makes a point of clarifying doctrinal issues related to the duty of good faith. First, the court emphasizes that the failure to act in good faith is a condition to finding a breach of the fiduciary duty of loyalty and imposing fiduciary liability. The court explains that "a failure to act in good faith is not conduct that results, ipso facto, in the direct imposition of fiduciary liability. The failure to act in good faith may result in liability because the requirement to act in good faith 'is a subsidiary element[,]' i.e., a condition, 'of the fundamental duty of loyalty.' It follows that because a showing of bad-faith conduct . . . is essential to establish director oversight liability, the fiduciary duty violated by that conduct is the duty of loyalty." Second, and as a corollary, the duty to act in good faith does not establish an independent fiduciary duty that stands on the same footing as the duty of care and loyalty. A failure to act in good faith gives rise to liability only indirectly. Also, as a corollary, the fiduciary duty of loyalty is not limited to financial or similar conflicts of interest, but also encompasses cases where a director has failed to act in good faith.

Quicknotes

DEMAND REQUIREMENT Also referred to as "pre-suit demand," a requirement that a shareholder make a demand for corrective legal action by the board of directors before commencing a shareholder's derivative action.

DERIVATIVE SUIT Action asserted by a shareholder in order to enforce a cause of action on behalf of the corporation.

DUTY OF CARE Duty that an officer or director owes to the corporation, by virtue of their fiduciary relationship, to act for the benefit of the corporation.

DUTY OF LOYALTY A director's duty to refrain from self-dealing or to take a position that is adverse to the corporation's best interests.

FIDUCIARY DUTY A legal obligation to act for the benefit of another, including subordinating one's personal interests to that of the other person.

GOOD FAITH An honest intention to abstain from taking advantage of another.

Waltuch v. Conticommodity Services, Inc.

Officer (P) v. Corporation (D)

88 F.3d 87 (2d Cir. 1996)

NATURE OF CASE: Appeal from denial of indemnity claims.

FACT SUMMARY: Waltuch (P) sought indemnification of his legal expenses from his former employer, Conticommodity Services, Inc. (D), after lawsuits against him were dismissed.

RULE OF LAW

(1) A provision of a corporation's articles of incorporation that provides for indemnification without including a good-faith limitation runs afoul of a statute that permits indemnification only if the prospective indemnitee acted in good faith, even if the statute also permits the corporation to grant rights in addition to indemnification rights.

(2) A corporate director or officer who has been successful on the merits or otherwise vindicated from the claims asserted against them is entitled to indemnification from the corporation for expenses reasonably incurred.

FACTS: Waltuch (P), chief metals trader and vice president of Conticommodity Services, Inc. (Conti) (D), traded silver for the firm's clients, as well as for his own account. When the silver market collapsed, he became the subject of numerous lawsuits alleging fraud, market manipulation, and antitrust violations. All the lawsuits were eventually settled, and Waltuch (P) was dismissed from the suits with no settlement contribution imposed. His unreimbursed legal expenses in these actions totaled approximately $1.2 million. Waltuch (P) sued Conti (D), claiming that Article Ninth of Conti's (D) Articles of Incorporation required Conti (D) to indemnify him in both the private and Commodity Futures Trading Commission actions. Conti (D) alleged that this claim was barred by § 145(a) of Delaware's General Corporation Law, which permits indemnification only if the corporate officer acted in good faith. The district court ruled that Waltuch (P) could recover only if he met the good faith requirement of the Delaware statute. The parties stipulated that they would forego trial on the issue of Waltuch's (P) good faith and allow Waltuch (P) to take an immediate appeal of the judgment to the court of appeals. Waltuch's (P) second claim required Conti (D) to indemnify him under Delaware's General Corporation Law because he was successful on the merits or otherwise in the private lawsuits. The district court ruled for Conti (D) on this issue as well, reasoning that Waltuch (P) was not successful on the merits or otherwise because Conti's (D) settlement payments to the plaintiffs were partially on Waltuch's (P) behalf. Waltuch (P) appealed, and the court of appeals granted review.

ISSUE:

(1) Does a provision of a corporation's articles of incorporation that provides for indemnification without including a good-faith limitation run afoul of a statute that permits indemnification only if the prospective indemnitee acted in good faith, even if the statute also permits the corporation to grant rights in addition to indemnification rights?

(2) Is a corporate director or officer who has been successful on the merits or otherwise vindicated from the claims assessed against them entitled to indemnification from the corporation for expenses reasonably incurred?

HOLDING AND DECISION: [Judge not stated in casebook excerpt.]

(1) Yes. A provision of a corporation's articles of incorporation that provides for indemnification without including a good-faith limitation runs afoul of a statute that permits indemnification only if the prospective indemnitee acted in good faith, even if the statute also permits the corporation to grant rights in addition to indemnification rights. Section 145(a) limits a corporation's indemnification powers to situations where the officer or director to be indemnified acted in good faith. Critically, § 145(f) merely acknowledges that one seeking indemnification may be entitled to rights in addition to that of indemnification; it does not speak in terms of corporate power, and therefore cannot be read to free a corporation from the good faith limit explicitly imposed in § 145(a). To hold otherwise would require ignoring the explicit terms of § 145. Additionally, such an interpretation does not render § 145(f) meaningless, since a corporation may grant additional rights that are not inconsistent with § 145(a). For these reasons, Waltuch (P) is not entitled to indemnification under Article Ninth, which exceeds the scope of § 145(a). Affirmed as to this issue.

(2) Yes. A corporate director or officer who has been successful on the merits or otherwise vindicated from the claims asserted against them is entitled to indemnification from the corporation for expenses reasonably incurred. Conti (D) argued that the successful settlements could not be attributed to Waltuch (P) but

Continued on next page.

were the result of Conti's (D) efforts. This application is overbroad. Escape from an adverse judgment or other detriment, for whatever reason, is determinative. "Success is vindication." To go behind the "successful" result is inappropriate. Once Waltuch (P) achieved his settlement gratis, he achieved success "on the merits or otherwise." Accordingly, Conti (D) must indemnify Waltuch (P) under § 145(c) for the $1.2 million in unreimbursed legal fees he spent defending the private lawsuits. Reversed as to this issue.

ANALYSIS

Indemnification rights provided by contract cannot exceed the scope of a corporation's indemnification powers as set out by statute. Although indemnification rights may be broader than those set out in the statute, they cannot be inconsistent with the scope of the statute. Delaware case law suggests a consistency rule that was reinforced by the court's reading of the state statute as well.

Quicknotes

GOOD FAITH An honest intention to abstain from any unconscientious advantage of another.

INDEMNIFICATION Reimbursement for losses sustained or security against anticipated loss or damages.

Citadel Holding Corporation v. Roven

Corporation (D) v. Former director (P)

Del. Sup. Ct., 603 A.2d 818 (1992)

NATURE OF CASE: Appeal from award of damages for reimbursement of litigation expenses.

FACT SUMMARY: Roven (P) sought to have Citadel Holding Corporation (Citadel) (D) reimburse him for legal expenses he incurred defending a securities action filed against him by Citadel (D).

RULE OF LAW

A corporation may advance reasonable costs in defending a suit to a director even when the suit is brought by the corporation.

FACTS: Roven (P) was a director of Citadel Holding Corporation (Citadel) (D) from July 1985 to July 1988. Roven (P) owned over nine percent of Citadel's (D) common stock for most of that time. Roven (P) and Citadel (D) entered into an indemnity agreement in May 1987. In an effort to keep Roven (P) as a director, Citadel (D) agreed to provide Roven (P) with more protection than provided by Citadel's (D) Certificate of Incorporation, Bylaws, and Insurance. The resulting indemnification agreement promised to indemnify Roven (P) for expenses and liabilities incurred while serving Citadel (D). There was, however, an exception for expenses or liabilities incurred due to profits made by Roven (P) from the purchase or sale of Citadel (D) securities falling under § 16(b) of the Securities Exchange Act of 1934. The indemnification agreement also promised to advance Roven (P) costs in defending lawsuits or investigations. Roven (P) subsequently sought to have costs advanced when Citadel (D) brought suit against Roven (P) in federal court for violations of § 16(b) after Roven (P) purchased options to buy Citadel (D) stock while still a director. Citadel (D) argued that the advancement provision was not intended to cover the federal action brought by Citadel (D) against Roven (P). Citadel (D) also argued that the suit brought against Roven (P) was exempted under the § 16(b) exception to the indemnity agreement. The superior (trial) court disagreed and found in favor of Roven (P). Citadel (D) appealed, and the state's highest court granted review.

ISSUE: May a corporation advance reasonable costs of defending a suit to a director even when the suit is brought by the corporation?

HOLDING AND DECISION: [Judge not stated in casebook excerpt.] Yes. A corporation may advance reasonable costs of defending a suit to a director even when the suit is brought by the corporation. Reasonable expenses are expenses related to the corporation's business. In this case, the intent of the indemnification agreement was to provide Roven (P) with more protection than before. Under the General Corporation Law of Delaware, a corporation may advance such costs to a director. Moreover, the indemnification agreement between Roven (P) and Citadel (D) made this advancement mandatory. Since these proceedings are related to proceedings that deal with Citadel's (D) business, they are reasonable. Affirmed with prejudgment and postjudgment-interest awarded to Roven (P).

ANALYSIS

Corporations often enter into indemnification agreements in an effort to recruit key employees or retain them, as in the case of Roven (P). These agreements, however, are criticized by some as leading to irresponsible actions by the employees. This is because the employee would not really be personally liable for anything except intentional misconduct.

Quicknotes

8 DEL. C. § 145(E) Expressly allows corporations to advance the costs of defending a suit to a director.

COMMON STOCK A class of stock representing the corporation's ownership, the holders of which are entitled to dividends only after the holders of preferred stock are paid.

INDEMNIFICATION The payment by a corporation of expenses incurred by its officers or directors as a result of litigation involving the corporation.

In re Medtronic, Inc. Shareholder Litigation

[Parties not identified.]

Minn. Sup. Ct., 900 N.W.2d 401 (2017)

NATURE OF CASE: Appeal in shareholder class action from affirmance in part and reversal in part from judgment that various shareholder claims were all derivative.

FACT SUMMARY: Steiner (P), a shareholder in Medtronic, Inc. (D), contended that all claims he asserted challenging an acquisition of an Irish company, Covidien plc, which was structured as an inversion, were direct, rather than derivative, claims.

RULE OF LAW

In determining whether a shareholder claim is derivative or direct, a derivative claim is stated when shareholders are injured only indirectly, and a direct claim is stated when shareholders show an injury that is not shared with the corporation.

FACTS: Medtronic, Inc. (D), a Minnesota corporation, acquired Covidien plc, a public Irish company, in a transaction structured as an inversion. Medtronic (D) acquired Covidien through a new holding company, Medtronic plc, incorporated in Ireland, with Medtronic (D) and Covidien then becoming wholly owned subsidiaries of the Irish holding company ("new Medtronic"). Shareholders of Medtronic (D) had their stock converted into shares in new Medtronic on a one-for-one basis, while shareholders of Covidien received $35.19 and 0.956 shares of new Medtronic for every share of Covidien stock held. Ultimately, former Medtronic shareholders collectively owned approximately 70 percent of new Medtronic (D) and former Covidien shareholders collectively owned approximately 30 percent of new Medtronic. As a result of the transaction, Medtronic (D) operated as a wholly owned subsidiary of an Irish company and thus was subject to Ireland's tax laws. Steiner (P), a Medtronic (D) shareholder, brought a shareholder class action alleging that Medtronic (D) reduced the interest of its shareholders to 70 percent of new Medtronic in order to secure and protect the tax benefits it sought in this transaction. In addition, because the Internal Revenue Service treats an inversion transaction as a taxable event for the shareholders of the U.S. company, Medtronic (D) shareholders incurred a capital-gains tax on Medtronic (D) shares held in taxable accounts but received no compensation from the company for this tax liability. On the other hand, Steiner (P) alleged, Medtronic (D) officers and directors who incurred an excise-tax liability on their stock-based compensation as a result of the transaction were reimbursed by Medtronic (D) for that expense. Steiner (P) asserted the following injuries, which he claimed were direct, rather than derivative: (1) disparate treatment of Medtronic (D), as compared to Covidien, shareholders; (2) disparate treatment with respect to the tax liability incurred by Medtronic (D) shareholders and the lack of compensation for that liability as compared to the reimbursement paid to Medtronic's (D) officers and directors for their excise-tax liability; and (3) the possibility of a reduction of shareholders' interest in the combined company to 60 percent causing significant dilution to shareholders' interest in new Medtronic. Medtronic (D) moved to dismiss, on the grounds the claims were derivative, requiring Steiner (P) to make a demand on the Medtronic (D) board, which he failed to do. The state's trial court agreed with Medtronic (D) and dismissed the claims. The state's intermediate appellate court affirmed in part and reversed in part, holding that the excise-tax reimbursement claims alleged a harm that belonged to the corporation because voiding the Excise Tax Reimbursement would result in a return of funds to the corporation. However, the court concluded that the remaining claims were direct claims and should not have been dismissed. The state's highest court granted review.

ISSUE: In determining whether a shareholder claim is derivative or direct, is a derivative claim stated when shareholders are injured only indirectly, and is a direct claim stated when shareholders show an injury that is not shared with the corporation?

HOLDING AND DECISION: [Judge not stated in casebook excerpt.] Yes. In determining whether a shareholder claim is derivative or direct, a derivative claim is stated when shareholders are injured only indirectly, and a direct claim is stated when shareholders show an injury that is not shared with the corporation. To determine whether a shareholder claim is direct or derivative, the inquiry focuses on whether the complained-of injury was an injury to the shareholder directly, or to the corporation, looking not to the theory in which the claim is couched, but instead to the injury itself. Applying this test here, the excise-tax claim is derivative, but the claims asserting injuries due to the capital-gains tax liability and dilution of shareholders' interests are direct. The excise-tax claim alleged that Medtronic (D) improperly reimbursed corporate officers and directors for the excise-tax liability that resulted from the transaction, without following statutory procedures before doing so or in violation of duties owed to Medtronic (D) shareholders. Regardless of the specific theory for these claims, the

Continued on next page.

alleged wrongful conduct caused an injury to Medtronic (D) as a corporation, not to the individual shareholders, because corporate reimbursement of an excise-tax liability resulting from the transaction is at bottom an alleged waste of corporate assets. Further, if Steiner (P) were to prevail on these claims, the recovery would go to Medtronic (D) (as a return of the improperly paid funds) rather than to the shareholders. On the other hand, as to the capital-gains-tax claim, the allegations were that the shareholders were harmed because the tax liability was imposed on them solely in their status as shareholders. Medtronic (D) itself did not incur a capital-gains tax liability on the transaction, and therefore could not recover for the injury caused by this alleged harm. Because any recovery would go only to the shareholders who incurred a capital-gains tax liability, rather than to the corporation, the claims asserting this harm are direct. Finally, as to the dilution claims, Steiner (P) did not contend that the inversion diluted shareholders' interests in the company by decreasing the value of the corporation but instead alleged that Medtronic (D) structured the inversion to secure and then protect the corporation's expected tax benefit by taking from its shareholders a portion of their interest in the corporation, thus decreasing their ownership share in new Medtronic. In other words, rather than a simple loss of economic value, Steiner (P) alleged an injury based on the loss of certain rightful incidents of his ownership interest, which is an injury that falls only on shareholders and not on the corporation. Accordingly, this claim was also direct. Affirmed in part and reversed in part.

ANALYSIS

In reaching its decision, the Minnesota Court of Appeals relied on the Delaware Supreme Court's decision in *Tooley v. Donaldson, Lufkin & Jenrette, Inc.*, 845 A.2d 1031 (Del. 2004), and concluded that a direct claim is available when: (1) all shareholders share the same injury; (2) the shareholders would receive the benefit of the recovery or remedy; and (3) the injury is not suffered by the corporation. The Minnesota Supreme Court, however, explained that reliance on *Tooley* was misplaced, as the *Tooley* three-part test has been limited to claims asserting breach of fiduciary duty. Instead, the Supreme Court applied a test that distinguishes direct from derivative claims by identifying who suffered the injury and therefore who is entitled to the recovery for that injury.

Quicknotes

CAPITAL GAIN AND LOSS Gain or loss from the sale or exchange of a capital asset.

DERIVATIVE CLAIM Action asserted by a shareholder in order to enforce a cause of action on behalf of the corporation.

United Food and Commercial Workers Union v. Zuckerberg

Institutional shareholder (P) v. Director and controlling shareholder (D)

Del. Sup. Ct., 262 A.3d 1034 (2021)

NATURE OF CASE: Appeal from dismissal, based on failure to make pre-suit demand, of derivative action for breach of fiduciary duties.

FACT SUMMARY: After Facebook, Inc. (D), defended and settled a consolidated class action challenging a reclassification of Facebook (D) stock, and after Facebook (D) abandoned the reclassification, a Facebook (D) institutional shareholder, United Food and Commercial Workers Union [and Participating Food Industry Employers Tri-State Pension Fund] (Tri-State) (P) brought a derivative suit alleging that Facebook's directors (D) had breached their fiduciary duties by approving the reclassification, and seeking to recoup for Facebook (D) the amounts it had spent defending and settling the class action, amounting to around $90 million. However, Tri-State (P) did not make pre-suit demand, asserting that such demand would have been futile because the reclassification was not the product of a valid exercise of business judgment and because a majority of the board faced a substantial likelihood of liability and/or lacked independence. Facebook (D) and the director defendants (D) moved to dismiss based on Tri-State's (P) failure to make pre-suit demand or to prove that demand would have been futile prior to filing its action.

RULE OF LAW

(1) Exculpated care violations do not satisfy the second prong of the test for demand futility under Aronson v. Lewis, 473 A.2d 805 (Del. 1984).

(2) In determining whether demand is excused as futile for a given corporate director when a shareholder files a derivative action, the court must use a three-part test that asks whether the director: (1) received a material personal benefit from the alleged misconduct that is the subject of the litigation demand; (2) would face a substantial likelihood of liability on any of the claims that are the subject of the litigation demand; and (3) lacks independence from someone who received a material personal benefit from the alleged misconduct that is the subject of the litigation demand or who would face a substantial likelihood of liability on any of the claims that are the subject of the litigation demand.

FACTS: In 2016, the board of directors of Facebook, Inc. (D), voted in favor of a stock reclassification (the "Reclassification") that would allow Mark Zuckerberg (D)—Facebook's (D) controller, chairman, and chief executive officer (CEO)—to sell most of his Facebook (D) stock while maintaining voting control of the company. The board has nine members, six of whom served on the board when it approved the Reclassification. Zuckerberg (D) had proposed the Reclassification to allow him and his wife to fulfill a pledge to donate most of their wealth to philanthropic causes. The Reclassification had been researched, negotiated, and recommended by a special committee (Special Committee) of three purportedly independent directors, starting in August 2015. In April 2016, the Special Committee recommended that the full board approve the Reclassification, which the board approved the next day, and, a couple of weeks later, the Reclassification was publicly announced. Starting two days later, numerous stockholders filed lawsuits in the Delaware Court of Chancery, alleging that Facebook's (D) board of directors violated their fiduciary duties by negotiating and approving a purportedly one-sided deal that put Zuckerberg's (D) interests ahead of the company's interests. The Court of Chancery consolidated more than a dozen of these lawsuits into a single class action (the "Reclassification Class Action"), which was scheduled for trial in September 2017. However, at Zuckerberg's (D) request, a week before trial, Facebook (D) withdrew the Reclassification and mooted the fiduciary-duty Reclassification Class Action. Facebook (D) had spent more than $20 million defending against the Reclassification Class Action and had paid plaintiffs' counsel more than $68 million in attorneys' fees under the corporate benefit doctrine. Following the settlement, another Facebook (D) stockholder—the United Food and Commercial Workers Union [and Participating Food Industry Employers Tri-State Pension Fund] (Tri-State) (P)—filed a derivative complaint in the Court of Chancery. This new action rehashed many of the allegations made in the prior Reclassification Class Action but sought compensation for the money Facebook (D) spent in connection with that action. However, Tri-State (P) did not make a pre-suit litigation demand on Facebook's (D) board prior to filing its action. Instead, Tri-State (P) pleaded that demand was futile because the board's negotiation and approval of the Reclassification was not a valid exercise of its business judgment and because a majority of the directors (D) were beholden to Zuckerberg (D). Facebook (D) and the other defendants (D) moved to dismiss Tri-State's (P) complaint under Court of Chancery Rule 23.1, arguing that Tri-State

Continued on next page.

(P) did not make demand or prove that demand was futile. Both sides agreed that the demand futility test established in *Aronson v. Lewis,* 473 A.2d 805 (Del. 1984), applied to Tri-State's (P) complaint.

Other than Zuckerberg (D), the directors (Director Defendants (D)) whose independence was at issue for demand futility were:

- Peter Thiel (D), who served as a Facebook (D) director since April 2005 and who voted in favor of the Reclassification, was a partner at the venture capital firm Founders Firm.
- Reed Hastings (D), who began serving as a Facebook (D) director in June 2011 and was still a director when Tri-State (P) filed its complaint. Hastings (D), who voted in favor of the Reclassification, had founded and served as the chairman and CEO of Netflix, Inc.
- Erskine B. Bowles (D), who began serving as a Facebook (D) director in September 2011 and was still a director when Tri-State (P) filed its complaint. Bowles (D) was a member of the Special Committee that negotiated and recommended that the full board approve the Reclassification.

In October 2020, the Court of Chancery dismissed Tri-State's (P) complaint under Rule 23.1. The court held that exculpated care claims do not excuse demand under *Aronson's* second prong because they do not expose directors to a substantial likelihood of liability. The court also held that the complaint failed to raise a reasonable doubt that a majority of the demand board lacked independence from Zuckerberg (D). In reaching these conclusions, the Court of Chancery applied a three-part test for demand futility that blended the *Aronson* test with the test articulated in *Rales v. Blasband,* 634 A.2d 927 (Del. 1993). Tri-State (P) appealed, and the Delaware Supreme Court granted review.

ISSUE:

(1) Do exculpated care violations satisfy the second prong of the test for demand futility under *Aronson v. Lewis,* 473 A.2d 805 (Del. 1984)?

(2) In determining whether demand is excused as futile for a given corporate director when a shareholder files a derivative action, must the court use a three-part test that asks whether the director: (1) received a material personal benefit from the alleged misconduct that is the subject of the litigation demand; (2) would face a substantial likelihood of liability on any of the claims that are the subject of the litigation demand; and (3) lacks independence from someone who received a material personal benefit from the alleged misconduct that is the subject of the litigation demand or who would face a substantial likelihood of liability on any of the claims that are the subject of the litigation demand?

HOLDING AND DECISION: [Judge not stated in casebook excerpt.]

(1) No. Exculpated care violations do not satisfy the second prong of the test for demand futility under *Aronson v. Lewis,* 473 A.2d 805 (Del. 1984). Section 102(b)(7) of the Delaware General Corporation Law (DGCL) authorizes corporations to adopt a charter provision insulating directors from liability for breaching their duty of care, and Facebook's (D) charter has such a provision. Therefore, the Director Defendants (D) faced no risk of personal liability from the allegations asserted by Tri-State (P). Accordingly, the question becomes whether the Defendant Directors' (D) exculpated duty of care violations alone satisfy the second prong of the *Aronson* test. The Court of Chancery held that exculpated care claims do not excuse demand because the second prong of the *Aronson* test focuses on whether a director faces a substantial likelihood of liability. Tri-State (P) argues that this analysis was wrong because *Aronson's* second prong focuses on whether the challenged transaction "satisfies the applicable standard of review," not on whether directors face a substantial likelihood of liability. Tri-State's (P) position rests on the language in *Aronson* stating that the Court of Chancery in a demand futility case must determine whether the particularized facts alleged by the plaintiff create a reasonable doubt as to the soundness of the challenged transaction sufficient to rebut the presumption that the business judgment rule attaches to the transaction by assessing "the substantive nature of the challenged transaction and the board's approval thereof." Although later opinions issued by the Delaware Supreme Court contain similar language that can be read to suggest that *Aronson's* second prong focuses on the propriety of the challenged transaction, those decisions do not address why *Aronson* used the standard of review as a proxy for whether the board could impartially consider a litigation demand. The likely answer is that, before the General Assembly adopted Section 102(b)(7) in 1986 [the casebook incorrectly states "1995"], rebutting the business judgment rule through allegations of care violations exposed directors to a substantial likelihood of liability. Thus, even if the demand board was independent and disinterested with respect to the challenged transaction, the litigation presented a threat that would "sterilize [the board's] discretion" with respect to a demand. After the enactment of § 102(b)(7), the Court's decisions increasingly held that *Aronson's* second prong focuses on whether

Continued on next page.

director-defendants face a substantial likelihood of liability, and, in *In re Cornerstone Therapeutics, Inc. Stockholder Litigation,* 115 A.3d 1173 (Del. 2015), the Court left no doubt that exculpated care violations do not satisfy the second prong. When *Aronson* was decided, raising a reasonable doubt that directors breached their duty of care exposed them to a substantial likelihood of liability and protracted litigation, raising doubt as to their ability to impartially consider demand. The ground shifted, and exculpated breach of care claims no longer pose a threat that neutralizes director discretion. These developments must be factored into demand-futility analysis, and Tri-State (P) failed to provide a reasoned explanation of why rebutting the business judgment rule should automatically render directors incapable of impartially considering a litigation demand if their duty of care violations are exculpated. Nevertheless, Tri-State (P) argues that construing the second prong to focus on whether directors face a substantial likelihood of liability erases any distinction between the two prongs of the *Aronson* test, because if directors face a substantial likelihood of liability for approving the challenged transaction, then they are interested with respect to the challenged transaction, which is addressed by the first prong, so that construing the second prong to require a substantial risk of liability makes it redundant. This argument misconstrues *Aronson.* The first prong focuses on whether the directors had a personal interest in the challenged transaction (i.e., a personal financial benefit from the challenged transaction that is not equally shared by the stockholders). This is a different consideration than whether the directors face a substantial likelihood of liability for approving the challenged transaction, even if they received nothing personal from the challenged transaction. Thus, the first and second prongs perform separate functions, even if those functions are complementary. For these reasons, the Court of Chancery's judgment is affirmed as to this issue.

(2) Yes. In determining whether demand is excused as futile for a given corporate director when a shareholder files a derivative action, the court must use a three-part test that asks whether the director: (1) received a material personal benefit from the alleged misconduct that is the subject of the litigation demand; (2) would face a substantial likelihood of liability on any of the claims that are the subject of the litigation demand; and (3) lacks independence from someone who received a material personal benefit from the alleged misconduct that is the subject of the litigation demand or who would face a substantial likelihood of liability on any of the claims that are the subject of the litigation demand. When the Court decided *Aronson,* raising a reasonable doubt that the business judgment standard of review would apply exposed directors to a substantial likelihood of liability for care violations. The General Assembly's enactment of Section 102(b)(7) and other developments in corporate law have weakened the connection between rebutting the business judgment standard and exposing directors to a risk that would sterilize their judgment with respect to a litigation demand. Further, the *Aronson* test has proved difficult to apply in many contexts, such as where there is turnover on a corporation's board, or director abstention, as happened in the case at bar. The Court of Chancery's refined articulation of the *Aronson* standard helps to address these issues. Nonetheless, this refined standard is consistent with *Aronson, Rales v. Blasband,* 634 A.2d 927 (Del. 1993), and their progeny. Thus, cases properly applying those holdings remain good law.

Accordingly, to determine whether Tri-State's (P) complaint pleaded with particularity facts establishing that a litigation demand on Facebook's (D) board would be futile, the Court will apply this three-part test on a director-by-director basis. Tri-State (P) conceded that of the nine members of the board on whom demand would have to be made, two could have impartially considered a litigation demand, and Facebook (D) did not argue that three others could have impartially considered a litigation demand. Thus, to show that demand was futile, Tri-State (P) had to sufficiently allege that two of the following directors could not impartially consider demand: Thiel (D), Hastings (D), Bowles (D), and Desmond-Hellmann (D). Whether a director is independent is a fact-specific determination that depends upon the context of a particular case. To show a lack of independence, a derivative complaint must plead with particularity facts creating a reasonable doubt that a director is so beholden to an interested director that their discretion would be sterilized. A plaintiff must allege that the director in question had ties to the person whose proposal or actions the director is evaluating that are sufficiently substantial to prevent the director from objectively discharge their fiduciary duties. A variety of motivations, including friendship, may influence the demand futility inquiry. Nonetheless, to render a director unable to consider demand, a relationship must be of a bias-producing nature. Alleging that a director had a personal friendship with someone else, or that a director had an outside business relationship, are insufficient to raise a reasonable doubt that the director lacked independence, and the existence of some financial ties between the interested party and the director, without more, is not disqualifying. Applying these principles here leads to the conclusion that Tri-State (P) failed to raise a reasonable doubt that either Hastings (D), Thiel (D), or Bowles (D) was beholden to Zuckerberg (D).

Continued on next page.

Hastings (D): According to the complaint, Hastings (D) was not independent because Netflix purchased advertisements from Facebook (D); Netflix had ongoing and potential future business relationships with Facebook(D); Facebook (D) gave to Netflix intrusive access to users' personal data, effectively exempting Netflix from privacy rules; Hastings (D) (as a Netflix founder) was biased in favor of founders maintaining control of their companies; and Hastings (D) publicly supported large philanthropic donations by founders during their lifetimes and made significant contributions to the same foundation as Zuckerberg (D). These allegations do not raise a reasonable doubt that Hastings (D) was beholden to Zuckerberg (D). Even if Netflix purchased advertisements from Facebook (D), the complaint does not allege that those purchases were material to Netflix or that Netflix received anything other than arm's length terms under those agreements. Similarly, the complaint does not make any particularized allegations explaining how obtaining special access to Facebook (D) user data was material to Netflix's business interests, or that Netflix used its special access to user data to obtain any concrete benefits in its own business. Further, having a bias in favor of founder-control does not mean that Hastings (D) lacks independence from Zuckerberg (D), as Hastings (D) might have a good-faith belief that founder control maximizes a corporation's value over the long-haul. If so, that good-faith belief would play a valid role in Hasting's (D) exercising impartial business judgment. Moreover, alleging that Hastings (D) and Zuckerberg (D) have a track record of donating to similar causes falls short of showing that Hastings (D) is beholden to Zuckerberg (D).

Thiel (D): The complaint alleged that Thiel (D) was not independent because: Thiel (D) was one of the early investors in Facebook (D); Thiel (D) is the longest-tenured board member besides Zuckerberg (D); Thiel (D) has been instrumental to Facebook's (D) business strategy and direction over the years; Thiel (D) has a personal bias in favor of keeping founders in control of the companies they created; Founders Fund, the venture capital firm at which Thiel (D) is a partner, gets good deal flow from its high-profile association with Facebook (D); Facebook (D) shares owned by the Founders Fund, and, therefore, by Thiel (D) will be released from escrow in connection with an acquisition; Thiel (D) is Zuckerberg's (D) close friend and mentor; despite Thiel's (D) involvement with a scandal that exposed Facebook (D) to regulatory investigations and litigation, Zuckerberg (D) did not try to remove Thiel (D) from the board; and, despite Thiel's (D) attempt to bankrupt a media organization and concomitant widespread calls for Zuckerberg (D) to remove Thiel (D) from Facebook's (D) board given Thiel's (D) apparent antagonism toward a free press, Zuckerberg (D) ignored those calls and did not seek to remove Thiel (D) from Facebook's (D) board. These allegations do not raise a reasonable doubt that Thiel (D) is beholden to Zuckerberg (D). The complaint does not explain why Thiel's (D) status as a long-serving board member, early investor, or his contributions to Facebook's (D) business strategy make him beholden to Zuckerberg (D). Similarly, a director's good-faith belief that founder controller maximizes value does not raise a reasonable doubt that the director lacks independence from a corporation's founder. Lastly, the allegations that suggest that, because Zuckerberg (D) stood by Thiel (D) in the face of public scandals, Thiel (D) feels a sense of obligation to Zuckerberg (D), can only raise a reasonable doubt about Thiel's (D) independence if remaining a Facebook (D) director was financially or personally material to Thiel (D). However, given Thiel's (D) wealth and stature, these allegations, without more, support neither an inference that Thiel's (D) service on the board is financially material to him, nor that serving as a Facebook (D) director confers such cachet that his independence is compromised.

Bowles (D): According to the complaint, Bowles (D) was not independent because: Bowles (D) is beholden to the entire board because it granted a waiver of the mandatory retirement age for Facebook (D) directors; Morgan Stanley—a company for which Bowles (D) served as a longstanding board member at the time—directly benefited by receiving over $2 million in fees for its work in connection with the Reclassification; Bowles (D) ensured that Evercore and his close friend Altman financially benefitted from the Special Committee's engagement without properly vetting Evercore's competency or considering alternatives. These allegations do not raise a reasonable doubt that Bowles (D) is beholden to Zuckerberg (D) or the other members of the Demand Board (D). The complaint does not make any particularized allegation explaining why the board's decision to grant Bowles (D) a waiver from the mandatory retirement age would compromise his ability to impartially consider a litigation demand or engender a sense of debt to the other directors. The other allegations likewise are ill-supported, as none of these suggest that Bowles (D) received a personal benefit from the Reclassification, or that his ties to these financial advisors made him beholden to Zuckerberg (D) as a condition of sending business to Morgan Stanley, Evercore, or Altman. Affirmed.

ANALYSIS

With *Zuckerberg,* the Delaware Supreme Court adopted a new three-part test as "the universal test" for assessing whether pre-suit demand should be excused as futile. As the Court indicates, this test is a blend of the *Aronson* test, which applied when the same board that made the challenged decision also considered the

Continued on next page.

litigation demand, and the *Rales* test, which applied in all other circumstances. As the Court also emphasized, the refined test refocuses the inquiry on the decision regarding the litigation demand, rather than the decision being challenged, explaining that notwithstanding text focusing on the propriety of the challenged transaction, this approach is consistent with the overarching concern that *Aronson* identified: whether the directors on the demand board cannot be considered proper persons to conduct litigation on behalf of the corporation because they are under an influence that sterilizes their discretion. The purpose of the demand-futility analysis is to assess whether the board should be deprived of its decision-making authority because there is reason to doubt that the directors would be able to bring their impartial business judgment to bear on a litigation demand, which is a different consideration than whether the derivative claim is strong or weak because the challenged transaction is likely to pass or fail the applicable standard of review. The Court noted that it is helpful to keep those inquiries separate. Going forward, at the very least, the new test can be expected to eliminate disputes or doubts as to whether the *Aronson* test or the *Rales* test controls the demand futility inquiry.

Quicknotes

BUSINESS JUDGMENT RULE Standard of review that presumes that in making a business decision, the directors of a corporation acted on an informed basis, in good faith, and in the honest belief that the action taken was in the best interests of the company.

DEMAND FUTILITY Exception to the requirement that a shareholder make a prior demand for corrective legal action by the board of directors before commencing a derivative action if the plaintiff pleads particularized facts demonstrating that such demand would be futile as a consequence of a conflict of interest, lack of independence, or breach of fiduciary duty on the part of a majority of the board.

DEMAND REQUIREMENT Also referred to as "pre-suit demand," a requirement that a shareholder make a demand for corrective legal action by the board of directors before commencing a shareholder's derivative action.

DUTY OF CARE Duty that an officer or director owes to the corporation, by virtue of their fiduciary relationship, to act for the benefit of the corporation.

DUTY OF LOYALTY A director's duty to refrain from self-dealing or to take a position that is adverse to the corporation's best interests.

EXCULPATED CARE VIOLATIONS PROVISION A corporate charter provision insulating a corporation's directors from personal liability for breaching their duty of care.

SHAREHOLDER'S DERIVATIVE ACTION Action asserted by a shareholder to enforce a cause of action on behalf, and in the name, of the corporation.

Auerbach v. Bennett

Shareholder (P) v. Corporate directors (D)

N.Y. Ct. App., 47 N.Y.2d 619, 393 N.E.2d 994 (1979)

NATURE OF CASE: Appeal from reversal of dismissal on summary judgment of a shareholder derivative action.

FACT SUMMARY: A shareholder (P) of General Telephone and Electronics Corporation (GTE) (D) challenged the decision by a board-appointed special litigation committee to terminate a shareholder's derivative action.

RULE OF LAW

While the substantive aspects of a decision to terminate a shareholder's derivative action against defendant corporate directors made by a committee of disinterested directors appointed by the corporation's board of directors is beyond judicial inquiry under the business judgment doctrine, the court may inquire as to the disinterested independence of the members of that committee and as to the appropriateness and sufficiency of the investigative procedures chosen and pursued by the committee.

FACTS: With the assistance of special counsel and Arthur Andersen & Co. (D), the General Telephone and Electronics Corporation (GTE) (D) audit committee conducted an investigation into GTE's (D) worldwide operations. The audit committee subsequently released its report, which stated that evidence had been found that, in the period from 1971 to 1975, GTE (D) had made payments abroad and in the United States constituting bribes and kickbacks totaling more than $11,000,000, and that some directors (D) had been involved. Auerbach (P), a shareholder, instituted a derivative action on behalf of GTE (D) against GTE's directors (D), Arthur Andersen (D), and GTE (D), alleging breach of corporate duties and seeking damages as reimbursement for the wrongful payments. The board of directors then adopted a resolution creating a special litigation committee to investigate the derivative action and determine what position GTE (D) should take. The committee comprised three disinterested directors who had joined the board after the alleged transactions had occurred. The committee concluded that Arthur Andersen (D) had acted in accordance with generally accepted auditing standards and in good faith and that no proper interest of GTE (D) or its shareholders would be served by continuing the claim against it. The committee also found that the claims against the individual directors (D) were without merit. [GTE (D) was granted summary judgment. Another shareholder, Wallenstein (P), was substituted as plaintiff and appealed. The state's intermediate appellate court reversed.] The state's highest court granted review.

ISSUE: While the substantive aspects of a decision to terminate a shareholder's derivative action against defendant corporate directors made by a committee of disinterested directors appointed by the corporation's board of directors is beyond judicial inquiry under the business judgment doctrine, may the court inquire as to the disinterested independence of the members of that committee and as to the appropriateness and sufficiency of the investigative procedures chosen and pursued by the committee?

HOLDING AND DECISION: (Jones, J.) Yes. While the substantive aspects of a decision to terminate a shareholder's derivative action against defendant corporate directors made by a committee of disinterested directors appointed by the corporation's board of directors is beyond judicial inquiry under the business judgment doctrine, the court may inquire as to the disinterested independence of the members of that committee and as to the appropriateness and sufficiency of the investigative procedures chosen and pursued by the committee. The business judgment doctrine recognizes that courts are ill-equipped to evaluate what are and essentially must be business judgments. However, the rule shields the deliberations and conclusions of a special committee only if its members possess disinterested independence and do not stand in a dual relation that would prevent an unprejudicial exercise of judgment. In this case there is nothing in the record to raise a triable issue of fact as to the independence and disinterested status of the three directors on the special litigation committee, or as to the sufficiency and appropriateness of the investigative procedures they employed. The derivative suit was brought against only four members of the fifteen-member board, and the three members of the special litigation committee joined the board after the alleged transactions occurred. To disqualify an entire board would be to render a corporation powerless to make an effective business judgment with respect to prosecution of a derivative action. The decision of the disinterested special litigation committee forecloses further judicial inquiry. Affirmed.

DISSENT: (Cooke, C.J.) Summary judgment should not be granted prior to disclosure proceedings, because the continuation of the suit is so dependent upon the

Continued on next page.

motives and actions of the board members (D) and the special litigation committee, who are in exclusive possession of much of the factual information concerning the case.

ANALYSIS

While the court did not make it impossible for a derivative action to survive a special litigation committee's decision to terminate it, it did make it extremely difficult. Other courts have been far less deferential to the business judgment of such committees. In Delaware and other jurisdictions, the court first determines whether the committee is disinterested, independent, and acting in good faith, and then applies its own business judgment in evaluating the evidence presented and the committee's recommendation.

Quicknotes

BUSINESS JUDGMENT RULE Standard of review that presumes that in making a business decision, the directors of a corporation acted on an informed basis, in good faith, and in the honest belief that the action taken was in the best interests of the company.

SHAREHOLDER'S DERIVATIVE ACTION Action asserted by a shareholder in order to enforce a cause of action on behalf of the corporation.

Zapata Corp. v. Maldonado

Corporation (D) v. Shareholder (P)

Del. Sup. Ct., 430 A.2d 779 (1981)

NATURE OF CASE: Appeal from dismissal of derivative action.

FACT SUMMARY: Maldonado (P), a shareholder of the Zapata Corp. (D), sought to prevent the dismissal of his derivative action against Zapata (D) following the recommendation for dismissal by a corporation-appointed investigation committee.

RULE OF LAW

When assessing a special litigation committee's motion to dismiss a derivative action, a court must: (1) determine whether the committee acted independently, in good faith, and made a reasonable investigation; and (2) apply the court's own independent business judgment.

FACTS: In June 1975, Maldonado (P) instituted a derivative action against ten officers and/or directors of Zapata Corp. (D), alleging breaches of fiduciary duty. Maldonado (P) did not first demand that the board bring the action, believing that demand would be futile because all directors (D) were named as defendants and allegedly participated in the wrongful acts. By June 1979, four of the directors (D) named in the action were no longer on the board, and the remaining directors (D) appointed two new outside directors to the board. The board then created an independent investigation committee, comprised solely of the two new directors, to investigate Maldonado's (P) allegations and determine whether Zapata (D) should continue the litigation. The committee's determination was intended to be final and binding upon Zapata (D). In September 1979, the committee concluded that the action should be dismissed because it was not in Zapata's (D) best interests. Zapata (D) filed a motion for dismissal or summary judgment, which was granted by the Court of Chancery. The state's highest court granted review.

ISSUE: When assessing a special litigation committee's motion to dismiss a derivative action, must a court: (1) determine whether the committee acted independently, in good faith, and made a reasonable investigation, with the burden of proof on the corporation; and (2) apply the court's own independent business judgment?

HOLDING AND DECISION: (Quillen, J.) Yes. When assessing a special litigation committee's motion to dismiss a derivative action, a court must: (1) determine whether the committee acted independently, in good faith, and made a reasonable investigation, with the burden of proof on the corporation; and (2) apply the court's own independent business judgment. A board has the power to choose not to pursue litigation when demand is made upon it, so long as the decision is not wrongful. Where demand has been excused, courts have struggled between allowing the independent business judgment of a board committee to prevail and yielding to unbridled plaintiff stockholder control. The test promulgated here allows for the balancing of these competing interests under appropriate court supervision. While courts should be mindful of judicial overreaching, the interests at stake necessitate the fresh view of a judicial outsider. Reversed and remanded.

ANALYSIS

The approach set forth in this Delaware case has been adopted by many jurisdictions searching for a compromise between demand-required and demand-excused cases. New York courts, on the other hand, have applied a more deferential standard of review in cases challenging the recommendations of special litigation committees. New York courts apply only the first half of the *Zapata* test, relying on the business judgment of a committee so long as the committee members are disinterested, independent, and have conducted a reasonable investigation.

Quicknotes

BUSINESS JUDGMENT RULE Standard of review that presumes that in making a business decision, the directors of a corporation acted on an informed basis, in good faith, and in the honest belief that the action taken was in the best interests of the company.

FIDUCIARY DUTY A legal obligation to act for the benefit of another, including subordinating one's personal interests to that of the other person.

SHAREHOLDER'S DERIVATIVE ACTION Action asserted by a shareholder in order to enforce a cause of action on behalf of the corporation.

Securities and Exchange Commission v. Texas Gulf Sulphur Co.

Government regulatory agency (P) v. Corporation (D)

401 F.2d 833 (2d Cir.), *cert. denied sub nom.* Coates v. S.E.C, 394 U.S. 976 (1969)

NATURE OF CASE: Appeal from dismissal of Securities and Exchange Commission (SEC) enforcement action for violations of federal securities laws.

FACT SUMMARY: Texas Gulf Sulphur Co. (TGS) (D) maintained that, because its employees were ordered not to disclose material information to the public, those employees were entitled to trade on that information prior to its dissemination to the public. TGS (D) further maintained that, because its press release was not issued in order to affect the market price of TGS's (D) stock, it could not form the basis for a violation of the federal securities laws.

RULE OF LAW

(1) Anyone in possession of material inside information must either disclose it to the investing public, or, if ordered not to disclose it to protect a corporate confidence, abstain from trading in the securities concerned while such inside information remains undisclosed.

(2) A company press release is considered to have been issued in connection with the purchase or sale of a security for purposes of imposing liability under the federal securities laws, and liability will flow if a reasonable investor, in the exercise of due care, would have been misled by it.

FACTS: Employees of Texas Gulf Sulphur Co. (TGS) (D), doing exploratory drilling in Canada, discovered unusually rich ore deposits. To facilitate purchase of all the land containing those deposits, Stephens, president of TGS (D), instructed the exploratory team not to disclose the results of their drilling to anyone else, including other TGS employees, directors, and officers, and drilling ceased. During a period of about four months, some of those with knowledge of the drilling results purchased TGS (D) stock or calls thereon. Also, during this period TGS (D) issued stock options to 26 of its officers and employees whose salaries exceeded a specified amount, five of whom knew or had some knowledge of the drilling results. At this point, neither the board nor the compensation committee knew of the drilling results. Drilling then resumed, and rumors began to circulate in the press of a rich ore strike. TGS (D) issued a press release to downplay these rumors and stated that the work done to date was not sufficient to reach definite conclusions as to the size and grade of any ore discovered. The TGS (D) official who issued the press release knew of the developments to date. Four days later, TGS (D) officially announced a major strike. During those four days, certain TGS (D) employees and officers who knew about the strike purchased substantial amounts of TGS (D) stock and call options. After the strike announcement, the price of TGS (D) stock increased dramatically. The SEC (P) sued, alleging that TGS's (D) conduct constituted insider trading in violation of § 10(b) of the Securities Exchange Act (the Act) and Securities and Exchange Commission (SEC) Rule 10b-5. It sought to compel the rescission of those securities transactions that violated the Act. The district court concluded that the results of the first drill core were too remote to be deemed material or to have had any significant impact on the market. The SEC (P) appealed, and the court of appeals granted review.

ISSUE:

(1) Must anyone in possession of material inside information either disclose it to the investing public, or, if ordered not to disclose it to protect a corporate confidence, abstain from trading in the securities concerned while such inside information remains undisclosed?

(2) Is a company press release considered to have been issued in connection with the purchase or sale of a security for purposes of imposing liability under the federal securities laws and will liability flow therefrom if a reasonable investor, in the exercise of due care, would have been misled by it?

HOLDING AND DECISION: [Judge not stated in casebook excerpt.]

(1) Yes. Anyone in possession of material inside information must either disclose it to the investing public, or, if ordered not to disclose it to protect a corporate confidence, abstain from trading in the securities concerned while such inside information remains undisclosed. Rule 10b-5 is based on the justifiable expectation of the securities marketplace that all investors have equal access to material information. Material facts include those that may affect the desire of investors to buy, sell, or hold the company's securities. Here, knowledge of the possible existence of a remarkably rich drill core would certainly have been an important fact to a reasonable investor in deciding whether he should buy, sell, or hold. A survey of the facts found by the trial court conclusively establishes that knowledge of the results of the discovery hole constituted material information. Therefore, all transactions in TGS (D) stock by individuals apprised

Continued on next page.

of the drilling results were made in violation of SEC Rule 10b-5. Reversed as to this issue.

(2) Yes. A company press release is considered to have been issued in connection with the purchase or sale of a security for purposes of imposing liability under the federal securities laws, and liability will flow therefrom if a reasonable investor, in the exercise of due care, would have been misled by it. The purchase or sale requirement under § 10(b) of the Securities Exchange Act requires merely that the deceptive device employed be likely to cause a reasonable investor, exercising due care, to have been misled. TGS's (D) press release could satisfy this test, although the lower court did not properly apply this standard to the facts before it. Reversed in part. Remanded as to this issue.

ANALYSIS

The purchase or sale requirement of § 10(b) operates to limit those who can recover under that section to actual purchasers or sellers of a company's securities. However, consider the case of persons who choose not to purchase or sell a company's stock because of misrepresentations or omissions of material information. These persons are no less injured as a result of the offending conduct. They will not, however, have private cause of action against the corporation under § 10(b) and Rule 10b-5. See *Blue Chip Stamps v. Manor Drug Stores*, 421 U.S. 723 (1975).

Quicknotes

RULE 10b-5 Unlawful to defend or make untrue statements in connection with purchase or sale of securities.

Dirks v. Securities and Exchange Commission

Broker (D) v. Government regulatory agency (P)

463 U.S. 646 (1983)

NATURE OF CASE: Securities and Exchange Commission (SEC) action for violation of § 10(b).

FACT SUMMARY: Dirks (D) contended that he should not be censured under Rule 10b-5 for openly discussing with investors inside information he had been given by Secrist, the insider, for the purpose of investigating and verifying fraud by Equity Funding of America.

RULE OF LAW

A tippee will not be liable for disclosing nonpublic information received from an insider where the insider will not personally benefit from the disclosure so as not to be in breach of the insider's fiduciary duty.

FACTS: Dirks (D), the tippee, and an officer of a brokerage firm, was told by Secrist, a former officer of Equity Funding of America (Equity Funding), that Equity Funding was engaging in fraud. Secrist urged Dirks (D) to verify the fraud and disclose it publicly. Neither Dirks (D) nor his firm owned Equity Funding stock. Dirks (D) investigated, and as he did, he openly discussed the information he had received from Secrist with clients and investors, some of whom sold Equity Funding securities, causing the price of its stock to drop from $26 to $15 per share. After the Equity Funding fraud came to light, the Securities and Exchange Commission (SEC)—notwithstanding that it was able to successfully convict Equity Funding's officers for securities fraud—censured Dirks (D) for aiding and abetting Rule 10b-5 violations. The court of appeals affirmed, and the United States Supreme Court granted certiorari.

ISSUE: Will a tippee be liable for disclosing nonpublic information received from an insider where the insider will not personally benefit from the disclosure so as not to be in breach of the insider's fiduciary duty?

HOLDING AND DECISION: (Powell, J.) No. A tippee will not be liable for disclosing nonpublic information received from an insider where the insider will not personally benefit from the disclosure so as not to be in breach of the insider's fiduciary duty. In determining whether a tippee is under an obligation to disclose or abstain from using inside information, it is necessary to determine whether the insider's tip constituted a breach of the insider's fiduciary duty, and the test for this is whether the insider personally will benefit, directly or indirectly, from their disclosure. Absent some personal gain, there has been no breach of duty to stockholders. And absent a breach by the insider, there is no derivative breach. Here, unless Secrist breached his duty to shareholders in disclosing the nonpublic information to Dirks (D), Dirks (D) breached no duty when he passed it on to investors. Since Secrist did not violate his fiduciary duty to the corporation's shareholders, given that he was motivated by a desire to expose the fraud, there cannot be a derivative breach by Dirks (D). Reversed.

ANALYSIS

This case is consistent with the Court's decision in *Chiarella v. United States*, 445 U.S. 222 (1980), where the Court found that there is no general duty to disclose before trading on material nonpublic information and held that a duty to disclose under § 10(b) does not arise from mere possession of nonpublic market information. Rather, such a duty, the Court found, arises from the existence of a fiduciary relationship.

Quicknotes

FIDUCIARY DUTY A legal obligation to act for the benefit of another.

FRAUD A false representation of facts with the intent that another will rely on the misrepresentation to their detriment.

RULE 10b-5 It is unlawful to defend or make untrue statements in connection with purchase or sale of securities.

SECURITIES EXCHANGE ACT § 10(b) Makes it unlawful for any person to use manipulation or deception in the buying or selling of securities.

Salman v. United States

Convicted insider trader (D) v. Federal government (P)

580 U.S. 39 (2016)

NATURE OF CASE: Appeal from affirmance of conviction for conspiracy and securities fraud based on insider trading.

FACT SUMMARY: Salman (D) contended that an insider's gift of confidential information to a trading relative or friend is insufficient by itself to constitute securities fraud, and that the tipper must also receive something of a pecuniary value to benefit from the transaction.

RULE OF LAW

An insider's gift of confidential information to a trading relative or friend is sufficient by itself to constitute securities fraud.

FACTS: Salman (D) was indicted for federal securities-fraud crimes for trading on inside information he received from a friend and relative-by-marriage, Michael Kara, who, in turn, received the information from his brother, Maher Kara, a former investment banker at Citigroup. Maher testified at Salman's (D) trial that he shared inside information with his brother Michael to benefit him and expected him to trade on it, and Michael testified to sharing that information with Salman (D), who knew that it was from Maher. Salman (D) was convicted. The court of appeals affirmed, and the United States Supreme Court granted certiorari.

ISSUE: Is an insider's gift of confidential information to a trading relative or friend sufficient by itself to constitute securities fraud?

HOLDING AND DECISION: [Judge not stated in casebook excerpt.] Yes. An insider's gift of confidential information to a trading relative or friend is sufficient by itself to constitute securities fraud. Salman (D) contends that a gift of confidential information to a friend or family member alone is insufficient to establish the personal benefit required for tippee liability, claiming that a tipper does not personally benefit unless the tipper's goal in disclosing information is to obtain money, property, or something of tangible value. The Government (P) counters that a gift of confidential information to anyone, not just a "trading relative or friend," is enough to prove securities fraud. The holding in *Dirks v. SEC*, 463 U.S. 646 (1983), easily resolves the case at hand, as it held that when an insider makes a gift of confidential information to a trading relative or friend, the tip and trade resemble trading by the insider themself followed by a gift of the profits to the recipient. In these situations, the tipper personally benefits because giving a gift of trading information to a trading relative is the same thing as trading by the tipper followed by a gift of the proceeds. Here, by disclosing confidential information as a gift to his brother with the expectation that he would trade on it, Maher breached his duty of trust and confidence to Citigroup and its clients—a duty acquired and breached by Salman (D) when he traded on the information with full knowledge that it had been improperly disclosed. Moreover, contrary to Salman's (D) argument, the *Dirks* gift-giving standard is not unconstitutionally vague, but instead is a simple and clear "guiding principle" for determining tippee liability. [Affirmed.]

ANALYSIS

While Salman's (D) appeal to the Ninth Circuit was pending, the Second Circuit decided that *Dirks* did not permit a factfinder to infer a personal benefit to the tipper from a gift of confidential information to a trading relative or friend, unless there is "proof of a meaningfully close personal relationship" between tipper and tippee "that generates an exchange that is objective, consequential, and represents at least a potential gain of a pecuniary or similarly valuable nature," *United States v. Newman*, 773 F.3d 438 (2014), *cert. denied*, 577 U.S. 874, 136 S. Ct. 242, 193 L.Ed.2d 133 (2015). Pointing to *Newman*, Salman (D) argued that his conviction should be reversed. In its decision in *Salman*, the Supreme Court expressly rejected this approach and overruled *Newman* to the extent that it required that the tipper would have to also receive something of a "pecuniary or similarly valuable nature" in exchange for a gift to family or friends for there to be securities fraud.

Quicknotes

TIPPEE A person who obtains material nonpublic information from another standing in a fiduciary relationship to the corporation that is the subject of such information.

TIPPER A person standing in a fiduciary duty to a corporation who discloses material nonpublic information for personal benefit.

United States v. O'Hagan

Federal government (P) v. Lawyer (D)

521 U.S. 642 (1997)

NATURE OF CASE: Appeal of the reversal of convictions for violations of § 10(b) and § 14(e) of the Securities Exchange Act.

FACT SUMMARY: O'Hagan (D) began purchasing call options on Pillsbury stock when his law firm was retained to handle a potential tender offer by Grand Met for Pillsbury stock. When the tender offer was announced, O'Hagan (D) sold his options, profiting by more than $4.3 million.

RULE OF LAW

(1) A person who trades in securities for personal profit, using confidential information misappropriated in breach of a fiduciary duty to the source of the information, is guilty of violating Securities Exchange Act § 10(b) and Rule 10b-5.

(2) The Securities and Exchange Commission (SEC) did not exceed its rulemaking authority by promulgating Rule 14e-3(a), which prohibits trading on undisclosed information in a tender offer situation, even where the person has no fiduciary duty to disclose the information.

FACTS: Dorsey & Whitney, a law firm, was retained by Grand Metropolitan PLC (Grand Met) as counsel in a proposed tender offer for the stock of Pillsbury. O'Hagan (D), a partner in Dorsey & Whitney, was not assigned to the case. However, during the course of the representation, O'Hagan (D) purchased a total of 2,500 Pillsbury call options and 5,000 shares of common stock. Following the announcement of the tender offer, he sold his interests, at a profit of more than $4.3 million. The SEC (P) commenced an investigation of O'Hagan (D) and indicted him on fifty-seven counts of mail and securities fraud, fraudulent trading, and money laundering. He was convicted on all fifty-seven counts and sentenced to forty-one months of imprisonment. The Eighth Circuit Court of Appeals reversed all the convictions on the basis that Rule 10b-5 liability may not be based on a misappropriation theory. Furthermore, the court held that SEC Rule 14e-3(a) was beyond the scope of the SEC's (P) rulemaking power. As a result, none of the convictions could stand since they were based on the underlying securities fraud violations. The United States Supreme Court granted certiori to determine the propriety of the misappropriation theory, and the authority of the SEC (P) to promulgate Rule 14e-3(a).

ISSUE:

(1) Is a person who trades in securities for personal profit, using confidential information misappropriated in breach of a fiduciary duty to the source of the information, guilty of violating Securities Exchange Act § 10(b) and Rule 10b-5?

(2) Did the SEC exceed its rulemaking authority by promulgating Rule 14e-3(a), which prohibits trading on nondisclosed information in a tender offer situation, even where the person has no fiduciary duty to disclose the information?

HOLDING AND DECISION: [Judge not stated in casebook excerpt.]

(1) Yes. A person who trades in securities for personal profit, using confidential information misappropriated in breach of a fiduciary duty to the source of the information, is guilty of violating Securities Exchange Act § 10(b) and Rule 10b-5. Section 10(b) prohibits the use of any deceptive device in conjunction with the purchase or sale of securities. The "traditional" theory holds an insider liable for trading in securities of their corporation based on relevant, nonpublic information. Such trading satisfies the requirement of deception due to the relationship of trust and confidence reposed in the insider by virtue of their position. Such entrustment requires the insider to disclose or abstain from trading in the securities of the corporation in order to protect unsuspecting shareholders. This duty applies to officers and directors, as well as to anyone else who acts in a fiduciary capacity towards the corporation, including attorneys, accountants, and consultants. In contrast, the "misappropriation" theory holds a person liable for the misappropriation of material, nonpublic information for the purpose of trading thereon, in breach of a fiduciary duty due to the provider of the information. The misappropriation theory extends liability to include corporate outsiders who owe no duty to the shareholders of the corporation, but who nonetheless have access to the confidential information by virtue of their fiduciary position. A fiduciary's undisclosed, self-serving use of a principal's information to purchase or sell securities, in breach of a duty of loyalty and confidentiality, defrauds the principal of the exclusive use of that information. O'Hagan (D) did not owe a duty to the

Continued on next page.

shareholders of Pillsbury since he was not an attorney involved in the case, but he owed a duty of loyalty and confidentiality to his law firm and the firm's client. O'Hagan (D) took information that was the exclusive property of the client and used it to make securities trades. His actions fall squarely within behaviors that the Exchange Act sought to eliminate to "insure the maintenance of fair and honest markets." While prior cases have held that there is no general duty to disclose between members of the marketplace, when a special relationship exists, misappropriation is a sufficient basis upon which to rest a conviction for violations of § 10(b) and Rule 10b-5. Reversed as to this issue.

(2) No. The SEC (P) did not exceed its rulemaking authority in promulgating Rule 14e-3(a), which prohibits trading on undisclosed information in a tender offer situation, even where the person has no fiduciary duty to disclose the information. Under § 14(e) of the Securities Exchange Act, the SEC (P) is granted the authority to pass such rules and regulations as are necessary to prevent the commission of fraud or deception in connection with the sale of securities. The rationale supporting the rule is the protection of uninformed shareholders involved in a potential tender offer situation. The rule imposes a duty on the trader to disclose the confidential information or abstain from trading on it. This rule is consistent with the legislative goal of proscribing fraudulent or deceptive acts in the purchase or sale of securities. The SEC (P) has broad latitude under § 14(e), so that under that section, it may prohibit acts, not themselves fraudulent under the common law or § 10(b), if doing so will prevent fraudulent acts or practices. Moreover, the SEC's (P) assessment that Rule 14e-3(a) is reasonably designed to prevent fraudulent acts is not arbitrary, capricious, or manifestly contrary to the statute, so this assessment is controlling. In reviewing the propriety of SEC (P) regulations, the Court must give great deference to the SEC's (P) judgment absent a patently contrary intent. Reversed as to this issue.

ANALYSIS

Chiarella v. United States, 445 U.S. 222 (1980), which involved securities trades by a printer privy to corporate takeover plans, had left open the questions posed in this case. In *Chiarella*, the Court held that there was no general duty between all participants in market transactions to forgo action based on material, nonpublic information. The Court suggested that a special relationship was necessary to give rise to a duty to disclose or abstain from trading. However, the Court did not specify whether the only relationship prompting liability was the relationship between a corporation's insiders and shareholders. Another issue left undecided until *O'Hagan* was whether misappropriation of information could be a basis for criminal liability. The validity of the misappropriation theory turned on whether it satisfied the requirement of a "deceptive device" under § 10(b). The Court holds that a misappropriator of confidential information necessarily effectuates a deception on the source of that information through his nondisclosure of his intent to trade on it. Such deception involves illusory loyalty to the company that has the exclusive right to use of the information and is equivalent to an act of embezzlement.

Quicknotes

EMBEZZLEMENT The fraudulent appropriation of property lawfully in one's possession.

FIDUCIARY DUTY A legal obligation to act for the benefit of another, including subordinating one's personal interests to that of the other person.

MISAPPROPRIATION The unlawful use of another's property or funds.

RULE 10B-5 It is unlawful to defend or make untrue statements in connection with purchase or sale of securities.

RULE 14E-3(A) Makes it unlawful to make false statements in connection with tender offers.

TENDER OFFER An offer made by one corporation to the shareholders of a target corporation to purchase their shares subject to number, time, and price specifications.

Reliance Electric Co. v. Emerson Electric Co.

Corporation (D) v. Corporate shareholder (P)

404 U.S. 418, *rehearing denied*, 405 U.S. 969 (1972)

NATURE OF CASE: Discretionary review on certiorari of reversal of declaratory judgment finding liability for damages under § 16(b) of the Securities Exchange Act of 1934.

FACT SUMMARY: Reliance Electric Co. (D) argued that since Emerson Electric Co. (P) intentionally disposed of its stock in two separate sales in an effort to avoid liability under § 16(b) of the Securities Exchange Act of 1934 as to the bulk of its short-swing profits, the two sales should be treated as one.

RULE OF LAW

When a holder of more than 10 percent of the stock in a corporation sells enough shares to reduce its holdings to less than 10 percent, and then sells the balance of its shares to another buyer within six months of its original purchase, it is not liable to the corporation for the profit it made on the second sale.

FACTS: On June 16, 1967, Emerson Electric Co. (Emerson) (P) acquired 13.2 percent of the outstanding common stock of Dodge Manufacturing Co. (Dodge) pursuant to a tender offer it made in an unsuccessful attempt to take over Dodge. Shortly thereafter, Dodge merged with Reliance Electric Co. (Reliance) (D). Emerson (P), desiring to dispose of its Dodge stock, decided to first sell enough shares to bring its holdings below 10 percent, thereby immunizing the sale of the remainder of its shares from liability under § 16(b) of the Securities Exchange Act of 1934. On August 28, Emerson (P) sold to a brokerage house enough of its stock in Dodge to reduce its holdings to 9.96 percent. The remaining shares were then sold to Dodge on September 11. Reliance (D) then demanded from Emerson (P) all the profits Emerson (P) made on both sales. Emerson (P) then filed an action for a declaratory judgment as to its liability under § 16(b). The district court held Emerson (P) was liable for the profits from both sales. The court of appeals reversed as to the profits from the second sale. The United States Supreme Court granted certiorari.

ISSUE: When a holder of more than 10 percent of the stock in a corporation sells enough shares to reduce its holdings to less than 10 percent, and then sells the balance of its shares to another buyer within six months of its original purchase, is it liable to the corporation for the profit it made on the second sale?

HOLDING AND DECISION: [Judge not stated in casebook excerpt.] No. When a holder of more than 10 percent of the stock in a corporation sells enough shares to reduce its holdings to less than 10 percent, and then sells the balance of its shares to another buyer within six months of its original purchase, it is not liable to the corporation for the profit it made on the second sale. In enacting § 16(b) of the Securities Exchange Act of 1934, Congress chose a relatively arbitrary rule, capable of easy administration, in an effort to take the profits out of a class of transactions in which the possibility of abuse was believed to be intolerably great. Section 16(b) imposes strict liability, regardless of the intent of the insider; and yet Congress did not reach every transaction in which an investor actually relies on inside information. A person avoids liability if he does not meet the statute's definition of "insider," or if he sells more than six months after purchase. Section 16(b) clearly states that a 10 percent owner must be such "both at the time of the purchase and sale . . . of the security involved." This language clearly contemplates that a person might sell enough shares to bring their holdings below 10 percent, and later, but still within six months, sell additional shares free from liability under the statute. In fact, commentators on the securities laws have recommended this exact procedure for a 10 percent owner who wishes to dispose of their holdings within six months of purchase. Affirmed.

ANALYSIS

Note that under *Foremost-McKesson, Inc. v. Provident Securities Co.*, 423 U.S. 232 (1976), a purchaser who becomes a 10 percent owner only by virtue of the purchase is not subject to § 16(b) of the Securities Exchange Act of 1934. Thus, Emerson (P) would not have been liable for the profit on either sale had its purchase of the stock taken place after the decision in *Foremost-McKesson.*

Quicknotes

COMMON STOCK A class of stock representing the corporation's ownership, the holders of which are entitled to dividends only after the holders of preferred stock are paid.

DECLARATORY JUDGMENT An adjudication by the courts that grants not relief but is binding over the legal status of the parties involved in the dispute.

SECURITIES EXCHANGE ACT § 16(b) Provides that corporations may recover profits realized by an owner of more

Continued on next page.

than 10 percent of shares when that owner buys and sells stock within a six-month period.

STRICT LIABILITY Liability for all injuries proximately caused by a party's conducting of certain inherently dangerous activities without regard to negligence or fault.

Foremost-McKesson, Inc. v. Provident Securities Company

Acquiring company (D) v. Purchased company (P)

423 U.S. 232 (1976)

NATURE OF CASE: Appeal from affirmance of summary judgment for plaintiff in declaratory judgment action seeking a declaration of no liability under § 16(b) of the Securities and Exchange Act of 1934.

FACT SUMMARY: Provident Securities Co. (P) brought suit seeking a declaration that it was not liable to Foremost-McKesson, Inc. (D) under § 16(b) of the Securities and Exchange Act of 1934 for any profits it realized on the sale of a $25 million debenture to underwriters.

RULE OF LAW

In a purchase-sale sequence, a beneficial owner must account for profits only if they were a beneficial owner before the purchase.

FACTS: Provident Securities Co. (Provident) (P), a personal holding company, decided to liquidate and dissolve. Foremost-McKesson, Inc. (Foremost) (D) was a potential purchaser, but the parties disagreed as to the form of consideration to be paid. The parties reached a compromise and executed a purchase agreement, providing that Foremost (D) would buy two-thirds of Provident's (P) assets for $4.25 million in cash and $49.75 million in convertible subordinated debentures. The agreement also provided Foremost (D) would register $25 million and participate in an underwriting agreement by which the debentures would be sold to the public. Provident (P), Foremost (D), and a group of underwriters executed an underwriting agreement on October 28, after which Provident (P) distributed the cash proceeds to its stockholders and dissolved. Provident's (P) holdings in Foremost (D) debentures on October 20 were large enough to make it a beneficial owner of Foremost (D) within the meaning of section 16. Thus, Foremost (D) could potentially sue Provident (P) to recover any profits realized on the sale of the $25 million debenture to the underwriters under the statute. Provident (P) sued for a declaration that it would not be liable to Foremost (D) under Section 16(b). The district court granted summary judgment for Provident (P) and the court of appeals affirmed. Foremost (D) appealed.

ISSUE: In a purchase-sale sequence, must a beneficial owner account for profits only if they were a beneficial owner before the purchase?

HOLDING AND DECISION: [Judge not stated in casebook excerpt.] Yes. In a purchase-sale sequence, a beneficial owner must account for profits only if they were a beneficial owner before the purchase. Section 16(b) of the Securities and Exchange Act of 1934 does not require that a person purchasing securities placing their holdings above the 10 percent level is a beneficial owner at the time of the purchase so that he must account for their profits realized on the same of those securities within six months. Section 16(b) was intended to prevent corporate officers and directors or the beneficial owner of more than 10 percent of a corporation from profiteering through short-swing securities transactions due to inside information. The section allows a corporation to retain profits realized on a purchase and sale, or sale and purchase, of its securities within six months by a director, officer, or beneficial owner. The last sentence, however, provides that the provision should "not be construed to cover any transaction where such beneficial owner was not such, both at the time of the purchase and sale, or the sale and purchase, of the security involved." Jurisdictions are divided as to whether the "time of sale" means before or immediately after the purchase. The legislative record indicates that this provision was intended to preserve the requirement of beneficial ownership before the purchase. Affirmed.

ANALYSIS

The Court noted that its holding was also confirmed by the legislature's differentiation between short-term trading by shareholders and trading by corporate officers and directors. In the latter case, such trading has greater potential for abuse due to the officers' and directors' extensive involvement in the corporation. Such abuse by shareholders was only in issue when the extent of their holdings permitted them access to insider information. This was not a risk in a situation in which the purchase was made prior to achieving insider status.

Quicknotes

DEBENTURES Long-term unsecured debt securities issued by a corporation.

SECURITIES EXCHANGE ACT § 16(b) Provides that corporations may recover profits realized by an owner of more than 10 percent of shares when that owner buys and sells stock within a six-month period.

CHAPTER 5

Problems of Control

Quick Reference Rules of Law

CHAPTER 5

Stroh v. Blackhawk Holding Corp.

Shareholder (P) v. Corporation (D)

Ill. Sup. Ct., 48 Ill. 2d 471, 272 N.E.2d 1 (1971)

NATURE OF CASE: Appeal from judgment for defendant in shareholder derivative suit seeking to declare shares of stock invalid.

FACT SUMMARY: Shareholders (P) of Class B stock in Blackhawk Holding Corp. (D) claimed that a limitation on their rights at dissolution rendered their shares invalid.

RULE OF LAW

A corporation may prescribe whatever restrictions or limitations it deems necessary in regard to the issuance of stock, provided that it not limit or negate the voting power of any share.

FACTS: Blackhawk Holding Corp.'s (Blackhawk) (D) articles of incorporation provided for the issuance of three million shares of Class A stock and 500,000 shares of Class B stock. Each share was entitled to one vote. The articles also provided that in the case of liquidation, shares of Class B stock were not entitled to dividends. The shareholders (P) sued claiming this limitation on their economic interest in the shares rendered the shares invalid. A lower court rendered judgment for Blackhawk (D), and the state's highest court granted review.

ISSUE: May a corporation prescribe whatever restrictions or limitations it deems necessary in regard to the issuance of stock, provided that it not limit or negate the voting power of any share?

HOLDING AND DECISION: [Judge not stated in casebook excerpt.] Yes. A corporation may prescribe whatever restrictions or limitations it deems necessary in regard to the issuance of stock, provided that it not limit or negate the voting power of any share. State statute defines "shares" to mean the units into which the proprietary interests in a corporation are divided. Contrary to shareholders' (P) contention, "proprietary" does not necessarily denote economic or asset rights. The definition can also encompass the right to participate in the corporation's control, or in surplus profits. Therefore, a corporation may remove the right to earnings and assets from its shares of stock, provided the voting rights are preserved. Under the applicable statute, § 14 of the Illinois Business Corporation Act, a corporation may prescribe the relative rights of its classes of shares in its articles of incorporation, subject to their absolute right to vote. A corporation is expressly afforded the right to establish classes of stock in regards to preferential distribution of the corporation's assets. However, the shareholder's right to vote is guaranteed, and must be in proportion to the number of shares possessed. Here the Class B stock possessed equal voting rights, though it did not possess the right to share in the dividends or assets of the company. Thus the stock is valid. Affirmed and remanded.

DISSENT: (Schaefer, J.) When the economic or asset rights are removed from shares of stock, thus leaving only management rights, there is no longer incentive to manage, as the economic interest is divorced from the managerial power. What is left is not a share of stock.

ANALYSIS

The shareholders (P) and Blackhawk Holding Corp. (D) differed on the definition of the term "proprietary" in respect to the statutory definition of shares. Shareholders (P) defined this as a property right, necessarily encompassing a correlating economic interest in the corporation. However, the court adopted Blackhawk's (D) definition as merely the right to management or control. The dissent considered this disembodied right to manage as insufficient to constitute corporate stock.

Quicknotes

DISSOLUTION Annulment or termination of a formal or legal bond, tie, or contract.

ILL. BUS. CORP. ACT, § 14 Allows the stock in Illinois corporations to be divided into classes.

VOTING RIGHTS A shareholder's right to vote their shares with respect to corporate matters.

Espinoza v. Zuckerberg

Shareholder (P) v. Company CEO and controlling shareholder (D)

Del. Ct. Ch., 124 A.3d 47 (2015)

NATURE OF CASE: Motion for summary judgment in derivative action challenging the fairness of compensation to a company's outside, non-management directors.

FACT SUMMARY: Espinoza (P), a shareholder of Facebook, Inc. (D), contended that a self-dealing transaction related to the compensation of Facebook's (D) outside non-management directors could not be ratified by Zuckerberg (D), Facebook's (D) controlling shareholder and a disinterested director as to the challenged transaction, absent Zuckerberg's (D) compliance with the formalities for ratification set forth in the Delaware General Corporation Law (DGCL).

RULE OF LAW

A disinterested controlling stockholder cannot ratify a transaction approved by an interested board of directors, so as to shift the standard of review from entire fairness to the business judgment presumption, by expressing assent to the transaction informally without using one of the methods the Delaware General Corporation Law prescribes to take stockholder action, i.e., either formally by a vote at a meeting of stockholders or by written consent.

FACTS: Facebook, Inc.'s (D) board approved equity awards and a compensation plan for its outside, non-management directors, who comprised six of the board's eight members. Espinoza (P), a Facebook (D) shareholder, brought a derivative action challenging the fairness of the compensation plan. A couple of months later, the defendant directors (D) moved for summary judgment as to this claim, and, on that same day, Zuckerberg (D), one of the two inside directors who did not receive the challenged compensation, and who is Facebook's (D) controlling shareholder, filed an affidavit in support of the summary judgment motion declaring that he ratified the compensation, and would have done so formally at a stockholder vote or if presented with a written consent. Espinoza (P) argued that such informal ratification was insufficient to transform the standard of review from entire fairness to the business judgment presumption, and that only shareholder ratification made under Delaware General Corporation Law (DGCL) § 228, either through a shareholder vote or written consent, would suffice. The defendant directors (D) countered that Zuckerberg's (D) informal ratification was sufficient to bring the board action within the business judgment rule, as there was no case or statute that required a formal stockholder vote or written consent to effect ratification of board action by a controlling, disinterested shareholder. The Delaware Court of Chancery decided the issue.

ISSUE: Can a disinterested controlling stockholder ratify a transaction approved by an interested board of directors, so as to shift the standard of review from entire fairness to the business judgment presumption, by expressing assent to the transaction informally without using one of the methods the Delaware General Corporation Law prescribes to take stockholder action, i.e., either formally by a vote at a meeting of stockholders or by written consent?

HOLDING AND DECISION: [Judge not stated in casebook excerpt.] No. A disinterested controlling stockholder cannot ratify a transaction approved by an interested board of directors, so as to shift the standard of review from entire fairness to the business judgment presumption, by expressing assent to the transaction informally without using one of the methods the Delaware General Corporation Law (DGCL) prescribes to take stockholder action, i.e., either formally by a vote at a meeting of stockholders or by written consent. Under DGCL § 228, unless the certificate of incorporation restricts the use of written consents, any action that may be taken at any annual or special meeting of stockholders may be taken by majority stockholder consent (or whatever other voting threshold applies for a particular act) "without a meeting, without prior notice and without a vote." Significantly, although § 228 permits stockholders to take action by written consent without prior notice, prompt notice of the taking of the corporate action by written consent must be provided to the non-consenting stockholders so as to ensure some level of transparency for non-consenting stockholders. Thus, the requirements of § 228 must be strictly complied with if any semblance of corporate order is to be maintained. Although neither case law nor statute permit or preclude ratification by informal means, it is noteworthy that many Delaware courts that have used stockholder ratification to apply the business judgment rule or to cure unauthorized conduct have done so when the act of ratification occurred at a formal meeting of stockholders. More importantly, references in existing case law to ratification in the context of a stockholder "vote," as well as policy considerations underlying the provisions of the DGCL for taking stockholder action, support the conclusion that adherence to formalities should be required in this context. To hold

Continued on next page.

otherwise, by permitting ratification absent adherence to corporate formalities, would impinge on the rights of minority stockholders. In traditional agency relationships, a single principal's ratification of an agent's conduct comes at a cost to that principal only. However, in the corporate context, the ratification decisions of a controlling stockholder affect the minority stockholders. Although minority stockholders have no power to alter a controlling stockholder's binding decisions absent a fiduciary breach, they are entitled to the benefits of the formalities imposed by the DGCL, including prompt notification under § 228(e). This requirement promotes transparency and enables minority stockholders to stay abreast of corporate decision making and maintain the accountability of boards of directors and controlling stockholders. Accordingly, even if a controlling shareholder manifests a clear intent to ratify a decision outside of a stockholder meeting, the ratification will not be effective unless it complies with the technical requirements of § 228. Applying this rule here, Zuckerberg's (D) attempted ratification was insufficient, and the entire fairness standard of review applies. Because the directors (D) have not demonstrated as yet the entire fairness of the challenged compensation decisions, their motion for summary judgment is denied. [Espinoza (P) had also asserted a claim for corporate waste, but the court concluded that he failed to adequately state the claim, and, therefore, the court dismissed it.]

ANALYSIS

This case presented an issue of first impression. The Court of Chancery rejected the argument made by the defendants that common-law ratification rules should apply in the corporate context and also rejected their argument that although formal processes such as a stockholder vote or a written consent can be convenient methods of ratification for groups of stockholders, who may suffer from collective action difficulties, such formalities are not necessary for a controlling stockholder whose will can be clearly expressed without formalities. In rejecting these arguments, the Court of Chancery emphasized that once the statutory framework is removed, the possibilities for ambiguity in expressing approval are seemingly limitless, and that such an approach would require directors, stockholders, and courts to engage in the inefficient exercise of divining the intentions of a controlling stockholder, and would cut away at the certainty and precision that make the formalities of stockholder meetings or statutorily compliant written consents beneficial. The Court also observed that the rights of a controlling stockholder as a stockholder are no greater than the rights of any other stockholder, other than that the controlling shareholder simply holds more voting power. The court reasoned that, consequently, just as a majority group of stockholders must follow the requirements of Delaware General Corporation Law § 228 in fairness to the minority stockholders, a single holder of a majority of voting power must do so as well.

Quicknotes

BUSINESS JUDGMENT RULE Standard of review that presumes that in making a business decision, the directors of a corporation acted on an informed basis, in good faith, and in the honest belief that the action taken was in the best interests of the company.

DERIVATIVE SUIT Action asserted by a shareholder to enforce a cause of action on behalf of the corporation.

ENTIRE FAIRNESS Standard of review that places the burden on a corporate defendant to demonstrate that a corporate transaction is entirely fair to the corporation and its stockholders both as to the transaction's process ("fair dealing") and economics ("fair price").

Rosenfeld v. Fairchild Engine & Airplane Corp.

Shareholder (P) v. Corporation (D)

N.Y. Ct. App., 309 N.Y. 168, 128 N.E.2d 291 (1955)

NATURE OF CASE: Appeal from affirmance of dismissal of a shareholder's derivative suit seeking the return of proxy contest costs.

FACT SUMMARY: Rosenfeld (P) brought a derivative suit to have the $261,522 that had been paid to both sides of a proxy contest returned to the corporation (D).

RULE OF LAW

In a contest over policy, corporate directors have the right to make reasonable and proper expenditures from the corporate treasury for the purpose of persuading the stockholders of the correctness of their position and soliciting their support for policies that the directors believe, in all good faith, are in the best interests of the corporation.

FACTS: $261,522 was paid out of Fairchild Engine & Airplane Corp.'s (D) corporate treasury to reimburse both sides in a proxy contest. Of the $261,522 at issue, $106,000 of corporate funds was spent by the old board of directors in defense of their positions in the proxy contest. The new board paid $28,000 to the old board for the remaining expenses incurred after the proxy contest was over. The new board found this to be fair and reasonable. The new board was paid expenses in the proxy contest. This was ratified by stockholders. Stockholder Rosenfeld (P) admitted the sums were reasonable. Rosenfeld (P), however, argued that they were not legal charges that could be reimbursed and sued to compel the return of the $261,522. The state's intermediate appellate court affirmed the judgment of an official referee, who had dismissed Rosenfeld's (P) complaint, having concluded that this was a contest over corporate policy. Rosenfeld (P) appealed, and the state's highest court granted review.

ISSUE: In a contest over policy, do directors have a right to make reasonable and proper expenditures from the corporate treasury for the purpose of persuading the stockholders of the correctness of their position and soliciting their support for policies that the directors believe, in all good faith, are in the best interests of the corporation?

HOLDING AND DECISION: (Froessel, J.) Yes. In a contest over policy, directors have a right to make reasonable and proper expenditures from the corporate treasury for the purpose of persuading the stockholders of the correctness of their position and soliciting their support for policies that the directors believe, in all good faith, are in the best interests of the corporation. If not, incumbent directors would be unable to defend their positions and corporate policies. As such, the old board was reimbursed for reasonable and proper expenditures in defending their positions. Stockholders also have the right to reimburse successful contestants for their reasonable expenses. As such, the new board was also reimbursed for its expenditures by the stockholders. Affirmed.

DISSENT: (Van Voorhis, J.) Incumbent directors have the burden of going forward with evidence explaining and justifying their expenditures. Only those reasonably related to fully informing stockholders of corporate affairs should have been allowed. Here, however, personal expenses were also allowed, and the case should have been remanded to the trial court to sort out which expenses should have been allowed and which should not. Moreover, as to the expenses paid to the insurgent group, the question is whether those expenses were for a corporate purpose. However, it is very difficult to distinguish between corporate policy questions and those regarding corporate personnel. Sometimes a change in personnel is indispensable to a change in policy; often, the distinction is meaningless.

ANALYSIS

This case reflects the popularity of proxy contests in the 1950s. One of the advantages of proxy contests is that they are considered to be cheaper than tender offers where a bidder offers to buy voting shares at a particular price. Another advantage is that insurgent groups may be reimbursed for their expenses, as in this case. Lastly, proxy contests are often considered successful in contests alleging incompetence.

Quicknotes

PROXY A person authorized to act for another.

SHAREHOLDER'S DERIVATIVE ACTION Action asserted by a shareholder in order to enforce a cause of action on behalf, and in the name, of the corporation.

J.I. Case Co. v. Borak

Corporation (D) v. Shareholder (P)

377 U.S. 426 (1964)

NATURE OF CASE: Appeal from reversal of judgment dismissing, other than as to declaratory relief, a civil action brought by a shareholder against the corporation for violation of federal securities laws prohibiting false and misleading proxy statements.

FACT SUMMARY: Borak (P) was a shareholder of J.I. Case Co. (D). The company's shareholders approved a merger with another corporation, and Borak (P) contended the proxy statements violated federal securities laws and sought private relief.

RULE OF LAW

A federal cause of action is available to a shareholder for rescission or damages with respect to a consummated merger that was authorized pursuant to the use of a proxy statement alleged to contain false and misleading statements in violation of the federal securities laws.

FACTS: The management of J.I. Case Co. (Case) (D) submitted a proposal of merger to the shareholders for their approval. In connection with this proposal, management solicited shareholder proxies in support of the merger. Borak (P) contended that the proxy solicitations were false and misleading in violation of § 14(a) of the Securities Exchange Act of 1934 (the Act), and he sought rescission of the consummated merger plus damages for himself and all other shareholders similarly situated and any other appropriate equitable relief. The district court held that the federal statute authorized only declaratory relief, and any other remedies would have to be sought under state law. Borak (P) appealed, contending that § 27 of the Act authorized a private right of action by implication and that he was not limited to the state courts for other than declaratory relief, and the court of appeals reversed. On further appeal by Case (D), the United States Supreme Court granted certiorari.

ISSUE: Is a federal cause of action available to a shareholder for rescission or damages with respect to a consummated merger that was authorized pursuant to the use of a proxy statement alleged to contain false and misleading statements in violation of the federal securities laws?

HOLDING AND DECISION: [Judge not stated in casebook excerpt.] Yes. A federal cause of action is available to a shareholder for rescission or damages with respect to a consummated merger that was authorized pursuant to the use of a proxy statement alleged to contain false and misleading statements in violation of the federal securities laws. It is clear private parties have a right under § 27 to bring suit for violations of § 14(a). The purpose of § 14(a) is to prevent management or others from obtaining authorization for corporate action through the use of false or misleading proxy solicitations. The Act under which the rule was promulgated authorized the Securities and Exchange Commission (SEC) to enact whatever rules and regulations are deemed necessary to protect both the public interest and interests of shareholders. The congressional mandate to protect the interests of the investors requires an available judicial remedy to enforce that protection. The SEC states that it is not equipped to probe the accuracy of all proxy statements submitted for registration. If the investors' interests are to be protected in the spirit of the congressional mandate, a private right of action for shareholders who believe they have been wronged must be afforded. Since the statute does not provide for specific types of relief, the court must determine for itself what remedies are appropriate to redress the alleged wrong. In this regard, any remedy available to a federal court can be utilized to provide relief for the plaintiff, and such remedies are not limited to prospective relief. To hold that the plaintiff is restricted to declaratory relief in federal courts, with any other relief to be pursued in a state court, could conceivably leave the plaintiff without an effective remedy. Once having obtained the federal declaration of his rights, the plaintiff might find that the state does not recognize the defendant's actions as unlawful. This would leave the plaintiff without a means to enforce his judicially declared rights. The case is remanded to the trial court for a hearing on the merits with relief to be granted abiding the outcome. Affirmed.

ANALYSIS

By completely removing state law from consideration in cases alleging violations of federal securities laws, the court relieved plaintiffs of a tremendous burden in many instances. A large number of jurisdictions have a requirement that the plaintiff post a security for expenses on behalf of the defendant. The posting of such security can be an onerous burden, particularly if the case involves complex issues that would result in prolonged litigation. Had Borak (P) been required to proceed under state law, he would have had to post $75,000. This type of burden might very well stop the plaintiff from proceeding with his case, no matter how meritorious. Further, the court's ruling greatly expands the remedies available to

Continued on next page.

a plaintiff shareholder. Most state statutes limit a shareholder who dissents from a merger to a right of appraisal for his shares. The federal court could conceivably rescind the merger completely if that action was warranted. This decision greatly expanded the effectiveness of the federal securities regulations by providing a broad range of enforcement techniques, notwithstanding that nothing in the Act or the SEC's rules thereunder created an express private cause of action for proxy violations.

Quicknotes

SECURITIES EXCHANGE ACT, § 14(a) Prevents management from obtaining illegal proxies.

Mills v. Electric Auto-Lite Co.

Shareholder (P) v. Corporation (D)

396 U.S. 375 (1970)

NATURE OF CASE: Derivative suit and class action to set aside a merger.

FACT SUMMARY: Mills (P) brought a derivative suit and class action against the management of Electric Auto-Lite Co. (D) and other companies to set aside a merger obtained through allegedly misleading proxy solicitations.

RULE OF LAW

Where a trial court makes a finding that a proxy solicitation contains a materially false or misleading statement under § 14(a) of the Securities Exchange Act of 1934, a stockholder seeking to establish a cause of action under such finding does not have to further prove that their reliance on the contents of the defects in the proxy solicitation caused them to vote for proposed transactions that later proved unfair to their interests in the corporation.

FACTS: In 1963, Electric Auto-Lite Co. (Auto-Lite) (D) sought merger with Mergenthaler Linotype Co. The day before shareholders were to vote on the merger, Mills (P) and other shareholders (P) of Auto-Lite (D) sought an injunction against Auto-Lite's (D) management to stop them from voting proxies obtained by means of an allegedly misleading proxy solicitation. The suit also named American Manufacturing Co., which owned about one-third of Mergenthaler's shares and had voting control of Mergenthaler. Mergenthaler owned about 50 percent of Auto-Lite's (D) common stock and had control of that company. But, since Mills (P) failed to seek a temporary restraining order, the voting on the merger proceeded and the merger was approved. Subsequently, Mills (P) amended his complaint, seeking to set aside the merger and to obtain other relief. The district court found that a two-thirds vote of Auto-Lite's (D) shares was required to approve the merger. Since Mergenthaler and American Manufacturing controlled about 54 percent of Auto-Lite's (D) shares, it was necessary to gain the approval of a substantial minority shareholder vote. At the stockholder's meeting, about 950,000 of 1,160,000 shares were voted in favor of the merger; 317,000 of these votes were obtained by the allegedly misleading proxy solicitation from minority shareholders. The district court found these votes necessary and indispensable to the approval of the merger and granted an interlocutory judgment in favor of Mills (P) on grounds that a causal relationship had been shown between the solicitation and the injury. An interlocutory appeal was taken to the court of appeals. The court of appeals affirmed the district court's conclusion that the proxy statement was materially misleading, but reversed on the causation issue, holding that Mills (P) must further show that there was a causal connection between the injury suffered by Auto-Lite (D) stockholders (P) and the misleading proxy solicitations. The court of appeals held that the causation issue should be determined on the fairness of the terms of the merger. Mills (P) appealed from this reversal. The United States Supreme Court granted review.

ISSUE: Where a trial court makes a finding that a proxy solicitation contains a materially false or misleading statement under § 14(a) of the Securities Exchange Act of 1934, does a stockholder seeking to establish a cause of action under such finding have to further prove that their reliance on the contents of the defects in the proxy solicitation caused them to vote for proposed transactions that later proved unfair to their interests in the corporation?

HOLDING AND DECISION: [Judge not stated in casebook excerpt.] No. Where a trial court makes a finding that a proxy solicitation contains a materially false or misleading statement under § 14(a) of the Securities Exchange Act of 1934, a stockholder seeking to establish a cause of action under such finding does not have to further prove that their reliance on the contents of the defects in the proxy solicitation caused them to vote for proposed transactions that later proved unfair to their interests in the corporation. Where the misstatement or omission in a proxy statement is shown to be material, as is the case here, that determination alone embodies the conclusion that the defective statement was such that it might have been considered important enough by a shareholder to use it as a basis for deciding how to vote. Section 14(a) contains the express requirement that the defect have a significant propensity to affect the voting process. There is no need to add to this requirement, as the court of appeals attempted to do, the further requirement of proof as to whether the defect did in fact have a decisive effect on voting. Where there has been a finding of materiality, a shareholder has made a sufficient showing of causal relationship between the violation of § 14(a) and the resulting injury, but only if there is proof by the plaintiff that the proxy solicitation and not the defect was the deciding link in causing such injury. The court of appeals "fairness test" as a defense to a violation of § 14(a) would confront small shareholders with an added obstacle to establishing a cause of action to a defective proxy statement. Whether or not the merger

Continued on next page.

was fair has no bearing on establishing a cause of action under that section. As held in *J.I. Case Co. v. Borak,* 377 U.S. 426 (1964), the purpose of § 14(a) is the promotion of the free exercise of stockholder voting rights by requiring that proxy solicitations contain explanations of the real nature of the questions for which authority to cast the proxies is sought. In the present case, once the causal relationship of the proxy material and the merger were established at trial—essentially questions of fact—the only related legal issue is whether the facts on which that conclusion was reached were sufficient at law to establish Mills's (P) cause of action under § 14(a). Here, those facts are sufficient. Where the misstatement or omission in the proxy statement is found to be material, as it was found to be here, that conclusion on its own implies that the defect was such that a reasonable shareholder would have considered it important when deciding how to vote. Contrary to the court of appeals' approach, there is no need to require additional proof that the defect actually had a decisive impact on voting. As to the appropriate remedy, this Court held in *Borak* that on finding a violation of § 14(a), remedies must affect the congressional purpose behind the act. Such remedies are not limited to prospective relief but may include retrospective relief based on factors governing relief in similar fraud cases. Possible terms of relief could be the setting aside of the merger or granting other equitable relief with fairness of the merger a contributing factor. But the courts are not required to unscramble a corporate transaction. A merger can't be set aside merely because the merger agreement is a void contract, compelling a conclusion that no enforceable rights are created even when a party is innocent of the violation. But the guilty party is precluded from enforcing the contract against the unwilling innocent party. Thus, the contract becomes voidable at the option of the innocent party. As to monetary relief, if the defect in the proxy solicitations relates to specific terms of the merger, an accounting may be ordered; but if the misleading aspect does not relate to the merger terms, monetary relief is available to shareholders to the extent they can be shown. Concerning the awarding of attorney fees and litigation expenses, although the general American rule does not allow for such recovery, one primary judge-made exception is to award such expenses where a plaintiff has successfully maintained a class action suit benefitting a group of others as he is benefitted. Mills (P) has rendered a substantial service to Auto-Lite (D) shareholders. The benefit furnished all the shareholders here, is enforcement of the proxy statute. Vacated and remanded.

ANALYSIS

The rationale behind § 14(a) is to create an informed electorate of shareholders and, thus, further the ideal of corporate democracy. The Court in the present case realized, however, that the purpose of the rule would be destroyed if oppressive burdens of proof of misuse of proxy statements were placed on shareholders in attempting to establish a cause of action against management. If stockholders in the present case were required to prove that they had actually relied on the false proxy statements, the burden of proof would be so heavy that many potentially valid causes of actions would be dropped before they were even started. This would give management an effective shield against shareholder action and prosecution for misuse of corporate proxy solicitations. The Court in this case refused to encourage such wrongdoing.

Quicknotes

CLASS ACTION A suit commenced by a representative on behalf of an ascertainable group that is too large to appear in court, shares a commonality of interests, and will benefit from a successful result.

MATERIALITY Importance; the degree of relevance or necessity to the particular matter.

PROXY STATEMENT A statement, containing specified information by the Securities and Exchange Commission, in order to provide shareholders with adequate information upon which to make an informed decision regarding the solicitation of their proxies.

SECURITIES EXCHANGE ACT, § 14(a) Prevents management from obtaining illegal proxies.

SECURITIES EXCHANGE ACT, § 29(b) Contracts made in violation of the Act are void.

Lovenheim v. Iroquois Brands, Ltd.

Shareholder (P) v. Corporation (D)

618 F. Supp. 554 (D.D.C. 1985)

NATURE OF CASE: Motion for preliminary injunction.

FACT SUMMARY: Lovenheim (P) sought an injunction barring Iroquois Brands, Ltd. (D) from excluding from its proxy statements a proposed resolution he intended to offer at the upcoming shareholders meeting.

RULE OF LAW

A shareholder proposal can be significantly related to the business of a securities issuer for noneconomic reasons, including social and ethical issues, and therefore may not be omitted from the issuer's proxy statement even if it relates to operations that account for less than 5 percent of the issuer's total assets.

FACTS: Iroquois Brands, Ltd. (Iroquois) (D) was engaged in the business of importing foie gras, and Lovenheim (P), a shareholder, intended to offer a resolution at the next shareholders meeting relating to the procedure used to force-feed geese for production of the pâté de foie gras in France. A rule promulgated by the Securities and Exchange Commission under § 14(a) of the Securities Exchange Act of 1934 required that Iroquois (D) allow information regarding the proposal to be included in proxy materials sent to all shareholders. Iroquois (D) refused to allow information concerning Lovenheim's (P) proposal to be included in the proxy materials being sent in connection with the annual shareholders meeting because its foie gras sales implicated less than .05 percent of its assets, and an exception to the rule thus precluded application of the shareholders proposal rule. Lovenheim (P) asserted that the rule and statute on which it was based did not permit omission simply because a proposal is not economically significant where a proposal has either ethical or social significance, and he sought an injunction in federal court.

ISSUE: Can a shareholder proposal be significantly related to the business of a securities issuer for noneconomic reasons, including social and ethical issues, and may it therefore not be omitted from the issuer's proxy statement even if it relates to operations that account for less than 5 percent of the issuer's total assets?

HOLDING AND DECISION: [Judge not stated in casebook excerpt.] Yes. A shareholder proposal can be significantly related to the business of a securities issuer for noneconomic reasons, including social and ethical issues, and therefore may not be omitted from the issuer's proxy statement even if it relates to operations that account for less than 5 percent of the issuer's total assets. Economic considerations are not the only factors to be taken into account in deciding whether to include information in a proxy statement. In an exception to the general requirement of Rule 14a-8 of the SEC regulations, found in Rule 14a-8(c)(5), management may omit information from a proxy statement if it concerns a matter relating to less than 5 percent of its net earnings and gross sales, or is not "otherwise significant." Accordingly, Lovenheim (P) argues that omission of a shareholder proposal is not permitted merely because the proposal is not economically significant where the proposal has "ethical or social significance." On the other hand, Iroquois Brands (D) argues that because corporations are economic entities, the exception must be interpreted in only economic terms. The issue is a close one, because there is lack of clarity in the exception itself. However, the legislative history provides guidance. In 1983, the SEC adopted the 5 percent test as an objective yardstick in deciding whether information in a shareholder proposal merited inclusion in a proxy statement. In adopting this objective standard, the Commission stated that proposals would be includable notwithstanding their "failure to reach the specified economic thresholds if a significant relationship to the issuer's business" is demonstrated on the face of the proposal. Thus, the history of the rule shows that the meaning of "significant" is not limited to economic significance and factors of noneconomic significance, such as those of ethical and social relevance, may be considered. In light of the ethical and social significance of Lovenheim's (P) proposal and the fact it implicates significant levels of sales, Lovenheim (P) has shown a likelihood of prevailing on the merits with regard to the issue of whether his proposal is otherwise significantly related to Iroquois's (D) business. Lovenheim (P) will suffer irreparable injury without such relief, Iroquois (D) will not suffer any undue harm, and the public interest is served by granting the injunction. Motion granted.

ANALYSIS

The court in this case discussed the requirements for an injunction to issue. First, the proponent must demonstrate a likelihood he will prevail on the merits. Then a determination must be made as to whether plaintiff will suffer irreparable injury without such relief, whether

Continued on next page.

issuance of the requested relief will substantially harm other parties, and the public interest.

Quicknotes

INJUNCTION An equitable remedy requiring a person, entity, or governmental unit to do, or prohibiting that person, entity, or governmental unit from doing, a specific act.

IRREPARABLE INJURY Such harm that because it is either too great, too small, or of a continuing character that it cannot be properly compensated in damages, and the remedy for which is typically injunctive relief.

SECURITIES EXCHANGE ACT OF 1934 Regulates the conduct of shareholder meetings.

Trinity Wall Street v. Wal-Mart Stores, Inc.

Shareholder (P) v. Public corporation (D)

792 F.3d 323 (3d Cir. 2015)

NATURE OF CASE: Appeal from judgment and injunction requiring the inclusion in proxy materials of a shareholder proposal.

FACT SUMMARY: Wal-Mart Stores, Inc. (Wal-Mart) (D) contended that the proxy materials proposed to be included for shareholder consideration by Trinity Wall Street (Trinity) (P), one of its public shareholders, related to its ordinary business operations, and, therefore, was properly excludable under the Securities and Exchange Commission's "ordinary business" rule.

RULE OF LAW

A corporation may exclude a shareholder proposal from proxy materials under Securities and Exchange Commission Rule 14a–8(i)(7) as relating to the corporation's ordinary business where the proposal, even if it raises sufficiently significant social and corporate policy issues, does not transcend the corporation's ordinary business operations.

FACTS: Wal-Mart Stores, Inc. (Wal-Mart) (D), a publicly traded company and the world's largest retailer, sells among its thousands of retail products the Bushmaster AR-15, a type of assault rifle. One of Wal-Mart's (D) shareholders, Trinity Wall Street (Trinity) (P), believing such sale was inconsistent with certain of Wal-Mart's (D) policies, and indicated a lack of Board oversight and a lack of consistent written policies, submitted a proxy proposal requesting that the Board provide oversight concerning the formulation and implementation of policies and standards that determine whether or not the company should sell a product that: (1) especially endangers public safety and well-being; (2) has the substantial potential to impair the reputation of the company; and/or (3) would reasonably be considered by many offensive to the family and community values integral to the company's promotion of its brand. The proposal also requested that such policies be publicly reported. The narrative part of the proposal made clear it was intended to cover Wal-Mart's (D) sale of high-capacity firearms. Trinity's (P) perception that Wal-Mart (D) was taking an unprincipled approach in deciding which products to sell was based on Wal-Mart's (D) policy of not selling adult-rated movie titles or similarly rated video or computer games, not selling to children under 17 R-rated movies or "Mature" rated video games, or not selling music bearing a Parental Advisory Label because of concerns about the music containing strong language or depictions of violence, sex, or substance abuse, on the one hand, but on the other hand continuing to sell high-capacity firearms, notwithstanding that, apparently due to safety concerns, Wal-Mart (D) had stopped selling (1) handguns in the United States; (2) high-capacity magazines separate from a gun; and (3) guns through its website. Wal-Mart (D) obtained a no-action letter from the Securities and Exchange Commission (SEC), thus signaling that there would be no recommendation of an enforcement action against the company if it omitted the proposal from its proxy materials. The no-action letter was based on SEC Rule 14a–8(i)(7), known as the "ordinary business" exclusion rule, which provides that a company may omit a shareholder proposal from its proxy materials if the proposal relates to its ordinary business operations. Trinity (D) thereafter filed suit in federal court, seeking to enjoin Wal-Mart's (D) exclusion of the proposal. The district court ruled for Trinity (P), concluding that the proposal concerned the company's Board (rather than its management) and focused principally on governance (rather than how Wal-Mart (D) decides what to sell), so that related to matters outside Wal-Mart's (D) ordinary business operations. In the alternative, the district court held that even if the proposal did tread on the core of Wal-Mart's (D) business—the products it sells—it nonetheless focused on sufficiently significant social policy issues that transcended the day-to-day business matters of the company, making the proposal appropriate for a shareholder vote. Wal-Mart (D) appealed, and the court of appeals granted review.

ISSUE: May a corporation exclude a shareholder proposal from proxy materials under Securities and Exchange Commission Rule 14a–8(i)(7) as relating to the corporation's ordinary business where the proposal, even if it raises sufficiently significant social and corporate policy issues, does not transcend the corporation's ordinary business operations?

HOLDING AND DECISION: [Judge not stated in casebook excerpt.] Yes. A corporation may exclude a shareholder proposal from proxy materials under Securities and Exchange Commission Rule 14a–8(i)(7) as relating to the corporation's ordinary business where the proposal, even if it raises sufficiently significant social and corporate policy issues, does not transcend the corporation's ordinary business operations. The term "ordinary business" in Rule 14a–8(i)(7) is neither self-defining nor consistent in its meaning across different corporate contexts. Neither the courts nor Congress has offered a corrective. The SEC has explained that the term "ordinary

Continued on next page.

business operations" has been wrongly interpreted to include certain matters that have significant policy, economic, or other implications inherent in them. Thus, to determine whether Trinity's (P) proposal deals with a matter relating to the company's ordinary business operations a two-step analysis is made. Under the first step, the "subject matter" of the proposal is determined. Under the second step, it is determined whether that subject matter relates to Wal-Mart's (D) ordinary business operations. If the answer to the second question is yes, Wal-Mart (D) must still prove that Trinity's proposal does not raise a significant policy issue that transcends the nuts and bolts of the retailer's business. As to the first step, substance rules over form, and, here, regardless of how the proposal was styled—as a request for Board action versus a directive to management—the subject matter of the proposal is its ultimate consequence—here a potential change in the way Wal-Mart (D) decides which products to sell. Thus, the subject matter is not ultimately about corporate governance, but how Wal-Mart (D) approaches merchandising decisions involving products that (1) especially endanger public safety and well-being, (2) have the potential to impair the reputation of the Company, and/or (3) would reasonably be considered by many to be offensive to the family and community values integral to the company's promotion of the brand. A contrary holding—that the proposal's subject matter is improved corporate governance—would allow drafters to evade Rule 14a–8(i)(7)'s reach by styling their proposals as requesting board oversight or review. The second step in the analysis is whether the subject matter of Trinity's (P) proposal relates to day-to-day matters of Wal-Mart's (D) business. It does, since a retailer's approach to its product offerings is the bread and butter of its business, so that, in effect, Trinity's (P) proposal is in reality a referendum on how Wal-Mart (D) selects its inventory. Moreover, a proposal need relate only to a company's ordinary business to be excludable; it need not dictate any particular outcome. Because the subject matter of the proposal concerns Wal-Mart's (D) ordinary business operations, it must next be determined whether the proposal falls within the significant social policy exception to the default rule of excludability for proposals that relate to a company's ordinary business operations. Here, it is fairly evident that the proposal touches on significant societal concerns about gun violence and public safety in an age of mass shootings. Therefore, the next question is whether that policy issue transcends Wal-Mart's (D) ordinary business operations. Because the proposal goes to the core of Wal-Mart's (D) ordinary business operations, i.e., crafting a product mix that satisfies consumer demand, it cannot be said that the issue addressed by the proposal transcends such ordinary business operations. In other words, how a retailer weighs safety in deciding which products to sell is too enmeshed with its day-to-day business, since the essence of a retailer's business is deciding what products to put on its shelves—decisions made daily that involve a careful balancing of financial, marketing, reputational, competitive, and other factors. The emphasis management places on safety to the consumer or the community is fundamental to its role in managing the company in the best interests of its shareholders and cannot, as a practical matter, be subject to direct shareholder oversight. Although shareholders perform a valuable service by creating awareness of social issues, they are not well positioned to opine on basic business choices made by management. This conclusion is consistent with the SEC's approach, which consistently allows retailers to omit proposals that address their product menus. Although Trinity's (P) proposal is not strictly a stop-selling proposal, it still targets the same basic business decision: how to weigh safety risks in the merchandising calculus. That is because the relevant question relative to a retailer, such as Wal-Mart (D), that sells thousands of products is whether the consideration of the risk that certain products pose to its "economic success" and "reputation for good corporate citizenship" is enmeshed with the way it runs its business and the retailer-consumer interaction. The answer to that question is yes in the context of a large retailer. Decisions relating to what products Wal-Mart (D) sells in its rural locations versus its urban sites will vary considerably, and these are quintessentially calls made by management. Wal-Mart (D) serves different Americas with different values. Its customers in rural America want different products than its customers in cities, and that management decides how to deal with these differing desires is not an issue typical for its Board. Whether to put emphasis on brand integrity and brand protection, or none at all, is naturally a decision shareholders and directors entrust management to make in the exercise of their experience and business judgment. For these reasons, the policy issues raised by Trinity's (P) proposal do not transcend Wal-Mart's (D) ordinary business operations, and the proposal is excludable under Rule 14a–8(i)(7). [Reversed.]

ANALYSIS

Rule 14a-8(i)(7) has been interpreted broadly, and the court in this case continues that approach, in an apparent effort to ensure that shareholders do not micromanage day-to-day business operations and decisions. Arguably, the district court's decision could have had troubling ramifications for public companies and manufacturers because it potentially opened the door to the possibility that any lawful product that could draw some social objection would be ripe for shareholder consideration. The Third Circuit in this case foreclosed that possibility.

Quicknotes

ORDINARY COURSE OF BUSINESS The conducting of business in accordance with standard customs and practices.

AFSCME v. AIG, Inc.

Shareholder (P) v. Corporation (D)

462 F.3d 121 (2d Cir. 2006)

NATURE OF CASE: Appeal from denial of injunctive and declaratory relief in action to compel inclusion of a shareholder proposal in a proxy statement.

FACT SUMMARY: The American Federation of State, County and Municipal Employees (AFSCME) (P) contended that its shareholder proposal—to require American International Group (AIG) (D) to amend its bylaws to require AIG (D), under certain circumstances, to publish the names of shareholder-nominated candidates for director positions together with any candidates nominated by AIG's (D) board of directors—could not be excluded from AIG's (D) proxy statement under Securities and Exchange Commission Rule 14a-8(i)(8) as relating to an election.

RULE OF LAW

Under Securities Exchange Commission Rule 14a-8(i)(8), a shareholder proposal does not relate "to an election," and is therefore not excludable from a proxy statement, if it seeks to amend the corporate bylaws to establish a procedure by which certain shareholders are entitled to include in the corporate proxy materials their nominees for the board of directors.

FACTS: The American Federation of State, County and Municipal Employees (AFSCME) (P), a large shareholder of American International Group (AIG) (D), submitted a shareholder proposal for inclusion in AIG's (D) proxy statement for the company's annual meeting that if passed would require AIG (D) to amend its bylaws to require AIG (D), under certain circumstances, to publish the names of shareholder-nominated candidates for director positions together with any candidates nominated by AIG's (D) board of directors. AIG (D) received a no-action letter from the Securities and Exchange Commission's (SEC's) Division of Corporate Finance (Division) indicating that it would not take action against AIG (D) if it excluded the proposal from its proxy statement, on the basis that under SEC Rule 14a-8(i)(8), the proposal could be excluded as relating "to an election." For nearly 16 years, the SEC's interpretation of Rule 14a-8(i)(8) had been that it related only to shareholder proposals used to oppose solicitations dealing with an identified board seat in an upcoming election and rejected the somewhat broader interpretation that the Rule's election exclusion applied to shareholder proposals that would institute procedures making such election contests more likely. The SEC then changed course and, as indicated by its no-action letter to AIG (D), interpreted the Rule to apply to proxy access bylaw proposals. Based on the no-action letter, AIG (D) excluded the proposal from its proxy statement, and AFSCME (P) brought suit seeking a court order compelling AIG (D) to include the proposal in its next proxy statement. The district court denied AFSCME's (P) request for declaratory and injunctive relief and dismissed the action. The court of appeals granted review.

ISSUE: Under SEC Rule 14a-8(i)(8), does a shareholder proposal relate "to an election," and is therefore excludable from a proxy statement, if it seeks to amend the corporate bylaws to establish a procedure by which certain shareholders are entitled to include in the corporate proxy materials their nominees for the board of directors?

HOLDING AND DECISION: [Judge not stated in casebook excerpt.] No. Under SEC Rule 14a-8(i)(8) (the Rule), a shareholder proposal does not relate "to an election," and is therefore not excludable from a proxy statement, if it seeks to amend the corporate bylaws to establish a procedure by which certain shareholders are entitled to include in the corporate proxy materials their nominees for the board of directors. Rule 14a-8(i)(8) is ambiguous. It permits a corporation to exclude a shareholder proposal—a recommendation(s) or requirement(s) that the company and/or its board of directors take some action, which the submitting shareholder(s) intend to present at a meeting of the company's shareholders—if the proposal "relates to an election" for membership on the board. The relevant language, "relates to an election," could be read as creating a distinction between proposals addressing a particular seat in a particular election, and those—such as AFSCME's (P)—that simply set the background rules governing elections generally. It is a plausible reading of the language, which uses the article "an" preceding "election," that the Rule was intended to cover only particular elections, rather than elections generally. It is, however, also plausible that the phrase was intended to create a comparatively broader exclusion, one covering "a particular election or elections generally" since any proposal that relates to elections in general will necessarily relate to an election in particular. Because the Rule itself provides no reason to adopt one interpretation over the other, the Rule is ambiguous on its face. When the language of a regulation is ambiguous, courts typically look for guidance in any interpretation made by the agency that promulgated the regulation in question,

Continued on next page.

and usually defers to that agency's interpretation. Here, however, the SEC has over time rendered two distinctly different and conflicting interpretations of the Rule. The earlier interpretation took a narrower view of the Rule's exclusion, whereas the later interpretation took a significantly broader view of the exclusion. Because the SEC has taken these conflicting views, it does not merit the usual deference reserved for an agency's interpretation of its own regulations. Moreover, the SEC has not provided reasons for its changed position, despite a "duty to explain its departure from prior norms." Therefore, it is appropriate to defer to the SEC's earlier interpretation, which deems proxy access bylaw proposal non-excludable. If the SEC wants to change its earlier position, it should do so by explaining its shift in position or amending the Rule. Reversed.

ANALYSIS

Rule 14a-8(i)(8), also known as "the town meeting rule," is one of the 13 substantive bases upon which a company may rely to exclude a shareholder proposal from its proxy materials. In response to the *AIG* decision, the SEC in 2007 adopted an amendment to Rule 14a-8(i)(8) that codified the agency's more recent interpretation of the rule. The language of the rule, as amended, specifies that a company may exclude a proposal "If the proposal relates to a nomination or an election for membership on the company's board of directors or analogous governing body or a procedure for such nomination or election." This amendment effectively overturned the effect of the *AIG* case. In addition, the adopting release for this rule clarifies that the amended rule text relates only to procedures that would result in a contested election, either in the year in which the proposal is submitted or in subsequent years and does not affect or address any other aspect of the agency's prior interpretation of the exclusion. The agency subsequently further amended Rule 14a-8 so that, currently, shareholders who want proxy access can now propose to amend the corporation's bylaws to permit shareholder nominees to be on the proxy card.

Quicknotes

NO-ACTION LETTER A letter issued by an attorney of a governmental agency stating that if the facts are as stated, the attorney would not advise the agency to prosecute.

CA, Inc. v. AFSCME Employees Pension Plan

[No judicial adversarial parties.]

Del. Sup. Ct., 953 A.2d 227 (2008)

NATURE OF CASE: Questions certified to the state's highest court by the Securities and Exchange Commission in proceeding for a no-action letter.

FACT SUMMARY: The Securities and Exchange Commission was asked to provide a no-action letter to a corporation, stipulating that it would not recommend an enforcement action against the company if the company accepted a shareholder proposal to amend the company's bylaws. The shareholders proposed to amend the bylaws to require the company to reimburse shareholders for expenses incurred in certain elections of directors.

RULE OF LAW

(1) A proposal seeking to require a company to reimburse shareholders for expenses incurred in the elections of directors is a proper subject for inclusion in proxy statements as a matter of Delaware law.

(2) A proposal seeking to require a company to reimburse shareholders for expenses incurred in the elections of directors, if adopted, would cause the company to violate any Delaware law to which it is subject.

FACTS: [This decision answers certified questions to the Delaware Supreme Court that were submitted by the Securities and Exchange Commission (SEC). There are no plaintiffs or defendants.] AFSCME, a CA, Inc. stockholder associated with the American Federation of State, County and Municipal Employees, submitted a proposal for inclusion in proxy materials for CA Inc.'s annual shareholders meeting. The proposal sought to require CA to reimburse expenses incurred by stockholders in elections of directors, provided that at least one nominee was elected. CA argued that the proposal could be excluded pursuant to 1934 Securities Exchange Act Rule 14a-8 because it related to an election of directors, conflicted with Delaware law, was inconsistent with SEC proxy rules, and conflicted with the company's certificate of incorporation, which provided that the management of the company was vested in its board of directors. A no-action request was submitted by the company to ensure that acceptance of the proposal would not result in an SEC enforcement action. The SEC asked the Delaware high court to weigh in on the topic.

ISSUE:

(1) Is a proposal seeking to require a company to reimburse shareholders for expenses incurred in the elections of directors a proper subject for inclusion in proxy statements as a matter of Delaware law?

(2) Would a proposal seeking to require a company to reimburse shareholders for expenses incurred in the elections of directors, if adopted, cause the company to violate any Delaware law to which it is subject?

HOLDING AND DECISION: [Judge not stated in casebook excerpt.]

(1) Yes. A proposal seeking to require a company to reimburse shareholders for expenses incurred in the elections of directors is a proper subject for inclusion in proxy statements as a matter of Delaware law. Both the board of directors and the shareholders of a corporation are empowered by law to adopt, amend, or repeal the corporation's bylaws. However, such power is not coextensive, because only the board has management powers. Well-established Delaware law provides that a proper function of bylaws is not to mandate how the board should decide specific substantive business decisions, but to define the process and procedures by which those decisions are made. Such bylaws are appropriate for shareholder action. Contrary to CA's argument, it cannot be that any bylaw that in any respect might be viewed as limiting or restricting the power of the board of directors automatically falls outside the scope of permissible bylaws. That reasoning, taken to its logical extreme, would result in eliminating altogether the shareholders' statutory right to adopt, amend, or repeal bylaws. Applying these principles here, the AFSCME bylaw, even though couched as a substantive-sounding mandate to expend corporate funds, has both the intent and the effect of regulating the process for electing directors of CA. Therefore, the bylaw is a proper subject for shareholder action.

(2) Yes. A proposal seeking to require a company to reimburse shareholders for expenses incurred in the elections of directors, if adopted, would cause the company to violate any Delaware law to which it is subject. As answered in response to the first certified question, the proposed bylaw does not facially violate any provision of Delaware statutory law or the company's certificate of incorporation. Thus, the issue is whether the bylaw would violate any common-law rule. The bylaw would prevent the directors from exercising their full managerial power

Continued on next page.

in circumstances where their fiduciary duties would otherwise require them to deny reimbursement. The challenged bylaw contains no language or provision that would reserve to CA's directors their full power to exercise their fiduciary duty to decide whether or not it would be appropriate, in a specific case, to award reimbursement at all. AFSCME's argument that it is unfair to claim that the bylaw prevents the CA board from discharging its fiduciary duty where the effect of the bylaw is to relieve the board entirely of those duties in this specific area must be rejected as more semantic than substantive, since it concedes the very proposition that renders the bylaw, as written, invalid: the bylaw mandates reimbursement of election expenses in circumstances that a proper application of fiduciary principles could preclude. This is significant given that one of the most basic tenets of Delaware corporate law is that the board of directors has the ultimate responsibility for managing the business and affairs of a corporation.

ANALYSIS

Following this case, the Delaware legislature enacted new §§ 112 and 113 to the Delaware G.C.L. specifying that bylaws can include provisions requiring a corporation's proxy and proxy solicitation to include individuals nominated by shareholders (§ 112) and providing for the reimbursement by the corporation of expenses incurred in connection with the election of directors (§ 113). The statute is permissive, rather than mandatory, and includes a list of procedures or conditions that may be included. The American Bar Association (ABA) has passed similar provisions in amendments to the MBCA § 2.06 that authorize both shareholder-expense-reimbursement bylaws and shareholder-proxy access bylaws.

Quicknotes

NO-ACTION LETTER A letter issued by an attorney of a governmental agency stating that if the facts are as stated, the attorney would not advise the agency to prosecute.

AmerisourceBergen Corporation v. Lebanon County Employees' Retirement Fund

Wholesale distributor of opioid medication (D) v. Shareholders (P)

Del. Sup. Ct., 243 A. 3d 417 (2020)

NATURE OF CASE: Appeal from order to produce a corporation's books and records in action brought under Section 220 of the Delaware General Corporation Law (DGCL).

FACT SUMMARY: Stockholders (P) of AmerisourceBergen Corporation (AmerisourceBergen) (D)—one of the country's largest opioid distributors that had been investigated by numerous law-enforcement and government agencies and that had spent more than $1 billion in connection with opioid-related lawsuits and investigations—sought to inspect the company's books and records for corporate wrongdoing and mismanagement. In rejecting the inspection demand, AmerisourceBergen (D) contended that the stockholders' (P) stated purpose was improper, and that even if it were proper, it was overbroad. AmerisourceBergen (D) also contended that the stockholders (P) were required to state their objectives for the use of the information they would obtain from inspecting the requested books and records, and that the stockholders had to establish that the wrongdoing they sought to investigate was actionable.

RULE OF LAW

(1) When a stockholder's purpose in making a demand for inspection of books and records pursuant to Section 220 of the Delaware General Corporation Law (DGCL) is to investigate corporate wrongdoing, mismanagement, or waste, the stockholder need not state the ends to which it might use the inspected books and records.

(2) When a stockholder's purpose in making a demand for inspection of books and records pursuant to Section 220 of the Delaware General Corporation Law (DGCL) is to investigate corporate wrongdoing, mismanagement, or waste, the stockholder need not establish that the wrongdoing, mismanagement, or waste is actionable.

FACTS: AmerisourceBergen Corporation (AmerisourceBergen *or* the company) (D), one of the country's largest opioid distributors, had been investigated by numerous law-enforcement and government agencies. In 2007, the federal Drug Enforcement Administration (DEA) determined that AmerisourceBergen (D) had not maintained effective controls to ensure that its distribution of opioids stayed within legitimate channels, and suspended the company's (D) license at one of its distribution centers. Although AmerisourceBergen (D) settled with the DEA and agreed to implement and maintain at all its facilities a compliance program designed to detect and prevent diversion of controlled substances, AmerisourceBergen (D) continued to be the subject of several governmental reports, investigations, and state and federal lawsuits. The company (D) spent over $1 billion in connection with such lawsuits, and analysts estimated it could spend up to $100 billion to reach a global settlement. In 2019, stockholders (P) of AmerisourceBergen (D) served a demand on the company (D) pursuant to Section 220 of the Delaware General Corporation Law (DGCL) seeking to inspect 13 categories of books and records (the Demand). The Demand listed four investigatory purposes: (1) to investigate possible breaches of fiduciary duty, mismanagement, and other violations of law by members of the company's (D) board of directors and management; (2) to consider any remedies to be sought in respect of any breaches of duty, mismanagement, or wrongdoing; (3) to evaluate the independence and disinterestedness of the directors; and (4) to use information obtained through inspection of the company's (D) books and records to evaluate possible litigation or other corrective measures with respect to some or all of these matters. AmerisourceBergen (D) rejected the Demand in its entirety, claiming that the Demand did not state a proper purpose and that, even if the stockholders' (P) purpose were proper, the scope of the inspection was overbroad. AmerisourceBergen (D) also contended that the stockholders (P) were required to state their objectives for the use of the information they would obtain from inspecting the requested books and records, and that the stockholders had to establish that the wrongdoing they sought to investigate was actionable. The stockholders (P) then filed suit in the Delaware Court of Chancery, seeking to compel production of the requested documents. The Court of Chancery determined that the stockholders' (P) purpose was proper, and ordered production of the documents. AmerisourceBergen (D) appealed, and the Delaware Supreme Court granted review.

ISSUE:

(1) When a stockholder's purpose in making a demand for inspection of books and records pursuant to Section 220 of the Delaware General Corporation Law (DGCL) is to investigate corporate wrongdoing,

Continued on next page.

mismanagement, or waste, must the stockholder state the ends to which it might use the inspected books and records?

(2) When a stockholder's purpose in making a demand for inspection of books and records pursuant to Section 220 of the Delaware General Corporation Law (DGCL) is to investigate corporate wrongdoing, mismanagement, or waste, must the stockholder establish that the wrongdoing, mismanagement, or waste is actionable?

HOLDING AND DECISION: [Judge not stated in casebook excerpt.]

(1) No. When a stockholder's purpose in making a demand for inspection of books and records pursuant to Section 220 of the Delaware General Corporation Law (DGCL) is to investigate corporate wrongdoing, mismanagement, or waste, the stockholder need not state the ends to which it might use the inspected books and records. AmerisourceBergen (D) contends that, unless a plaintiff's objectives are explicitly disclosed in a books and records demand, the corporation will be impaired, if not entirely thwarted, in its efforts to evaluate the propriety of the demand's purpose without resorting to litigation. Although this is a question of first impression, this Court has ruled that a stockholder's request to inspect a company's list of stockholders for the purpose of communicating with other stockholders is an inadequate purpose under Section 220, unless accompanied by a statement of the intended communication. The case at bar, however, is distinguishable, because a request to inspect a list of stockholders is fundamentally different than a request to inspect books and records in furtherance of an investigation of corporate wrongdoing. A corporation cannot discern whether the inspection of its list of stockholders for the purpose of communicating with other stockholders is related to the stockholder's interest as a stockholder without a disclosure of the substance of the intended communication. By contrast, when a stockholder investigates meritorious allegations of possible mismanagement, waste, or wrongdoing, it serves the interests of all stockholders, and the purpose is proper. Accordingly, the stockholder seeking inspection is not required to specify the ends to which it might use the books and records. Nevertheless, the stockholder's intended uses are not irrelevant, and it may be advisable, in the interest of enhancing litigation efficiencies, to state the intended uses in the stockholder's demand. In any event, such a statement is not mandatory, and a stockholder making an inspection demand is entitled to pursue a variety of responses to the information it obtains, without being confined by statements made in the demand of the stockholder's objectives or its intended uses of the information.

(2) No. When a stockholder's purpose in making a demand for inspection of books and records pursuant to Section 220 of the Delaware General Corporation Law (DGCL) is to investigate corporate wrongdoing, mismanagement, or waste, the stockholder need not establish that the wrongdoing, mismanagement, or waste is actionable. First, a stockholder may state more than one purpose for inspection and use the information obtained for more than one purpose. Thus, a stockholder may use the information supporting a claim of mismanagement obtained through an inspection for purposes other than bringing litigation. Here, for example, the Demand contemplated the possibility that the stockholders (P) would take action in several ways, not just bringing a derivative action against the company (D). Although inspections for the purpose of investigating mismanagement and wrongdoing have been disallowed when the stockholder's sole objective is to pursue litigation that faces an insurmountable procedural obstacle, such as standing or the statute of limitations, that is not the case here. In the rare cases where litigation is the stockholder's sole objective but an insurmountable procedural obstacle unrelated to the suspected corporate wrongdoing bars the stockholder's path, it cannot be said the stockholder's stated purpose is its actual purpose. In such instances, given the obvious futility of the litigation the stockholder claims to have in mind, the investigation can only be seen as assuaging the stockholder's idle curiosity or a fishing expedition. In all other cases, such as the one at bar, however, the court should defer adjudicating merits-based defenses, and the stockholder need not demonstrate that the alleged mismanagement or wrongdoing is actionable.

[We affirm the Court of Chancery's interlocutory judgment as set forth in its January 13, 2020 Memorandum Opinion and remand for further proceedings consistent with this opinion.]

ANALYSIS

To avoid indiscriminate "fishing expeditions," a bare allegation of possible waste, mismanagement, or breach of fiduciary duty, without more, will not entitle a stockholder to a Section 220 inspection. Rather, a stockholder seeking to investigate wrongdoing must show, by a preponderance of the evidence, a credible basis from which the court can infer there is possible mismanagement as would warrant further investigation. Although not an insubstantial threshold, the credible basis standard is the lowest possible burden of proof. A stockholder need not show that corporate wrongdoing or mismanagement has occurred in fact,

Continued on next page.

but rather the threshold may be satisfied by a credible showing, through documents, logic, testimony or otherwise, that there are legitimate issues of wrongdoing. Once a stockholder has established a proper purpose, the stockholder will be entitled only to those books and records that are necessary and essential to accomplish the stated, proper purpose. Here, the Court of Chancery found that the stockholders (P) had established a credible basis, through strong circumstantial evidence, to suspect that AmerisourceBergen's (D) situation did not result from any ordinary business decision that, in hindsight, simply turned out poorly, but instead may have been the product of the company's (D) violation of positive law. In other words, the stockholders (P) had not engaged in an indiscriminate fishing expedition or out of mere curiosity when making the Demand.

Quicknotes

BREACH OF FIDUCIARY DUTY The failure of a fiduciary to observe the standard of care exercised by professionals of similar education and experience.

BURDEN OF PROOF The duty of a party to introduce evidence to support a fact that is in dispute in an action; made up of the burden of production and the burden of persuasion.

OVERBROAD Refers to a statute that proscribes lawful as well as unlawful conduct.

Crane Co. v. Anaconda Co.

Shareholder (P) v. Company (D)

N.Y. Ct. App., 39 N.Y.2d 14, 346 N.E.2d 507 (1976)

NATURE OF CASE: Appeal from judgment reinstating petition to compel inspection of a corporation's shareholder list.

FACT SUMMARY: Crane Co. (P), a stockholder, demanded access to Anaconda Co.'s (D) shareholder list for the purpose of informing other shareholders of a pending tender offer Crane (P) was planning to make.

RULE OF LAW

A shareholder wishing to inform other shareholders regarding a pending tender offer the shareholder plans to make should be permitted access to the company's shareholder list for that purpose unless the list is sought for an objective adverse to the company or its stockholders.

FACTS: Crane Co. (P) proposed a tender offer of Anaconda Co.'s (D) stock. Crane (P) requested a copy of Anaconda's (D) shareholder list for the purposes of informing other shareholders of the tender offer, and to rebut misleading statements disseminated by Anaconda (D). Crane (P) had acquired over 11 percent of Anaconda's (D) common stock, making Crane (P) Anaconda's (D) single largest shareholder. Anaconda (D) refused to furnish the shareholder list, claiming that Crane's (P) motives were not for a purpose relating to the business of the corporation. The trial court dismissed, but the state's intermediate appellate court reversed. Anaconda (D) appealed. The state's highest court granted review.

ISSUE: Should a shareholder wishing to inform other shareholders regarding a pending tender offer the shareholder plans to make be permitted access to the company's shareholder list for that purpose unless the list is sought for an objective adverse to the company or its stockholders?

HOLDING AND DECISION: [Judge not stated in casebook excerpt.] Yes. A shareholder wishing to inform other shareholders regarding a pending tender offer the shareholder plans to make should be permitted access to the company's shareholder list for that purpose unless the list is sought for an objective adverse to the company or its stockholders. The state's statute permits access to qualified shareholders on written demand accompanied by an affidavit stating the inspection is not unrelated to the business of the company and that the shareholder has not sold stock lists within the previous five years. The pendency of a tender offer necessarily relates to the business of the corporation and to the safeguarding of the shareholders' investment. Anaconda's (D) shareholders should be afforded the opportunity to make an informed judgment regarding the sale. Affirmed.

ANALYSIS

Note that the shareholders' right to examine the corporation's shareholder list is derived from both state statute and the common-law right of inspection. Federal proxy rules do not provide for stockholder access to a corporation's shareholder list; however, they do not preclude the right either. Most states require that the shareholder meet minimum percentage or period of ownership prerequisites, and that the inspection further a "proper purpose."

Quicknotes

BUSINESS CORPORATION LAW, § 1315 Provides that access to shareholder lists must be permitted to qualified stockholdings.

State ex rel. Pillsbury v. Honeywell, Inc.

Stockholder (P) v. Company (D)

Minn. Sup. Ct., 291 Minn. 322, 191 N.W.2d 406 (1971)

NATURE OF CASE: Appeal from district court judgment denying writ of mandamus.

FACT SUMMARY: Stockholder Pillsbury (P) purchased shares in Honeywell, Inc. (D) for the sole purpose of persuading Honeywell (D) to cease its production of munitions for use in the Vietnam War.

RULE OF LAW

In order for a stockholder to inspect shareholder lists and corporate records, the stockholder must demonstrate a proper purpose relating to an economic interest.

FACTS: After learning of Honeywell Inc.'s (D) involvement in the production of munitions for use in the Vietnam War, Pillsbury (P) bought a sufficient number of shares to give him a voice in Honeywell's (D) affairs for the purpose of altering its policies. Pillsbury (P) submitted two formal requests for the inspection of Honeywell's (D) shareholder list and corporate records. Honeywell (D) refused, and Pillsbury (P) initiated suit. The trial court dismissed the petition on the basis that the demand to inspect Honeywell's (D) records was not in furtherance of a proper purpose related to Pillsbury's (P) interest as a shareholder. Pillsbury (P) appealed. The state's highest court granted review.

ISSUE: In order for a stockholder to inspect shareholder lists and corporate records, must the stockholder demonstrate a proper purpose relating to an economic interest?

HOLDING AND DECISION: [Judge not stated in casebook excerpt.] Yes. In order for a stockholder to inspect shareholder lists and corporate records, the stockholder must demonstrate a proper purpose relating to an economic interest. This standard is derived from both Delaware statute and the common law. The requisite of a proper purpose is also necessary to compel shareholder inspection of corporate records other than the shareholder list. A proper purpose constitutes those relating to a shareholder's economic interest in the corporation. In this case, Pillsbury's (P) sole purpose in obtaining access to Honeywell's (D) shareholder list and corporate records was for the furtherance of his personal political views, regardless of any economic implications to himself or the corporation. Affirmed.

ANALYSIS

Note that Pillsbury (P) could have accomplished his goal had his motivation been different. A shareholder with legitimate concerns for the economic implications of Honeywell's (D) armament production on his investment would have a purpose germane to his investment. Likewise, a shareholder concerned with the negative effects of ceasing such production could also request review of Honeywell's (D) records.

Quicknotes

WRIT OF MANDAMUS A court order issued commanding a public or private entity, or an official thereof, to perform a duty required by law.

In re Match Group Inc. Derivative Litigation

[Minority shareholders of controlled subsidiary (P) v. Controlling shareholder (D)

Del. Sup. Ct., 315 A.3d 446, 2024 WL 1449815 (2024)

NATURE OF CASE: Appeal from dismissal of stockholder action challenging the fairness of a controlling shareholder's separation from its controlled subsidiary through a reverse spinoff.

FACT SUMMARY: Minority stockholders (P) of Match Group, Inc. (Old Match) (D) challenged as unfair IAC/InterActiveCorp's (Old IAC's) (D) separation from Old Match (D), its controlled subsidiary, through a reverse spinoff, alleging that Old IAC (D), as the controlling stockholder of Old Match (D), received benefits in the transaction at the expense of the Old Match minority stockholders (P), so that the entire fairness standard of review was applicable. Old IAC (D) countered that the business judgment standard of review was applicable because a separation committee, the majority of members of which were independent, had recommended the separation deal. The Old Match minority stockholders (P) disagreed, contending that because one of the committee's members, Thomas McInerney (D), was not independent or was conflicted, the separation committee failed to function as an independent negotiating body, thus necessitating the application of entire fairness review to the entire transaction.

RULE OF LAW

Where a controlling stockholder stands on both sides of a non-freezeout transaction and receives non-ratable benefits therefrom, the use of a special separation committee, composed of a majority of members who are independent of the controlling stockholder and a minority of members who are not independent, is insufficient to render the committee an independent negotiating body for the purpose of shifting the standard of review from entire fairness to the business judgment rule.

FACTS: IAC/InterActiveCorp (Old IAC) (D) was a Delaware internet and media company. In 1999, Old IAC (D) acquired Match Group, Inc., which owned the Match.com business, a market leader in online dating products in the United States and Europe. In 2009, Old IAC (D) incorporated a new subsidiary, Old Match (D), to hold the Match.com business and the other dating platforms held by Old IAC (D). In 2015, Old Match (D) offered shares to the public through an initial public offering (IPO) of its common stock. In August 2019, Old IAC (D) announced in a letter to its stockholders that it was considering separating from Old Match (D), and the Old IAC (D) board informed Old Match (D) that any transaction would be conditioned from the start upon both the recommendation of an Old Match (D) board special committee and the approval of the holders of a majority of the shares held by Old Match's (D) unaffiliated stockholders. The Old Match board appointed directors Thomas McInerney (D), Pamela Seymon (D), and Ann McDaniel (D) to a "Separation Committee" to assess a proposed transaction. McInerney (D) was Old IAC's (D) former CFO and, at the time, CEO of Altaba, Inc. (formerly Yahoo! Inc.). The Old Match (D) board empowered the Separation Committee to retain its own financial and legal advisors, oversee and consider potential separation transactions with Old IAC (D), and, in its sole discretion, to direct, negotiate, and approve or disapprove any separation transaction. Old IAC (D) proposed the creation of two separate public companies—New IAC and New Match—via a reverse spin-off of Old Match (D). The parties negotiated, respectively, through McInerney (D) and Joey Levin (D), Old IAC's CEO. On November 22, 2019, McInerney (D) and Levin (D) reached a preliminary agreement on the key transaction terms. On December 18, 2019, the parties reached a final agreement, and the Separation Committee recommended that the Old Match (D) board approve the separation transaction ("Separation"). At the time of the reverse spinoff, Old IAC (D) held 98.2 percent of Old Match's (D) voting power through ownership of 24.9 percent of Old Match's (D) common stock, and all of Old Match's Class B high-vote common stock. Barry Diller (D) who was the Chairman, Senior Executive, and a large stockholder of Old IAC (D), supported the final transaction, the key terms of which were:

- New Match would be reclassified into a widely held public corporation with a single class of common stock and no controlling stockholder;
- Old IAC's (D) stockholders would receive stock in New IAC and New Match based on an exchange ratio adjusted for the rest of the consideration comprising the Separation;
- Old Match's (D) minority stockholders would receive, in exchange for one share of their common stock, the right to receive one share of New Match common stock and, at the holder's election either $3.00 in cash or a fraction of a share of New Match stock with a value of $3.00;
- Old Match (D) would issue an $850 million dividend to its existing stockholders, with Old IAC (D) receiving approximately $680 million of that amount because of its equity in Old Match (D). New IAC would retain the dividend proceeds;

Continued on next page.

- New Match would retain and guarantee various Old IAC (D) debt obligations, which were valued at about $1.7 billion;
- New Match would be subject to certain governance restrictions, giving New IAC a degree of control over New Match for the near future; and
- Old IAC (D) would have the right to engage in an equity offering where it would raise $1.5 billion for New IAC by selling shares of Old IAC (D) stock convertible into shares of New Match stock following the completion of the Separation. The proceeds of the equity offering would be transferred into New IAC. At their respective special meetings, the stockholders of Old IAC (D) and Old Match (D) voted in favor of the Separation and its related transactions. On June 30, 2020, Old IAC (D) carried out the Separation, whereby New IAC was spun-off from Old IAC (D). Old Match (D) was merged into a subsidiary held by Old IAC (D), and therefore ceased to exist as a legal entity, and Old IAC (D) was renamed to Match Group, Inc., and reclassified into a corporation with one class of common stock, thereby becoming New Match. Old IAC (D) stockholders received shares in both New IAC and New Match. Old Match (D) minority stockholders received shares in New Match. The New Match minority stockholders thus owned common stock in a widely held and highly leveraged corporation, subject to short-term restrictive governance provisions, and also gained an additional two percent of the Match business. Old IAC (D) stockholders received most of the interest in New Match, as well as shares in a cash-rich corporation with little to no debt, New IAC. Former Old Match stockholders (P) challenged the Separation in the Delaware Court of Chancery, alleging, inter alia, that the Separation was a conflicted transaction in which Old IAC (D), as Old Match's (D) controlling stockholder, stood on both sides of the transaction, that that Old IAC (D) obtained significant non-ratable benefits in the Separation to the detriment of Old Match (D) and its minority stockholders, and that the Separation Committee had been conflicted. The plaintiff stockholders (P) also claimed that this allegedly unfair process yielded an unfair price given to Old Match's (D) minority stockholders, who were left with a "slightly larger piece of a much less substantial pie." The Chancery Court determined that the transaction met the standards for fairness, accordingly applied the business judgment rule standard of review, and dismissed the complaint. In reaching its decision, the Chancery Court found that, although McInerney (D) was conflicted, a majority of the Separation Committee was independent, and that McInerney (D) did not "infect" or "dominate" the Separation Committee process. The Chancery Court also determined that the proxy statement adequately disclosed McInerney's (D) conflicts. The plaintiff stockholders (P) appealed, arguing, inter alia, that the Court of Chancery's analysis was flawed, contending that, if the goal of having a special separation committee is to replicate arm's length negotiation, each committee member must be independent. The Delaware Supreme Court granted review.

ISSUE: Where a controlling stockholder stands on both sides of a non-freezeout transaction and receives non-ratable benefits therefrom, is the use of a special separation committee, composed of a majority of members who are independent of the controlling stockholder and a minority of members who are not independent, sufficient to render the committee an independent negotiating body for the purpose of shifting the standard of review from entire fairness to the business judgment rule?

HOLDING AND DECISION: [Judge not stated in casebook excerpt.] No. Where a controlling stockholder stands on both sides of a non-freezeout transaction and receives non-ratable benefits therefrom, the use of a special separation committee, composed of a majority of members who are independent of the controlling stockholder and a minority of members who are not independent, is insufficient to render the committee an independent negotiating body for the purpose of shifting the standard of review from entire fairness to the business judgment rule. The default standard of review of directors' conduct for compliance with their fiduciary duties is the business judgment rule, whereby the court will not second-guess the decisions of disinterested and independent directors. If the plaintiff rebuts the business judgment rule, the court will apply the entire fairness standard of review, which reviews whether the challenged act or transaction was the product of fair dealing and resulted in a fair price. Fair dealing looks at questions of when the transaction was timed, how it was initiated, structured, negotiated, disclosed to the directors, and how the approvals of the directors and the stockholders were obtained. Fair price looks at the economic and financial considerations of the proposed act or transaction, including all relevant factors such as assets, market value, earnings, future prospects, and any other elements that affect the intrinsic or inherent value of a company's stock. When a controlling stockholder stands on both sides of a transaction and receives a non-ratable benefit, the controlling stockholder bears the burden of demonstrating the most scrupulous inherent fairness of the bargain. This rule applies when a parent company, by virtue of its domination of a subsidiary, causes the subsidiary to act in such a way that the parent receives something from the subsidiary to the exclusion of, and detriment to, the minority stockholders of the subsidiary. With the evolution of the Delaware Supreme Court's precedents in this area, as it now stands, the

Continued on next page.

business judgment rule will apply when: (i) a controlling stockholder conditions a transaction from the start on the approval of both a special committee and a majority of the minority stockholders; (ii) the special committee is independent; (iii) the special committee is fully empowered; (iv) the special committee meets its duty of care; (v) the vote of the minority is informed; and (vi) there is no coercion of the minority. The defendants argue that, outside the context of freeze out mergers, any one of three cleansing mechanisms—approval by (i) a board with an independent director majority; (ii) a special committee of independent directors; or (iii) a majority of the unaffiliated stockholders—suffices to invoke the business judgment standard of review in a conflict transaction. The Court of Chancery agreed with the defendants, finding that notwithstanding McInerney's (D) lack of independence, because a majority of the Separation Committee was independent, and McInerney (D) did not "infect" or "dominate" the separation committee process, the Separation met the requirements for application of the business judgment rule. The plaintiffs, however, contended persuasively that if the goal is to replicate arm's length negotiation, each Separation Committee member must be independent, so that the Chancery Court erred in concluding that only a majority of the Separation Committee had to be independent. To apply the business judgment rule when a controlling stockholder transacts with the corporation and receives a non-ratable benefit, the inherently coercive presence of the controlling stockholder requires it to irrevocably and publicly disable itself from using its control to dictate the outcome of the negotiations to ensure an "arm's-length" outcome. A controlling stockholder's influence is not "disabled" when the special committee is staffed with members loyal to the controlling stockholder. As the Delaware Supreme Court stated in *Kahn v. M & F Worldwide Corp.*, 88 A.3d 635 (Del. 2014) ("*MFW*"), the special committee must be independent, not that only a majority of the committee must be independent. Also, as the Supreme Court also stated, fairness can be equated to conduct by a theoretical, wholly independent, board of directors acting upon the matter before them. Because the complaint pleaded particularized facts that raised a reasonable doubt as to McInerney's (D) independence from Old IAC (D) and, therefore, as to the entire Separation Committee's independence, the Court of Chancery's decision to apply the business judgment rule and dismiss the plaintiffs' claims was erroneous. Reversed.

ANALYSIS

In this case, it seems fairly clear that IAC/InterActiveCorp (Old IAC) (D) had sought to ensure that any legal challenges to the conflicted-controller reverse spinoff would be dismissed at the pleading stage, given that it seemingly sought to comply with the *MFW* requirements by informing Old Match (D) that any transaction would be conditioned from the start upon both the recommendation of an Old Match (D) board special committee and the approval of the holders of a majority of the shares held by Old Match's (D) unaffiliated stockholders. It also seems that counsel for Old IAC (D) underestimated just how exacting the Delaware Supreme Court would be in construing the *MFW* requirements. The Court agreed with the Chancery Court that McInerney (D) could be deemed conflicted because he had a "longstanding" business affiliation with Old IAC (D) and Diller (D)—one developed over a period of decades with "personal ties of respect, loyalty, and affection" that was based on "mutual respect." In this regard, the Court said, "[d]irectors who owe their success to another will conceivably feel as though they owe a 'debt of gratitude' to the individual," and noted that the plaintiffs had adequately pleaded that McInerney (D) may have had such a relationship with Old IAC (D) and Diller (D), so that it was a reasonable inference that he was not independent of Old IAC (D) when negotiating the Separation. Accordingly, going forward in Delaware, counsel in a conflicted-controller transaction should advise that any member of a special committee considering the transaction should be heavily vetted for any potential conflicts based on ties with the controller, even those going back many years, and based on unquantifiable interpersonal qualities such as respect, loyalty, and affection.

Quicknotes

BUSINESS JUDGMENT RULE Standard of review that presumes that in making a business decision, the directors of a corporation acted on an informed basis, in good faith, and in the honest belief that the action taken was in the best interests of the company.

ENTIRE FAIRNESS Standard of review that places the burden on a corporate defendant to demonstrate that a corporate transaction is entirely fair to the corporation and its stockholders both as to the transaction's process ("fair dealing") and economics ("fair price").

INITIAL PUBLIC OFFERING (IPO) Process by which a private company for the first time sells shares of its stock to the public on a stock exchange, thereby becoming a publicly traded company.

NON-RATABLE TRANSACTION Corporate transaction that provides benefits that are not shared equally among all shareholders, often favoring a controlling stockholder.

RATABLE TRANSACTION Corporate transaction that provides benefits that are distributed evenly among all shareholders.

SPINOFF Divestment by a parent company of a subsidiary and its business through the creation of a new, independent entity, the shares of which are distributed to existing shareholders on a predetermined exchange rate, usually pro rata.

Zahn v. Transamerica Corporation

Shareholder (P) v. Corporation (D)

162 F.2d 36 (3d Cir. 1947)

NATURE OF CASE: Appeal from judgment for defendant in action to recover payments to be made upon liquidation of corporation.

FACT SUMMARY: Transamerica Corp. (D), owning a majority of voting stock of Axton-Fisher Tobacco Co. (Axton-Fisher) and thereby controlling the board of directors, had some of Axton-Fisher's stock redeemed so that Transamerica (D) would benefit from the liquidation.

RULE OF LAW

Majority shareholders owe minority shareholders a duty similar to the duty owed by a director, and, when a controlling stockholder is voting as a director, the controlling stockholder violates their duty if they vote for their personal benefit at the expense of the minority stockholders.

FACTS: Axton-Fisher Tobacco Co.'s (Axton-Fisher's) stock was divided into three groups: Preferred, Class A, and Class B. The charter provided that, upon liquidation of the corporation, a set amount was to be paid to the preferred shareholders, with the remainder of the assets to be divided between the Class A and Class B shareholders. The Class A shareholders were to receive twice the amount per share as were the Class B shareholders. The charter also provided that the board of directors could redeem the Class A stock at its option by paying $60 per share and all unpaid dividends to the shareholders. Over a period of time Transamerica Corp. (D) acquired 80 percent of the Class B stock and two-thirds of the overall voting stock of Axton-Fisher and thereby controlled the board of directors. When the value of Axton-Fisher's assets increased greatly, the Transamerica (D) controlled board redeemed the Class A stock and then sold the assets of the corporation, thereby liquidating it and benefiting Transamerica (D), who owned most of the remaining non-preferred stock. The district court ruled for Transamerica (D), and the court of appeals granted review.

ISSUE: Do majority shareholders owe minority shareholders a duty similar to the duty owed by a director, and, when a controlling stockholder is voting as a director, does the controlling stockholder violate their duty if they vote for their personal benefit at the expense of the minority stockholders?

HOLDING AND DECISION: [Judge not stated in casebook excerpt.] Yes. Majority shareholders owe minority shareholders a duty similar to the duty owed by a director, and, when a controlling stockholder is voting as a director, the controlling stockholder violates their duty if they vote for their personal benefit at the expense of the minority stockholders. There are two bases for the maintenance of such a suit. First, a dominant shareholder is held to the same duty as is a director, and when the dominant shareholder benefits from dealings with the corporation, they have the burden of proving good faith of the transaction and fairness to minority interests. Second, when a director votes for the benefit of an outside interest, rather than for the benefit of the shareholders as a whole, there has been a breach of duty. Here, the vote of the board of directors was to benefit Transamerica (D), the majority shareholder, rather than the total shareholders of Axton-Fisher, and, by exercising such power through the board, Transamerica (D) breached its duty as a majority shareholder and is thereby liable to the minority interests. Reversed.

ANALYSIS

This case points up the rule that, in some cases, a majority shareholder owes some fiduciary duty to the minority. (At common law no such duty was recognized.) However, the court makes clear that when a majority shareholder votes purely in their capacity as a shareholder, they may vote with only his self-interest in mind, at the expense of the minority shareholders, without violating any fiduciary duties—otherwise there would be little value in being a controlling shareholder.

Quicknotes

DELAWARE C. § 144 Interested transactions are not voidable if approved in good faith by a majority of disinterested stockholders.

DUTY OF CARE Duty that an officer or director owes to the corporation, by virtue of their fiduciary relationship, to act for the benefit of the corporation.

DUTY OF LOYALTY A director's duty to refrain from self-dealing or to take a position that is adverse to the corporation's best interests.

FIDUCIARY DUTY A legal obligation to act for the benefit of another.

VOTING STOCK Stock that entitles its holders to vote for the corporation's directors and with respect to other matters.

Zetlin v. Hanson Holdings, Inc.

Minority shareholder (P) v. Corporation (D)

N.Y. Ct. App., 48 N.Y.2d 684, 397 N.E.2d 387 (1979)

NATURE OF CASE: Appeal from an order in favor of the defendants in an action involving the sale of majority shares of a corporation.

FACT SUMMARY: When Hanson Holdings, Inc. (D) and the Sylvestri family (D) sold their controlling interest in Gable Industries for a premium price, Zetlin (P), a minority shareholder, brought suit, contending that minority shareholders were entitled to an opportunity to share equally in any premium paid for a controlling interest.

RULE OF LAW

Absent looting of corporate assets, conversion of a corporate opportunity, fraud, or other acts of bad faith, a controlling stockholder is free to sell, and a purchaser is free to buy, that controlling interest at a premium price without the minority shareholders being entitled to share in that premium.

FACTS: Zetlin (P) held a two percent interest in Gable Industries. Hanson Holdings, Inc. (D) and members of the Sylvestri family (D) owned 44 percent of Gable's shares. After the Sylvestri family (D) and Hanson Holdings (D) sold their controlling interest at a premium price per share, Zetlin (P) brought suit, contending that minority stockholders were entitled to an opportunity to share equally in any premium paid for a controlling interest in the corporation. The appellate division disagreed. Zetlin (P) appealed.

ISSUE: Absent looting of corporate assets, conversion of a corporate opportunity, fraud, or other acts of bad faith, is a controlling stockholder free to sell, and is a purchaser free to buy, that controlling interest at a premium price without the minority shareholders being entitled to share in that premium?

HOLDING AND DECISION: [Judge not stated in casebook excerpt.] Yes. Absent looting of corporate assets, conversion of a corporate opportunity, fraud, or other acts of bad faith, a controlling stockholder is free to sell, and a purchaser is free to buy, that controlling interest at a premium price without the minority shareholders being entitled to share in that premium. Certainly, minority shareholders are entitled to protection against abuse by controlling shareholders. They are not entitled, however, to inhibit the legitimate interests of the other stockholders. It is for this reason that control shares usually command a premium price. The premium is the added amount an investor is willing to pay for the privilege of directly influencing the corporation's affairs. Order affirmed.

ANALYSIS

Zetlin's (P) contention would profoundly affect the manner in which controlling stock interests are now transferred. It would require, essentially, that a controlling interest be transferred only by means of an offer to all stockholders, that is, a tender offer. The New York Court of Appeals declared that this would be contrary to existing law and that the legislature is best suited to make radical changes.

Quicknotes

CONTROLLING SHAREHOLDER A person who has power to vote a majority of the outstanding shares of a corporation, or who is able to direct the management of the corporation with a smaller block of stock because the remaining shares are scattered among small, disorganized holdings.

CORPORATE OPPORTUNITY An opportunity that a fiduciary to a corporation has to take advantage of information acquired by virtue of their position for the individual's benefit.

MINORITY SHAREHOLDER A shareholder in a corporation controlling such a small portion of those shares outstanding that the shareholder's votes have no influence in the management of the corporation.

Perlman v. Feldmann

Minority shareholder (P) v. Former controlling shareholder (D)

219 F.2d 173 (2d Cir.), *cert. denied*, 349 U.S. 952 (1955)

NATURE OF CASE: Appeal from a judgment in an action to compel an accounting in the sale of a controlling corporate interest.

FACT SUMMARY: After Feldmann (D) sold his controlling interest in the Newport Steel Corporation, Perlman (P) and other minority stockholders (P) brought a derivative action to compel accounting for, and restitution of, allegedly illegal gains accruing to Feldmann (D) as a result of the sale.

RULE OF LAW

Directors and dominant stockholders stand in a fiduciary relationship to the corporation and to the minority stockholders as beneficiaries thereof.

FACTS: Newport Steel Corporation (Newport) operated mills for the production of steel sheets for sale to manufacturers of steel products. Feldmann (D), the dominant stockholder, chairman of the board of directors, and Newport's president, negotiated a sale of the controlling interest in Newport to a syndicate organized as Wilport Company. A steel shortage existed at the time as a result of demand during the Korean War. Perlman (P) and other minority stockholders (P) brought a derivative action to compel an accounting for, and restitution of, allegedly illegal gains accruing to Feldmann (D) and the other majority stockholders as a result of the sale. The district court found the share price to be a fair one for a control block of stock. Perlman (P) and the others (P) appealed, and the court of appeals granted review.

ISSUE: Do directors and dominant stockholders stand in a fiduciary relationship to the corporation and to the minority stockholders as beneficiaries thereof?

HOLDING AND DECISION: (Clark, C.J.) Yes. Directors and dominant stockholders stand in a fiduciary relationship to the corporation and to the minority stockholders as beneficiaries thereof. However, a majority stockholder can dispose of their controlling block of stock to outsiders without having to account to their corporation for profits. But when the sale necessarily results in a sacrifice of an element of corporate good will and consequently unusual profit to the fiduciary that caused the sacrifice, that fiduciary should account for their gains. In a time of market shortage, where a call on a corporation's product commands an unusually large premium, a fiduciary may not themself appropriate the value of this premium. There need not be an absolute certainty that a corporate opportunity is involved; only a possibility of corporate gain is necessary to trigger the fiduciary duty and recovery for breach of that duty. Hence, to the extent that the price received by Feldmann (D) and the others included such a gain, he is accountable to the minority stockholders (P), who are entitled to a recovery in their own right, instead of in the right of Newport Steel. Reversed.

DISSENT: (Swan, J.) The majority's opinion does not specify exactly the fiduciary duty Feldmann (D) violated, either as a director or as a dominant shareholder. As a dominant shareholder, Feldmann (D) did not have a duty to refrain from selling the stock he controlled. There was also no indication that Wilport would use its newly acquired power to injure Newport, and there is nothing illegal in a dominant shareholder purchasing products made by the company at the same price offered to other customers—which is what the Wilport members did. The majority says that the price paid for the stock included compensation for a "corporate asset," which it describes as "the ability to control the allocation of the corporate product in a time of short supply, through control of the board of directors." If the implication of this is that during tight market conditions a dominant shareholder has a fiduciary duty not to sell his stock to users of the corporation's products who wish to buy a controlling block of stock in order to be able to purchase part of the corporation's output at the same mill list prices as are offered to other customers, such a holding should not stand. Only if Feldmann (D) received value in excess of what his stock was worth, for performing duties he was already under an obligation to perform, should he account for the difference in value. However, the record and district court findings support that Feldmann (D) did not receive such excess value, since a controlling block of stock is worth significantly more than a block without such control. Finally, the majority is incorrect in holding that the shareholders (P) are entitled to recover in their own right instead of in the corporation's right. This holding contradicts the majority's theory that the price of the stock "included compensation for the sale of a corporate asset." If indeed a corporate asset was sold, then the corporation, not its shareholders, should be entitled to the proceeds from the sale of that asset.

ANALYSIS

The court found no fraud, no misuse of confidential information, and no outright looting of a helpless corporation. On the other hand, it did not find compliance

Continued on next page.

with the high standard applied as the rule of law, which other courts have come to expect and demand of corporate fiduciaries. In the words of Judge Cardozo, many forms of conduct permissible in a workaday world for those acting at arm's length are forbidden to those bound by fiduciary ties.

Quicknotes

CORPORATE OPPORTUNITY An opportunity that a fiduciary to a corporation has to take advantage of information acquired by virtue of their position for the individual's benefit.

FIDUCIARY DUTY A legal obligation to act for the benefit of another, including subordinating one's personal interests to that of the other person.

MINORITY SHAREHOLDER A shareholder in a corporation controlling such a small portion of those shares outstanding that the shareholder's votes have no influence in the management of the corporation.

RESTITUTION The return or restoration of what the defendant has gained in a transaction to prevent the unjust enrichment of the defendant.

Essex Universal Corporation v. Yates

Corporation (P) v. Director (D)

305 F.2d 572 (2d Cir. 1962)

NATURE OF CASE: Appeal from summary judgment dismissing action seeking damages for breach of contract.

FACT SUMMARY: A contract calling for a sale of stock in Republic Pictures Corp. (Republic) to Essex Universal Corp. (Essex) (P) included a provision calling for eight of Republic's fourteen directors to resign and be replaced by Essex (P) nominees.

RULE OF LAW

A sale of a controlling interest in a corporation may include immediate transfer of control.

FACTS: Yates (D) was a shareholder and president of Republic Pictures Corp. (Republic), which operated a film studio. He owned less than a majority of shares, but a sufficient amount to exercise de facto majority control. At one point he contracted to sell his interest to Essex Universal Corporation (Essex) (P). The contract called for a transfer of Yates's (D) shares, which equaled roughly 28 percent of voting shares and for the resignation of a majority of Republic's board, to be filled by individuals of Essex's (P) choice. At the last minute, the deal fell through, due to disagreement on the value of shares. Essex (P) filed suit in New York state court, seeking damages for breach of contract. The matter was removed to federal court. Yates (D) successfully moved for summary judgment, arguing that the clause calling for immediate transfer of control was illegal and voided the contract. Essex (P) appealed, and the court of appeals granted review.

ISSUE: May a sale of a controlling interest in a corporation include immediate transfer of control?

HOLDING AND DECISION: (Lumbard, C.J.) Yes. A sale of a controlling interest in a corporation may include immediate transfer of control. It is the law that control of a corporation may not be sold absent the sale of sufficient shares to transfer such control. This is based on the notion that control of a corporation derives from corporate voting and is not a personal right. There can be no question but that if a block of stock is sold which is sufficient to transfer control, the buyer can, through the normal directorate voting process, install a directorate of their choosing. This being so, there is no reason why such transfer should not be assignable upon sale. Transfer of control is inevitable in such a situation, and goals of corporate efficiency will be promoted by allowing it in circumstances such as these. Because of this, the better rule is that immediate transfer of control will not void a sale of a controlling block of stock. Remanded.

CONCURRENCE: (Clark, J.) The action should be remanded for trial, but great discretion should be left to the trial court as to how to deal with the present issue.

CONCURRENCE: (Friendly, J.) In this case, a mass seriatim resignation was directed by a selling stockholder. He filled the vacancies with his henchmen at the dictation of a purchaser and without any consideration of the character of the latter's nominees. This is beyond what the stockholders contemplated or should have been expected to contemplate. And, therefore, the transaction here should be considered illegal. However, this rule should not be applied retrospectively, and would therefore not void this particular transaction.

ANALYSIS

This particular decision produced no majority—each justice wrote his own separate opinion. It is clear Justice Lumbard approved of immediate transfer of control, and Justice Friendly did not. Justice Clark's view is not at all clear, so the precedential value of the present opinion is dubious.

Quicknotes

CONTROLLING SHAREHOLDER A person who has power to vote a majority of the outstanding shares of a corporation, or who is able to direct the management of the corporation with a smaller block of stock because the remaining shares are scattered among small, disorganized holdings.

SERIATIM In order; successively.

Frandsen v. Jensen-Sundquist Agency, Inc.

Minority shareholder (P) v. Corporation (D)

802 F.2d 941 (7th Cir. 1986)

NATURE OF CASE: Appeal from dismissal of action for breach of a stockholder agreement.

FACT SUMMARY: Frandsen (P), a minority shareholder in Jensen-Sundquist Agency, Inc. (D), brought suit after his attempt to exercise his right of first refusal to buy the majority bloc's shares at the offer price in a proposed acquisition failed.

RULE OF LAW

In a transfer of control of a company, the rights of first refusal to buy shares at the offer price are to be interpreted narrowly.

FACTS: Frandsen (P) was a minority shareholder of Jensen-Sundquist Agency, Inc. (Jensen-Sundquist) (D), a holding company whose principal asset was the First Bank of Grantsburg. If the Jensen (D) family majority bloc ever offered to sell its shares, Frandsen (P) had a right to buy the shares at the offer price, or, if he declined, the majority had to buy Frandsen's (P) shares at the same price at which it sold its own shares. First Wisconsin (D) negotiated to acquire Jensen-Sundquist (D) because it wanted the bank. Frandsen (P) then announced that he was exercising his right of first refusal to buy the majority shares. When the deal was restructured, Frandsen (P) brought suit, charging Jensen-Sundquist (D) with breach of the stockholder agreement, and First Wisconsin (D) with tortious interference with his contract rights. The district court granted summary judgment for Jensen-Sundquist (D) and First Wisconsin (D). Frandsen (P) appealed, and the court of appeals granted review.

ISSUE: In a transfer of control of a company, are the rights of first refusal to buy shares at the offer price to be interpreted narrowly?

HOLDING AND DECISION: (Posner, J.) Yes. In a transfer of control of a company, the rights of first refusal to buy shares at the offer price are to be interpreted narrowly. In this case, there never was an offer within the scope of the stockholder agreement. Thus Frandsen's (P) right of first refusal was never triggered. First Wisconsin (D) was never interested in becoming a majority shareholder of Jensen-Sundquist (D); it simply wanted to acquire the bank. Therefore, a sale of stock was never contemplated. A sale of the majority bloc's stock is different from a sale of the holding company's assets. The sale of assets does not result in substituting a new majority bloc, and that possibility was the one that the contract was aimed at—not the sale of assets. If no contractual right of Frandsen's (P) was violated by the transaction, it is difficult to see how First Wisconsin (D) could have been guilty of a tortious interference with his contractual rights. Affirmed.

ANALYSIS

The effect of a right of first refusal is to add a party to a transaction, which increases the costs of transacting exponentially. If all the costs of the more complicated transaction were borne by the parties, it would not be a matter of social concern. However, since some of the costs are borne by the taxpayers who support the court system, the courts are not hospitable to such rights.

Quicknotes

MAJORITY SHAREHOLDER A shareholder of a corporation who holds in excess of 50 percent of the corporation's shares.

MINORITY SHAREHOLDER A shareholder in a corporation controlling such a small portion of those shares outstanding that the shareholder's votes have no influence in the management of the corporation.

RIGHT OF FIRST REFUSAL Allows one to meet the terms of a proposed contract before it is executed.

TORTIOUS INTERFERENCE WITH CONTRACT RIGHTS An intentional tort whereby a defendant intentionally elicits the breach of a valid contract resulting in damages.

Ringling Bros.-Barnum & Bailey Combined Shows v. Ringling

Corporation (D) v. Shareholder (P)

Del. Sup. Ct., 29 Del. Ch. 610, 53 A.2d 441 (1947)

NATURE OF CASE: Appeal from decision ordering a new directors' election.

FACT SUMMARY: Edith Ringling (P) and Aubrey Haley (D) entered into a written agreement to act jointly in regard to all matters pertaining to ownership of their stock.

RULE OF LAW

Shareholders may lawfully contract with each other to vote their stock in a stock pooling arrangement that is not illegal and does not violate public policy.

FACTS: Edith Ringling (P) and Aubrey Haley (D) entered into a voting trust agreement binding them to act jointly in all matters relating to their stock and ownership interests in Ringling Bros.-Barnum & Bailey Combined Shows (D). The contract further provided in the event that the parties failed to reach a joint conclusion in respect to the exercise of their voting rights, the issue would be submitted to an arbitrator and they would vote their stock in accordance with the arbitrator's decision. Prior to the 1946 annual shareholders meeting, Ringling (P) and Haley (D) failed to agree on the selection of a fifth director. Haley (D) was absent from the shareholders meeting, and the arbitrator directed that the stock of both women be voted for an adjournment of 60 days. Notwithstanding that the motion for adjournment was ruled to have carried, the meeting proceeded to the election of directors, and the candidates proposed by the arbitrator were ruled to have been elected. Haley's (D) faction disputed the results, and the director purportedly elected by the Haley (D) faction attempted to join in the voting as a director for different slates of officers. Edith Ringling (P) sued to review the election, contending that Haley (D) was bound to have voted her stock either for an adjournment or for the slate of directors put forth by the arbitrator. The Court of Chancery held that the agreement to vote in accordance with the determination of the arbitrator was valid and ordered a new election before a master. The state's highest court granted review.

ISSUE: May shareholders lawfully contract with each other to vote their stock in a stock pooling arrangement that is not illegal and does not violate public policy?

HOLDING AND DECISION: [Judge not stated in casebook excerpt.] Yes. Shareholders may lawfully contract with each other to vote their stock in a stock pooling arrangement that is not illegal and does not violate public policy. Both the common law and statutes recognize the right of a shareholder to contract away his voting rights while still retaining other rights incident to stock ownership. Similarly, agreements between shareholders purporting to bind the exercise of their voting rights have also been upheld as a valid means of obtaining the advantages of concerted action. The provision submitting the decision to the arbitrator in the case of disagreement or deadlock is consistent with this goal of joint action and is neither illegal nor revocable. The provision is reasonable and does not enable the parties to take any unlawful advantage of any of the non-party shareholders, and it otherwise offends no rule or public policy of the state. Haley's (D) failure to vote consistent with the arbitrator's decision was a breach of this contract. However, contrary to the Court of Chancery's order, the election should not be held invalid. Instead, the appropriate relief is to hold the election valid, but not count Haley's (D) votes. Doing this leaves a vacancy, but such vacancy might be filled in the 1947 election. Order modified in accordance with this opinion.

ANALYSIS

Although the agreement provided for concerted action, the court ruled that there was no express grant of authority to either the other shareholders or to the arbitrator authorizing them to vote the dissenting stockholders' shares in accordance with the majority. The arbitrator was not vested with the power to enforce his decision. Instead, each party to the agreement merely promised to vote her own shares in accordance with the arbitrator's decision. The agreement, however, was silent as to the exercise of the voting rights of one party by the other. Though such agreements to transfer one's voting rights are upheld as valid, this was not what the parties in this case bargained for.

Quicknotes

ARBITRATION An agreement to have a dispute heard and decided by a neutral third party, rather than through legal proceedings.

FIDUCIARY SHAREHOLDER A shareholder who owes a legal obligation to deal fairly with, and not to exploit or oppress, minority shareholders.

VOTING RIGHTS A shareholder's right to vote their shares with respect to corporate matters.

VOTING TRUST An agreement establishing a trust, whereby shareholders transfer their title to shares to a trustee who is authorized to exercise their voting powers.

McQuade v. Stoneham

Minority shareholder (P) v. Majority shareholder (D)

N.Y. Ct. App., 263 N.Y. 323, 189 N.E. 234 (1934)

NATURE OF CASE: Appeal from affirmance of award of damages in action to compel specific performance.

FACT SUMMARY: McQuade (P), officer and director of National Exhibition Company, was voted out of office in violation of a shareholder agreement he entered into with Stoneham (D) and McGraw (D), and McQuade (P) sought specific performance of the agreement.

RULE OF LAW

A shareholder agreement entered into by directors as shareholders is illegal and void where the agreement purports to abrogate the directors' independent judgment.

FACTS: Stoneham (D) owned a majority of shares in the National Exhibition Company, also known as the New York Giants. McQuade (P) and McGraw (D) each purchased seventy shares of Stoneham's (D) stock, and the three shareholders entered into a shareholder agreement to preserve themselves as directors and officers of the corporation. The agreement further prohibited the amendment of salaries, shares, or bylaws of the corporation except with unanimous consent of the three aforementioned parties. The board of directors consisted of seven men including Stoneham (D), McGraw (D), and McQuade (P). McQuade (P) was named treasurer, until he was discharged from the corporation in his capacities both as officer and director. In contravention of the agreement with McQuade (P), Stoneham (D) and McGraw (D) both abstained from voting. The trial court refused specific performance of McQuade's (P) reinstatement but gave him damages for wrongful discharge and a cause of action for future damages, and the state's intermediate appellate court affirmed. The state's highest court granted review.

ISSUE: Is a shareholder agreement entered into by directors as shareholders illegal and void where the agreement purports to abrogate the directors' independent judgment?

HOLDING AND DECISION: (Pound, C.J.) Yes. A shareholder agreement entered into by directors as shareholders is illegal and void where the agreement purports to abrogate the directors' independent judgment. Shareholders of a corporation possess an inalienable right to elect directors and may combine to achieve this purpose. Stockholders may form a voting trust and thereby elect directors who they believe will manage consistent with the stockholders' views. However, shareholders may not enter into agreements interfering with the directors' powers to exercise their independent judgment in the management of the corporation's affairs. There is no evidence in this case that Stoneham (D) and McGraw (D) did not act consistent with their business judgment. They were not trustees for McQuade (P) as an individual, and they were under no legal obligation to deal righteously with him if doing so was contrary to public policy. A second reason the contract is unenforceable is because McQuade (P) was a city magistrate at the time the contract was entered. The law governing magistrates prohibits them from engaging in any business while they are magistrates. Therefore, the performance of the contract constituted a violation of this law. Reversed.

CONCURRENCE AND DISSENT: (Lehman, J.) The majority's second ground for reversal is correct insofar as the contract is unenforceable because it resulted in an employment that was illegal. However, the majority's first ground is incorrect. Shareholders owning a majority of the stock may combine to obtain and exercise any control that a single majority owner could exercise, because what may be done lawfully by one may be done lawfully by a combination of individuals. Here, the contract did not restrict the powers of the board of directors, except regarding the election and remuneration of officers and the adhesion by the corporation to established policies. The directors retain the power to exercise their business judgment, subject to the majority shareholder(s) removal. Thus, in reality, majority stockholders have effective control of the board of directors, except to the extent that the board may check the stockholders when their will is arbitrary. A contract that destroys this check is illegal, but a contract that provides that the stockholders shall use their power to achieve a legitimate purpose is not illegal. The directors may not disregard the best interests of the corporation, but within that limitation, they may be swayed by the wishes of the majority. The contract here is within that limitation, and is, therefore, valid, because it provides for the election of fit officers and adhesion to a particular policy determined in advance; it is designed to protect legitimate interests without prejudicing the corporation.

ANALYSIS

Courts are suspicious of contracts purporting to limit directors' discretion. Such contracts violate a foundation

Continued on next page.

of corporate law that management of a corporation shall be centralized in a board of directors. Courts will decline to validate agreements not approved by all the shareholders in an effort to protect the interests of the minority.

Quicknotes

BUSINESS JUDGMENT RULE Standard of review that presumes that in making a business decision, the directors of a corporation acted on an informed basis, in good faith, and in the honest belief that the action taken was in the best interests of the company.

SPECIFIC PERFORMANCE An equitable remedy whereby the court requires the parties to perform their obligations pursuant to a contract.

VOTING TRUST An agreement establishing a trust, whereby shareholders transfer their title to shares to a trustee who is authorized to exercise their voting powers.

Clark v. Dodge

Minority shareholder (P) v. Majority shareholder (D)

N.Y. Ct. App., 269 N.Y. 410, 199 N.E. 641 (1936)

NATURE OF CASE: Appeal in suit for specific performance of a shareholder agreement.

FACT SUMMARY: Clark (P) and Dodge (D), sole shareholders in two pharmaceutical companies, entered into a shareholders' agreement regarding Clark's (P) continuation as manager and director.

RULE OF LAW

Where the directors are also the sole stockholders of a corporation, a contract between them to vote for specified persons to serve as directors is legal, and not in contravention of public policy.

FACTS: Clark (P) and Dodge (D) owned 25 percent and 75 percent, respectively, of the stock of two pharmaceutical corporations in the business of manufacturing medicinal compounds from secret formulas. Though he was a director, Dodge (D) did not take an active role in the management of the companies. Clark (P) served as director, treasurer, and manager of Bell & Co. and also managed most of the business of Hollings-Smith Company. Clark (P) possessed sole knowledge of the formulas. Both entered a written contract that Dodge (D) should vote so that Clark (P) would continue as director of Bell, he would receive one-fourth net income from the corporations, and that no unreasonable salaries would be paid to other officers of the corporations. Clark in turn (P) agreed to disclose the formula to one of Dodge's (D) sons, and to bequeath his interest in the companies to Dodge's (D) wife and sons should he have no heirs of his own. Clark (P) claimed Dodge (D) breached the contract by failing to continue Clark (P) as a director, preventing Clark's (P) receipt of his income, and paying excessive salaries. Clark (P) sought reinstatement, an accounting, and an injunction against future violations. The state's intermediate appellate court dismissed, on the grounds the agreement was illegal as against public policy, and he appealed. The state's highest court granted review.

ISSUE: Where the directors are also the sole stockholders of a corporation is a contract between them to vote for specified persons to serve as directors legal, and not in contravention of public policy?

HOLDING AND DECISION: [Judge not stated in casebook excerpt.] Yes. Where the directors are also the sole stockholders of a corporation, a contract between them to vote for specified persons to serve as directors is legal, and not in contravention of public policy. The general rule is that the board of directors has the unfettered responsibility of managing the daily operation of the corporation's business. Courts have held that any departure from this standard is illegal as against public policy. However, in a case such as this, where the directors are also the sole shareholders of the corporation, where the agreement does not attempt to sterilize the board, and where there is no harm to anyone, policy concerns of shareholder interference with management decisions are no longer applicable. Reversed.

ANALYSIS

The *Clark* court distinguished its decision from the decision rendered in *McQuade v. Stoneham*, 189 N.E. 234 (1934). The court read that decision as allowing for no variation from the statutory norm that the corporation be governed exclusively by its board of directors, but chose to confine its broad statements to its facts. The court then determined that if a contract presents no harm of injury to anyone, there is no reason for holding it invalid, even though it departs from the general rule.

Quicknotes

INJUNCTION An equitable remedy requiring a person, entity, or governmental unit to do, or prohibiting that person, entity, or governmental unit from doing, a specific act.

SPECIFIC PERFORMANCE An equitable remedy whereby the court requires the parties to perform their obligations pursuant to a contract.

Galler v. Galler

Shareholder (P) v. Shareholder (D)

Ill. Sup. Ct., 32 Ill. 2d 16, 203 N.E.2d 577 (1964)

NATURE OF CASE: Appeal in suit for specific enforcement of a shareholder agreement.

FACT SUMMARY: Benjamin and Isadore (D) Galler entered into a shareholder agreement for the purpose of maintaining themselves and their spouses as officers of the company, and for the continued support and maintenance of their families.

RULE OF LAW

Shareholders in a closely held corporation are free to contract regarding the management of the corporation absent the presence of an objecting minority, and threat of public injury.

FACTS: Benjamin and Isadore (D) Galler, partners who each owned an equal share of stock in Galler Drug Company, entered into a shareholder agreement providing for the support and maintenance of both their families. The agreement further bound the shareholders to elect as directors Isadore, Benjamin, and each of their spouses. Benjamin transferred his shares into his wife, Emma's (P), possession as trustee. Isadore (D) sought to have Emma (P) modify the shareholder agreement and remove herself as a director. She refused and initiated suit. The state's intermediate appellate court held the shareholder agreement void due to indefinite duration, election of officers, salary continuation, and mandatory declaration of dividends. The state's highest court granted review.

ISSUE: Are shareholders in a closely held corporation free to contract regarding the management of the corporation absent the presence of an objecting minority, and threat of public injury?

HOLDING AND DECISION: [Judge not stated in casebook excerpt.] Yes. Shareholders in a closely held corporation are free to contract regarding the management of the corporation absent the presence of an objecting minority, and threat of public injury. The general rule is that majority shareholders in a corporation have the right to select its managers. Shareholders' interests in publicly held corporations must be distinguished from those in closely held corporations. The shareholder in the closely held corporation is in greater need of methods of protecting their investment, as they do not have the option of selling their shares on the open market. Moreover, shareholders in a closely held corporation often also serve as its directors and officers. Consequently, such shareholder agreements are the result of informed decisions, and the safeguards afforded shareholders in a publicly held corporation do not apply. There is no reason to extend the durational limits imposed on voting trusts to a straight voting control agreement in the absence of fraud or disadvantage to minority interests. Likewise, the provision for the election of ascertained persons as officers for a definite period should be upheld. The purpose of the contract to provide for maintenance and support of the two families is a valid purpose, and the provisions for minimum earned surplus requirement and salary continuation are valid means of protecting the corporation's interests. [Reversed.]

ANALYSIS

Some jurisdictions differentiate in their treatment of closely held corporations from other corporate entities. The purpose of the distinction is to alleviate the potentially adverse consequences of the close corporation's failure to comply with statutory regulations, and to promote fair dealing among the parties. Jurisdictions recognizing the distinction hold shareholders in the closely held corporation to the standard of care of partners and impart to them the correlating fiduciary duties of good faith and fair dealing.

Quicknotes

CLOSELY HELD CORPORATION A corporation whose shares (or at least voting shares) are held by a closely knit group of shareholders or a single person.

FAIR DEALING An implied warranty the parties will deal honestly in the satisfaction of their obligations and without intent to defraud.

Ramos v. Estrada

Shareholder (P) v. Director (D)

Cal. Ct. App., 8 Cal. App. 4th 1070, 10 Cal. Rptr. 2d 833 (1992)

NATURE OF CASE: Appeal from judgment for plaintiffs in breach of contract action seeking specific performance.

FACT SUMMARY: Tila Estrada (D) violated a shareholder voting agreement by voting her shares in opposition to the majority.

RULE OF LAW

Voting agreements binding individual shareholders to vote in concurrence with the majority constitute valid contracts.

FACTS: Broadcast Group and Ventura 41 combined to form Television, Inc., for the purpose of establishing a Spanish-language television station. Broadcast Group was owned 50 percent by the Ramoses (P), and the Estradas (D) and four other couples each owned 10 percent. The shareholders of Broadcast Group entered an agreement to vote their shares in Television, Inc., in accordance with the majority view. In addition, the contract placed restrictions on transfer, and treated a shareholder's noncompliance with the voting provision as an election to sell his shares. Tila Estrada (D) voted in opposition to Broadcast Group's majority and declared the agreement void. Ramos (P) sued Estrada (D) for breach of contract. The trial court held the Estradas (D) in breach of contract, ordered their shares in Television, Inc., sold, and restrained them from further voting their shares in violation of the shareholders' agreement. The Estradas (D) appealed, and the state's intermediate appellate court granted review.

ISSUE: Do voting agreements binding individual shareholders to vote in concurrence with the majority constitute valid contracts?

HOLDING AND DECISION: [Judge not stated in casebook excerpt.] Yes. Voting agreements binding individual shareholders to vote in concurrence with the majority constitute valid contracts. Although Broadcast Group did not qualify as a closely held corporation, the contract will be upheld, since voting agreements are valid in various other corporate forms. The agreement purports to limit transferability of shares consistent with the theme of effectuating the majority's interests. It expressly provides that in the event of a member's failure to vote in accordance with the majority, the member effectively elects to sell his shares to the other members. The agreement further provides for the remedy of specific performance in the event of a breach. The Estradas' (D) departure from the majority constituted a breach of the agreement, and, effectively constituted an election to sell their interest in Television, Inc., in accordance with the agreement's buy-sell provisions. Affirmed.

ANALYSIS

Closely held corporations present an unusual situation requiring departure from the corporate norm. Shareholders in large, publicly held corporations necessarily relinquish their control over mundane, daily activities to the board of directors, and function only to elect the board and decide on fundamental transactions. Shareholders who disagree with corporate management may elect a new board or sell their shares. In a closely held corporation, however, shareholders often serve also as directors and officers of the corporation, and do not have available the alternative of selling their shares on the open market. Thus, shareholder agreements regarding the transfer of shares, voting rights, and election of directors are necessary for investors in close corporations to safeguard their investment.

Quicknotes

CAL. CORP. CODE, § 706 An agreement between two or more stockholders in a close corporation may prescribe voting agreements.

CLOSELY HELD CORPORATION A corporation whose shares (or at least voting shares) are held by a closely knit group of shareholders or a single person.

SPECIFIC PERFORMANCE An equitable remedy whereby the court requires the parties to perform their obligations pursuant to a contract.

Wilkes v. Springside Nursing Home, Inc.

Director (P) v. Corporation (D)

Mass. Sup. Jud. Ct., 370 Mass. 842, 353 N.E.2d 657 (1976)

NATURE OF CASE: Appeal from dismissal of claim for damages resulting from shareholders' breach of fiduciary duty.

FACT SUMMARY: Wilkes (P) was terminated as director and officer of Springside Nursing Home, Inc. (D) in violation of a shareholder agreement that each investor would serve as a director and receive a salary from the corporation.

RULE OF LAW

In a closely held corporation, the majority stockholders have a duty to deal with the minority in accordance with a good-faith standard.

FACTS: Wilkes (P), Riche, Quinn, and Pipkin joined forces to purchase a building and operate it as a nursing home. They formed Springside Nursing Home, Inc. (Springside) (D), a corporation in which ownership of the property was vested. Each invested and received an equal share in Springside (D). They agreed that each would serve as a director and take an active role in management. As Springside (D) became profitable, each received a weekly stipend. However, as relations among the parties became strained, Wilkes (P) notified Springside (D) of his intention to sell his shares. The board ceased Wilkes's (P) salary and did not reelect him as director or officer. Wilkes (P) sued for damages based on breach of the fiduciary duty owed him by the other shareholders. The lower court dismissed the complaint. Wilkes (P) appealed, and the state's highest court granted review.

ISSUE: In a closely held corporation, do the majority stockholders have a duty to deal with the minority in accordance with a good-faith standard?

HOLDING AND DECISION: [Judge not stated in casebook excerpt.] Yes. In a closely held corporation, the majority stockholders have a duty to deal with the minority in accordance with a good-faith standard. Determination of whether there was a breach of this duty is decided on a case-by-case basis. The burden of proof is on the majority to show a legitimate purpose for its decision related to the operation of the business. Then the minority may answer that the same objective could be reached through less harmful means. In reaching a determination, the court must balance the legitimacy of the intended purpose against the practicability of the less harmful alternative. In this case, there was no legitimate business purpose proffered for Wilkes's (P) termination, nor was there any evidence in the record legitimizing the majority's action. Here, the duty of utmost good faith and loyalty would require, at a minimum, that the majority consider that their action was in disregard of a long-standing policy of the stockholders that each would be a director of Springside (D) and that employment would be coterminous with stock ownership. Because the issue of damages was not considered below, the case is remanded to the lower court to determine the appropriate damages for the majority's breaches of their fiduciary duties. Reversed and remanded.

ANALYSIS

Courts traditionally decline to intercede in the business affairs of a corporation, such as the election and removal of officers and directors, which are subject to review by the majority of shareholders. Such noninterference has led to abuse of minority shareholders under the close corporation structure. Thus, shareholders in a closely held corporation are held to a similar standard as is required between partners. This is necessary due to the unavailability of a ready market for the minority shareholder to dispose of his shares, and the greater dependency on the corporation to safeguard the shareholders' investment.

Quicknotes

CLOSELY HELD CORPORATION A corporation whose shares (or at least voting shares) are held by a closely knit group of shareholders or a single person.

FIDUCIARY DUTY A legal obligation to act for the benefit of another, including subordinating one's personal interests to that of the other person.

GOOD FAITH An honest intention to abstain from any unconscientious advantage of another.

MINORITY SHAREHOLDER A shareholder in a corporation controlling such a small portion of those shares outstanding that the shareholder's votes have no influence in the management of the corporation.

Brodie v. Jordan

Minority shareholder (P) v. Majority shareholder (D)

Mass. Sup. Jud. Ct., 447 Mass. 866, 857 N.E.2d 1076 (2006)

NATURE OF CASE: Appeal from affirmance of buyout of minority shareholder ordered in action for freeze-out.

FACT SUMMARY: Jordan (D) and Barbuto (D), who collectively were the majority shareholders (D) of Malden, a closely held corporation, contended that Brodie (P) was not entitled to a forced buyout of her shares, even though she had been frozen out by Jordan (D) and Barbuto (D), because this remedy would grant her a windfall and excessively penalize Jordan (D) and Barbuto (D).

RULE OF LAW

A forced buyout is an inappropriate remedy for the freeze-out of a minority shareholder in a close corporation where such a remedy effectively grants the minority a windfall or excessively penalizes the majority.

FACTS: Brodie (P), a minority shareholder in the close corporation Malden, brought suit claiming that Jordan (D) and Barbuto (D), the corporation's two other shareholders who collectively owned a majority share, had "frozen her out" from participation in the company, refused her access to company information, and denied her any economic benefit from her shares. Jordan (D) and Barbuto (D), who did receive economic benefits from their ownership, had also failed to hold an annual shareholders meeting for the previous five years, and hindered Brodie's (P) attempts to sell her interest in the open market. The trial court found that Jordan (D) and Barbuto (D) had breached their fiduciary duties to Brodie (P) and had frustrated her reasonable expectations of benefit. Accordingly, it concluded that they were liable to Brodie (P) for freezing her out. As a remedy, the trial court ordered that Jordan (D) and Barbuto (D) purchase Brodie's (P) shares in the corporation at a price equal to her share of the corporation's net assets, as valuated by an expert, even though neither the articles of organization nor any corporate bylaw obligated Malden or Jordan (D) and Barbuto (D) to purchase Brodie's (P) shares. The state's intermediate appellate court affirmed. The state's highest court granted review.

ISSUE: Is a forced buyout an appropriate remedy for the freeze-out of a minority shareholder in a close corporation where such a remedy effectively grants the minority a windfall or excessively penalizes the majority?

HOLDING AND DECISION: [Judge not stated in casebook excerpt.] No. A forced buyout is an inappropriate remedy for the freeze-out of a minority shareholder in a close corporation where such a remedy effectively grants the minority a windfall or excessively penalizes the majority. The lower courts correctly determined that Brodie (P) had been frozen-out and that Jordan (D) and Barbuto (D) had breached their fiduciary duties to her. Nonetheless, the forced buyout in this case was not an appropriate remedy. The appropriate remedy for a freeze-out should, to the extent possible, restore to the minority shareholder those benefits that she reasonably expects, but has not received because of the fiduciary breach. The remedy should neither grant the minority a windfall nor excessively penalize the majority. Here, the problem with the trial court's remedy was that it placed Brodie (P) in a significantly better position than she would have enjoyed absent the wrongdoing, and well exceeded her reasonable expectations of benefit from her shares. In ordering Jordan (D) and Barbuto (D) to purchase Brodie's (P) stock at the price of her share of the company, the trial court created an artificial market for her minority share of a close corporation—an asset that, by definition, has little or no market value. It was undisputed that neither the articles of organization nor any corporate bylaw obligated Malden or Jordan (D) and Barbuto (D) to purchase Brodie's (P) shares. Thus, there was nothing in the background law, the governing rules of Malden, or any other circumstance that could have given Brodie (P) a reasonable expectation of having her shares bought out. Thus, the trial court's remedy had the perverse effect of placing Brodie (P) in a position superior to that which she would have enjoyed had there been no wrongdoing. Accordingly, the case must be remanded for a remedy that will restore to Brodie (P) those benefits she could reasonably have expected by being a minority shareholder in a close corporation such as Malden. For quantifiable deprivations, monetary damages will be appropriate. Prospective injunctive relief may be granted to ensure that Brodie (P) is allowed to participate in company governance, and to enjoy financial or other benefits from the business, to the extent that her ownership interest justifies. If it is determined that Jordan (D) and Barbuto (D) drained off Malden's earnings from themselves, it may be appropriate to order the declaration of dividends. Reversed and remanded.

ANALYSIS

This case illustrates the benefit of having a shareholder agreement—especially in a close corporation—that requires the corporation to purchase a minority

Continued on next page.

shareholder's shares upon the occurrence of certain events, such as the death of a shareholder, and that otherwise spells out shareholder expectations. Here, Brodie (P) inherited her interest from her deceased husband, who had tried, but failed, to have Malden purchase his shares when his relationship with Jordan (D) and Barbuto (D) deteriorated while he was alive. If the Malden shareholders had a Shareholders Agreement in place prior to the breakdown of their relationship, the costly lawsuit in this case could have been avoided and the parties could have had established expectations regarding the liquidity of their shares. In addition, this decision arguably represents a retreat from the Massachusetts Supreme Judicial Court's seminal decision in *Donahue v. Rodd Electrotype Co. of New England, Inc.*, 328 N.E.2d 505 (1975), which recognized a direct right of action between shareholders of a close corporation, and broad equitable relief, for breach of the fiduciary duty of utmost good faith and loyalty (i.e., "freeze-out" claims). The *Donahue* court remedied a freeze-out by ordering that the minority's shares be purchased on terms as favorable as those that the controlling shareholders offered to another shareholder. However, by adopting a "reasonable expectation" standard for both assessing liability and determining the scope of equitable relief available in freeze-out disputes, the court seems to have aligned itself with the current trend in other jurisdictions.

Quicknotes

FIDUCIARY DUTY A legal obligation to act for the benefit of another, including subordinating one's personal interests to that of the other person.

MINORITY SHAREHOLDER A shareholder in a corporation controlling such a small portion of those shares outstanding that the shareholder's votes have no influence in the management of the corporation.

Smith v. Atlantic Properties, Inc.

Shareholder (P) v. Corporation (D)

Mass. App. Ct., 12 Mass. App. Ct. 201, 422 N.E.2d 798 (1981)

NATURE OF CASE: Appeal from a judgment for the plaintiff in an action for breach of a fiduciary duty owed other stockholders.

FACT SUMMARY: After disagreements arose between the parties who had formed Atlantic Properties, Inc. (D), three (P) of the four shareholders filed suit, seeking a determination of dividends to be paid and the removal of the fourth shareholder (D) as a director.

RULE OF LAW

Stockholders in a close corporation owe one another the same fiduciary duty in the operation of the enterprise that partners owe to one another.

FACTS: Smith (P), Wolfson (D), Zimble (P), and Burke (P) formed Atlantic Properties, Inc. (Atlantic) (D) for the purpose of acquiring real estate. All four held an equal number of shares. A clause in the articles of incorporation had the effect of giving to any one of the four original shareholders a veto in corporate decisions. Wolfson (D) wanted earnings devoted to making building repairs, while the other three wanted a declaration of dividends in order to avoid penalty taxes. Wolfson (D) refused to vote for any dividends, leading to an Internal Revenue Service (IRS) assessment of a penalty tax. Smith (P) and the others (P) filed suit, seeking a court determination of the dividends to be paid, the removal of Wolfson (D) as a director, and an order that Atlantic (D) be reimbursed by Wolfson (D) for the penalty taxes assessed against it and for related expenses. The trial court ruled in favor of Smith (P). Wolfson (D) appealed, and the state's intermediate appellate court granted review.

ISSUE: Do stockholders in a close corporation owe one another the same fiduciary duty in the operation of the enterprise that partners owe to one another?

HOLDING AND DECISION: [Judge not stated in casebook excerpt.] Yes. Stockholders in a close corporation owe one another the same fiduciary duty in the operation of the enterprise that partners owe to one another. In this case, a clause required an affirmative vote of 80 percent of the capital stock issued outstanding and entitled to vote in order to effect a change. Therefore, the minority becomes an ad hoc controlling interest, thus reversing the usual roles of the majority and the minority shareholders. Wolfson (D) requested the 80 percent provision to protect himself from the other shareholders (P). With respect to the past damage caused to Atlantic (D), the trial judge was justified in finding that Wolfson's (D) conduct went beyond what was reasonable. In addition, the court may require information necessary to direct the adoption of a specific dividend and capital improvements policy, and reserve jurisdiction to ensure compliance. Affirmed.

ANALYSIS

The possibilities of shareholder disagreement made the 80 percent provision seem a sensible precaution. However, to what extent may such a veto power, possessed by a minority stockholder, be exercised as its holder may wish without a violation of that shareholder's fiduciary duty? The court found this a difficult area of the law, best developed on a case-by-case basis.

Quicknotes

CLOSELY HELD CORPORATION A corporation whose shares (or at least voting shares) are held by a closely knit group of shareholders or a single person.

FIDUCIARY DUTY A legal obligation to act for the benefit of another, including subordinating one's personal interests to that of the other person.

MINORITY SHAREHOLDER A shareholder in a corporation controlling such a small portion of those shares outstanding that the shareholder's votes have no influence in the management of the corporation.

Ingle v. Glamore Motor Sales, Inc.

Former officer (P) v. Corporation (D)

N.Y. Ct. App., 73 N.Y.2d 183, 535 N.E.2d 1311 (1989)

NATURE OF CASE: Appeal from dismissal of action for wrongful termination and breach of fiduciary duty.

FACT SUMMARY: Ingle (P), a shareholder, officer, and business manager of Glamore Motor Sales (Glamore) (D), was terminated by Glamore's (D) board of directors, and his shares therein repurchased, consistent with a shareholders' agreement he entered with James Glamore.

RULE OF LAW

A minority shareholder in a closely held corporation, who is also employed by the corporation, is not afforded a fiduciary duty on the part of the majority against the termination of their employment.

FACTS: Ingle (P), sales manager of Glamore Motor Sales (D), entered into a shareholders' agreement with owner James Glamore providing for the purchase by Ingle (P) of 22 of James Glamore's shares, with an option to purchase an additional 18. James Glamore agreed to nominate and vote for Ingle (P) as director and secretary of Glamore Motor Sales (D). James Glamore (D) retained the right to repurchase Ingle's (P) shares if he should terminate employment with Glamore Motor Sales (D) for any cause. Ingle (P) later exercised the option, and the parties executed a second shareholder agreement. James Glamore (D) subsequently issued an additional 60 shares, which were purchased by Glamore and his sons. The board of directors then voted to remove Ingle (P) as director and secretary and terminated him as operating manager. James Glamore then exercised his option to repurchase Ingle's (P) shares. Ingle (P) initiated two actions claiming breach of fiduciary duty and breach of contract. The trial court dismissed, the state's intermediate appellate court affirmed, and the state's highest court granted review.

ISSUE: Is a minority shareholder in a closely held corporation, who is also employed by the corporation, afforded a fiduciary duty on the part of the majority against the termination of their employment?

HOLDING AND DECISION: (Bellacosa, J.) No. A minority shareholder in a closely held corporation, who is also employed by the corporation, is not afforded a fiduciary duty on the part of the majority against the termination of their employment. A minority shareholder does not derive from that status protection against their termination in the absence of contractual provision. A court must distinguish between the fiduciary duties owed by the corporation to a minority shareholder as a shareholder, in contrast to its duties owed to the shareholder as an employee. Here Ingle (P) served as an employee at will, there being no evidence of the existence of an employment contract. The common law does not recognize an implied duty of good faith and fair dealing in such employment situations. Ingle (P) voluntarily accepted employment without the protection of a contract as to duration, without any restrictions on the Glamore Motor Sales's (D) corporation's right to terminate him and providing for the repurchase of his shares in the event of such termination. Affirmed.

DISSENT: (Hancock, J.) The majority erroneously applied the employment-at-will rule to a minority shareholder in a closely held corporation situation. An employee's status as a minority shareholder necessitates special safeguards to protect their investment in the corporation.

ANALYSIS

Courts have differed on their treatment of wrongful termination claims brought by minority shareholders in closely held corporations. Jurisdictions recognizing the fiduciary duty of good faith and fair dealing allow the claim on the demonstration that the termination was not justified by good cause, and that it frustrated the expectations of the minority shareholder. Other jurisdictions do not recognize breaches of fiduciary duty in the absence of statutory violations or the breach of express contractual provisions.

Quicknotes

CLOSELY HELD CORPORATION A corporation whose shares (or at least voting shares) are held by a closely knit group of shareholders or a single person.

EMPLOYEE AT WILL An employee who works pursuant to the agreement that either the employee or the employer may terminate the employment relationship at any time and for any cause.

FIDUCIARY DUTY A legal obligation to act for the benefit of another, including subordinating one's personal interests to that of the other person.

GOOD FAITH An honest intention to abstain from any unconscientious advantage of another.

MINORITY SHAREHOLDER A shareholder in a corporation controlling such a small portion of those shares outstanding that the shareholder's votes have no influence in the management of the corporation.

Jordan v. Duff and Phelps, Inc.

Former employee (P) v. Corporation (D)

815 F.2d 429 (7th Cir. 1987)

NATURE OF CASE: Appeal from a grant of summary judgment for the defendants in an action for fraud and breach of fiduciary duty.

FACT SUMMARY: When Jordan (P) heard of a merger announcement that would have increased the value of stock he had sold back to Duff and Phelps (D) upon leaving their employ, he filed suit, asking for damages measured by the value his stock would have had under the terms of the acquisition.

RULE OF LAW

Close corporations buying their own stock have a fiduciary duty to disclose material facts.

FACTS: Jordan (P), a securities analyst employed at will by Duff and Phelps (D), purchased stock in the company at book value. After informing Duff and Phelps (D) that he was resigning to take a new job, Jordan (P) stayed on until the end of the year in order to receive book value for his stock as of the end of that year rather than the prior year. After leaving, Jordan (P) was startled to learn of a pending merger between Duff and Phelps (D) and another company. Under the terms of the merger, Jordan's (P) stock would have been worth a great deal more. Jordan (P) refused to cash the check, demanding his stock back. Duff and Phelps (D) refused. The merger proposal was abandoned in January. Jordan (P) filed suit in March, asking for damages measured by the value his stock would have had under the terms of the acquisition. The district court awarded summary judgment to Duff and Phelps (D). Jordan (P) appealed. The court of appeals granted review.

ISSUE: Do close corporations buying their own stock have a fiduciary duty to disclose material facts?

HOLDING AND DECISION: (Easterbrook, J.) Yes. Close corporations buying their own stock have a fiduciary duty to disclose material facts. Jordan (P) sold his stock in ignorance of facts that would have established a higher value. The relevance of the fact does not depend on how things turn out. Thus, a failure to disclose an important beneficent event is a violation even if things later go sour. The news here that some firm was willing to pay $50 million for Duff and Phelps (D) in an arm's-length transaction allows investors to assess the worth of the stock. Less than a year later, Duff and Phelps (D) sold the firm to a trust for about $40 million. To recover, Jordan (P) must establish that on learning of the merger negotiations, he would have dropped plans to change jobs and stayed for another year, finally receiving payment from the leveraged buyout. A jury would be entitled to conclude that Jordan (P) would have remained. Reversed and remanded.

DISSENT: (Posner, J.) The mere existence of a fiduciary relationship between a corporation and its shareholders does not require disclosure of material information to the shareholders. The contingent nature of Jordan's (P) status as a shareholder, that is, dependent upon his continued employment, negates the existence of a right to be informed and hence a duty to disclose. By signing the stockholder agreement, Jordan (P) gave Duff and Phelps (D), in effect, an option to buy back his stock at any time at a fixed price. That option denied Jordan (P) the right to profit from any information that Duff and Phelps (D) might have about its prospects but preferred not to give him.

ANALYSIS

Doubtless the news of the impending merger was the reason Jordan (P) filed this suit. If one deal for $50 million falls through, another may be possible at a similar price. Just because the first deal for $50 million fell through does not mean that the company is worth only $2.5 million, which was the book value.

Quicknotes

CLOSELY HELD CORPORATION A corporation whose shares (or at least voting shares) are held by a closely knit group of shareholders or a single person.

EMPLOYEE AT WILL An employee who works pursuant to the agreement that either the employee or the employer may terminate the employment relationship at any time and for any cause.

FIDUCIARY DUTY A legal obligation to act for the benefit of another, including subordinating one's personal interests to that of the other person.

MATERIALITY Importance; the degree of relevance or necessity to the particular matter.

Alaska Plastics, Inc. v. Coppock

Corporation (D) v. Minority shareholder (P)

Alaska Sup. Ct., 621 P.2d 270 (1980)

NATURE OF CASE: Appeal from a judgment for the plaintiff in an action to compel purchase of minority shares.

FACT SUMMARY: After Alaska Plastics, Inc. (D) failed to notify Muir (P) of annual shareholders meetings, she filed suit, seeking to compel Alaska Plastics (D) to purchase its stock she had received in a divorce settlement.

RULE OF LAW

The breach of the fiduciary duty of utmost good faith and loyalty owed by majority shareholders to minority shareholders in a close corporation does not support an appraisal remedy whereby the corporation is required to purchase the minority shareholder's stock at fair value.

FACTS: As part of a property settlement related to her divorce from one of Alaska Plastics Inc.'s (D) directors, Muir (P) (who previously had gone by the last name Coppock) received one-sixth of the shares issued by Alaska Plastics (D). Alaska Plastics (D) subsequently failed to notify Muir (P) of annual shareholders meetings, paid her no dividends, did not allow her to participate in the business, and later offered to buy her shares for $15,000. An accountant hired by Muir (P) appraised the shares as having a value between $23,000 and $40,000. One of the directors later offered Muir (P) $20,000, but a purchase never took place. Muir (P) filed suit, individually and derivatively, after further negotiations failed. The trial court concluded that Alaska Plastics (D) was obligated to buy Muir's (P) shares at fair value, plus pay her attorney fees, interest, and costs. Both sides appealed. The state's highest court granted review.

ISSUE: Does the breach of the fiduciary duty of utmost good faith and loyalty owed by majority shareholders to minority shareholders in a close corporation support an appraisal remedy whereby the corporation is required to purchase the minority shareholder's stock at fair value?

HOLDING AND DECISION: [Judge not stated in casebook excerpt.] No. The breach of the fiduciary duty of utmost good faith and loyalty owed by majority shareholders to minority shareholders in a close corporation does not support an appraisal remedy whereby the corporation is required to purchase the minority shareholder's stock at fair value. The majority in a close corporation owes minority shareholders a duty of utmost good faith and loyalty, akin to the duty owed by partners to each other. Here, the trial court concluded that once the corporation made an offer to Muir (P), it was obligated to purchase her stock at a "fair" price. However, Muir (P) rejected the corporation's offers, and there is no authority that would allow a court to order specific performance on the basis of an unaccepted offer. Nevertheless, Muir's (P) remedy may lie in the fact that the majority shareholders enjoyed benefits that were not shared with her—but that should have been shared with her. But, in this case, payments were made to the directors, and personal expenses were paid for their wives. Such payments could be characterized as constructive dividends. Whether these payments were a distribution of dividends, whether Muir (P) was deprived of other corporate benefits, or whether the majority shareholders violated Alaska law should be determined by the trial court. The trial court did, however, properly dismiss Muir's (P) derivative complaint, since she failed to allege that Alaska Plastics (D) itself was harmed. Remanded.

ANALYSIS

On remand, the court awarded Muir (P) the same amount for her shares that it had awarded her initially. The Alaska Supreme Court upheld the trial court's findings on appeal. The court noted that while Alaska law allows the superior court to liquidate a corporation when the acts of those in control are oppressive or fraudulent, courts retain equitable authority to fashion a less drastic remedy to fit the parties' situation.

Quicknotes

ALASKA CORP. CODE § 10.05.540 Shareholders may bring a liquidation action upon a showing that director's actions are illegal, fraudulent, or wasteful.

CLOSELY HELD CORPORATION A corporation whose shares (or at least voting shares) are held by a closely knit group of shareholders or a single person.

FIDUCIARY DUTY A legal obligation to act for the benefit of another, including subordinating one's personal interests to that of the other person.

GOOD FAITH An honest intention to abstain from any unconscientious advantage of another.

MAJORITY SHAREHOLDER A shareholder of a corporation who holds in excess of 50 percent of the corporation's shares.

MINORITY SHAREHOLDER A shareholder in a corporation controlling such a small portion of those shares outstanding that the shareholder's votes have no influence in the management of the corporation.

Pedro v. Pedro

Minority shareholder (P) v. Majority shareholder (D)

Minn. Ct. App., 489 N.W.2d 798 (1992)

NATURE OF CASE: Appeal from a judgment for the plaintiff in an action requesting dissolution of a closely held corporation.

FACT SUMMARY: After Alfred Pedro (P) was fired from his position in the company by his two brothers, Carl (D) and Eugene (D), he filed this suit seeking to dissolve the company.

RULE OF LAW

Shareholders in closely held corporations have a fiduciary duty to deal openly, honestly, and fairly with one another.

FACTS: Alfred (P), Carl (D), and Eugene (D) Pedro, brothers who each owned a one-third interest in The Pedro Companies, had worked for the company all their lives, and planned to continue doing so. When Alfred (P) discovered a large discrepancy in the company's internal accounting records, he was told that if he did not cooperate and forget about the apparent discrepancy, his brothers (D) would fire him. After a second independent accountant identified a discrepancy, Alfred (P) was placed on mandatory leave of absence and subsequently fired. He brought suit, seeking dissolution of the company. His brothers (D) moved that the action proceed as a buyout under Minnesota law. Alfred (P) was awarded damages for his one-third ownership of the company, for breach of fiduciary duty, and for wrongful termination, plus attorney costs and prejudgment interest on the awards. Carl (D) and Eugene (D) appealed.

ISSUE: Do shareholders in closely held corporations have a fiduciary duty to deal openly, honestly, and fairly with one another?

HOLDING AND DECISION: [Judge not stated in casebook excerpt.] Yes. Shareholders in closely held corporations have a fiduciary duty to deal openly, honestly, and fairly with one another. Carl (D) and Eugene (D) admitted in their motion requesting a buyout that they had acted in a manner unfairly prejudicial toward Alfred (P). This admission supports a finding of breach of fiduciary duty. Furthermore, there was evidence in the record to support the measure of damages for the buyout. Finally, the unique facts in the record support the trial court's finding of an agreement to provide lifetime employment to Alfred (P). Thus, the award of lost wages was proper. Once the court found that Carl (D) and Eugene (D) had breached their fiduciary duties, the court had discretion to award attorney fees. Affirmed.

ANALYSIS

In a closely held corporation, the nature of the employment of a shareholder may create a reasonable expectation by the employee-owner that his employment is not terminable at will. Here, the three brothers had worked in the company all their lives, Carl (D) since 1940, Eugene (D) since 1939, and Alfred (P) since 1942. It was thus reasonable for the court to find that they did in fact have a contract that was not terminable at will.

Quicknotes

CLOSELY HELD CORPORATION A corporation whose shares (or at least voting shares) are held by a closely knit group of shareholders or a single person.

FIDUCIARY DUTY A legal obligation to act for the benefit of another, including subordinating one's personal interests to that of the other person.

CHAPTER 6

Mergers, Acquisitions, and Takeovers

Quick Reference Rules of Law

CHAPTER 6

14. *CTS Corporation v. Dynamics Corporation of America.* (1) A law permitting in-state corporations to require shareholder approval prior to significant shifts in corporate control is consistent with the provisions and purposes of the Williams Act and is not preempted thereby. (2) A law permitting in-state corporations to require shareholder approval prior to significant shifts in corporate control is constitutional as not violating the Commerce Clause. *196*

Weinberger v. UOP, Inc.

Minority shareholder (P) v. Corporation (D)

Del. Sup. Ct., 457 A.2d 701 (1983) (*en banc*)

NATURE OF CASE: Appeal from judgment finding merger and price paid to shareholders fair in class action challenging cash-out merger.

FACT SUMMARY: The Signal Companies, Inc. (D) effected a freeze-out merger with subsidiary UOP, Inc. (D) without disclosing to minority shareholders the value of UOP (D) shares.

RULE OF LAW

A freeze-out merger approved without full disclosure of share value to minority shareholders is invalid.

FACTS: The Signal Companies, Inc. (Signal) (D) acquired, through both market purchases and a tender offer, a majority interest in UOP, Inc. (D). Signal (D) paid $21 per share. Signal (D) later decided to acquire all shares in UOP (D). A report generated by two directors of both corporations concluded that a share price of up to $24 would be a beneficial deal for Signal (D). Signal (D) announced to minority shareholders in UOP (D) that it was offering $21 per share to acquire all shares in UOP (D). At the annual shareholder meeting of UOP (D), a majority of the minority shareholders approved the sale, which resulted in a forced sale of all shares. Weinberger (P), a minority shareholder who had voted against the sale, filed an action seeking to enjoin the merger. The Court of Chancery held the merger valid, and an appeal was taken. The state's highest court granted review.

ISSUE: Is a freeze-out merger approved without full disclosure of share value to minority shareholders valid?

HOLDING AND DECISION: [Judge not stated in casebook excerpt.] No. A freeze-out merger approved without full disclosure of share value to minority shareholders is invalid. For a freeze-out merger to be valid, the transaction must be fair. A plaintiff in a suit challenging a cash-out merger must allege specific acts of fraud, misrepresentation, or other items of misconduct to demonstrate the unfairness of the merger terms to the minority. To be considered fair, two conditions must be met: shareholders must be informed of all relevant facts prior to voting and the price given must be fair. There must be fair dealing as to timing, initiation, structuring, negotiation, disclosure to the board, and board approval, as well as to price, which addresses financial and economic factors such as assets, market value, earnings, prospects, and any other elements that affect the intrinsic or inherent value of company stock. Initially, the burden is on the plaintiff to demonstrate some basis for invoking the fairness obligation, and then the burden is on the majority shareholder to prove fairness. Where corporate action has been approved by an informed vote of a majority of the minority, the burden shifts to the plaintiff to show the transaction was unfair to the minority. Throughout, the majority shareholder retains the burden of showing that all material facts were completely disclosed. Here, however, the record does not support a conclusion that the minority stockholder vote was an informed one, as material information was withheld, in breach of the fiduciary duty of disclosure. When important information is withheld from minority shareholders, their consent to the merger cannot be informed. In this particular instance a report existed that showed that a share price of as much as $24 would be advantageous to Signal (D); had they known this, the minority shareholders might not have voted in favor of a cash-out at $21 per share. Therefore, as material information was withheld, the merger was not fair, both as to fair dealing and fair price, and therefore must be voided. In such a situation, the appropriate remedy is that of appraisal, but with a valuation process that accounts for proof of value by all current and widely accepted methods of valuation, including, but not limited to, discounted cash flow. The injured minority shareholders are entitled to fair value based on all relevant factors, including elements of future value that are not speculative and that are susceptible of proof. In addition to this remedy, the Court of Chancery, in the exercise of its equitable powers, may grant whatever other relief it deems appropriate. Finally, the prior business purpose test is hereby abolished, as it no longer provides any additional, meaningful protection to minority shareholders in a cash-out merger. Reversed and remanded.

ANALYSIS

The *Weinberger* case is a pivotal case in the jurisprudence on squeeze-outs, and most of its rulings are still good law in Delaware. In cases like these, burden of proof can often determine the winner. In the instance of a challenge to a freeze-out merger, the rule in this jurisdiction was that the ultimate burden to show unfairness was on Weinberger (P) and the others challenging the transaction, but the burden was on the corporations (D) to show the vote had been done with full disclosure.

Continued on next page.

Quicknotes

FAIR DEALING The duty owed by a controlling shareholder to a company's minority shareholders to deal fairly and not to act in a manner so as to exploit or oppress the minority shareholders.

FREEZE-OUT MERGER Merger whereby the majority shareholder forces minority shareholders into the sale of their securities.

TENDER OFFER An offer made by one corporation to the shareholders of a target corporation to purchase their shares subject to number, time, and price specifications.

Kahn v. M & F Worldwide Corp.

Minority shareholder (P) v. Corporation (D)

Del. Sup. Ct., 38 A.3d 635 (2014)

NATURE OF CASE: Appeal from judgment for defendants in action challenging a going private transaction.

FACT SUMMARY: Kahn (P) and other minority shareholders (P) of M & F Worldwide Corp. (MFW) (D) challenged a going private, controller buyout merger by MacAndrews & Forbes (M & F) (D), asserting that the appropriate standard of review should be entire fairness, rather than business judgment, notwithstanding that the transaction was conditioned on approval by an independent special committee and a vote of a majority of the minority shareholders. Kahn (P) also asserted that there were triable issues of fact as to the independence of some of the members of the special committee that approved the merger.

RULE OF LAW

A going private, controller buyout merger will be reviewed under the business judgment standard of review if, and only if: (i) the controller conditions the procession of the transaction on the approval of both a special committee and a majority of the minority stockholders; (ii) the special committee is independent; (iii) the special committee is empowered to freely select its own advisors and to say no definitively; (iv) the special committee meets its duty of care in negotiating a fair price; (v) the vote of the minority is informed; and (vi) there is no coercion of the minority.

FACTS: MacAndrews & Forbes (M & F) (D), which owned 43 percent of M & F Worldwide Corp. (MFW) (D), sought to take MFW (D) private in a merger initially valued at $24 per share. The merger was conditioned on approval by an independent special committee and a vote of the majority-of-the-minority stockholders. The MFW (D) board formed an independent special committee to negotiate with M & F (D). The special committee, comprised of four members, selected its own legal and financial advisors, met several times over several months, and negotiated vigorously with M & F (D). As a result of the negotiations the special committee obtained an offer of $25 per share. In a vote of shareholders excluding M & F (D), 65.4 percent of the shares voted in favor of the transaction, and the transaction was consummated. Kahn (P) and other MFW minority shareholders (P) brought suit in the Delaware Court of Chancery challenging the transaction. The Court of Chancery ruled that the appropriate standard of review was business judgment, rather than entire fairness, where the controller buyout was conditioned on both the approval of an independent special committee and a vote of a majority of the minority. Kahn (P) appealed, maintaining that notwithstanding the dual deal protections, the appropriate standard of review should be entire fairness, and that, in any event, three of the four special committee members were not independent. In this regard, Kahn (P) claimed that these three members—Webb (D), Dinh (D), and Byorum (D)—were beholden to Perelman (D), the owner of M & F (D), and a director of MFW (D), because of their prior business and/or social dealings with Perelman (D) or Perelman-related entities. As to Webb (D), Kahn (P) claimed he was not independent because he and Perelman (D) had shared a lucrative business partnership nine years earlier. As to Dinh (D), an attorney and law professor, Kahn (P) adduced evidence that Dinh's (D) law firm had advised M & F (D) and its affiliates, but such engagements were inactive by the time the merger was announced, and they had been disclosed to the special committee. Kahn (P) also claimed that Dinh (D) was influenced by another board member of M & F (D), Schwartz (D), who sat on the board of Dinh's (D) law school. However, at the time of the merger, Dinh (D) was fully tenured, and had been so even before he ever knew Schwartz (D). Schwartz (D) invited Dinh (D) to join the board of another company after the merger, which Kahn (P) alleged showed an ongoing relationship between Dinh (D) and Schwartz (D). Finally, as to Byorum (D), Kahn (D) adduced evidence that she had had prior dealings with Perelman (D) but failed to show there was an ongoing economic relationship with Perelman (D) that was material to her in any way. Advisory work she had done years prior to the merger for an M & F (D) affiliate had also been fully disclosed to the special committee. The Delaware Supreme Court granted review.

ISSUE: Will a going private, controller buyout merger be reviewed under the business judgment standard of review if, and only if: (i) the controller conditions the procession of the transaction on the approval of both a special committee and a majority of the minority stockholders; (ii) the special committee is independent; (iii) the special committee is empowered to freely select its own advisors and to say no definitively; (iv) the special committee meets its duty of care in negotiating a fair price; (v) the vote of the minority is informed; and (vi) there is no coercion of the minority?

HOLDING AND DECISION: [Judge not stated in casebook excerpt.] Yes. A going private, controller

Continued on next page.

buyout merger will be reviewed under the business judgment standard of review if, and only if: (i) the controller conditions the procession of the transaction on the approval of both a special committee and a majority of the minority stockholders; (ii) the special committee is independent; (iii) the special committee is empowered to freely select its own advisors and to say no definitively; (iv) the special committee meets its duty of care in negotiating a fair price; (v) the vote of the minority is informed; and (vi) there is no coercion of the minority. This case presents an issue of first impression: what should be the standard of review for a merger between a controlling stockholder and its subsidiary, where the merger is conditioned ab initio upon the approval of both an independent, adequately empowered special committee that fulfills its duty of care, and the uncoerced, informed vote of a majority of the minority stockholders. The Court of Chancery reasoned that by giving controlling stockholders the opportunity to have a going private transaction reviewed under the business judgment rule, a strong incentive is created to give minority stockholders both procedural protections. Having both protections is critically different than a structure that uses only one of the procedural protections, as the "both" structure effects arm's-length merger steps by requiring two independent approvals. Nevertheless, Kahn (P) argues that neither procedural protection is adequate to protect minority stockholders, because possible ineptitude and timidity of directors may undermine the special committee protection, and because majority-of-the-minority votes may be unduly influenced by arbitrageurs that have an institutional bias to approve virtually any transaction that offers a market premium, however insubstantial it may be. Such a skeptical view is rejected, because independent directors are viewed largely as being effective at protecting public stockholders—and it is the exception when an independent director has little regard for their duties. Also, regarding the majority-of-the-minority vote, Kahn (P) is not saying that minority stockholders will vote against a going private transaction because of fear of retribution, but merely that investors like a premium and will tend to vote for a deal that delivers one. Thus, the standard adopted by the Court of Chancery is affirmed. Where the controller irrevocably and publicly disables itself from using its control to dictate the outcome of the negotiations and the shareholder vote, the controlled merger then acquires the shareholder-protective characteristics of third-party, arm's-length mergers, which are reviewed under the business judgment standard. Also, the dual procedural protection merger structure optimally protects the minority stockholders in controller buyouts. Finally, applying the business judgment standard to the dual protection merger structure is consistent with the central tradition of Delaware law, which defers to the informed decisions of impartial directors, especially when those decisions have been approved by the disinterested stockholders on full information and without coercion. Such a structure is in the best interests of the minority shareholders and enables them to get the best price, which typically is the preponderant merger consideration for an investor. A controller that uses only one of the dual procedural protections continues to receive burden shifting within the entire fairness standard of review framework. At this point, having set forth the standard for business judgment review of a controlled merger, it must be determined whether the standard has been met in this case. Kahn (P) claims three of the four special committee members were not independent, but the Court of Chancery correctly ruled that he failed to adduce sufficient evidence that they were so beholden, or so controlled by, Perelman (D) that they would not be able to make independent decisions regarding the merger. The mere fact that Webb (D) engaged in business dealings with Perelman (D) nine years earlier did not raise a triable fact issue regarding his ability to evaluate the merger impartially. As to Dinh (D), the fees that his law firm obtained from its engagements with M & F (D) and its affiliates was de minimis and would not have influenced his decision making with respect to the M & F (D) proposal. The relationship between Dinh (D) and M & F's (D) Schwartz (D) also did not create a triable issue of fact as to Dinh's independence, since Schwartz (D) could not influence Dinh's (D) tenure, and Schwartz's (D) invitation to Dinh (D) to join the board of another company came months after the merger was consummated. Finally, as to Byorum (D), the evidence presented similarly did not create a triable issue of fact as to her independence, since no evidence was presented that she had an ongoing economic relationship with Perelman (D) that was material to her in any way. Additionally, any moneys she received while advising an affiliate of M & F (D) were not material to her, and no evidence to the contrary was presented. In sum, it is well established that bare allegations that directors are friendly with, travel in the same social circles as, or have past business relationships with the proponent of a transaction or the person they are investigating are not enough to rebut the presumption of independence. Here, there was insufficient evidence, applying a subjective standard, that the directors' ties with Perelman (D) or M & F (D) and its affiliates were material, in the sense that the alleged ties could have affected the impartiality of any individual director. Accordingly, the special committee was independent. The committee was also empowered to hire its own advisors, and to negotiate with M & F (D) over the deal terms. The committee also had the power to reject the deal outright if it believed the deal was not in the minority shareholders' best interests. Although the committee did not have the authority to sell MFW (D) to buyers other than M & F (D), the committee nevertheless explored other sales options that might have generated more value for the shareholders. The committee also exercised due

Continued on next page.

care, meeting often, and reviewing a rich body of financial information relevant to whether and at what price a going private transaction was advisable. Finally, it was undisputed that the majority-of-the-minority vote was informed and uncoerced. Therefore, all conditions under the standard are met. Affirmed.

ANALYSIS

If a plaintiff such as Kahn (P) were able to plead a reasonably conceivable set of facts showing that any or all the enumerated conditions set forth in the court's holding did not exist, that complaint would state a claim for relief that would entitle the plaintiff to proceed and conduct discovery. If, after discovery, triable issues of fact remained whether either or both dual procedural protections were established, or if established were effective, the case would proceed to a trial in which the court would conduct an entire fairness review. Here, because Kahn (P) was unable to convince the court that any of the conditions for business judgment review were not met, Kahn (P) was unable to advance his case.

Quicknotes

AB INITIO From its inception or beginning.

BUSINESS JUDGMENT RULE Standard of review that presumes that in making a business decision, the directors of a corporation acted on an informed basis, in good faith, and in the honest belief that the action taken was in the best interests of the company.

DE MINIMIS Insignificant; trivial; not of sufficient signif - cance to require legal action.

DUTY OF CARE Duty that an officer or director owes to the corporation, by virtue of their fiduciary relationship, to act for the benefit of the corporation.

ENTIRE FAIRNESS Standard of review that places the burden on a corporate defendant to demonstrate that a corporate transaction is entirely fair to the corporation and its stockholders both as to the transaction's process ("fair dealing") and economics ("fair price").

Coggins v. New England Patriots Football Club, Inc.

Shareholder (P) v. Corporation (D)

Mass. Sup. Jud. Ct., 397 Mass. 525, 492 N.E.2d 1112 (1986)

NATURE OF CASE: Appeal from judgment holding freeze-out merger illegal and assessing rescissionary damages.

FACT SUMMARY: A freeze-out merger of the New England Patriots Football Club, Inc. (D) into a parent corporation was challenged as having been affected solely for the benefit of the majority shareholder.

RULE OF LAW

Controlling stockholders violate their fiduciary duties when they cause a merger to be made for the sole purpose of eliminating minority shareholders on a cash-out basis.

FACTS: In 1959, Sullivan (D) purchased a franchise in the newly formed American Football League, later named the Boston Patriots. The team was owned by the New England Patriots Football Club, Inc. (Old Patriots) (D), in which Sullivan (D) held a controlling, but nonmajority, interest. To foster public interest in the team, nonvoting stock was sold to the public. In 1974 Sullivan (D) was ousted as president of the corporation. The following year he managed to acquire all voting shares. He then formed a new corporation, also called the New England Patriots Football Club, Inc. (New Patriots) (D). In a transaction effected primarily to pay off Sullivan's (D) personal debts incurred in acquiring the voting stock, New Patriots (D) acquired 100 percent of Old Patriots' (D) voting stock, Sullivan (D) retained 100 percent of the voting stock of New Patriots (D), the two corporations were merged, and the nonvoting shares of Old Patriots (D) were to be exchanged for cash at the rate of $15.00 a share. Coggins (P), who owned ten nonvoting shares of Old Patriots (D), challenged the transaction in a class action. The trial court held the merger illegal, but rather than void the transaction, ordered rescissory damages. An appeal was taken, and the state's highest court granted review.

ISSUE: Do controlling stockholders violate their fiduciary duties when they cause a merger to be made for the sole purpose of eliminating minority shareholders on a cash-out basis?

HOLDING AND DECISION: [Judge not stated in casebook excerpt.] Yes. Controlling stockholders violate their fiduciary duties when they cause a merger to be made for the sole purpose of eliminating minority shareholders on a cash-out basis. To be valid, a freeze-out merger must be "fair." To be fair, two conditions must be met: fair dealing and fair price. Fair dealing means that the majority shareholder must act not only for their own benefit, but for the benefit of the corporation as a whole. In other words, it must serve a business purpose. If the majority shareholder acts solely for their own benefit, then fair dealing is not present. The burden to show fairness is on the majority shareholder. In this particular instance it appears that the sole reason for the freeze-out merger was that, under state corporation laws, the nonvoting stock had to be extinguished in order for the New Patriots (D) to assume Sullivan's (D) personal liabilities incurred in his quest to regain control of the franchise. This clearly was a purpose beneficial to Sullivan (D) personally and not to the corporation, and therefore the transaction was illegal. As to the appropriate remedy, because ten years have passed since the merger was affected, voiding the merger would be unduly harsh. Instead, on remand, the lower court should consider the present value of the Patriots in awarding rescissory damages, i.e., what the stockholders would have if the merger were rescinded. Reversed and remanded.

ANALYSIS

What constitutes a business purpose can be a matter of some dispute. If, for instance, Sullivan (D) had reacquired the franchise out of a concern that the rebels that ousted him were harming the franchise, a business purpose in incurring the debts he did might have existed. There was no hint in the published opinion as to what Sullivan's (D) ulterior motives might have been, however.

Quicknotes

BUSINESS JUDGMENT RULE Standard of review that presumes that in making a business decision, the directors of a corporation acted on an informed basis, in good faith, and in the honest belief that the action taken was in the best interests of the company.

CASH-OUT MERGER The acquisition of one company by another by exchanging cash for the shares of the target corporation, after which the acquired company ceases to exist as an independent entity.

CONTROLLING SHAREHOLDER A person who has power to vote a majority of the outstanding shares of a corporation, or who is able to direct the management of the corporation with a smaller block of stock because the

Continued on next page.

remaining shares are scattered among small, disorganized holdings.

FAIR DEALING An implied warranty that the parties will deal honestly in the satisfaction of their obligations and without intent to defraud.

FIDUCIARY DUTY A legal obligation to act for the benefit of another, including subordinating one's personal interests to that of the other person.

FREEZE-OUT Merger whereby the majority shareholder forces minority shareholders into the sale of their securities.

RESCISSION The canceling of an agreement and the return of the parties to their positions prior to the formation of the contract.

Farris v. Glen Alden Corporation

Shareholder (P) v. Corporation (D)

Pa. Sup. Ct., 393 Pa. 427, 143 A.2d 25 (1958)

NATURE OF CASE: Appeal from judgment enjoining performance of a corporate reorganization agreement.

FACT SUMMARY: Glen Alden Corp. (D) and List Industries Corporation (List) entered into a reorganization agreement under which Glen Alden (D) was to acquire List's assets. Farris (P), a stockholder in Glen Alden (D), sued to enjoin performance of this agreement on grounds that the notice of the annual meeting failed to conform to statutory merger provisions.

RULE OF LAW

A transaction that is in the form of a sale of corporate assets, but that is in effect a de facto merger of two corporations, must meet the statutory merger requirements in order to protect the rights of minority shareholders.

FACTS: List Industries Corp. (List), a holding company, purchased 38.5 percent of the outstanding stock of Glen Alden Corp. (D), a corporation engaged in mining and manufacture, and placed three of its directors on the Glen Alden (D) board. The two corporations entered into a "reorganization agreement" under which Glen Alden (D) was to purchase the assets of List and take over List's liabilities. List shareholders would receive stock in Glen Alden, and List would be dissolved. Notice of this agreement was sent to the shareholders of Glen Alden (D), who approved the agreement at their annual meeting. Farris (P), a shareholder of Glen Alden (D), filed suit to enjoin performance of the agreement on grounds that the notice to the shareholders of the proposed agreement did not conform to the statutory requirements for a proposed merger. Glen Alden (D) defended on the basis that the form of the transaction was a sale of assets rather than a merger, so the merger statute was inapplicable. The trial court, concluding the transaction was a de facto merger, so that the failure of the annual meeting notice to conform to the pertinent statutory requirements rendered all proceedings in furtherance of the merger void, granted Farris's (P) requested injunctive relief. The state's highest court granted review.

ISSUE: Must a transaction that is in the form of a sale of corporate assets, but that is in effect a de facto merger of two corporations, meet the statutory merger requirements in order to protect the rights of minority shareholders?

HOLDING AND DECISION: [Judge not stated in casebook excerpt.] Yes. A transaction that is in the form of a sale of corporate assets, but that is in effect a de facto merger of two corporations, must meet the statutory merger requirements in order to protect the rights of minority shareholders. To decide whether a transaction is in fact a merger or only a sale of assets, a court must look not to the formalities of the agreement but to its practical effect. Under Pennsylvania law, a shareholder of a corporation that is planning to merge has a right to dissent and to get paid fair value for their shares but has no such rights if their corporation is merely purchasing the assets of another corporation. A transaction is a de facto merger, and these rights must be granted to dissenting shareholders, if the agreement will so change the corporate character that to refuse to allow the shareholder to dissent will, in effect, force him to give up their shares in one corporation and accept shares in an entirely different corporation. If this agreement is performed, Farris (P) will become a shareholder in a larger corporation that is engaged in an entirely different type of business. The new corporation will have a majority of directors appointed by List, Farris (P) will have a smaller percentage of ownership because of the shares issued to the List shareholders, and the market value of his shares will decrease. This, then, is a de facto merger, and Glen Alden (D) must follow the statutory merger requirements even though the transaction is in the form of a purchase of List's assets. Also, even if this were a purchase of assets, the reality of the agreement is that List is acquiring Glen Alden, despite the form that states that Glen Alden (D) is acquiring List, and under Pennsylvania law shareholders of a purchased corporation also have a statutory right to dissent. Therefore, even if this were not a de facto merger, Farris (P) still has a right to dissent. Affirmed.

ANALYSIS

Because of the statutory merger requirements, corporations will try to achieve the effect of a merger by alternative methods, such as a sale of assets or a sale of stock. The formal merger requirements are consent by the shareholders of both corporations and majority approval by the directors. *Glen Alden* illustrates the resulting rights of a dissenting shareholder to demand appraisal – requiring the corporation to purchase their shares before the merger can take place. The rationale of the appraisal right is that the shareholder purchased the shares of a specific corporation, and to force them to exchange their stock in the corporation they chose

Continued on next page.

for stock in an entirely different corporation is to deprive them of their property.

Quicknotes

DE FACTO MERGER DOCTRINE The acquisition of one company by another without compliance with the requirements of a statutory merger but treated by the courts as such.

PENNSYLVANIA BUS. CORP. LAW § 908 Shareholders objecting to a merger are entitled to sell at market value.

Hariton v. Arco Electronics, Inc.

Shareholder (P) v. Corporation (D)

Del. Sup. Ct., 41 Del. Ch. 74, 188 A.2d 123 (1963)

NATURE OF CASE: Appeal from summary judgment dismissing an action seeking to enjoin sale of stock.

FACT SUMMARY: Loral Electronics and Arco Electronics, Inc. (D) agreed to an assets sale that constituted a de facto merger.

RULE OF LAW

A sale of assets involving dissolution of the selling corporation and distribution of the shares to its shareholders is legal.

FACTS: Loral Electronics and Arco Electronics, Inc. (Arco) (D) entered into an agreement wherein Arco (D) was to sell all its assets to Loral. Loral was then to issue 230,000 shares of stock, to be transferred to Arco (D). Arco (D) was then to distribute the shares to its own shareholders. Hariton (P), a shareholder of Arco (D), filed an action seeking to enjoin the transaction, contending that it was a de facto merger and, as such, was subject to certain regulations that the transaction avoided by not officially being called a merger. The Court of Chancery held the transaction valid, and the Delaware Supreme Court granted review.

ISSUE: Is a sale of assets involving dissolution of the selling corporation and distribution of the shares to its shareholders legal?

HOLDING AND DECISION: [Judge not stated in casebook excerpt.] Yes. A sale of assets involving dissolution of the selling corporation and distribution of the shares to its shareholders is legal. The statutes controlling mergers and those controlling asset sales are independent of each other and are equal in terms of validity. If an asset sale meets the legal requirements of such a sale, the fact that it might be a de facto merger should not invalidate it any more than an otherwise legal merger should be invalidated because it is a de facto asset sale. To hold otherwise would be to create unnecessary uncertainty and litigation. Affirmed.

ANALYSIS

Generally speaking, legislatures tend to place greater scrutiny on mergers than on asset sales. The perception appears to be that the chances of injuring minority shareholders are greater in a merger. For that reason, restrictions may be placed on mergers that are not placed on asset sales. Here, for instance, a right of appraisal attached to mergers, but not to asset sales.

Quicknotes

8 DEL. C. § 271 Governs mergers where purchasing corporation buys with its own shares.

DE FACTO MERGER DOCTRINE The acquisition of one company by another without compliance with the requirements of a statutory merger but treated by the courts as such.

Rauch v. RCA Corporation

Shareholder (P) v. Corporation (D)

861 F.2d 29 (2d Cir. 1988)

NATURE OF CASE: Appeal from judgment dismissing challenge to merger.

FACT SUMMARY: Shareholders (P) of acquired corporation RCA Corp. (D) contended that a merger that involved a forced sale of their shares triggered redemption rights contained in RCA's Articles of Incorporation.

RULE OF LAW

A cash-out merger that is otherwise legal does not trigger any right the shareholders may have with respect to share redemption.

FACTS: In 1985, General Electric Co. (GE) (D), a majority shareholder in RCA Corp. (D), merged the latter into itself. A certain class of preferred stock was valued at $40 per share, and the shareholders thereof were paid this amount per share. Rauch (P), holder of 250 of these shares, challenged the merger on the grounds the Articles of Incorporation of RCA (D) contained a provision that his class of stock, if redeemed, was to be paid at $100 per share. Rauch (P) argued that the merger had the same effect as redemption. The district court ruled in favor of the merger and dismissed. Rauch (P) appealed. The Second Circuit Court of Appeals granted review.

ISSUE: Does a cash-out merger that is otherwise legal trigger any right the shareholders may have with respect to share redemption?

HOLDING AND DECISION: [Judge not stated in casebook excerpt.] No. A cash-out merger that is otherwise valid does not trigger any right the shareholders may have with respect to share redemption. It has long been the law in Delaware that when a corporate reorganization leads to a particular result, any consequence thereof is not invalidated by the mere fact that a similar result could have been reached by a different type of reorganization that would have been more advantageous to a particular plaintiff. Under Delaware law, mergers are governed by certain laws and redemptions by others, and they are considered equal in terms of validity. Having affected a cashing out of Rauch's (P) interest by a merger, the fact that Rauch (P) could have been cashed out in a redemption on terms more advantageous to Rauch (P) does no good to Rauch (P) where, as here, there is no allegation that the merger itself was unfair or otherwise tainted. Affirmed.

ANALYSIS

In this instance, the merger could have been accomplished by a sale of assets of RCA (D), along with redemption of preferred shares. This would have led to the same result but would have triggered redemption rights. It is not clear if GE (D) effected the transaction as it did to avoid paying preferred shareholders their redemption amounts, but the opinion makes it clear that it makes no difference if it did.

Quicknotes

CASH-OUT MERGER The acquisition of one company by another by exchanging cash for the shares of the target corporation, after which the acquired company ceases to exist as an independent entity.

DE FACTO MERGER DOCTRINE The acquisition of one company by another without compliance with the requirements of a statutory merger but treated by the courts as such.

DEL. GEN. CORP. LAW § 251(b) Governs merger agreements in which shares are converted to cash.

REDEMPTION The repurchase of a security by the issuing corporation according to the terms specified in the security agreement specifying the procedure for the repurchase.

Unocal Corporation v. Mesa Petroleum Co.

Target corporation (D) v. Corporation (P)

Del. Sup. Ct., 493 A.2d 946 (1985)

NATURE OF CASE: Appeal from judgment enjoining a tender offer.

FACT SUMMARY: To ward off a hostile takeover by Mesa Petroleum Co. (P), directors of Unocal Corporation (D) instituted a selective exchange offer.

RULE OF LAW

A selective tender offer effected to thwart a takeover is not in itself invalid.

FACTS: Unocal Corporation (D) was faced with a hostile tender offer by Mesa Petroleum Co. (Mesa) (P). The tender offer was of a "two-tier" structure such that the shareholders first tendering their stock obtained much greater value than those who tendered theirs later in the offer. The purpose of the plan was to motivate the shareholders to sell their shares lest they find themselves in the second tier of the offering. Following consultations with financial professionals, the board of directors of Unocal (D) approved a defensive tactic wherein Unocal (D) issued an exchange offer for its own stock, at an amount higher than that offered by Mesa (P). Mesa (P) was specifically excluded from the offer. Mesa (P) then filed an action seeking to enjoin Unocal's (D) selective exchange offer. The Court of Chancery issued a temporary restraining order halting the proposed offer, which it extended into an injunction. Unocal (D) appealed, and the state's highest court granted review.

ISSUE: Is a selective tender offer effected to thwart a takeover in itself invalid?

HOLDING AND DECISION: [Judge not stated in casebook excerpt.] No. A selective tender offer effected to thwart a takeover is not in itself invalid. In the context of a battle for corporate control, the usual deference given to the decisions of the board of directors under the business judgment rule is somewhat circumscribed by the fact that directors in such a situation are in an inherent conflict of interest, as self-preservation is an issue they face. In spite of this threat to their corporate survival, directors must continue to put the interests of shareholders first. Therefore, acts of the directors to defeat a takeover must be shown to have been done because the takeover represented a danger to corporate policy and effectiveness. Further, the conclusion that such a threat existed must have been made after reasonable investigation and in good faith. Finally, the severity of the tactic must be reasonable in relation to the level of perceived threat. Here, the directors of Unocal (D) were faced with a situation where a coercive tender offer had been made by a reputed "greenmailer." The response was to affect a counteroffer that excluded the would-be acquirer to ward off the takeover. Given the facts available to the board, it appears that their response was commensurate to the threat, and therefore was valid. Reversed.

ANALYSIS

This case established what has come to be known as the "*Unocal* Rule," which is a standard used in assessing a takeover defense. As the opinion states, the business judgment rule is not automatically applied to defensive tactics. Rather, a reviewing court must look at the reasonableness of the defensive tactic employed, due to the high possibility of interested acts on the part of the board.

Quicknotes

8 DEL. CODE § 160 Corporations have the right to buy and sell shares of their own stock.

BUSINESS JUDGMENT RULE Standard of review that presumes that in making a business decision, the directors of a corporation acted on an informed basis, in good faith, and in the honest belief that the action taken was in the best interests of the company.

TENDER OFFER An offer made by one corporation to the shareholders of a target corporation to purchase their shares subject to number, time, and price specifications.

Revlon, Inc. v. MacAndrews & Forbes Holdings, Inc.

Target corporation (D) v. Corporation (P)

Del. Sup. Ct., 506 A.2d 173 (1985)

NATURE OF CASE: Appeal from judgment enjoining stock purchase.

FACT SUMMARY: Directors of target corporation Revlon, Inc. (D) instituted an antitakeover strategy that favored corporate bondholders over shareholders.

RULE OF LAW

Lockups and related defensive measures are permitted where their adoption is untainted by director interest or other breaches of fiduciary duty and where value to shareholders is maximized.

FACTS: Revlon, Inc. (D) became the object of interest of potential buyer Pantry Pride, Inc. (P). Pantry Pride (P) initially made an overture to Revlon (D) to purchase the corporation at $45 per share. Revlon's (D) board rejected the offer. As part of a defensive strategy, Revlon's (D) board adopted a plan whereby shareholders exchanged their shares for bonds. Pantry Pride (P) made a series of ever-increasing tender offers, which the board of Revlon (D) continuously opposed. The board then announced a leveraged buyout by "white knight" Forstmann (D) at $57.25 per share. Part of the deal was a lockup provision relating to a division of Revlon (D) that would have made any acquisition of Revlon (D) by another concern unprofitable. Also, Forstmann (D) agreed to support the value of the notes, which were sagging in the bond market. At this point Pantry Pride (P) filed an action seeking to enjoin the agreement between Revlon (D) and Forstmann (D). The Court of Chancery so ordered and Revlon (D) appealed. The state's highest court granted review.

ISSUE: Are lockups and other defensive measures permitted where their adoption is untainted by director interest or other breaches of fiduciary duty and where value to shareholders is maximized?

HOLDING AND DECISION: [Judge not stated in casebook excerpt.] Yes. Lockups and related defensive measures are permitted where their adoption is untainted by director interest or other breaches of fiduciary duty and where value to shareholders is maximized. The actions taken by the Revlon directors (D) did not meet this standard, however. While a board is not required to be blind to all others having an interest in a corporation, their main responsibility is to the shareholders. This usually means maximizing share prices. When, as here, it becomes clear that a corporation is going to be taken over and the only issue remaining is the price that is to be paid, this duty of the directors becomes an obligation to maximize the sale price, not unlike an auctioneer. Here, the board of Revlon (D), to thwart an unfriendly takeover, negotiated a sale to a suitor that effectively ended the bidding for the corporation, which in turn prevented a higher share price. It had become clear that Revlon (D) was going to be sold, so it was incumbent upon the directors to maximize share price. Instead, they worked out a deal that favored the noteholders to the detriment of the shareholders, which was improper. This invalidated the entire transaction with Forstmann (D). Affirmed.

ANALYSIS

Although not the central holding of this opinion, this case gave rise to what has become called the "*Revlon* Rule." This rule holds that when it is clear a target is going to be sold, the directors become little more than auctioneers and their duty becomes to maximize shareholder value. Long-term corporate interests are no longer considered. While not binding in other states, this rule is widely followed around the nation due to the influence of the Delaware Supreme Court in matters of corporate law.

Quicknotes

BUSINESS JUDGMENT RULE Standard of review that presumes that in making a business decision, the directors of a corporation acted on an informed basis, in good faith, and in the honest belief that the action taken was in the best interests of the company.

FIDUCIARY DUTY A legal obligation to act for the benefit of another, including subordinating one's personal interests to that of the other person.

HOSTILE TAKEOVER Refers to a situation in which an outside group attempts to seize control of a target corporation against the will of the targeted company's officers, directors, or shareholders.

LOCKUP OPTION A defensive strategy to a takeover attempt whereby a target corporation sets aside a specified portion of the company's shares for purchase by a friendly investor.

TENDER OFFER An offer made by one corporation to the shareholders of a target corporation to purchase their shares subject to number, time, and price specifications.

Paramount Communications, Inc. v. Time Incorporated

Corporation (P) v. Target corporation (D)

Del. Sup. Ct., 571 A.2d 1140 (1989)

NATURE OF CASE: Appeal from judgment rejecting challenge to corporate merger.

FACT SUMMARY: Directors of Time, Inc. (D), seeing a threat by a bid for control by Paramount Communications, Inc. (P), undertook measures to defeat the takeover effort.

RULE OF LAW

Directors of a corporation involved in an ongoing business enterprise may take into account all long-term corporate objectives in responding to an offer to take over the corporation.

FACTS: Time, Inc. (D), publisher of a major newsmagazine, developed the intention of making inroads into the entertainment industry. After considering several established entertainment companies, Time's (D) board began merger discussions with the board of Warner Brothers, Inc. (Warner) (D), a motion picture studio. A merger was agreed upon, consisting of a stock-for-stock swap in which Warner (D) would be merged into Time (D) with Warner (D) shareholders receiving 0.465 shares of Time (D) stock for each share of Warner (D) stock owned. Unexpectedly, Paramount Communications (P) announced an all-cash offer to purchase Time (D) for $175 per share. This led to a restructuring of the proposed Time (D)–Warner (D) merger into a cash and securities acquisition. Time's (D) board, citing concerns about Paramount's (P) acquisition posing a threat to Time's (D) corporate culture, continually rejected Paramount's (P) overtures, which eventually increased to an offer of $200 per share. The original Time (D)–Warner (D) agreement had included a "no shop" clause that prevented Time's (D) board from considering other options. Both Paramount (P) and various shareholders of Time (D) filed suit, alleging breach of fiduciary duty by Time's (D) board. The Court of Chancery rejected the claims and dismissed. An appeal was taken. The state's highest court granted review.

ISSUE: May directors of a corporation involved in an ongoing business enterprise take into account all long-term corporate objectives in responding to an offer to take over the corporation?

HOLDING AND DECISION: [Judge not stated in casebook excerpt.] Yes. Directors of a corporation involved in an ongoing business enterprise may take into account all long-term corporate objectives in responding to an offer to take over the corporation. When a corporation is an ongoing enterprise, and is not effectively "up for sale," directors are more than mere auctioneers trying to obtain the highest price possible. A board's decision to reject a takeover offer will be upheld under the business judgment rule if the directors can show their decision was not dictated by a selfish desire to retain their jobs, but rather was in the best interests of the corporation. Share price is a component of this analysis but is not the sole criterion. If the directors arrived at the decision to reject an offer after appropriate analysis and consideration of legitimate factors, a court will not substitute its judgment for that of the directors. Here, the directors elected to continue with a deliberately conceived corporate plan for long-term growth rather than accept an opportunity for short-term profits, which is a legitimate decision. The acts of Time's (D) board were therefore appropriate. Affirmed.

ANALYSIS

The court here applied what is known as the "*Unocal*" analysis, after the case *Unocal Corp. v. Mesa Petroleum Co.,* 493 A.2d 946 (Del. 1985). In that opinion, the Delaware Supreme Court established the rule that a board's defensive tactics will not be given the deferential business judgment rule test but will be subject to a higher level of scrutiny due to the possibility of self-interest.

Quicknotes

BUSINESS JUDGMENT RULE Standard of review that presumes that in making a business decision, the directors of a corporation acted on an informed basis, in good faith, and in the honest belief that the action taken was in the best interests of the company.

FIDUCIARY DUTY A legal obligation to act for the benefit of another, including subordinating one's personal interests to that of the other person.

TENDER OFFER An offer made by one corporation to the shareholders of a target corporation to purchase their shares subject to number, time, and price specifications.

Paramount Communications, Inc. v. QVC Network, Inc.

Target corporation (D) v. Corporation (P)

Del. Sup. Ct., 637 A.2d 34 (1994)

NATURE OF CASE: Appeal from judgment enjoining certain defensive measures taken in response to a takeover threat.

FACT SUMMARY: Directors of target corporation Paramount Communications, Inc. (D) instituted as deterrents to an unfriendly acquisition a no-shop clause, a "poison pill" termination fee, and a stock option agreement favoring friendly suitor Viacom (D).

RULE OF LAW

The directors of a corporation targeted by two or more suitors may not institute tactics that favor one suitor in such a manner as to allow the favored suitor to offer less than it otherwise would have.

FACTS: Paramount Communications, Inc. (Paramount) (D) instituted talks with Viacom, Inc. (D) for a friendly merger. An agreement was reached that included several devices to discourage other potential suitors. One was a "no-shop" agreement barring Paramount (D) directors from discussing mergers with any other suitor, absent certain specific circumstances. The second was a fee of $100,000,000 to be paid to Viacom (D) if Paramount (D) terminated the agreement. Finally, a stock option was granted to Viacom (D), which, if exercised, would be so advantageous that any party acquiring Paramount (D) would be subject to the danger of large losses. QVC Network, Inc. (QVC) (P) announced a tender offer and filed an action seeking the defensive measures declared invalid. The Court of Chancery held the measures invalid, and Paramount (D) appealed. The state's highest court granted review.

ISSUE: May the directors of a corporation targeted by two or more suitors institute tactics that favor one suitor in such a manner as to allow the favored suitor to offer less than it otherwise would have?

HOLDING AND DECISION: [Judge not stated in casebook excerpt.] No. The directors of a corporation targeted by two or more suitors may not institute tactics that favor one suitor in such a manner as to allow the favored suitor to offer less than it otherwise would have. Generally speaking, the actions of a directorate are given great deference, under the business judgment rule. However, one exception to this rule is the area of tactics employed to defeat an unfriendly takeover. This is because the board is in an inherent conflict in that there is a likelihood if an unfriendly takeover is affected they will be ousted. The specter of self-interest, rather than corporate interest, is therefore present. When control of a corporation is up for sale, the duty of the board is to seek a transaction that gives the shareholders the best value possible. Directors are not limited in this regard to cash value only, but may analyze the entire situation, both in the short and long term. Nonetheless, when directors by their acts do something that has the effect of lessening the value shareholders would otherwise receive, they have breached their fiduciary duty. Here, the directors of Paramount (D) were faced with the all-but-inevitable sale of control to either Viacom (D) or QVC (P); one of those two entities was going to end up with control of Paramount (D). While the Paramount (D) directors were free to conclude that Viacom (D) offered Paramount (D) the best deal in the long run, they took steps that effectively cut off the bidding process. It seems clear that Viacom (D) would have raised the ante had it needed to do so to gain control, and by cutting off the bidding, the directors of Paramount (D) made it unnecessary for it to do so. In doing this, the directors breached their duties to Paramount's (D) shareholders. Affirmed.

ANALYSIS

The present case was something of an extension of a previous case, *Revlon, Inc. v. MacAndrews & Forbes Holdings*, 506 A.2d 173 (1985). In that case, the Delaware Supreme Court held that the directors of a corporation whose sale and breakup were inevitable were under a duty to maximize share value. The present action extended this rule to sales of control where breakup is not a certainty. After the Delaware Supreme Court rendered its decision, Paramount (D) adopted procedures, in keeping with the decision, that encouraged the suitors to bid against each other. Ultimately, Viacom (D) prevailed with a $10 billion package—which was about $2 billion more than the value of the original package negotiated with Viacom (D).

Quicknotes

BUSINESS JUDGMENT RULE Standard of review that presumes that in making a business decision, the directors of a corporation acted on an informed basis, in good faith, and in the honest belief that the action taken was in the best interests of the company.

POISON PILL A tactic employed by a company, which is the target of a takeover attempt, to make the purchase of its shares less attractive to a potential buyer by requiring

Continued on next page.

the issuance of a new series of shares to be redeemed at a substantial premium over their stated value if a party purchases a specified percentage of voting shares of the corporation.

TENDER OFFER An offer made by one corporation to the shareholders of a target corporation to purchase their shares subject to number, time, and price specifications.

Corwin v. KKR Financial Holdings LLC

Stockholders (P) v. Company (D)

Del. Sup. Ct., 125 A.3d 304 (2015)

NATURE OF CASE: Appeal from grant of a motion to dismiss.

FACT SUMMARY: Corwin (P) was a stockholder in KKR Financial Holdings LLC (Financial Holdings) (D). Financial Holdings merged into KKR & Co. L.P. (KKR) in a stock-for-stock transaction approved by a majority of fully informed stockholders. Corwin (P) alleged KKR was a controlling stockholder of Financial Holdings (D) and the merger was subject to the entire fairness standard.

RULE OF LAW

A merger approved by a fully informed, uncoerced, majority of stockholders is subject to the business judgment rule rather than the entire fairness standard.

FACTS: KKR & Co. L.P. (KKR) specializes in leveraged buyouts and KKR Financial Holdings LLC's (Financial Holding's) (D) primary business is financing KKR's leveraged buy-out activities. Financial Holdings (D), in turn, was managed by KKR Financial Advisors, an affiliate of KKR, under a management agreement subject to a termination fee if canceled. Financial Holdings (D) merged into KKR in a stock-for-stock transaction duly approved by a majority vote of the stockholders. Corwin (P) alleged that Financial Holdings' (D) business reliance on KKR and the termination fee in the management agreement were enough to render KKR a controlling shareholder of Financial Holdings (D). Corwin (P) asserted that the merger was subject to review under the stringent entire fairness standard rather than the deferential business judgment rule because KKR was a controlling shareholder. KKR owned less than one percent of Financial Holdings' (D) stock prior to the merger, did not have the right to appoint directors, and had no contractual veto rights over the actions of the board. The unusual relationship between KKR and Financial Holdings (D) was known to investors. Financial Holdings (D) moved for dismissal arguing that KKR was not a controlling shareholder and that a stockholder approved merger was not subject to the entire fairness standard. The trial court granted the motion and Corwin (P) appealed.

ISSUE: Is a merger approved by a fully informed, uncoerced, majority of stockholders subject to the business judgment rule rather than the entire fairness standard?

HOLDING AND DECISION: [Judge not stated in casebook excerpt.] Yes. A merger approved by a fully informed, uncoerced, majority of stockholders is subject to the business judgment rule rather than the entire fairness standard. The trial court correctly held that in the absence of management control or veto power over the KKR Financial Holdings LLC (D) board, KKR & Co. L.P. was not a controlling shareholder. Corwin's (P) argument in the alternative that the *Revlon v. MacAndrews & Forbes Holdings Inc.*, 506 A.2d 173 (Del. 1986) standard applies was rejected as it was not properly raised in the trial court, and even if it were, it was not necessary to reach *Revlon*. Affirmed.

ANALYSIS

Shareholder ratification in this case requires those shareholders to be both fully informed and uncoerced. Should material facts respecting the transaction not be disclosed to the shareholders, the business judgment rule does not apply. When a transaction is not subject to the entire fairness standard, the business judgment rule presumptively applies.

Quicknotes

BUSINESS JUDGMENT RULE Standard of review that presumes that in making a business decision, the directors of a corporation acted on an informed basis, in good faith, and in the honest belief that the action taken was in the best interests of the company.

ENTIRE FAIRNESS Standard of review that places the burden on a corporate defendant to demonstrate that a corporate transaction is entirely fair to the corporation and its stockholders both as to the transaction's process ("fair dealing") and economics ("fair price").

Omnicare, Inc. v. NCS Healthcare, Inc.

Acquiring corporation (P) v. Target corporation (D)

Del. Sup. Ct., 818 A.2d 914 (2003)

NATURE OF CASE: Appeal from decision holding that lockup deal protection measures were reasonable.

FACT SUMMARY: Omnicare, Inc. (Omnicare) (P) sought to acquire NCS Healthcare, Inc. (NCS) (D). Genesis Health Ventures, Inc. (Genesis) had made a competing bid for NCS (D) that the NCS board had originally recommended, but the NCS board withdrew its recommendation and instead recommended that stockholders accept the Omnicare (P) offer, which was worth more than twice the Genesis offer. However, the agreement between Genesis and NCS (D) contained a provision that the agreement be placed before the NCS (D) shareholders for a vote, even if the board no longer recommended it. There was also no fiduciary-out clause in the agreement. Pursuant to voting agreements, two NCS shareholders who held a majority of the voting power agreed unconditionally to vote all their shares in favor of the Genesis merger, thus assuring that the Genesis transaction would prevail. Omnicare (P) challenged the defensive measures that were part of the Genesis transaction.

RULE OF LAW

Lockup deal protection devices, which when operating in concert are coercive and preclusive, are invalid and unenforceable in the absence of a fiduciary-out clause.

FACTS: In late 1999, NCS Healthcare, Inc. (NCS) (D) began to experience serious liquidity problems that led to a precipitous decline in the market value of its stock. As a result, it began to explore strategic alternatives to address its situation. In the summer of 2001, Omnicare, Inc. (Omnicare) (P), an NCS (D) competitor, made a series of offers to acquire NCS's (D) assets in a bankruptcy sale—at less than face value of NCS's (D) outstanding debts, and with no recovery for NCS stockholders. NCS (D) rejected Omnicare's (P) offers. By early 2002, NCS's (D) financial condition was improving, and the NCS board began to believe it might be able to realize some value for its shareholders. An Ad Hoc Committee of NCS (D) creditors contacted Genesis Health Ventures, Inc. (Genesis), an Omnicare (P) competitor, and Genesis expressed interest in bidding on NCS (D). Genesis made it clear that it did not want to be a "stalking horse" for NCS (D) and demanded an exclusivity agreement. After Genesis steadily increased its offers, NCS (D) granted Genesis the exclusivity it sought. The NCS board consisted of Outcalt and Shaw, who together controlled more than 65 percent of voting power in NCS (D), and Sells and Osborne, both of whom were disinterested, outside directors. In its negotiations, Genesis sought an agreement that would require, as permitted by Delaware General Corporation Law (DGCL) § 251(c), NCS (D) to submit the merger to NCS stockholders regardless of whether the NCS Board recommended the merger; an agreement by Outcalt and Shaw to vote their NCS stock in favor of the merger; and omission of any effective fiduciary-out clause from the agreement. Meanwhile, Omnicare (P) learned that NCS (D) was negotiating with Genesis and made a proposed bid for a transaction in which all NCS's (D) debt would be paid off and NCS stockholders would receive greater value than offered by Genesis. This offer was conditioned on satisfactory completion of due diligence. Fearing that Genesis might abandon its offer, NCS (D) refused to negotiate with Omnicare (P) but used Omnicare's (P) proposal to negotiate for improved terms with Genesis, which Genesis provided. However, in exchange, Genesis conditioned its offer on approval the next day. The NCS board gave such approval to the merger, in which NCS stockholders would receive Genesis stock and all NCS (D) debt would be paid off. The merger transaction included the provisions that Genesis had sought during negotiations, as well as the voting agreements with Outcalt and Shaw. Thus, the combined terms of the merger agreement and voting agreement guaranteed that the transaction proposed by Genesis would be approved by the NCS stockholders. Omnicare (P) filed suit to enjoin the merger and then launched a tender offer for all NCS (D) stock at a value of more than twice the then current market value of the shares to be received in the Genesis transaction. Otherwise, its offer equaled that of Genesis. Several months later, but before the NCS stockholders were to vote on the Genesis merger, as a result of Omnicare (P) irrevocably committing itself to its offer, the NCS board withdrew its recommendation of the Genesis merger and recommended, instead, that NCS shareholders vote for the Omnicare (P) merger because it was a superior proposal. The Court of Chancery ruled that the voting agreements with Outcalt and Shaw, combined with the provision requiring a stockholder vote regardless of board recommendation, constituted defensive measures, but found that, under the enhanced judicial scrutiny standard of *Unocal Corp. v. Mesa Petroleum Co.*, 493 A.2d 946 (Del. 1985), these measures were reasonable. The Delaware Supreme Court granted review.

ISSUE: Are lockup deal protection devices, which when operating in concert are coercive and preclusive,

Continued on next page.

invalid and unenforceable in the absence of a fiduciary-out clause?

HOLDING AND DECISION: (Holland, J.) Yes. Lockup deal protection devices, which when operating in concert are coercive and preclusive, are invalid and unenforceable in the absence of a fiduciary-out clause. The Chancery Court concluded that because the Genesis transaction did not result in a change of control, the transaction would be reviewed under the business judgment rule standard. Under this standard, the Chancery Court concluded that the NCS board had not breached its duty of care in approving the transaction. The Chancery Court's decision to use the business judgment rule standard, rather than enhanced scrutiny, is not outcome-determinative and this court will assume that the NCS board exercised due care when it approved the Genesis transaction. However, as to the defensive measures, enhanced scrutiny is required because of the inherent potential conflict of interest between a board's interest in protecting a merger transaction it has approved and the shareholders' statutory right to make the final decision to either approve or not approve a merger. This requires a threshold determination that the board approved defensive measures comport with the directors' fiduciary duties. In applying enhanced judicial scrutiny to defensive measures designed to protect a merger agreement, a court must first determine that those measures are not preclusive or coercive before its focus shifts to a "range of reasonableness" proportionality determination. When the focus shifts to the range of reasonableness, *Unocal* requires that any devices must be proportionate to the perceived threat to the corporation and its stockholders if the merger transaction is not consummated. Here, the voting agreements were inextricably intertwined with the defensive aspects of the Genesis merger agreement, and under *Unocal*, the defensive measures require special scrutiny. Under such scrutiny, these measures were neither reasonable nor proportionate to the threat NCS (D) perceived from the potential loss of the Genesis transaction. The threat identified by NCS (D) was the possibility of losing the Genesis offer and being left with no comparable alternative transaction. The second part of the *Unocal* analysis requires the NCS directors to demonstrate that their defensive response was reasonable in response to the threat posed. This inquiry itself involves a two-step analysis. The NCS directors must first establish that the deal protection devices adopted in response to the threat were not "coercive" or "preclusive," and then must demonstrate that their response was within a "range of reasonable responses" to the threat perceived. Here, the defensive measures were both preclusive and coercive, and, therefore, draconian and impermissible. That is because any stockholder vote would be "robbed of its effectiveness" by the impermissible coercion that predetermined the outcome of the merger without regard to the merits of the Genesis transaction at the time the vote was scheduled to take place. They were also preclusive because they accomplished a fait accompli. Accordingly, the defensive measures are unenforceable. They are alternatively unenforceable because the merger agreement completely prevented the board from discharging its fiduciary responsibilities to the minority stockholders when Omnicare (P) presented its superior transaction. Here, the NCS board could not abdicate its fiduciary duties to the minority by leaving it to the stockholders alone to approve or disapprove the merger because Outcalt and Shaw had combined to establish a majority of the voting power that made the outcome of the stockholder vote a foregone conclusion. Thus, the NCS board did not have authority to accede to the Genesis demand for an absolute "lockup." Instead, it was required to negotiate a fiduciary-out clause to protect the NCS shareholders if the Genesis transaction became an inferior offer. Therefore, the defensive measures—the voting agreements and the provision requiring a shareholder vote regardless of board recommendation—when combined to operate in concert in the absence of an effective fiduciary-out clause are invalid and unenforceable. [Reversed.]

DISSENT: (Veasey, C.J.) The NCS board's actions should have been evaluated based on the circumstances present at the time the Genesis merger agreement was entered into—before the emergence of a subsequent transaction offering greater value to the stockholders. The lockups were reached at the conclusion of a lengthy search and intense negotiation process in the context of insolvency, at a time when Genesis was the only viable bidder. Under these facts the NCS board's action before the emergence of the Omnicare (P) offer, reflected the actions of "a quintessential, disinterested, and informed board" made in good faith, and was within the bounds of its fiduciary duties and should be upheld. Moreover, situations arise where business realities demand a lockup so that wealth enhancing transactions may go forward. Accordingly, any bright-line rule prohibiting lockups, such as the one put forth by the majority, could, in circumstances such as those faced by the NCS board, chill otherwise permissible conduct. Here, the deal protection measures were not preclusive or coercive in the context of what they were intended for. They were not adopted to fend off a hostile takeover but were adopted so that Genesis—the "only game in town"—would save NCS (D), its creditors, and stockholders. Still, here there was no meaningful minority stockholder vote to coerce, given Outcalt and Shaw's majority position, so that the "preclusive" label has no application. Thus, giving Genesis an absolute lockup under the circumstances, by agreeing to omit a fiduciary-out clause, was not a per se violation of fiduciary duty. Hopefully, the rule announced by the majority will be interpreted narrowly and seen as sui generis.

Continued on next page.

ANALYSIS

One of the primary troubling aspects of the majority opinion, as voiced by the dissent, is the majority's suggestion that it can make a *Unocal* determination after-the-fact with a view to the superiority of a competing proposal that may subsequently emerge. Many commentators agree with the dissent that the lockups in this case should not have been reviewed in a vacuum. In a separate dissent, Justice Steele argued that when a board agrees rationally, in good faith, without conflict and with reasonable care to include provisions in a contract to preserve a deal in the absence of a better one, their business judgment should not be second-guessed in order to invalidate or declare unenforceable an otherwise valid merger agreement. Given the tension between the majority's and dissenters' positions, the full impact of the court's decision will need to await further judicial development.

Quicknotes

BUSINESS JUDGMENT RULE Standard of review that presumes that in making a business decision, the directors of a corporation acted on an informed basis, in good faith, and in the honest belief that the action taken was in the best interests of the company.

FIDUCIARY DUTY A legal obligation to act for the benefit of another, including subordinating one's personal interests to that of the other person.

LOCKUP OPTION A defensive strategy to a takeover attempt whereby a target corporation sets aside a specified portion of the company's shares for purchase by a friendly investor.

SUI GENERIS Peculiar to its own type or class.

Coster v. UIP Companies, Inc.

Shareholder (P) v. Corporation (D)

Del. Sup. Ct., 300 A.3d 656 (2023)

NATURE OF CASE: Appeal from judgment, following remand, upholding dilutive stock sale as entirely fair, not made for inequitable purposes, and made for compelling reasons.

FACT SUMMARY: Marion Coster (Coster) (P), who had been a 50 percent shareholder in UIP Companies, Inc. (UIP) (D), and who had been deadlocked with the other 50 percent shareholder to elect directors, petitioned for the appointment of a custodian for UIP (D). The UIP board (D) responded by issuing stock to Bonnell (D), a long-time employee, representing a one-third interest in UIP (D). The stock issuance diluted Coster's (P) ownership interest, broke the deadlock, and mooted the custodian action. Coster (P) claimed that the dilutive stock sale had not been entirely fair, had been made for inequitable purposes, and had not been made for compelling reasons.

RULE OF LAW

A dilutive stock sale will be upheld where it is entirely fair, was not made for inequitable purposes, and was made for compelling reasons.

FACTS: UIP Companies, Inc. (UIP) (D), a real estate services company, was founded in 2007 by Steven Schwat (D), Cornelius Bruggen, and Wout Coster ("Wout") and operated through various subsidiaries that provided a range of services to investment properties, many of which were held in special purpose entities ("SPEs") that UIP (D) owned alongside third-party investors. Each of the three founders initially controlled a third of UIP's (D) shares. In 2011, Bruggen left and tendered his shares to UIP (D) at no cost. This left Schwat (D) and Wout as half owners of UIP (D). In 2013, Wout notified Schwat (D) and Peter Bonnell (D), a senior UIP executive, that he had been diagnosed with leukemia. Shortly after, the group began negotiations for a buyout in which Bonnell (D) and Heath Wilkinson, another UIP (D) executive, would purchase Wout's shares in the company. Bonnell (D) had previously been promised equity in UIP (D) on multiple occasions, but as the prospect for promotion had stalled, Bonnell (D) and Wilkinson had both considered leaving UIP (D). Therefore, beyond providing Wout with an exit, the buyout was also useful in incentivizing Bonnell (D) and Wilkinson to stay. Unfortunately, negotiations were unsuccessful. Wout passed away in April 2015, and his widow, Marion Coster ("Coster") (P), inherited his UIP (D) interests. Immediately after Wout's death, Schwat (D) and Bonnell (D) continued exploring buyout options with Coster (P). Negotiations between the parties continued throughout 2016 and into 2017 as Coster (P) sought an independent valuation of UIP (D). In August 2017, Coster (P) provided UIP with a $7.3 million valuation and demanded to inspect UIP (D) books and records and then followed up with a second inspection demand in October 2017. Then, after much back and forth about the adequacy of the documents provided, in April 2018, Coster (P) called for a UIP (D) stockholders special meeting to elect new board members. At this time, UIP (D) had a five-member board composed of Schwat (D), Bonnell (D), and Stephen Cox (D), UIP's (D) Chief Financial Officer. Two seats were vacant as a result of Wout's passing and Cornelius Bruggen's departure in 2011. The stockholder meeting took place the following month. Coster (P), represented by counsel, raised multiple motions affecting the size and composition of the board. Predictably, each of Coster's (P) motions failed as a consequence of Schwat's (D) opposition. Later that day, the UIP board (D) reduced the number of board seats to three through unanimous written consent. A second stockholder meeting followed in June 2018, and also ended in deadlock, thus leaving Schwat (D), Bonnell (D), and Cox (D) as UIP's (D) directors. Afterward, Coster (P) filed a complaint in the Delaware Court of Chancery seeking appointment of a custodian under 8 Del. C. § 226(a)(1) (the "Custodian Action"). Coster's (P) complaint mainly sought to impose a neutral tie-breaker to facilitate director elections, but it also lodged allegations against Schwat (D) about the lack of distributions and transparency into the company's affairs and sought the appointment of a custodian with broad oversight and managerial powers. However, this request for a "broadly empowered" custodian rather than one specifically tailored to target the stockholder deadlock posed new risks to UIP (D), because the appointment of a custodian with such powers would have given rise to broad termination rights in SPE contracts and threatened UIP's (D) revenue stream. Facing this threat to UIP (D), the UIP board (D) decided to issue the equity that they had long promised to Bonnell (D). Having conducted its own valuation that valued a 100-percent, noncontrolling equity interest in UIP at $123,869, the board offered, and Bonnell (D) purchased, a one-third interest in the company for $41,289.67 (the "Stock Sale"). The Stock Sale diluted Coster's (P) ownership interest from one half to one third and negated her ability to block stockholder action as a half owner of the company. The Stock Sale also mooted the Custodian Action. In response, Coster (P) filed suit, seeking to cancel the Stock Sale. In its opinion

Continued on next page.

following trial, the Court of Chancery upheld the Stock Sale under the entire fairness standard of review. Coster (P) appealed, but the Delaware Supreme Court did not disturb the Court of Chancery's entire fairness decision, instead remanding with instructions to review the Stock Sale under Schnell and Blasius. As explained in our first decision, while entire fairness is "Delaware's most onerous standard of review," it is "not [a] substitute for further equitable review" under two precedents. The first, *Schnell v. Chris-Craft Industries, Inc.* 285 A.2d 437, 439 (Del. 1971), held that inequitable action does not become permissible simply because it is legally possible, and that management cannot inequitably manipulate corporate machinery to perpetuate itself in office and disenfranchise the stockholders. The second, *Blasius Industries, Inc. v. Atlas Corp.*, 564 A.2d 651, 659-661 (Del. Ch. 1988), held that directors who interfere with board elections, even if in good faith, must have a compelling justification for their actions. On remand, the Court of Chancery found that the UIP board (D) had not acted for inequitable purposes under *Schnell* and had compelling justifications for the Stock Sale under *Blasius*. The court found that the threat posed by the Custodian Action was "an existential crisis" that justified the UIP board's (D) actions and that the Stock Sale was appropriately tailored to achieve the goal of mooting the Custodian Action while also achieving other important goals, such as implementing the succession plan that Wout favored, and rewarding Bonnell (D). Coster (P) appealed the Court of Chancery's rulings on remand, and the Delaware Supreme Court granted review.

ISSUE: Will a dilutive stock sale be upheld where it is entirely fair, was not made for inequitable purposes, and was made for compelling reasons?

HOLDING AND DECISION: [Judge not stated in casebook excerpt.] Yes. A dilutive stock sale will be upheld where it is entirely fair, was not made for inequitable purposes, and was made for compelling reasons. The Court of Chancery correctly cabined *Schnell's* equitable review to those cases where the board acts within its legal power but is motivated for selfish reasons to interfere with the stockholder franchise. The Court of Chancery also properly folded its review under *Schnell* and *Blasius* into enhanced review under *Unocal Corp. v. Mesa Petroleum Co.*, 493 A.2d 946, 955 (Del. 1985), where the Supreme Court used an enhanced standard of review to decide whether the directors had reasonable grounds for believing that a danger to corporate policy and effectiveness existed and that the board's response was reasonable in relation to the threat posed. In this regard, a court first should review whether the board faced a threat to an important corporate interest or to the achievement of a significant corporate benefit. The threat must be real and not pretextual, and the board's motivations must be proper and not selfish or disloyal. Second, the court should review whether the board's response to the threat is preclusive or coercive to the stockholder franchise. To guard against unwarranted interference with corporate elections or stockholder votes in contests for corporate control, a board that is properly motivated and has identified a legitimate threat must tailor its response to only what is necessary to counter the threat. The board's response to the threat cannot deprive the stockholders of a vote, i.e., be preclusive, or coerce the stockholders to vote a particular way, i.e., be coercive. Applying these principles on remand, the Court of Chancery, after making additional findings, determined that the UIP board (D) faced a threat—which the court described as an "existential crisis"—to UIP's (D) existence through a deadlocked stockholder vote and the risk of a custodian appointment. Although the court thought that some of the board's reasons for approving the Stock Sale were problematic, on balance the court held that the board was properly motivated in responding to the threat. According to the court, the UIP board (D) acted in good faith to advance UIP's (D) best interests by rewarding and retaining Bonnell (D), an essential employee, implementing a succession plan that Wout had favored, and mooting the Custodian Action to avoid risk of default under key contracts. The court also relied on its earlier finding that the UIP board (D) issued UIP (D) stock to Bonnell (D) at an entirely fair price. The Court of Chancery also found that the UIP board (D) had responded reasonably and proportionately to the threat posed when it approved the Stock Sale and mooted the Custodian Action, given the exceptionally unique circumstances of the case. The court held that the Stock Sale had been appropriately tailored to achieve the goal of mooting the Custodian Action while implementing the succession plan and retaining Bonnell (D), noting that there were more aggressive options that could have been, but were not, pursued to break the deadlock. Finally, the UIP board's (D) response to the existential threat posed by the stockholder deadlock and custodian action was not preclusive or coercive. Although the Stock Sale effectively foreclosed Coster (P) from perpetuating the deadlock facing UIP (D), the new three-way ownership of the company presented a potentially more effective way for her to exercise actual control, because Schwat (D) and Bonnell (D) were not bound to vote together, meaning Coster (P) could cast a swing vote at stockholder meetings. As an equal one-third owner with the two other stockholders, Coster (P) would be able to join forces with either Schwat (D) and Bonnell (D) at some point in the future, and this realistic path to control of UIP (D) negated the preclusive impact of the Stock Sale. Affirmed.

Continued on next page.

ANALYSIS

As this case illustrates, enhanced scrutiny, or the *Unocal* doctrine, rests in part on an assiduous concern about defensive actions designed to thwart the essence of corporate democracy by disenfranchising shareholders. The *Unocal* standard is a flexible paradigm that jurists can apply to the myriad of fact scenarios that confront corporate boards, applying where the record reflects that a board of directors took defensive measures in response to a perceived threat to corporate policy and effectiveness that touches upon issues of control. This enhanced scrutiny standard of review requires a context-specific application of the directors' duties of loyalty, good faith, and care. Fundamentally, the standard to be applied is one of reasonableness. The defendants must identify the proper corporate objectives served by their actions and justify their actions as reasonable in relation to those objectives. If the incumbent directors' actions operate as a reasonable limitation upon the shareholders' right to nominate candidates for director, they will generally be validated. If, on the other hand, the directors' actions are unreasonable, notwithstanding that they are lawful and in compliance with the corporation's bylaws and other governing documents, they will be enjoined. The basis for such an outcome rests on the fiduciary duty imposed on directors and officers of a corporation to deal fairly, justly, and in good faith with the corporation and all of its shareholders, including minority shareholders.

Quicknotes

DUTY OF CARE Duty that an officer or director owes to the corporation, by virtue of their fiduciary relationship, to act for the benefit of the corporation.

DUTY OF LOYALTY A director's duty to refrain from self-dealing or to take a position that is adverse to the corporation's best interests.

ENTIRE FAIRNESS Standard of review that places the burden on a corporate defendant to demonstrate that a corporate transaction is entirely fair to the corporation and its stockholders both as to the transaction's process ("fair dealing") and economics ("fair price").

FIDUCIARY DUTY A legal obligation to act for the benefit of another, including subordinating one's personal interests to that of the other person.

GOOD FAITH An honest intention to abstain from taking advantage of another.

CTS Corporation v. Dynamics Corporation of America

Target corporation (D) v. Corporation (P)

481 U.S. 69 (1987)

NATURE OF CASE: Appeal from affirmance of invalidation of state corporate anti-takeover law.

FACT SUMMARY: Indiana enacted a statutory scheme requiring shareholder approval prior to significant shifts in corporate control.

RULE OF LAW

(1) A law permitting in-state corporations to require shareholder approval prior to significant shifts in corporate control is consistent with the provisions and purposes of the Williams Act and is not preempted thereby.

(2) A law permitting in-state corporations to require shareholder approval prior to significant shifts in corporate control is constitutional as not violating the Commerce Clause.

FACTS: Indiana enacted a control share acquisition statutory scheme whereby large Indiana public corporations, if they so opted, could require any entity acquiring shares that, but for the operation of the scheme, would bring its voting power in the corporation to or above a 20 percent, 33.33 percent, or 50 percent interest to be subjected to a shareholder referendum whereby voting power of those shares could be withheld. Dynamics Corp. of America (Dynamics) (P), holder of 9.6 percent of CTS Corporation's (D) shares, announced a tender offer that would have brought its control to 27.5 percent. Dynamics (P) challenged the statute as void as preempted by the federal Williams Act, 15 U.S.C. §§78m(d)-(e) and 78n(d)-(f), and as violating the Commerce Clause of the U.S. Constitution. The federal Williams Act and its implementing regulations, enacted by the Securities and Exchange Commission (SEC), govern hostile corporate stock tender offers by requiring, inter alia, that tender offers remain open for at least 20 business days. The district court found the statute was preempted by the Williams Act and violated the Commerce Clause, and the court invalidated the statute. The court of appeals affirmed. The court of appeals based its preemption finding on the view that the Indiana statute, in effect, imposed at least a 50-day delay on the consummation of tender offers and that this conflicted with the minimum 20-day, hold-open period under the Williams Act. The court also held that the state Act violated the Commerce Clause since it deprived nonresidents of the valued opportunity to accept tender offers from other nonresidents, and that it violated the conflict-of-laws "internal affairs" doctrine in that it had a direct, intended, and substantial effect on the interstate market in securities and corporate control. CTS (D) appealed, and the United States Supreme Court granted certiorari.

ISSUE:

(1) Is a law permitting in-state corporations to require shareholder approval prior to significant shifts in corporate control consistent with the provisions and purposes of the Williams Act and is not preempted thereby?

(2) Is a law permitting in-state corporations to require shareholder approval prior to significant shifts in corporate control constitutional as not violating the Commerce Clause?

HOLDING AND DECISION: (Powell, J.)

(1) Yes. A law permitting in-state corporations to require shareholder approval prior to significant shifts in corporate control is consistent with the provisions and purposes of the Williams Act and is not preempted thereby. The Indiana Act (the Act) protects independent shareholders from the coercive aspects of tender offers by allowing them to vote as a group, and thereby furthers the Williams Act's basic purpose of placing investors on an equal footing with takeover bidders. Moreover, the Indiana Act does not give either management or the offeror an advantage in communicating with shareholders, nor impose an indefinite delay on offers, nor allow the state government to interpose its views of fairness between willing buyers and sellers. Thus, the Indiana Act satisfies even broad interpretation of the Williams Act. The possibility that the Indiana Act will delay some tender offers does not mandate preemption. The state Act neither imposes an absolute 50-day delay on the consummation of tender offers nor precludes offerors from purchasing shares as soon as federal law permits. If an adverse shareholder vote is feared, the tender offer can be conditioned on the shares' receiving voting rights within a specified period. Furthermore, even assuming the Indiana Act does impose some additional delay, only "unreasonable" delays conflict with the Williams Act. Here, it cannot be said that a 50-day delay is unreasonable since that period falls within a 60-day period Congress established for tendering shareholders to withdraw their unpurchased shares. If the Williams Act were construed to preempt any state statute that caused delays, it would preempt a variety of state corporate

Continued on next page.

laws of hitherto unquestioned validity. The long-standing prevalence of state regulation in this area suggests that, if Congress had intended to preempt all such state laws, it would have said so. Reversed as to this issue.

(2) Yes. A law permitting in-state corporations to require shareholder approval prior to significant shifts in corporate control is constitutional as not violating the Commerce Clause. The Indiana Act's limited effect on interstate commerce is justified by the state's interests in defining attributes of its corporations' shares and in protecting shareholders. The principal objects of dormant commerce clause scrutiny are statutes discriminating against interstate commerce. The law in question here does not so discriminate, as it applies to both Indiana and non-Indiana would-be acquiring entities. Another type of law often struck down is that which would subject interstate commerce to inconsistent regulations. Such is not the case here, as Indiana's laws would be the only regulations applicable here. The court of appeals found the Indiana Act unconstitutional because it had great potential to hinder tender offers. This may be, but it is an insufficient reason to invalidate the state Act. Corporations are creatures of state law, and states are free to formulate policy regarding the internal operations of corporations, provided they do so in a non-discriminatory manner, which is the case here. Even if the Act did decrease the number of successful tender offers for Indiana corporations, this would not offend the Commerce Clause. The Act does not prohibit any resident or nonresident from offering to purchase, or from purchasing, shares in Indiana corporations, or from attempting thereby to gain control. It only provides regulatory procedures designed for the better protection of the corporations' shareholders. The Commerce Clause does not protect the particular structure or methods of operation in a market. Reversed as to this issue.

CONCURRENCE: (Scalia, J.) As long as a state's corporation law governs only its own corporations and does not discriminate against out-of-state-interests, it should survive this Court's scrutiny under the Commerce Clause, regardless of whether it promotes or inhibits corporate welfare; a law can be both economic folly and constitutional.

DISSENT: (White, J.) The law undermines the policy of the Williams Act by effectively preventing minority shareholders, in some circumstances, from acting in their own interests by selling their stock. The law also indirectly discriminates against interstate commerce in violation of the Dormant Commerce Clause.

ANALYSIS

The Court implies an acceptance of heavy regulation of the workings of a corporation by the state of its incorporation. States have, according to the Court, a great interest in their corporations, and this justifies the regulations under the "internal affairs" doctrine, under which a corporation's ownership structure and matters related thereto, is governed by the law of the state of incorporation.

Quicknotes

COMMERCE CLAUSE Article 1, section 8, clause 3 of the United States Constitution, granting Congress the power to regulate commerce with foreign countries and between the states.

DORMANT COMMERCE CLAUSE The regulatory effect of the Commerce Clause on state activity affecting interstate commerce, where Congress itself has not acted to control the activity; a provision inferred from, but not expressly present in, the language of the Commerce Clause.

INDIANA BUS. CORP. LAW 23-1-17-1 ET SEQ. Conditions acquisition of control of a corporation in approval of a majority of the preexisting disinterested shareholders.

TENDER OFFER An offer made by one corporation to the shareholders of a target corporation to purchase their shares subject to number, time, and price specifications.

CHAPTER 7

Corporate Debt

Quick Reference Rules of Law

Sharon Steel Corporation v. Chase Manhattan Bank, N.A.

Corporation (P) v. Debenture holders (D)

691 F.2d 1039 (2d Cir. 1982)

NATURE OF CASE: Appeal from dismissal of action to declare debentures not due or payable, and from judgment for indenture trustees and debenture holders that debentures were due and payable.

FACT SUMMARY: Sharon Steel Corp. (P) contended that certain debentures issued by UV Industries, a corporation whose assets it had purchased, were not due and payable because of a clause that exempted accelerated maturity if all or substantially all its assets were sold.

RULE OF LAW

A clause in a debt instrument preventing accelerated maturity in the event of a sale of all or substantially all the debtor's assets is inapplicable if the assets are sold piecemeal.

FACTS: UV Industries (UV) issued certain debentures. Subsequent to this, and before the debentures were due and payable, UV began to liquidate itself. UV consisted of three divisions. After two of the divisions had been sold, Sharon Steel Corporation (Sharon) (P) purchased the remaining division, which accounted for 38 percent of UV's revenues. The debentures were part of the package acquired by Sharon (P). Sharon (P) filed an action seeking a declaration that the maturity of the debentures had not been accelerated by the dissolution of UV due to a clause in the debentures that provided maturity would not be accelerated by a sale of "all or substantially all" of UV's assets. The district court dismissed Sharon's (P) complaint and awarded judgment to the indenture trustees and debenture holders on their claim that the debentures were due and payable, and Sharon (P) appealed. The court of appeals granted review.

ISSUE: Is a clause in a debt instrument preventing accelerated maturity in the event of a sale of all or substantially all the debtor's assets applicable if the assets are sold piecemeal?

HOLDING AND DECISION: [Judge not stated in casebook excerpt.] No. A clause in a debt instrument preventing accelerated maturity in the event of a sale of all or substantially all the debtor's assets is inapplicable if the assets are sold piecemeal. Such a clause is a "boilerplate" in that it is a common clause in instruments of this type. For this reason, it is to be construed in a manner uniform with the normal construction of the term. In this particular situation, the term "all or substantially all" of UV's assets means those assets existing at a time UV continues to act as an ongoing concern. Sharon (P) contends that since the assets it obtained were all of UV's assets after it had divested itself of most of its operations, it had in fact received "all" of UV's assets. This interpretation is incorrect. The common understanding of the term is that it refers to a debtor's operations before divestiture begins. Here, Sharon (P) obtained only 38 percent worth of the revenue-producing assets of UV, which does not come close to "all or substantially all" of UV's assets. Therefore, UV's obligations under the debentures became accelerated. Affirmed.

ANALYSIS

The reason that the maturity of the notes was at issue was their interest rate. As of the time of Sharon's (P) purchase of UV's assets, the market value of the notes was less than the amount payable upon maturity. Noteholders therefore wanted acceleration to receive the amount payable upon maturity. Had the interest rate been higher, the parties would each have argued for the opposite result.

Quicknotes

DEBENTURES Long-term unsecured debt securities issued by a corporation.

DISSOLUTION Annulment or termination of a formal or legal bond, tie, or contract.

DIVESTMENT The premature termination of an interest.

Metropolitan Life Insurance Company v. RJR Nabisco, Inc.

Bond holder (P) v. Bond issuer (D)

716 F. Supp. 1504 (S.D.N.Y. 1989)

NATURE OF CASE: Motion for summary judgment in action seeking contract damages on claims of breach of the implied covenant of good faith and fair dealing as well as equitable claims and claims for fraud.

FACT SUMMARY: Metropolitan Life Insurance Co. (P), holder of bonds issued by RJR Nabisco, Inc. (RJR) (D), contended that a downgrading of RJR's (D) credit rating due to a leveraged buyout (LBO), which had made the bonds less marketable, constituted breach of the implied covenant of good faith. RJR (D) defended by pointing to express provisions in the bond indentures that permitted mergers and the assumption of additional debt.

RULE OF LAW

The assumption of additional debt by a bond issuer in a leveraged buyout (LBO) that results in a downgrading of the bonds does not constitute a breach of the implied covenant of good faith and fair dealing.

FACTS: Metropolitan Life Insurance Co. (MetLife) (P) purchased over $340,000,000 in bonds from RJR Nabisco, Inc. (RJR) (D). Subsequent to this, RJR (D) was the subject of a highly publicized leveraged buyout (LBO). As part of the LBO, RJR (D) took on substantial additional debt. As a result of this debt assumption RJR's (D) creditworthiness was downgraded. This resulted in a significant decrease of the value of its corporate bonds in the bond market. MetLife (P), along with Jefferson-Pilot Life Insurance Co. (Jefferson-Pilot) (P), which had purchased over $9 million of RJR (D) bonds, filed an action in federal district court contending that this debt assumption constituted a breach of the implied covenant of good faith and fair dealing and gave rise to various equitable claims and claims for fraud. The bond indentures permitted mergers and the assumption of additional debt. Also, the bondholders (P), which were among the nation's most sophisticated investors and which were very familiar with the bond markets, the risks inherent in those markets, and bond indenture terms, were free to sell the bonds at any time. MetLife (P) and co-plaintiff bondholder moved for summary judgment, and RJR (D) moved to dismiss.

ISSUE: Does the assumption of additional debt by a bond issuer in a leveraged buyout that results in a downgrading of the bonds constitute a breach of the implied covenant of good faith and fair dealing?

HOLDING AND DECISION: [Judge not stated in casebook excerpt.] No. The assumption of additional debt by a bond issuer in a leveraged buyout that results in a downgrading of the bonds does not constitute a breach of the implied covenant of good faith and fair dealing. The law does recognize in all contracts an implied covenant of good faith and fair dealing. However, this covenant does not go so far as to give one party to a contract rights for which he did not bargain. The bonds in issue here contain specific language, common in corporate bonds, allowing the issuer to engage in merger transactions, which often results in additional debt. The bond indentures also expressly permitted the assumption of additional debt. Beyond this, internal memoranda generated within MetLife (P) indicate that it was aware of the potential of downgraded bonds subsequent to LBOs, and, in fact, contemplated attempting to insert language into the bonds it purchased prohibiting the incurrence of such debt. This plan was later dropped, based on a realization that bond issuers would likely balk at such language and insistence thereon might take MetLife (P) out of the bond market. Thus, MetLife (P) would have the court insert by operation of law a clause into its contract that it was unable or unwilling to do itself at the time the bonds were negotiated. In sum, the implied covenant of good faith and fair dealing arises out of the language of the contract at issue, which sets the rights of the parties. MetLife (P) wishes to extend the covenant to apply to rights it does not have under the contracts at issue, and therefore it must fail. Similarly, the bondholders' (P) equitable claims are merely restatements of their contract claim, and, therefore, must also be dismissed. Finally, the bondholders' (P) disclosure-related common-law fraud claim under Rule 10b-5 survives the motion to dismiss. With respect to all of the bondholders' (P) other claims, RJR's (D) motion to dismiss is granted, and the bondholders' (P) motion for summary judgment is denied.

ANALYSIS

The claims that survived dismissal (those for fraud and fraudulent conveyance) were ultimately settled, apparently restoring to MetLife (P) and Jefferson-Pilot (P) much of the value of the RJR (D) bonds that was lost after RJR (D) was taken private. Thus, while losing on their contract claims, the bondholders (P) prevailed, at least to some extent, with the threat of litigation on their other claims. That is not a bad outcome for the bondholders (P), given that typically bondholders ordinarily have not bargained for and do not expect any substantial

Continued on next page.

gain in the value of the security to compensate for the risk of loss. The holder can expect only interest at the prescribed rate plus the eventual return of the principal. Except for possible increases in the market value of the debt instrument as a result of changes in interest rates, the debt instrument will seldom be worth more than the holder paid for it. Moreover, the debt instrument may become worth much less. Therefore, the typical investor-holder in a long-term debt security is primarily interested in every reasonable assurance that the principal and interest will be paid when due. Any protections the bondholder seeks for timely repayment of interest and principal by the issuer must be provided for contractually in the bond agreement.

Quicknotes

IMPLIED COVENANT OF GOOD FAITH AND FAIR DEALING An implied warranty the parties will deal honestly in the satisfaction of their obligations and without intent to defraud.

INDENTURE A written instrument setting forth the terms pursuant to which a bond or debenture is issued.

LEVERAGED BUYOUT A transaction whereby corporate outsiders purchase the outstanding shares of a publicly held corporation mostly with borrowed funds.

RULE 10B-5 Unlawful to defend or make untrue statements in connection with purchase or sale of securities.

Bank of New York Mellon v. Realogy Corp.

Indenture trustee (P) v. Debenture issuer (D)

Del. Ct. Ch., 979 A.2d 1113 (2008)

NATURE OF CASE: Cross motions for summary judgment in action seeking declaration that terms of an exchange offer made by a debenture issuer are invalid under the indenture.

FACT SUMMARY: Bank of New York Mellon (Trustee) (P), the trustee for a class of unsecured debt holders of Realogy Corp. (D), contended that a proposed exchange offer, whereby a large amount of the unsecured indebtedness would be financed with a substantially smaller amount of a senior secured term loan, would violate the terms of the indenture, with the ultimate issue being whether the proposed borrowing satisfied the definition of "Permitted Refinancing Indebtedness" found in the bank credit agreement incorporated by reference into the indenture.

RULE OF LAW

A proposed exchange offer to refinance debt is void where some of its terms violate some of the debt indenture's and loan agreement's provisions.

FACTS: Realogy Corp. (D) had several levels of debt. Level I debt was the most senior and was secured by a first lien on substantially all of Realogy's (D) assets. Level II debt was unsecured and included two sets of obligations. One set covered payments to be made in cash (Cash Notes); the other covered payments to be made in either cash or in kind (Toggle Notes). Level III debt was also unsecured and was subordinated to the Level I and Level II debt. As a result of having gone private and in the face of recession all of Realogy Corp.'s (D) unsecured indebtedness was trading at a deep discount to face value. In response, Realogy (D) proposed a debt refinancing whereby a large amount of the unsecured indebtedness (Levels II and III) would be financed with a substantially smaller amount of a senior secured term loan. Specifically, eligible noteholders were invited to participate as lenders under a new term lending facility, which would consist of Term C and Term D Loans under the Other Term Loans accordion feature of the Credit Agreement and would be secured by a second lien on substantially all of Realogy's (D) assets. Instead of funding these term loans with cash, the participating noteholders would fund their obligations under the new term loans with the delivery of existing notes, with priority given to commitments funded with certain classes of notes. The new term loans were to be pari passu to the existing indebtedness under the Level I Credit Agreement as well as the Level II Notes, and were to be secured, thus giving holders of the new term loans higher priority than any of the Level II Notes or Level III Notes. Bank of New York Mellon (Trustee) (P), the trustee for the Level II Toggle Notes brought suit seeking a declaration that the proposed exchange would breach certain terms of the indenture, in particular, the Level I Credit Agreement's accordion provision. The question was whether the new "loan," funded by the cancellation of existing unsecured debt, was permitted under the accordion provision. The Trustee (P) also asserted that the new term loans did not qualify as "Loans" under the Credit Agreement because they were not funded in cash. The parties cross moved for summary judgment.

ISSUE: Is a proposed exchange offer to refinance debt void where some of its terms violate some of the debt indenture's and loan agreement's provisions?

HOLDING AND DECISION: [Judge not stated in casebook excerpt.] Yes. A proposed exchange offer to refinance debt is void where some of its terms violate some of the debt indenture's and loan agreement's provisions. First, contrary to the Trustee's (P) argument, the term "loan" does not necessarily imply cash funding. Loans may encompass non-cash funding, and there are many examples of commercial loans that are not funded in cash, but that are repaid in cash, such as traditional vendor and seller financing agreements. The next argument made by the Trustee (P) is that the Credit Agreement requires loans to be funded in cash. These arguments fundamentally fall into two categories: (1) arguments based on the use of loan denominations in terms of amounts of currency; and (2) arguments based on various procedural and ministerial provisions. As to the first category, the Trustee's (P) argument that loans must be funded in cash because the Credit Agreement frequently speaks about loans in terms of quantities of currency, is unconvincing. These currency terms, which require repayment in dollars, speak to the amounts that Realogy (D) will be required to repay upon maturation of the term loans. This is no different than any other term loan, whether originally funded in cash or by some other consideration. Similarly, with respect to the Trustee's (P) arguments that certain administrative and procedural provisions in the Credit Agreement require only cash-funded loans, those arguments are unconvincing; the Credit Agreement's requirement of an account into which funds are to be disbursed does not require cash-funded loans. Also, the proposed refinancing would be permissible if the term loans were funded in cash—which could be achieved by restructuring the transaction so that the noteholders

Continued on next page.

would commit to paying cash for the new term loans while at the same time having Realogy (D) agree to buy the existing notes from the noteholders for cash, at the proposed reduced price. The result would be identical to that of the proposed transaction. Notwithstanding these failed arguments by the Trustee (P), the Trustee (P) also argues that a covenant in the Credit Agreement prohibits the proposed transaction unless it comes within the definition of "Permitted Refinancing Indebtedness." That definition includes the provision that "no Permitted Refinancing Indebtedness shall have different obligors, or greater guarantees or security, than the Indebtedness being Refinanced." In this regard, the Trustee (P) successfully argues that the proposed transaction does not come within this definition, and, for that reason, must be granted judgment. Summary judgment for the Trustee (P).

ANALYSIS

With financing for companies becoming less available as a result of recession, companies, such as Realogy (D), are increasingly looking to debt exchange transactions such as the one proposed by Realogy (D) here to deal with liquidity problems, high leverage, and even to head off bankruptcy. Typically, these transactions involve the exchange of newly issued debt or equity in exchange for existing outstanding debentures. However, companies must be careful to avoid making these transactions overly coercive, or, as this case demonstrates, having the transactions violate the terms of the loan agreement and indenture.

Quicknotes

DEBENTURES Long-term unsecured debt securities issued by a corporation.

INDENTURE A written instrument setting forth the terms pursuant to which a bond or debenture is issued.

Katz v. Oak Industries, Inc.

Debt holder (P) v. Debt issuer (D)

Del. Ct. Ch., 508 A.2d 873 (1986)

NATURE OF CASE: Class action suit seeking a preliminary injunction.

FACT SUMMARY: Katz (P) sought to enjoin an exchange offer and consent solicitation made in connection with Oak Industries, Inc.'s (D) attempted reorganization and recapitalization efforts.

RULE OF LAW

An exchange offer and consent solicitation made by a corporation seeking to maximize the benefit to its stockholders, at the potential expense of its debt holders, does not constitute a breach of the directors' duty of loyalty to the corporation.

FACTS: In an attempt to reduce some of its $230 million in outstanding debentures, Oak Industries, Inc. (Oak) (D) made an exchange offer to its debt holders. Oak (D) entered into a contract with Allied-Signal, Inc., for the sale of a segment of its business (the Materials Segment) and continued to seek a buyer for another segment of its business. The companies entered into two agreements. The first involved the sale of Oak's (D) Materials Segment for cash. The second provided for the purchase by Allied-Signal of ten million shares of Oak's (D) common stock with warrants to purchase additional common stock. The second agreement was predicated upon the condition that at least 85 percent of Oak's (D) debt holders accept the exchange offer. If less than 85 percent of the aggregate principal amount of the debt, held in six classes of debt, accepted the offer, Allied-Signal had the option, but no obligation, to abide by the second agreement. Accordingly, Oak (D) extended an exchange offer to each of the holders of the six classes of its long-term debt. Oak (D) made two exchange offers providing for payment of less than the face value of the securities but above their market value. The exchange offers were also based on the conditions that a minimum amount of debt securities of each class be tendered, and that the holders thereof consent to amendments to the indentures. Katz (P), a holder of Oak's (D) long-term debt, sought to enjoin the exchange offer and consent solicitation, claiming that the terms of the exchange offer and consent solicitation constituted coercion and a breach of contract. The breach of contract claim was premised on the condition of the offer that tendering security holders would have to consent to amendments in the indentures governing the securities. Katz (P) claimed that those amendments would, if implemented, have the effect of removing significant negotiated protections to holders of Oak's (D) long-term debt, including the deletion of all financial covenants, and would adversely impact those debt holders who elected not to tender pursuant to the exchange offers. Katz (P) further asserted that no rational bondholder would refuse to tender and consent, because such refusal would face the bondholder with the risk of owning a security stripped of all financial covenant protections and for which there most likely would be no market. Thus, from this, Katz (P) concluded that the bondholders were being "forced" and coerced to tender and consent.

ISSUE: Does an exchange offer and consent solicitation, maximizing the interests of corporation's shareholders at the expense of its debt holders, constitute a breach of the directors' duty of loyalty?

HOLDING AND DECISION: [Judge not stated in casebook excerpt.] No. An exchange offer and consent solicitation made by a corporation seeking to maximize the benefit to its stockholders, at the potential expense of its debt holders, does not constitute a breach of the directors' duty of loyalty to the corporation. The proper standard to be applied is one of contract law, not that of fiduciary duties. The appropriate test is whether the corporation violated the implied covenants of good faith and fair dealing. In reaching this determination, the court must decide whether from the terms of the contract the parties involved would have proscribed the action in question as a breach of the implied covenant of good faith had they negotiated in respect thereto. If so, then the court may conclude that the implied covenant of good faith has been breached. Nothing in the indenture provisions at issue in this case precludes Oak (D) from offering the bondholders an inducement to consent to the proposed amendments. Nothing in the indenture provisions grants bondholders the power to veto proposed modifications in the relevant indenture that precludes Oak (D) from offering an inducement to bondholders to consent to such amendments. Furthermore, there is nothing in the agreement from which the court may infer that Oak's (D) act would have been prohibited as a breach of the implied covenant of good faith had the parties negotiated on the subject. The exchange offer is not in violation of either the express provisions of the indenture agreement nor does it violate the covenants of good faith and fair dealing. Katz (P) has failed to meet his burden of demonstrating a probability of success on the merits of his claim. Dismissed.

Continued on next page.

ANALYSIS

Note that holders of debt securities stand in a contractual relationship to the corporation's board of directors. This is so even for holders of convertible debt securities. The directors' primary concern in a tender offer situation is to advance the welfare of the company's shareholders and attempt to maximize the return on their investment. In the absence of statutory provisions or express contractual protections, shifting the risk of loss from the shareholders to the bondholders does not constitute a breach of the directors' fiduciary duties.

Quicknotes

BREACH OF CONTRACT Unlawful failure by a party to perform its obligations pursuant to contract.

CLASS ACTION A suit commenced by a representative on behalf of an ascertainable group that is too large to appear in court, shares a commonality of interests, and will benefit from a successful result.

COERCION The overcoming of a person's free will as a result of threats, promises, or undue influence.

DEBENTURES Long-term unsecured debt securities issued by a corporation.

DUTY OF LOYALTY A director's duty to refrain from self-dealing or to take a position that is adverse to the corporation's best interests.

EXCHANGE OFFER A form of takeover in which the acquiring company makes a public offer to exchange shares of its own company for those of the target corporation.

IMPLIED COVENANT OF GOOD FAITH AND FAIR DEALING An implied warranty the parties will deal honestly in the satisfaction of their obligations and without intent to defraud.

INDENTURE A written instrument setting forth the terms pursuant to which a bond or debenture is issued.

PRELIMINARY INJUNCTION An order issued by the court at the commencement of an action, requiring a party to refrain from conducting a specified activity that is the subject of the controversy, until the matter is determined.

Morgan Stanley & Co. v. Archer Daniels Midland Company

Debenture holder (P) v. Debenture issuer (D)

570 F. Supp. 1529 (S.D.N.Y. 1983)

NATURE OF CASE: Cross-motions for summary judgment in action to preliminarily enjoin a bond redemption.

FACT SUMMARY: Morgan Stanley & Co. (P) claimed that Archer Daniels Midland Co.'s (D) redemption of $125 million in debentures constituted a breach of contract and violated applicable securities law.

RULE OF LAW

An early redemption of debentures is lawful where the source of funds originates directly from the proceeds of a common stock offering.

FACTS: In May 1981, Archer Daniels Midland Co. (ADM) (D) issued $125 million in debentures. The debenture agreement provided ADM (D) would not redeem the debentures from the proceeds, or in the anticipation, of the issuance of debt if the interest rate fell below 16.08 percent. Following the issuance of the debentures, ADM (D) raised capital through borrowing at interest rates less than the stated 16.08 percent, and through two common stock offerings. In May 1983, Morgan Stanley & Co. (P) purchased $16 million worth in debentures. On June 1, ADM (D) called for the redemption of the debentures, the source of funds originating from the common stock offerings. Morgan Stanley (P) sought a preliminary injunction barring the redemption on the basis that it violated securities law and constituted breach of contract. The parties cross moved for summary judgment.

ISSUE: Is an early redemption of debentures lawful when it is funded directly from the proceeds of a common stock offering?

HOLDING AND DECISION: [Judge not stated in casebook excerpt.] Yes. An early redemption of debentures is lawful where the source of funds originates directly from the proceeds of a common stock offering. Where the contract in dispute involves "boilerplate" language, the court must construe the agreement so to create uniform treatment. In doing so, the court may examine surrounding facts and circumstances to determine the parties' intent. Furthermore, the court must consider existing law at the time the contract was entered as part of that contract. The only other court presented with this issue interpreted such standardized language to render redemption of stock lawful where the refunding was accomplished solely from the proceeds of an issuance of common stock. Here, the rules of contract construction are not helpful, and the equities are essentially in equilibrium. However, the court must still determine the actual source of the funds subsidizing the redemption. Here the redemption was lawful under the terms of the debenture agreement, the direct source of funds being the two common stock offerings. ADM's (D) motion for summary judgment is granted.

ANALYSIS

Note that in a case where a proposed redemption is indirectly funded by the issuance of debt borrowed at an interest rate prohibited by the debenture agreement, such redemption would be unlawful. Thus, if ADM (D) contemporaneously issued new debentures at a lower interest rate and used the proceeds of that issuance to repurchase the stock issued in the two common stock offerings, the attempted redemption would fail the test, having been indirectly funded through the proceeds of anticipated debt issued at a proscribed percentage. The result would place ADM (D) in an improved position, the new debt being repaid at a lower interest rate.

Quicknotes

BREACH OF CONTRACT Unlawful failure by a party to perform its obligations pursuant to contract.

COMMON STOCK A class of stock representing the corporation's ownership, the holders of which are entitled to dividends only after the holders of preferred stock are paid.

DEBENTURES Long-term unsecured debt securities issued by a corporation.

REDEMPTION The repurchase of a security by the issuing corporation according to the terms specified in the security agreement specifying the procedure for the repurchase.

SUMMARY JUDGMENT Judgment rendered by a court in response to a motion made by one of the parties, claiming that the lack of a question of material fact in respect to an issue warrants disposition of the issue without consideration by the jury.

CHAPTER 8

The Limited Liability Company (LLC)

Quick Reference Rules of Law

8. *Reese v. Newman.* Where a limited liability company (LLC) statute provides that a trial court may order a remedy other than dissolution, but also provides that "[a] person shall be dissociated as a member from a limited liability company" when the person commits certain actions described in the statute, and where a jury determines there are grounds supporting both dissolution of an LLC and the dissociation of a member from the LLC, a trial court has discretion to order either dissolution or dissociation. *226*

9. *Haley v. Talcott.* Where co-equal members of a limited liability company (LLC) are at an impasse, can no longer carry on the LLC's business, and are in disagreement whether to discontinue the business and how to dispose of its assets, and where an exit mechanism in the LLC's operating agreement is inequitable, dissolution is necessary. *228*

Duray Development, LLC v. Perrin

Developer (P) v. Contractor (D)

Mich. Ct. App., 288 Mich. App. 143, 792 N.W.2d 749 (2010)

NATURE OF CASE: Appeal from judgment for plaintiff in action for breach of contract.

FACT SUMMARY: Perrin (D), who had entered into a contract with Duray Development, LLC (P) on behalf of Outlaw Excavating, LLC (Outlaw) (D), at a time that the parties believed Outlaw (D) was a valid limited liability company (LLC), contended that, notwithstanding that in fact Outlaw (D) was not validly established when the contract was entered into, because the parties believed and acted as if Outlaw (D) had been validly established, the doctrine of limited liability company by estoppel should apply to shield Perrin (D) from personal liability for breach of contract.

RULE OF LAW

(1) The de facto corporation doctrine may be extended to a limited liability company where its incorporators have (a) proceeded in good faith, (b) under a valid statute, (c) for an authorized purpose, and (d) have executed and acknowledged articles of association pursuant to that purpose.

(2) A limited liability company by estoppel finding is appropriate where the parties enter into a contract believing that a limited liability company has been validly formed, and the parties proceed under that belief, notwithstanding that in fact the limited liability company was not validly formed at the time the contract was entered into.

FACTS: In September 2004, Duray Development, LLC (P) entered into a contract with Perrin (D) to supply excavating services for a development project. On October 27, 2004, Duray Development (P) entered into a second contract that was intended to supersede the earlier contract. This time, Perrin (D) signed on behalf of Outlaw Excavating, LLC (Outlaw) (D), which Perrin (D) had recently formed. Having signed the articles of organization for Outlaw (D) that same day, Perrin (D) believed that Outlaw (D) was a validly formed LLC, and the parties proceeded under this belief. Outlaw (D) billed Duray Development (P), which received a certificate of liability insurance for Outlaw (D). In fact, however, Outlaw (D) did not obtain "filed" status until November 29, 2004, so that under state law it was not a valid LLC until then. Outlaw (D) began performance under the contract, but did not perform satisfactorily or on time, and Duray Development (P) brought suit against Outlaw (D) and Perrin (D) for breach of contract. Through discovery, Duray Development (P) learned that Outlaw (D) had not been validly formed when Perrin (D) entered the contract in October 2004, and it obtained a judgment against Perrin (D) personally on this ground. The trial court rejected Perrin's (D) argument that the doctrine of de facto corporation should apply, since Outlaw (D) was not a corporation, and since the state's Limited Liability Company Act specifically provided for the time that an LLC comes into existence and has powers to contract, and, therefore, superseded the de facto corporation doctrine and made it inapplicable to LLCs altogether. The state's intermediate appellate court granted review.

ISSUE:

(1) May the de facto corporation doctrine be extended to a limited liability company where its incorporators have (a) proceeded in good faith, (b) under a valid statute, (c) for an authorized purpose, and (d) have executed and acknowledged articles of association pursuant to that purpose?

(2) Is a limited liability company by estoppel finding appropriate where the parties enter into a contract believing that a limited liability company has been validly formed, and the parties proceed under that belief, notwithstanding that in fact the limited liability company was not validly formed at the time the contract was entered into?

HOLDING AND DECISION: [Judge not stated in casebook excerpt.]

(1) Yes. The de facto corporation doctrine may be extended to a limited liability company (LLC) where its incorporators have (a) proceeded in good faith, (b) under a valid statute, (c) for an authorized purpose, and (d) have executed and acknowledged articles of association pursuant to that purpose. Under the state's Limited Liability Company Act (LLCA), an LLC is not formed until a specified administrator endorses the company's articles of organization with, among other things, the word "filed" and the date of filing. Only when the articles of organization are so endorsed do they become effective. Here, the articles were filed, and endorsed, on November 29, 2004. Thus, Outlaw (D) was not in existence on the date the second contract was signed by the parties. Therefore, Perrin (D) became personally liable for Outlaw's (D) obligations unless a de facto LLC existed or LLC by estoppel applied. To determine

Continued on next page.

whether either of these scenarios occurred, it is helpful to analogize from the de facto corporation and corporation by estoppel doctrines. The de facto corporation doctrine provides that a defectively formed corporation may attain the legal status of a de facto corporation if certain requirements are met, most important of which is that courts perceive and treat it in all respects as if it were a properly formed de jure corporation. By contrast, corporation by estoppel is an equitable remedy that does not concern legal status. Under this doctrine, where a body assumes to be a corporation and acts under a particular name, a third party dealing with it under such assumed name is estopped to deny its corporate existence. Thus, the de facto corporation doctrine establishes the legal existence of the corporation, whereas the corporation by estoppel doctrine merely prevents one from arguing against it and does nothing to establish its actual existence in the eyes of the rest of the world. Had Outlaw (D) been a corporation, it is likely that the de facto corporation doctrine would apply (and, in fact, the trial court indicated the belief that it would have applied had Outlaw (D) been organized as a corporation), since it requires incorporators to have (1) proceeded in good faith, (2) under a valid statute, (3) for an authorized purpose, and (4) have executed and acknowledged articles of association pursuant to that purpose. Perrin (D): (1) acted in good faith since he proceeded without fraudulent intent, (2) under the LLCA, (3) for starting a legitimate business, and (4) he executed the articles of organization. However, because Outlaw (D) was organized as an LLC, the trial court concluded that the LLCA governs when it came into existence, so there was no room for the de facto corporation doctrine to apply. However, the state's Business Corporation Act (BCA) also specifies when a corporation comes into existence, and that statute does not preclude application of the de facto corporation doctrine. Although neither this court nor the state's highest court has addressed this issue, there is no reason that the de facto corporation doctrine cannot be applied to an LLC. The similarities between the BCA and the LLCA support the conclusion that the de facto corporation doctrine applies to both. Because both statutes relate to the common purpose of forming a business and because both contemplate the moment of existence for each, they should be interpreted in a consistent manner. Therefore, the de facto corporation doctrine applies to Outlaw (D), and Outlaw (D), not Perrin (D), individually, is liable for the breach of the October 27, 2004 contract. Reversed as to this issue.

(2) Yes. A limited liability company (LLC) by estoppel finding is appropriate where the parties enter into a contract believing that a limited liability company has been validly formed, and the parties proceed under that belief, notwithstanding that in fact the limited liability company was not validly formed at the time the contract was entered into. Because corporation by estoppel is an equitable remedy, the purpose of which is to prevent one who contracts with a corporation from later denying its existence in order to hold the individual officers or partners liable, there is no reason or purpose to draw a distinction on the basis of corporate form. Furthermore, like de facto corporation, because corporation by estoppel coexists with the BCA, so too can it coexist with the LLCA. Here, the record supports a finding of "limited liability company by estoppel" through the extension of the "corporation by estoppel" doctrine. Only Outlaw (D) became a party to the second contract, which superseded the first, and all parties dealt with the second contract as though Outlaw (D) were a party. After the second contract, Duray Development (P) received billings from Outlaw (D), and not from Perrin (D). Duray Development also received a certificate of liability insurance for Outlaw (D), and there was evidence that Duray Development (D) only dealt with Outlaw (D) after the second contract was executed. Duray Development (P) continued to assume Outlaw (D) was a valid LLC even after filing its lawsuit and only learned of the filing and contract discrepancies once litigation began. [The court did not reverse as to this issue for procedural reasons.]

ANALYSIS

Although the de facto corporation doctrine (or de facto LLC doctrine) and corporation by estoppel (or LLC by estoppel) are two distinct and separate common-law doctrines, as in this case they are often discussed in tandem, and the discussion of the two is blended into a single analysis, since a common fact pattern continually emerges in the case law that triggers both doctrines: a party conducts business with an association that it believes to be a de jure corporation, but which was defective in some way and never truly incorporated. In that situation, both corporation by estoppel and de facto corporation naturally become relevant. As this case also illustrates, courts are reluctant to abolish these doctrines on the basis of the existence of business organization statutes.

Continued on next page.

Quicknotes

CORPORATION BY ESTOPPEL Arises when parties are estopped from denying the existence of the corporation as a result of their agreements or conduct.

DE FACTO CORPORATION A corporation arising from the good faith attempt to comply with the statutory requirements of establishing a corporation.

LIMITED LIABILITY COMPANY (LLC) A business entity combining the features of both a corporation and a general partnership; the LLC provides its members and managers with limited liability, but it is treated as a partnership for taxation purposes.

Elf Atochem North America, Inc. v. Jaffari

Joint venturer (P) v. Other joint venturer (D)

Del. Sup. Ct., 727 A.2d 286 (1999)

NATURE OF CASE: Appeal from dismissal for lack of jurisdiction under terms of a limited liability company agreement.

FACT SUMMARY: Elf Atochem North America Inc.'s (P) allegations of breach of contract, tortious interference with prospective business relations, and fraud were dismissed because, under the terms of the limited liability company agreement, all disputes were to be arbitrated in California.

RULE OF LAW

Because the policy of Delaware's Limited Liability Company Act (the Act) is to give maximum effect to the principle of freedom of contract and to the enforceability of limited liability company (LLC) agreements, the parties to LLC operating agreements may contract to avoid the applicability of certain provisions of the Act, including dispute resolution and forum selection provisions.

FACTS: Elf Atochem North America Inc. (Elf) (P), a manufacturer of solvent-based maskants to the aerospace industry, and Jaffari (D), who had developed an innovative, environmentally friendly alternative to the solvent-based maskants recently classified as hazardous by the Environmental Protection Agency, agreed to undertake a joint venture that would be carried out using a limited liability company (LLC) as the vehicle. A Delaware LLC (Malek LLC) was formed and the parties entered into several agreements. The LLC was not a signatory to the agreement detailing the governance of the new company. The agreement contained an arbitration clause and a forum selection clause providing California courts would have jurisdiction over any claims arising out of, under, or in connection with, the agreement. Elf (P) later sued Jaffari (D) directly and derivatively on behalf of Malek LLC for breach of fiduciary duty when he withdrew funds for personal use, interfered with business opportunities, failed to make disclosures, and threatened to violate environmental regulations. Elf (P) also alleged breach of contract, tortious interference, and fraud. The Delaware Court of Chancery dismissed, holding that Elf's (P) claims arose under the agreement and were subject to the provision mandating that all claims be settled in California. Elf (P) appealed, contending that the LLC was not a signatory and not a party to the agreement and therefore was not bound to its terms, and that the dispute resolution clauses were invalid because they violated the Delaware LLC Act (Act). The Delaware Supreme Court granted review.

ISSUE: Because the policy of Delaware's Limited Liability Company Act (the Act) is to give maximum effect to the principle of freedom of contract and to the enforceability of limited liability company (LLC) agreements, may the parties to LLC operating agreements contract to avoid the applicability of certain provisions of the Act, including dispute resolution and forum selection provisions?

HOLDING AND DECISION: (Veasey, C.J.) Yes. Because the policy of Delaware's Limited Liability Company Act (the Act) is to give maximum effect to the principle of freedom of contract and to the enforceability of limited liability company (LLC) agreements, the parties to LLC operating agreements may contract to avoid the applicability of certain provisions of the Act, including dispute resolution and forum selection provisions. The Act is designed to permit members maximum flexibility in entering into an agreement to govern their relationship. The parties specifically agreed that their disputes would be resolved by arbitration in California and that no judicial action could be brought, except in California, and then, only to enforce arbitration in California. There is no reason why the parties could not alter the default provisions of the statute and contract away their right to file suit in Delaware, since these provisions do not contravene any mandatory provisions of the Act. Such statutory provisions are likely to be those intended to protect third parties, not necessarily the contracting members. Also, the parties' arbitration provision fosters the Delaware policy favoring alternate dispute resolution mechanisms such as arbitration. Thus, there is no reason why the parties could not alter the Act's default jurisdictional provisions and contract away their right to file suit in Delaware. Elf (P) contends that the Chancery Court incorrectly characterized its claims against Malek (D) as direct rather than derivative, and that if the claims had been classified as derivative, they would not have been subject to the arbitration clause, since the Act expressly authorizes derivative actions. However, while the Act grants Delaware courts jurisdiction to hear derivative actions, and actions involving breaches of fiduciary duties and the removal of managers, there is no reason why these default jurisdictional provisions may not be altered. In other words, there is no "special" jurisdiction conferred on the Delaware courts in these areas, and parties may contractually alter such default provisions, especially where doing so promotes the state's policy interests,

Continued on next page.

as in promoting arbitration and other alternate dispute resolution mechanisms. Thus, it is irrelevant whether the claims at issue are characterized as direct or derivative, since the parties to the LLC agreement agreed not to institute any action at law or in equity based on any claim arising out of or relating to the agreement. Consequently, the Chancery Court did not err in holding that all claims, whether direct or derivative, arose out of or in connection with the agreement, and thus were covered by the arbitration clause. Affirmed.

ANALYSIS

The Uniform Limited Liability Company Act (ULLCA) was modeled on the popular Delaware Limited Partner Act. Many provisions of the Revised Uniform Limited Partners Act (RULPA) were also modeled on the Delaware Act. Almost all of the states have adopted some form of the RULPA.

Quicknotes

ARBITRATION An agreement to have a dispute heard and decided by a neutral third party, rather than through legal proceedings.

FIDUCIARY DUTY A legal obligation to act for the benefit of another, including subordinating one's personal interests to that of the other person.

JURISDICTION The authority of a court to hear and declare judgment in respect to a particular matter.

LIMITED LIABILITY COMPANY (LLC) A business entity combining the features of both a corporation and a general partnership; the LLC provides its members and managers with limited liability, but it is treated as a partnership for taxation purposes.

Fisk Ventures, LLC v. Segal

LLC member (P) v. LLC member (D)

Del. Ct. Ch., 2008 WL 1961156 (2008), *aff'd without opinion sub nom.*, Segal v. Fisk Ventures, LLC, Del. Sup. Ct., 984 A.2d 124 (2009)

NATURE OF CASE: Counterclaims and third-party claims for breach of contract and breach of the implied covenant of good faith and fair dealing in action for dissolution of a limited liability company (LLC).

FACT SUMMARY: Segal (D), a Class A member of Genitrix, LLC, brought counterclaims and third-party claims in an action for dissolution brought by Fisk Ventures, LLC (Fisk) (P), a Class B member, asserting, inter alia, that Class B members had breached the Limited Liability Company Agreement (the LLC Agreement) and its implied covenant of good faith and fair dealing by refusing to accede to certain requests he made of them as he tried to obtain financing for the company.

RULE OF LAW

(1) Where limited liability company (LLC) agreement vests power in more than one equity class and requires the classes to cooperate to effect LLC action, one class does not breach the LLC agreement by failing to acquiesce to the wishes of the other classes simply because the other classes believe their approach is superior or in the best interests of the LLC.

(2) Where a limited liability (LLC) company agreement vests power in more than one equity class and requires the classes to cooperate to effect LLC action, one class does not breach the LLC agreement's implied covenant of good faith and fair dealing by failing to acquiesce to the wishes of the other classes simply because the other classes believe their approach is superior or in the best interests of the LLC.

FACTS: Genitrix, LLC, had three equity classes: A, B, and C, with Class C being made up of mostly passive investors and with the company's power being split between Class A and Class B. Segal (D), the company's chief executive officer (CEO) and founder, was the key Class A member; and Johnson, Fisk Ventures, LLC (Fisk) (P), Rose, and Freund were the key Class B members. Although the Class B members had three representatives on the five-member board, and Class A had only two representatives, most actions required the approval of 75 percent of the board, thus requiring the cooperation of the Class A and B members. One of the provisions of the company's Limited Liability Company Agreement (LLC Agreement) was that Class B members could, at any time, force the company to purchase any or all of their Class B membership interests at a price determined by an independent appraisal. If the purchase price exceeded 50 percent of the company's tangible assets, the members who exercised this put right would receive notes secured by all of the assets of the company, thus subrogating what would otherwise be senior claims of new investors. Genitrix found itself strapped for cash and Segal (D) made numerous attempts to raise funds, whether from high-net-worth investors or other new investors. With each new effort, Segal (D) proposed that the Class B members agree to suspend their put right, but each time they refused. Many potential investors found the Class B put right to be a deal killer, and Segal (D) failed to raise the needed money. The Class B members, who had the right to replace Segal (D) as CEO under certain circumstances, did so. Eventually, the company ran out of operating cash. Throughout, Fisk (P) had kept making capital contributions, but after negotiations to buy out Segal (D) failed, and with the company not generating any revenue, Fisk (P) brought suit for dissolution. Segal (D) counterclaimed and brought third-party claims asserting, inter alia, that Class B members had breached the LLC Agreement and its implied covenant of good faith and fair dealing by refusing to accede to certain requests he made of them as he tried to obtain financing for the company. The counterclaim/third-party defendants moved to dismiss Segal's (D) claims for failure to state a claim.

ISSUE:

(1) Where a limited liability company (LLC) agreement vests power in more than one equity class and requires the classes to cooperate to effect LLC action, does one class breach the LLC agreement by failing to acquiesce to the wishes of the other classes simply because the other classes believe their approach is superior or in the best interests of the LLC?

(2) Where a limited liability company (LLC) agreement vests power in more than one equity class and requires the classes to cooperate to effect LLC action, does one class breach the LLC agreement's implied covenant of good faith and fair dealing by failing to acquiesce to the wishes of the other classes simply because the other classes believe their approach is superior or in the best interests of the LLC?

HOLDING AND DECISION: [Judge not stated in casebook excerpt.]

(1) No. Where a limited liability company (LLC) agreement vests power in more than one equity class and

Continued on next page.

requires the classes to cooperate to effect LLC action, one class does not breach the LLC agreement by failing to acquiesce to the wishes of the other classes simply because the other classes believe their approach is superior or in the best interests of the LLC. While Segal (D) may be correct that if only Class B members had not stood in the way of proposed funding, the company would be thriving, it also may very well be that the company would be thriving if only Segal (D) had gone along with what the Class B members wanted. It is not up to the court to decide which side's business judgment was more in keeping with the company's best interests—to do so would cripple the policy in the state's LLC Act promoting freedom of contract. Therefore, the breach of contract claim is dismissed.

(2) No. Where a limited liability company (LLC) agreement vests power in more than one equity class and requires the classes to cooperate to effect LLC action, one class does not breach the LLC agreement's implied covenant of good faith and fair dealing by failing to acquiesce to the wishes of the other classes simply because the other classes believe their approach is superior or in the best interests of the LLC. The implied covenant of good faith and fair dealing requires a party in a contractual relationship to refrain from arbitrary or unreasonable conduct that has the effect of preventing the other party to the contract from receiving the fruits of the bargain. In other words, it protects what was actually bargained and negotiated for in the contract. Here, Segal (D) argues that the Class B members breached this implied covenant by standing in the way of proposed financing. However, neither the LLC Agreement nor any other contract endowed Segal (D) with the right to unilaterally decide what fundraising or financing opportunities the company should pursue. Instead, financing decisions had to be made with approval of 75 percent of the board. Implicit in such a requirement is the right of the Class B board representatives to disapprove of and therefore block Segal's (D) proposals. Negotiating forcefully and within the bounds of rights granted by the LLC agreement does not translate to a breach of the implied covenant on the part of the Class B members. Therefore, the claim for breach of the implied covenant of good faith and fair dealing is dismissed.

ANALYSIS

The Delaware LLC statute stands out for its lack of mandatory rules and its express policy to give maximum effect to the principle of freedom of contract, allowing parties to alter default duties in their agreements as long as they are held to good faith compliance with their contracts. The decision in this case is in keeping with these principles, as there was no indication that the Class B members acted in bad faith; in their business judgment they merely disagreed with Segal (D) as to the best approach for promoting the company's best interests.

Quicknotes

IMPLIED COVENANT OF GOOD FAITH AND FAIR DEALING An implied warranty that the parties will deal honestly in the satisfaction of their obligations and without an intent to defraud.

LIMITED LIABILITY COMPANY (LLC) A business entity combining the features of both a corporation and a general partnership; the LLC provides its members and managers with limited liability, but it is treated as a partnership for taxation purposes.

NetJets Aviation, Inc. v. LHC Communications, LLC

Airplane lessor (P) v. Airplane lessee (D)

537 F.3d 168 (2d Cir. 2008)

NATURE OF CASE: Appeal from summary judgment dismissal of breach-of-contract and account-stated claims brought against an individual as the alter ego of a limited liability company.

FACT SUMMARY: NetJets Aviation, Inc. (NetJets) (P) contended that Zimmerman (D) could be held liable for the debts owed to NetJets (P) by LHC Communications, LLC (LHC) (D) as LHC's (D) alter ego, because there was sufficient evidence that Zimmerman (D) and LHC (D) operated as one, and that Zimmerman (D) conducted LHC's (D) affairs in a fraudulent, illegal, or unjust manner.

RULE OF LAW

Claims against the owner of a company for the debts of the company should be allowed to proceed on the theory that the owner is the company's alter ego where sufficient evidence has been presented that the owner and company operated as one, and that the owner conducted the company's affairs in a fraudulent, illegal, or unjust manner.

FACTS: NetJets Aviation, Inc. (NetJets) (P) leased fractional interests in airplanes and provided related air-travel services to LHC Communications, LLC (LHC) (D), a limited liability company (LLC) whose sole member-owner was Zimmerman (D). The companies entered a lease agreement and a management agreement in August 1999. The lease agreement was for five years, although LHC (D) had a qualified right of early termination. In July 2000, LHC (D) terminated the agreements, leaving a debt of $340,840.39. LHC (D) ceased operations in 2001. NetJets (P) brought suit in federal district court against LHC (D) and Zimmerman (D) for, inter alia, breach of contract, and account stated. NetJets (P) contended that Zimmerman (D) should be held liable for the debts of LHC (D) as its alter ego, based on evidence of, inter alia, the frequent use of LHC (D) air hours for personal travel by Zimmerman (D) and his friends and family, the frequent transfers of funds between LHC (D) and Zimmerman's (D) other companies, Zimmerman's (D) frequent withdrawal of funds from LHC (D) for his own personal use, and the fact that LHC (D) was no longer in business and had no assets with which to pay its debt to NetJets (P), a condition that NetJets (P) contended was caused by Zimmerman's (D) withdrawals. NetJets (P) presented evidence that Zimmerman (D) and LHC (D) operated as one, and that Zimmerman (D) conducted the company's affairs in a fraudulent, illegal, or unjust manner. This evidence included financial records of LHC (D) and deposition testimony from Zimmerman (D) and LHC's (D) CFO, Whittier. This evidence showed that LHC (D) started with a capitalization of no more than $20,100; that LHC (D) invested millions of dollars supplied by Zimmerman (D); and that Zimmerman (D) put money into LHC (D) as LHC (D) needed it and took money out of LHC (D) as he needed it. Zimmerman (D) owned other companies, and Whittier served as each of those companies' CFO. Whittier was paid either by one of those companies or by Zimmerman (D) personally. LHC (D) shared office space with some of Zimmerman's (D) other companies, and it employed no more than five to seven people at any given time. Some of its employees worked for both LHC (D) and Zimmerman's (D) other companies or for LHC (D) and Zimmerman (D) personally. Zimmerman (D) used LHC (D) as a personal investment vehicle and made all LHC's (D) financial decisions. LHC (D) operations run by Whittier apparently consisted only of making Zimmerman's (D) investments and carrying on Zimmerman's (D) personal business. Sometimes money came to LHC (D) from Zimmerman's (D) other companies, with which LHC (D) had no business connections. LHC (D) also transferred money to Zimmerman (D), or to third persons on his behalf, in connection with his living expenses, such as making mortgage payments, or paying cleaning people, or purchasing automobiles (e.g., LHC (D) purchased a Bentley automobile at a cost of approximately $350,000 for Zimmerman's personal use, placing title in his name). In addition, many of the air hours to which LHC (D) was entitled under its agreements with NetJets (P) were used by Zimmerman (D) personally, as for vacations for himself and/or his wife, or for transporting him and his family to and from Europe or to and from one of his five homes. Although transfers of money between LHC (D) and Zimmerman (D)—in either direction—were labeled "Loan receivable," they were so labeled regardless of whether Zimmerman's (D) payment to LHC (D) was to be used to make an investment or to be used for operating expenses. Whittier testified that the ledger treated Zimmerman's (D) payments to and withdrawals from LHC (D) as loans and loan repayments in order to allow Zimmerman (D) to make withdrawals as he needed money, without having to pay taxes on the moneys withdrawn. The decision to so characterize these payments was Zimmerman's (D) alone, and there were no written agreements as to these transfers. Other evidence showed that LHC's (D) only paying client began paying in the month that LHC (D) terminated its agreements with NetJets (P), and that, in toto, Zimmerman (D) and

Continued on next page.

his other companies withdrew from LHC (D) more than $3 million than he put into it. Despite this evidence, the district court sua sponte granted summary judgment to Zimmerman (D) dismissing all of NetJets' (P) claims against him. The Second Circuit Court of Appeals granted review.

ISSUE: Should claims against the owner of a company for the debts of the company be allowed to proceed on the theory that the owner is the company's alter ego where sufficient evidence has been presented that the owner and company operated as one, and that the owner conducted the company's affairs in a fraudulent, illegal, or unjust manner?

HOLDING AND DECISION: [Judge not stated in casebook excerpt.] Yes. Claims against the owner of a company for the debts of the company should be allowed to proceed on the theory that the owner is the company's alter ego where sufficient evidence has been presented that the owner and company operated as one, and that the owner conducted the company's affairs in a fraudulent, illegal, or unjust manner. Although the shareholders of a corporation and the members of a limited liability company (LLC) generally are not liable for the debts of the entity, the entity's corporate veil may be pierced to reach the owners where there is fraud or where the entity is in fact a mere instrumentality or alter ego of its owners. To prevail under the alter-ego theory of piercing the veil, a plaintiff need not prove that there was actual fraud but must show a mingling of the operations of the entity and its owner plus an overall element of injustice or unfairness. Thus, to determine whether LHC's (D) veil should be pierced to reach Zimmerman (D), there must be sufficient evidence presented that LHC (D) and Zimmerman (D) operated as one, and that there was an overall element of injustice or unfairness. Here, the evidence supports a finding that LHC (D) and Zimmerman (D) operated as one. There was evidence that, inter alia, Zimmerman (D) created LHC (D) to be one of his personal investment vehicles; that he was the sole decision maker (D) with respect to LHC's (D) financial actions; that Zimmerman (D) frequently put money into LHC (D) as LHC (D) needed it to meet operating expenses; that LHC (D) used some of that money, as well as some moneys it received from selling shares of one of its assets, to pay more than $4.5 million to third persons for Zimmerman's (D) personal expenses including margin calls, mortgage payments, apartment expenses, and automobiles; and that with no written agreements or documentation or procedures in place, Zimmerman (D) directly, on the average of twice a month for 2 ½ years, took money out of LHC (D) at will to make other investments or to meet his other personal expenses. This evidence is ample to permit a reasonable factfinder to find that Zimmerman (D) completely dominated LHC (D) and that he essentially treated LHC's (D) bank account as one of his pockets, into which he reached when he needed or desired funds for his personal use. Accordingly, Zimmerman's (D) contention that the district court properly granted summary judgment in his favor on the ground he and LHC (D) did not operate as a single economic entity is rejected. There was also sufficient evidence that Zimmerman's (D) conduct and the way he conducted LHC's (D) affairs resulted in fraud, illegality, or unfairness. There was evidence that Zimmerman (D) intentionally mischaracterized payments and transactions to avoid paying taxes, and that his withdrawals may have violated the state's Limited Liability Company Act (the Act). This Act provides that an LLC is prohibited from making a distribution to a member to the extent that at the time of the distribution, after giving effect to the distribution, all liabilities of the LLC exceed the fair value of its assets. Given that LHC (D) ceased operating and was unable to pay its debt to NetJets (P), if Zimmerman's (D) withdrawals left LHC (D) in that condition those withdrawals may well have been prohibited by the Act. A factfinder could infer that Zimmerman's (D) payments to LHC (D) were deliberately mischaracterized as loans in order to mask the fact that Zimmerman (D) was making withdrawals from LHC (D) that were forbidden by law and could thereby properly find fraud or an unfair siphoning of LHC's (D) assets. Other evidence also would support a finding by a reasonable factfinder that Zimmerman (D) operated LHC (D) in his own self-interest in a manner that unfairly disregarded the rights of LHC's (D) creditors, and that there was an overall element of injustice in Zimmerman's (D) operation of LHC (D). Accordingly, NetJets (P) adduced sufficient evidence of fraud, illegality, or unfairness to warrant a trial on its contract and account-stated claims against Zimmerman (D) as LHC's (D) alter ego. Vacated and remanded.

ANALYSIS

As this case indicates, numerous factors come into play when discussing whether separate legal entities should be regarded as alter egos, and the legal test for determining when a corporate form should be ignored in equity cannot be reduced to a single formula that is neither over- nor underinclusive. Stated generally, the inquiry initially focuses on whether those in control of a corporation or other business entity did not treat the corporation or entity as a distinct entity, and, if they did not, the court then seeks to evaluate the specific facts with a standard of fraud or misuse or some other general term of reproach in mind, such as whether the corporation was used to engage in conduct that was "inequitable." These principles are generally applicable

Continued on next page.

as well where one of the entities in question is an LLC rather than a corporation.

Quicknotes

ALTER EGO Other self; under the "alter ego" doctrine, the court disregards the corporate entity and holds the individual shareholders liable for acts done knowingly and intentionally in the corporation's name.

SUA SPONTE An action taken by the court by its own motion and without the suggestion of one of the parties.

McConnell v. Hunt Sports Enterprises

Investor (P) v. Sports team investor (D)

Ohio Ct. App., 132 Ohio App. 3d 657, 725 N.E.2d 1193 (1999)

NATURE OF THE CASE: Appeal from declaratory judgment for plaintiff in action to determine the scope of a limited liability company operating agreement.

FACT SUMMARY: Members of Columbus Hockey Limited, LLC (CHL)—a limited liability company formed to explore the possibility of applying for a new National Hockey League (NHL) franchise—sought a declaration for breach of contract against each other based on the exclusion of certain members' ownership interests in the franchise.

RULE OF LAW

(1) Extrinsic evidence will not be permitted for interpretation of a limited liability company operating agreement the terms of which are unambiguous and clear.

(2) A member of a limited liability company does not breach a fiduciary duty to the company by directly competing against it where the operating agreement expressly permits such competition.

(3) A directed verdict against a member of limited liability company, which is based on operating agreement violations, is appropriate where the evidence shows that the member has violated the operating agreement.

FACTS: Based on their involvement in professional sports, several wealthy individuals in Columbus, Ohio, including McConnell (P), were contacted by the city's mayor to examine the possibility of applying for a National Hockey League (NHL) hockey franchise for Columbus. McConnell's (P) colleagues approached Hunt (D) and his Hunt Sports Enterprises (HSE) (D) as a potential investor. Together, McConnell (P), HSE (D), and others formed Columbus Hockey Limited, LLC (CHL), a limited liability company (LLC) whose general character was to invest in and operate a franchise in the NHL. CHL's operating agreement permitted members to compete against it and did not require that CHL members contribute additional capital. Following an application for the franchise filed by CHL on behalf of the city of Columbus, difficulty arose when a planned tax to finance the construction of a required, appropriate arena failed to pass voter approval. When Hunt (D) and HSE (D) refused to accept an alternative lease proposal that would permit the required construction, McConnell (P) offered to lease the arena in Hunt's/HSE's (D) place. The offer was accepted, and the NHL required that an ownership group be identified pursuant to its granting of a franchise. McConnell (P) signed the required documents in an individual capacity, in the place intended for CHL's participation as franchise owner, thus identifying McConnell (P) as the majority owner. HSE (D) and Hunt (D) continued to find the existing terms unacceptable, and McConnell (P) filed suit requesting a declaration that his group had the legal right to the franchise without inclusion of CHL or Hunt (D) or HSE (D). The NHL awarded the franchise to Columbus with the McConnell (P) group as owner. The trial court proceedings included a jury trial and a directed verdict for McConnell (P). The trial court refused to allow introduction of extrinsic evidence of the meaning of the crucial language in the CHL operating agreement. The trial court also directed the jury that McConnell (P) had not violated any fiduciary duty by excluding Hunt/HSE (D) from participating in the franchise and by preparing to compete with CHL. In addition, the trial court entered a directed verdict in favor of McConnell (P) on its claim that HSE (D) breached the agreement by unilaterally rejecting the lease proposal, by failing to negotiate in good faith, by allowing the lease deadline to expire without response, by failing to advise or obtain the approval of the other members of CHL before unilaterally rejecting the lease offer, and by usurping control of CHL. The trial court's directed verdict rested on its finding that Hunt/HSE (D) violated the operating agreement in failing to ask for and obtain the authorization of CHL members—other than McConnell (P)—before filing the answer and counterclaim in the action and before filing a separate action. The state's intermediate appellate court granted review.

ISSUE:

(1) Will extrinsic evidence be permitted for interpretation of a limited liability company operating agreement the terms of which are unambiguous and clear?

(2) Does a member of a limited liability company breach a fiduciary duty to the company by directly competing against it where the operating agreement expressly permits such competition?

(3) Is a directed verdict against a member of limited liability company, which is based on operating agreement violations, appropriate where the evidence shows that the member has violated the operating agreement?

HOLDING AND DECISION: [Judge not stated in casebook excerpt.]

Continued on next page.

(1) No. Extrinsic evidence will not be permitted for interpretation of a limited liability company operating agreement the terms of which are unambiguous and clear. Section 3.3 of the operating agreement stated that "members may compete." However, Hunt/HSE (D) contend that members of CHL may compete only in any business venture that is different from the business of the company, which includes investing in and operating an NHL franchise. Such an interpretation goes beyond the plain language of section 3.3, which permits "any other venture of any nature." The terms of the operating agreement are clear and unambiguous, so that the trial court was correct in refusing to allow extrinsic evidence to aid in its interpretation. McConnell (P) and his group may therefore engage in activities that are competitive with CHL. Affirmed as to this issue.

(2) No. A member of a limited liability company does not breach a fiduciary duty to the company by directly competing against it where the operating agreement expressly permits such competition. The injury complained of is the direct competition of McConnell (P) as a member of CHL, against CHL and Hunt/HSE (D) as a co-member of the same limited liability company. By permitting such competition, the operating agreement defined the parties' general fiduciary duties as to competition. As to such competition, therefore, McConnell (P) and his group could not have breached their fiduciary duties to the other members. Moreover, they did not breach any other fiduciary duties to the other members. The evidence does not show McConnell (P) interfered with Hunt's/HSE's (D) own dealings with the NHL. Instead, McConnell (P) only agreed to lease the arena after Hunt/HSE (D) refused to do so. Thus, there was not sufficient evidence presented to suggest any breach of fiduciary duty on the part of McConnell (P) and his group to interfere tortiously with the business relationships of their limited liability parent. A directed verdict in favor of McConnell (P) and his group was therefore appropriate. Affirmed as to this issue.

(3) Yes. A directed verdict against a member of a limited liability company, which is based on operating agreement violations, is appropriate where the evidence shows that the member has violated the operating agreement. Hunt/HSE (D) incorrectly assert that they could only be liable for willful misconduct and that they were the operating member of CHL and, therefore, had full authority to act on CHL's behalf. First, there was no evidence at trial that Hunt/HSE (D) was the operating member of CHL. In fact, the operating agreement did not name any person or entity the operating or managing member of CHL. Instead, all members of CHL had an equal number of units in the company. Under the terms of the operating agreement, no member could take action on behalf of the company, unless such action was approved by at least a majority of the allocated units. Further, the approval of the members as to any action on behalf of CHL must have been evidenced by minutes of a meeting properly noticed and held or by an action in writing signed by the requisite number of members. Here, there was no evidence that Hunt/HSE (D) obtained the approval of CHL members prior to filing the actions at issue. There was also no evidence that they even asked permission of any member to file the actions, let alone held a meeting or requested approval in writing. Because Hunt/HSE (D) acted unilaterally, a directed verdict on the issue of breach of contract in favor of McConnell (P) was appropriate. Even if, as Hunt/HSE (D) claims, McConnell (P) had to show willful misconduct, McConnell (P) would have made such a showing, because the evidence showed that Hunt/HSE (D) engaged in willful misconduct in filing the actions at issue. Affirmed as to this issue.

ANALYSIS

Similar to a partnership, a limited liability company (LLC) involves a fiduciary relationship that precludes direct competition between the members of the company. However, because LLCs are creatures of contract, the members may agree to permit such competition. The court here and the lower court based their key rulings on the fact that the operating agreement explicitly permitted competition. The real dispute here rested in the ability of the operating agreement to define the scope of any individual member's fiduciary duties towards the company. In the present case, the court found that the operating agreement did in fact have the power to define these duties and gave the applicable clause appropriate weight when ruling in favor of McConnell (P) and other appellees.

Quicknotes

DECLARATORY JUDGMENT A judgment of the court establishing the rights of the parties.

EXTRINSIC EVIDENCE Evidence that is not contained within the text of a document or contract, but which is derived from the parties' statements or the circumstances under which the agreement was made.

FIDUCIARY DUTY A legal obligation to act for the benefit of another, including subordinating one's personal interests to that of the other person.

FRANCHISE An agreement whereby one party (the franchisor) grants another (the franchisee) the right to market its product or service.

PARTNERSHIP A voluntary agreement entered into by two or more parties to engage in business and to share any attendant profits and losses.

Racing Investment Fund 2000, LLC v. Clay Ward Agency, Inc.

Judgment debtor LLC (D) v. Insurance firm (P)

Ky. Sup. Ct., 320 S.W.3d 654 (2010)

NATURE OF CASE: Appeal from affirmance of order invoking a limited liability company's (LLC's) capital call provisions to fund a judgment against the LLC.

FACT SUMMARY: Clay Ward Agency, Inc. (P) succeeded in obtaining a judgment against Racing Investment Fund 2000, LLC (Racing Investment) (D), and the trial court ordered Racing Investment (D) to invoke its capital call provisions to require Racing Investment's (D) members to contribute capital so the LLC could satisfy its judgment.

RULE OF LAW

A limited liability company's (LLC's) capital call provision may not be invoked by a court in order to obtain funds from the LLC's members to satisfy a judgment against the LLC.

FACTS: Racing Investment Fund 2000, LLC (Racing Investment) (D) entered into an agreed judgment with its former insurance firm, Clay Ward Agency, Inc. (Clay Ward) (P). Shortly thereafter, Racing Investment (D) partially paid the judgment by tendering all of the remaining assets of the then-defunct LLC. When Racing Investment (D) failed to pay the remainder of the amount owed, Clay Ward (P) succeeded in having Racing Investment (D) held in contempt of court for its failure to pay the entire judgment amount. The trial court ruled that the capital call provision in Racing Investment's (D) operating agreement, which allowed Racing Investment's (D) manager to call for additional capital contributions, as needed, from all members on a pro rata basis for "operating, administrative, or other business expenses" provided a means of satisfying the judgment. Accordingly, the trial court ordered that Racing Investment (D) "act accordingly to satisfy the Judgment within a reasonable period of time" or face other sanctions. The state's intermediate appellate court affirmed, and the state's highest court granted review.

ISSUE: May limited liability company's (LLC's) capital call provision be invoked by a court in order to obtain funds from the LLC's members to satisfy a judgment against the LLC?

HOLDING AND DECISION: [Judge not stated in casebook excerpt.] No. A limited liability company's (LLC's) capital call provision may not be invoked by a court in order to obtain funds from the LLC's members to satisfy a judgment against the LLC. Racing Investment's (D) members did not agree to subject themselves to personal liability for the LLC's debts when they signed the operating agreement. Unless the members agree to the contrary, the LLC entity form provides members immunity from personal liability for the LLC's debts, and such immunity is strong. Here, Racing Investment's (D) members did not agree to waive this immunity. Under Clay Ward's (P) theory, any outstanding debt that remains unpaid by the LLC can be satisfied through application for a court-ordered capital call. Such a construction is contrary to the plain terms of the operating agreement and the letter and spirit of the state's LLC Act. It is clear that the capital call provision was not intended as a debt-collection mechanism and allowing a court to use it as such breaches the LLC's shield of limited liability to reach individual members. The LLC Act emphatically rejects personal liability for an LLC's debt unless the member or members, as the case may be, have agreed through the operating agreement or another written agreement to assume personal liability. Any such assumption of personal liability, which is contrary to the very business advantage reflected in the name "limited liability company," must be stated clearly in unequivocal language which leaves no room for doubt about the parties' intent. Here, the capital call provision does not begin to meet that standard: a provision designed to provide ongoing capital infusion as necessary, at the manager's discretion, for the conduct of the entity's business affairs is simply not an agreement "to be obligated personally for any of the debts, obligations, and liabilities of the limited liability company." Reversed.

ANALYSIS

One indicator of the strength of limited liability protection offered by the LLC form is that even the Internal Revenue Service has recognized that federal employment tax liabilities incurred by an LLC cannot be collected from the LLC's members. Some states however, have made exceptions to this rule for state taxes owed by an LLC: there can be personal liability on the part of members for sales taxes, payroll taxes, and other state taxes in such states.

Quicknotes

LIMITED LIABILITY An advantage of doing business in the corporate form by safeguarding shareholders from liability for the debts or obligations of the corporation.

LIMITED LIABILITY COMPANY (LLC) A business entity combining the features of both a corporation and a general partnership; the LLC provides its members and managers with limited liability, but it is treated as a partnership for taxation purposes.

VGS, Inc. v. Castiel

Newly formed company (D) v. Board member of original LLC (P)

Del. Ct. Ch., 2000 WL 1277372 (2000), *aff'd mem.*, Del. Sup. Ct., 781 A.2d 696 (2001)

NATURE OF CASE: Equity suit by an ousted manager of a limited liability company for rescission of a merger between his company and a new company.

FACT SUMMARY: When Sahagen (D) and Quinn (D), two managers of a limited liability company (LLC), took action to merge the LLC with another company, without notifying Castiel (P), who was the third manager, of the proposed action, the latter brought suit to rescind the merger, arguing that Sahagen (D) and Quinn (D) had breached their duty of loyalty and good faith.

RULE OF LAW

The managers of a limited liability company owe to one another a duty of loyalty to act in good faith.

FACTS: A Limited Liability Company Agreement (the Agreement) created a three-member board of managers with sweeping authority to govern the LLC. The managers were Castiel (P), Sahagen (D), and Quinn (D). Castiel (P) was also the majority shareholder and chief executive officer (CEO). The LLC statute, read literally, did not require notice to Castiel (P) before Sahagen (D) and Quinn (D) could act. Sahagen (D) and Quinn (D) acted to merge the original LLC with VGS, Inc. (D). They acted without notice to Castiel (P) of the proposed action, knowing that he would have blocked it. After the merger, Castiel (P) was relegated to the position of a minority shareholder and was no longer CEO. In short, the two managers acted without notice to the third under circumstances where they knew that with notice, the third could have acted to protect his majority interest. Castiel (P) brought suit in equity to have the merger declared invalid and rescinded on the ground it occurred based on the breach of the duty of loyalty of Sahagen (D) and Quinn (D) to have acted toward their fellow manager in good faith.

ISSUE: Do the managers of a limited liability company owe to one another a duty of loyalty to act in good faith?

HOLDING AND DECISION: [Judge not stated in casebook excerpt.] Yes. The managers of a limited liability company (LLC) owe to one another a duty of loyalty to act in good faith. Although the LLC statute, read literally, did not require notice to Castiel (P) before Sahagen (D) and Quinn (D) could act by written consent, and the LLC Agreement did not purport to modify the statute in this regard, such observations cannot here complete the analysis. Sahagen (D) and Quinn (D) knew what would happen if they notified Castiel (P) of their intention to act by written consent to merge the LLC into VGS, Inc. (D). Castiel (P) would have attempted to remove Quinn (D) and block the planned action. Regardless of his motivation in doing so, the removal of Quinn (D) in that circumstance would have been within Castiel's (P) rights as the LLC's controlling owner under the Agreement. The purpose of permitting action by written consent without notice is to enable LLC managers to take quick, efficient action in situations where a minority of managers could not block or adversely affect the course set by the majority even if they were notified of the proposed action and objected to it. The state legislature never intended to enable two managers to deprive, "clandestinely and surreptitiously," a third manager representing the majority interest in the LLC of an opportunity to protect that interest by taking an action that the third manager's member would surely have opposed if he had knowledge of it. Equity looks to the intent rather than to the form. In this hopefully unique situation, this application of the maxim requires construction of the statute to allow action without notice only by a constant or fixed majority. It cannot apply to an illusory, will-o'-the wisp majority that would implode should notice be given. Nothing in the statute suggests that a court of equity should blind its eyes to a shallow manipulative attempt to restructure an enterprise through an action taken by a "majority" that existed only so long as it could act in secrecy. Sahagen (D) and Quinn (D) owed Castiel (P) a duty to give him prior notice of the meeting even if he would have interfered with a plan that they conscientiously believed to be in the best interest of the LLC. They intentionally used a flawed process to merge the LLC into VGS, Inc. (D). Hence, they failed to discharge their duty of loyalty to him in good faith. The merger is invalid and is ordered rescinded.

ANALYSIS

The court in *VGS* noted that while many hours were spent at trial focusing on contentions that Castiel (P) had proved to be an ineffective leader in whom employees and investors had lost confidence, the issue of who was best suited to run the LLC should not be resolved in a court but in board meetings where all the managers are present and all members are appropriately represented. Furthermore, observed the court, the actions of Sahagen (D) and Quinn (D) constituted a breach of

Continued on next page.

their duty of loyalty; hence such actions did not entitle them to the benefit or protection of the business judgment rule.

Quicknotes

DUTY OF GOOD FAITH OF FAIR DEALINGS An implied duty in a contract that the parties will deal honestly in the satisfaction of their obligations and without intent to defraud.

DUTY OF LOYALTY A director's duty to refrain from self-dealing or to take a position that is adverse to the corporation's best interests.

LIMITED LIABILITY COMPANY (LLC) A business entity combining the features of both a corporation and a general partnership; the LLC provides its members and managers with limited liability, but it is treated as a partnership for taxation purposes.

Reese v. Newman

50 Percent LLC member (D) v. 50 Percent LLC member

D.C. Ct. App., 131 A.3d 880 (2016)

NATURE OF CASE: Appeal from order of dissolution of a limited liability company.

FACT SUMMARY: C. Allison Defoe Reese (Reese) (D) and Nicole Newman (Newman) (P) were co-owners of ANR Construction Management, LLC (ANR). After experiencing difficulties working together, Newman (P) wanted ANR dissolved, whereas Reese (D) wanted Newman (P) dissociated so Reese (D) could continue the business. After a jury found grounds for both judicial dissolution of ANR and for the forced dissociation of Newman (P), the trial court ordered dissolution. Reese (D) contended the trial court lacked discretion to order dissolution, and, instead, was required to order dissociation of Newman (P).

RULE OF LAW

Where a limited liability company (LLC) statute provides that a trial court may order a remedy other than dissolution, but also provides that "[a] person shall be dissociated as a member from a limited liability company" when the person commits certain actions described in the statute, and where a jury determines there are grounds supporting both dissolution of an LLC and the dissociation of a member from the LLC, a trial court has discretion to order either dissolution or dissociation.

FACTS: C. Allison Defoe Reese (Reese) (D) and Nicole Newman (Newman) (P) were co-owners of ANR Construction Management, LLC (ANR *or* the LLC). After they started experiencing substantial differences over the management of ANR, Newman (P) notified Reese (D) in writing that she intended to withdraw from, dissolve, and wind up the LLC. Reese (D) did not want to dissolve the LLC but preferred that Newman (P) simply be dissociated so that Reese (D) could continue the business herself. Shortly thereafter, Reese (D) allegedly locked Newman (P) out of the LLC's bank accounts, blocked her remote access to the LLC's files and email, and ended her salary and health benefits. Newman (P) then brought suit for breach of contract and sought to enjoin Reese (D) from any further action intended to dissociate Newman (P) from the LLC and for $500,000 in damages. Subsequently, Newman (P) amended her complaint to add many more claims, and Reese (D) counterclaimed, asserting many claims and seeking $500,000 in damages and the dissociation of Newman (P) from ANR. Reese (D) moved for summary judgment, which was denied. The parties' claims were resolved in a jury trial, which returned a $19,000 verdict for Newman (P) on her conversion claim and denied all other claims for both parties. The jury had been asked to make specific findings on the statutory grounds that permit both judicial dissolution of the LLC based on Reese's (D) conduct and judicial expulsion of a member with respect to Newman's (P) conduct. The jury returned findings that would support both judicial dissolution and dissociation of Newman (P) as a member. The trial judge chose to order dissolution of the LLC based on the evidence presented and the jury's findings and opted not to order the expulsion of Newman (P). Reese (D) appealed, contending that the trial judge erred in purporting to use discretion in choosing between dissolution of the LLC, as proposed by Newman (P), and forcing dissociation of Newman (P) from the LLC, as proposed by Reese (D). Reese (D) argued that the statute involved did not allow for any discretion by the court, and that, in fact, the statute mandated that the court order dissociation of Newman (P) based on the jury's findings. In relevant part, the dissociation section of the statute provided that "[a] person shall be dissociated" from an LLC when "the person is expelled as a member by judicial order" when the person has engaged in certain conduct described by the statute. The dissolution section of the statute provided that a trial court "may order a remedy other than dissolution." The District of Columbia intermediate appellate court granted review.

ISSUE: Where a limited liability company (LLC) statute provides that a trial court may order a remedy other than dissolution, but also provides that "[a] person shall be dissociated as a member from a limited liability company" when the person commits certain actions described in the statute, and where a jury determines there are grounds supporting both dissolution of an LLC and the dissociation of a member from the LLC, does a trial court have discretion to order either dissolution or dissociation?

HOLDING AND DECISION: [Judge not stated in casebook excerpt.] Yes. Where a limited liability company (LLC) statute provides that a trial court may order a remedy other than dissolution, but also provides that "[a] person shall be dissociated as a member from a limited liability company" when the person commits certain actions described in the statute, and where a jury determines there are grounds supporting both dissolution of an LLC and the dissociation of a member from the LLC, a trial court has discretion to order either dissolution or dissociation. Reese's (D) interpretation of the statute

Continued on next page.

is that, upon application to the court by a company, "a judge shall" dissociate a member of an LLC, when that member commits any one of the actions described in the statute. Although the introductory language of the dissociation section does use the word "shall"—that command is in no way directed at the trial judge. Instead, what the statute means is that when and if a judge has ordered a member expelled because the judge finds that any conditions of the statute have been established, e.g., the member to be expelled has engaged in certain conduct described by the statute, that member is then "dissociated." Thus, nothing in the statute's language strips a judge of discretion because it does not require the judge to expel the member if any of the enumerated conditions are established. In short, the dissociation section means when a judge has used discretion to expel a member of an LLC by judicial order, under any of the enumerated circumstances in the statute, that member "shall" be dissociated. Under Reese's (D) view, because the jury found grounds for dissociation, even though it also found grounds for dissolution, the judge necessarily had to dissociate Newman (P) because, Reese (D) argues, the language in the dissociation section is compulsory. However, Reese (D) attempts to read the dissolution section differently. Reese (D) differentiates the sections by pointing to the dissolution section's express authorization to order a remedy other than dissolution, and by then attempting to buttress her argument that the dissociation section is compulsory by pointing to the express provision in the dissolution section and the absence of a similar express provision in the dissociation section. This attempt is unavailing. First, the only "shall" in the dissociation section is in the introductory language, and the same "shall" can be found in the same place, in the dissolution section: "[a] limited liability company is dissolved, and its activities and affairs shall be wound up, upon the occurrence of any of the following." If that language does not make the rest of the section mandatory in the dissolution section, it cannot be said that the "shall" in the introduction of the dissociation section does the opposite. Thus, not only does the plain language necessitate an interpretation contrary to Reese's (D) interpretation, but additional authority also supports this conclusion. The statute at issue adopts language almost identical to the Revised Uniform Limited Liability Company Act (2013) (RULLCA). The RULLCA comments to its dissociation section states that "[w]here grounds exist for both dissociation and dissolution, a court has the discretion to choose between the alternatives." RULLCA § 602 cmt. ¶ 6. The notion that a judge has discretion to choose between alternatives (dissociation or dissolution) when grounds for both exist bolsters the view that the language in the District of Columbia's dissociation section is not compulsory. Otherwise, when grounds for both dissolution and dissociation were present, dissolution would never be mandated by a court because dissociation of a member would always necessarily trump it. For these reasons, that section can only be interpreted to mean that when a judge finds that any of the events described in the dissociation section have taken place, she may (i.e., has discretion to) expel by judicial order a member of an LLC, and when a judge has done so the member "shall be dissociated." Moreover, when both grounds for dissociation of a member and dissolution of the LLC exist, the trial judge has discretion to choose either alternative. Affirmed.

ANALYSIS

The trial court in the case found that in light of the jury finding that both statutory bases for judicial dissolution were met, (i.e., that Reese (D) acted or was acting in a manner that was illegal or fraudulent, and that she was acting in a manner that was or would be directly harmful to Newman (P)) it would be inappropriate to decline to order dissolution. The court further found that, although the jury did make findings that would allow her to order the dissociation of Newman (P), the jury also found that Newman (P) was not and had not willfully or persistently committed a breach of the LLC agreement or of her duty of loyalty to ANR. Therefore, the court reasoned, because the result of a dissociation order would be that Reese (D) alone (who was found to have been acting in a manner that was illegal or fraudulent) would be left to wind up ANR, such a result would not be equitable, and that a more equitable result would arise if she declined to expel Newman (P)–so that both parties would be on equal footing during the winding up of the company.

Quicknotes

BREACH OF CONTRACT Unlawful failure by a party to perform its obligations pursuant to contract.

DISCRETION The authority conferred upon a public official to act reasonably in accordance with their own judgment under certain circumstances.

DISSOLUTION Annulment or termination of a formal or legal bond, tie, or contract.

LIMITED LIABILITY COMPANY (LLC) A business entity combining the features of both a corporation and a general partnership; the LLC provides its members and managers with limited liability, but it is treated as a partnership for taxation purposes.

Haley v. Talcott

50 percent LLC owner (P) v. 50 percent LLC owner (D)

Del. Ct. Ch., 864 A.2d 86 (2004)

NATURE OF CASE: Action to dissolve limited liability company.

FACT SUMMARY: Haley (P) and Talcott (D), each 50 percent owners of a limited liability company (LLC), were at an impasse. Haley (P) argued that dissolution was necessary, whereas Talcott (D) argued that Haley (P) was limited to an exit mechanism provided in the LLC's operating agreement, even if such exit mechanism was not equitable regarding Haley's (P) interests.

RULE OF LAW

Where co-equal members of a limited liability company (LLC) are at an impasse, can no longer carry on the LLC's business, and are in disagreement whether to discontinue the business and how to dispose of its assets, and where an exit mechanism in the LLC's operating agreement is inequitable, dissolution is necessary.

FACTS: Haley (P) and Talcott (D) each owned 50 percent of Matt and Greg Real Estate, LLC (the LLC). A restaurant (the Redfin Grill) owned by Talcott (D) and operated by Haley (P) leased from the LLC the land on which the restaurant operated. Contractually, Haley (P) was supposed to receive 50 percent of the profits from the restaurant business, which the two men operated as a joint venture. Although pursuant to an employment contract Haley (P) was technically Talcott's (D) employee at the restaurant, the other terms of the contract established a relationship more similar to a partnership. Both men personally guaranteed the mortgage for the property owned by the LLC. Eventually, a rift developed between them, and the rift turned into deadlock and an impasse where the LLC could no longer carry on its business. In addition, the LLC property appreciated substantially in value (from the purchase price of $720,000 to an appraised value of $1.8 million). Absent court intervention, Haley (P) would be stuck with the status quo unless he chose to avail himself of the operating agreement's exit mechanism. This mechanism provided that upon notice of election to quit the LLC, the remaining member could elect to purchase the departing member's interest at fair market value. If the remaining member fails to elect to purchase the departing member's interest, the company is to be liquidated. However, the exit mechanism did not provide expressly for a release from the personal guarantees that the two men had given for the mortgage of the LLC's real property. Nor did the exit provision state that any member dissatisfied with the status quo had to break an impasse by exit rather than a suit for dissolution. Haley (P) brought suit for dissolution; Talcott (D) maintained that Haley's remedy (P) was limited to the contractual exit mechanism.

ISSUE: Where co-equal members of a limited liability company (LLC) are at an impasse, can no longer carry on the LLC's business, and are in disagreement whether to discontinue the business and how to dispose of its assets, and where an exit mechanism in the LLC's operating agreement is inequitable, is dissolution necessary?

HOLDING AND DECISION: [Judge not stated in casebook excerpt.] Yes. Where co-equal members of a limited liability company (LLC) are at an impasse, can no longer carry on the LLC's business, and are in disagreement whether to discontinue the business and how to dispose of its assets, and where an exit mechanism in the LLC's operating agreement is inequitable, dissolution is necessary. The applicable statute provides that on application by or for a member or manager, the court may decree dissolution of a limited liability company whenever it is not reasonably practicable to carry on the business in conformity with a limited liability company agreement. The elements of this statute are met here: the members are equal owners; they are engaged in a joint venture; and they are unable to agree upon whether to discontinue the business or how to dispose of its assets. Most important in this regard, Haley (P) never agreed to be a passive investor in the LLC who would be subject to Talcott's (D) unilateral dominion. Instead, the LLC agreement provided that "no member/managers may, without the agreement of a majority vote of the managers' interest, act on behalf of the company." Because the manifest weight of the evidence is that the parties are deadlocked, if the entity were a corporation, there would be no question that Haley's (P) request to dissolve the entity would be granted. However, here, the operating agreement's exit mechanism must also be considered. First, the state's LLC statute is grounded on principles of freedom of contract. For that reason, the presence of a reasonable exit mechanism bears on the propriety of ordering dissolution. When the agreement itself provides a fair opportunity for the dissenting member who disfavors the inertial status quo to exit and receive the fair market value of his interest, it is at least arguable that the limited liability company may still proceed to operate practicably under its contractual charter because the charter itself provides an equitable way to break the impasse. Thus, so long as Haley (P) can actually extract himself fairly, it arguably makes sense for the court to stay its hand in an LLC case and allow the contract itself to solve the problem. However,

Continued on next page.

forcing Haley (P) to exercise the contractual exit mechanism would not permit the LLC to proceed in a practicable way that accords with the LLC agreement, but would instead permit Talcott (D) to penalize Haley (P) without express contractual authorization. This is so because the exit mechanism would not relieve Haley (P) of his obligation under the personal guaranty that he signed to secure the mortgage on the LLC's property. If Haley (P) is forced to use the exit mechanism, Talcott (D) and he both believe that Haley (P) would still be left holding the bag on the guaranty. It is therefore not equitable to force Haley (P) to use the exit mechanism in this circumstance. Thus, the exit mechanism fails as an adequate remedy for Haley (P) because it does not equitably effect the separation of the parties. Rather, it would leave him with no potentiality and no protection over the considerable risk that he would have to make good on any future default by the LLC (over whose operations he would have no control) to its mortgage lender. For this reason, it is necessary for the court to intervene and order dissolution.

ANALYSIS

It is an interesting question whether the 50 percent member of an LLC that operates an ongoing business, and who does not favor inertial policy, must exit rather than force dissolution, particularly when the cost of the exit procedure would, as here, be borne solely by them. Arguably, it is economically more efficient—absent an explicit requirement that the party disfavoring inertia exit if they are dissatisfied—to order dissolution, and allow both parties to bid as purchasers, with the assets going to the highest bidder (inside or outside) who presumably will deploy the asset to its most valuable use. It is also concomitantly arguable that if parties wish to force the co-equal member disfavoring inertia to exit rather than seek dissolution, then they should explicitly contract upfront in the LLC agreement that exit (or the triggering of a buy-sell procedure, giving incentives for the business to be retained by the member willing to pay the highest value) is the required method of breaking any later-arising stalemate.

Quicknotes

DISSOLUTION Annulment or termination of a formal or legal bond, tie, or contract.

LIMITED LIABILITY COMPANY (LLC) A business entity combining the features of both a corporation and a general partnership; the LLC provides its members and managers with limited liability, but it is treated as a partnership for taxation purposes.

LIQUIDATION The reduction to cash of all assets for distribution to creditors.

STATUS QUO The existing circumstances at a particular moment.

Glossary

Common Latin Words and Phrases Encountered in the Law

A FORTIORI: Because one fact exists or has been proven, therefore a second fact that is related to the first fact must also exist.

A PRIORI: From the cause to the effect. A term of logic used to denote that when one generally accepted truth is shown to be a cause, another particular effect must necessarily follow.

AB INITIO: From the beginning; a condition that has existed throughout, as in a marriage that was void ab initio.

ACTUS REUS: The wrongful act; in criminal law, such action sufficient to trigger criminal liability.

AD VALOREM: According to value; an ad valorem tax is imposed upon an item located within the taxing jurisdiction calculated by the value of such item.

AMICUS CURIAE: Friend of the court. Its most common usage takes the form of an amicus curiae brief, filed by a person who is not a party to an action but is nonetheless allowed to offer an argument supporting their legal interests.

ARGUENDO: In arguing. A statement, possibly hypothetical, made for the purpose of argument is one made arguendo.

BILL QUIA TIMET: A bill to quiet title (establish ownership) to real property.

BONA FIDE: True, honest, or genuine. May refer to a person's legal position based on good faith or lacking notice of fraud (such as a bona fide purchaser for value) or to the authenticity of a particular document (such as a bona fide last will and testament).

CAUSA MORTIS: With approaching death in mind. A gift causa mortis is a gift given by a party who feels certain that death is imminent.

CAVEAT EMPTOR: Let the buyer beware. This maxim is reflected in the rule of law that a buyer purchases at their own risk because it is their responsibility to examine, judge, test, and otherwise inspect what they are buying.

CERTIORARI: A writ of review. Petitions for review of a case by the United States Supreme Court are most often done by means of a writ of certiorari.

CONTRA: On the other hand. Opposite. Contrary to.

CORAM NOBIS: Before us; writs of error directed to the court that originally rendered the judgment.

CORAM VOBIS: Before you; writs of error directed by an appellate court to a lower court to correct a factual error.

CORPUS DELICTI: The body of the crime; the requisite elements of a crime amounting to objective proof that a crime has been committed.

CUM TESTAMENTO ANNEXO, ADMINISTRATOR (ADMINISTRATOR C.T.A.): With will annexed; an administrator c.t.a. settles an estate pursuant to a will in which the administrator is not appointed.

DE BONIS NON, ADMINISTRATOR (ADMINISTRATOR D.B.N.): Of goods not administered; an administrator d.b.n. settles a partially settled estate.

DE FACTO: In fact; in reality; actually. Existing in fact but not officially approved or engendered.

DE JURE: By right; lawful. Describes a condition that is legitimate "as a matter of law," in contrast to the term "de facto," which connotes something existing in fact but not legally sanctioned or authorized. For example, de facto segregation refers to segregation brought about by housing patterns, etc., whereas de jure segregation refers to segregation created by law.

DE MINIMUS: Of minimal importance; insignificant; a trifle; not worth bothering about.

DE NOVO: Anew; a second time; afresh. A trial de novo is a new trial held at the appellate level as if the case originated there and the trial at a lower level had not taken place.

DICTA: Generally used as an abbreviated form of obiter dicta, a term describing those portions of a judicial opinion incidental or not necessary to resolution of the specific question before the court. Such nonessential statements and remarks are not considered to be binding precedent.

DUCES TECUM: Refers to a particular type of writ or subpoena requesting a party or organization to produce certain documents in their possession.

EN BANC: Full bench. Where a court sits with all justices present rather than the usual quorum.

EX PARTE: For one side or one party only. An ex parte proceeding is one undertaken for the benefit of only one party without notice to, or an appearance by, an adverse party.

EX POST FACTO: After the fact. An ex post facto law is alaw that retroactively changes the consequences of a prior act.

EX REL.: Abbreviated form of the term "ex relatione," meaning upon relation or information. When the state brings an action in which it has no interest against an individual at the instigation of one who has a private interest in the matter.

FORUM NON CONVENIENS: Inconvenient forum. Although a court may have jurisdiction over the case, the action should be tried in a more conveniently located court, one to which parties and witnesses may more easily travel, for example.

GUARDIAN AD LITEM: A guardian appointed by the court to represent a minor or incompetent person in a legal action.

HABEAS CORPUS: You have the body. The modern writ of habeas corpus is a writ directing that a person (body) being detained (such as a prisoner) be brought before the court so that the legality of their detention can be judicially ascertained.

IN CAMERA: In private, in chambers. When a hearing is held before a judge in their chambers or when all spectators are excluded from the courtroom.

IN FORMA PAUPERIS: In the manner of a pauper. A party who proceeds in forma pauperis because of their poverty is one who is allowed to bring suit without liability for costs.

INFRA: Below, under. A word referring the reader to a later part of a book. (The opposite of supra.)

IN LOCO PARENTIS: In the place of a parent.

IN PARI DELICTO: Equally wrong; a court of equity will not grant requested relief to an applicant who is in pari delicto, or as much at fault in the transactions giving rise to the controversy as is the opponent of the applicant.

IN PARI MATERIA: On like subject matter or upon the same matter. Statutes relating to the same person or things are said to be in pari materia. It is a general rule of statutory construction that such statutes should be construed together, i.e., looked at as if they together constituted one law.

IN PERSONAM: Against the person. Jurisdiction over the person of an individual.

IN RE: In the matter of. Used to designate a proceeding involving an estate or other property.

IN REM: A term that signifies an action against the res, or thing. An action in rem is basically one that is taken directly against property, as distinguished from an action in personam, i.e., against the person.

INTER ALIA: Among other things. Used to show that the whole of a statement, pleading, list, statute, etc., has not been set forth in its entirety.

INTER PARTES: Between the parties. May refer to contracts, conveyances, or other transactions having legal significance.

INTER VIVOS: Between the living. An inter vivos gift is a gift made by a living grantor, as distinguished from bequests contained in a will, which pass upon the death of the testator.

IPSO FACTO: By the mere fact itself.

JUS: Law or the entire body of law.

LEX LOCI: The law of the place; the notion that the rights of parties to a legal proceeding are governed by the law of the place where those rights arose.

MALUM IN SE: Evil or wrong in and of itself; inherently wrong. This term describes an act that is wrong by its very nature, as opposed to one which would not be wrong but for the fact that there is a specific legal prohibition against it (malum prohibitum).

MALUM PROHIBITUM: Wrong because prohibited, but not inherently evil. Used to describe something that is wrong because it is expressly forbidden by law but that is not in and of itself evil, e.g., speeding.

MANDAMUS: We command. A writ directing an official to take a certain action.

MENS REA: A guilty mind; a criminal intent. A term used to signify the mental state that accompanies a crime or other prohibited act. Some crimes require only a general mens rea (general intent to do the prohibited act), but others, like assault with intent to murder, require the existence of a specific mens rea.

MODUS OPERANDI: Method of operating; generally refers to the manner or style of a criminal in committing crimes, admissible in appropriate cases as evidence of the identity of a defendant.

NEXUS: A connection to.

NISI PRIUS: A court of first impression. A nisi prius court is one where issues of fact are tried before a judge or jury.

N.O.V. (NON OBSTANTE VEREDICTO): Notwithstanding the verdict. A judgment n.o.v. is a judgment given in favor of one party despite the fact that a verdict was returned in favor of the other party, the justification being that the verdict either had no reasonable support in fact or was contrary to law.

NUNC PRO TUNC: Now for then. This phrase refers to actions that may be taken and will then have full retroactive effect.

PENDENTE LITE: Pending the suit; pending litigation underway.

PER CAPITA: By head; beneficiaries of an estate, if they take in equal shares, take per capita.

PER CURIAM: By the court; signifies an opinion ostensibly written "by the whole court" and with no identified author.

PER SE: By itself, in itself; inherently.

PER STIRPES: By representation. Used primarily in the law of wills to describe the method of distribution where a person, generally because of death, is unable to take that which is left to them by the will of another, and therefore the person's divide such property between them rather than take under the will individually.

PRIMA FACIE: On its face, at first sight. A prima facie case is one that is sufficient on its face, meaning that the evidence supporting it is adequate to establish the case until contradicted or overcome by other evidence.

PRO TANTO: For so much; as far as it goes. Often used in eminent domain cases when a property owner receives partial payment for their land without prejudice to their right to bring suit for the full amount they claim his land to be worth.

QUANTUM MERUIT: As much as one deserves. Refers to recovery based on the doctrine of unjust enrichment in those cases in which a party has rendered valuable services or furnished materials that were accepted and enjoyed by another under circumstances that would reasonably notify the recipient that the rendering party expected to be paid. In essence, the law implies a contract to pay the reasonable value of the services or materials furnished.

QUASI: Almost like; as if; nearly. This term is essentially used to signify that one subject or thing is almost analogous to another but that material differences between them do exist. For example, a quasi-criminal proceeding is one that is not strictly criminal but shares enough of the same characteristics to require some of the same safeguards (e.g., procedural due process must be followed in a parole hearing).

QUID PRO QUO: Something for something. In contract law, the consideration, something of value, passed between the parties to render the contract binding.

RES GESTAE: Things done. In evidence law, this principle justifies the admission of a statement that would otherwise be hearsay when it is made so closely to the event in question as to be said to be a part of it, or with such spontaneity as not to have the possibility of falsehood.

RES IPSA LOQUITUR: The thing speaks for itself. This doctrine gives rise to a rebuttable presumption of negligence when the instrumentality causing the injury was within the exclusive control of the defendant, and the injury was one that does not normally occur unless a person has been negligent.

RES JUDICATA: A matter adjudged. Doctrine which provides that once a court of competent jurisdiction has rendered a final judgment or decree on the merits, that judgment or decree is conclusive upon the parties to the case and prevents them from engaging in any other litigation on the points and issues determined therein.

RESPONDEAT SUPERIOR: Let the master reply. This doctrine holds the master liable for the wrongful acts of their servant (or the principal for their agent) in those cases in which the servant (or agent) was acting within the scope of the master's authority at the time of the injury.

STARE DECISIS: To stand by or adhere to that which has been decided. The common law doctrine of stare decisis attempts to give security and certainty to the law by following the policy that once a principle of law as applicable to a certain set of facts has been set forth in a decision, it forms a precedent that will subsequently be followed, even though a different decision might be made were it the first time the question had arisen. Of course, stare decisis is not an inviolable principle and is departed from in instances where there is good cause (e.g., considerations of public policy led the Supreme Court to disregard prior decisions sanctioning segregation).

SUPRA: Above. A word referring a reader to an earlier part of a book. (The opposite of infra.)

ULTRA VIRES: Beyond the power. This phrase is most commonly used to refer to actions taken by a corporation that are beyond the power or legal authority of the corporation.

Addendum of French Derivatives

CHATTEL: Tangible personal property.

CY PRES: Doctrine permitting courts to apply trust funds to purposes not expressed in the trust but necessary to carry out the settlor's intent.

IN PAIS: Not pursuant to legal proceedings.

PER AUTRE VIE: For another's life; during another's life. In property law, an estate may be granted that will terminate upon the death of someone other than the grantee.

PROFIT A PRENDRE: A license to remove minerals or other produce from land.

VOIR DIRE: Process of questioning jurors as to their predispositions about the case or parties to a proceeding in order to identify those jurors displaying bias or prejudice.

www.ingramcontent.com/pod-product-compliance
Lightning Source LLC
LaVergne TN
LVHW080042210926
848481LV00011B/3261